DATE DUE			

SAMPLING
IN
ARCHAEOLOGY

James W. Mueller, editor

Collaborating
Authors

David L. Asch
Robert A. Benfer
Lewis R. Binford
James A. Brown
Robert G. Chenhall
Michael B. Collins
George L. Cowgill
James I. Ebert
Robert K. Hitchcock
W. James Judge
William D. Lipe
Richard G. Matson
Craig Morris
James W. Mueller
Jeffrey M. Neff
Dwight W. Read
Charles L. Redman
J. Jefferson Reid
Michael B. Schiffer
David Hurst Thomas

THE UNIVERSITY OF ARIZONA PRESS
Tucson, Arizona

THE UNIVERSITY OF ARIZONA PRESS

I.S.B.N. 0-8165-0482-2
L.C. No. 74-26372

Contents

Charts

Tables

Editor's Introduction

Archaeologists have been sampling – in the broadest sense of the term – regions, sites, artifacts, and attributes since the beginnings of the discipline. They have been forced to excavate one portion of a site and to exclude other portions. The location of a survey quadrat or block excavation has been a field decision, influenced by the archaeologist's knowledge and experience. The discipline of archaeology is developed to its present state because of accumulated fieldwork based on sampling in this general sense. However, this method of locating productive areas for evidence of ancient man and extinct cultures may be examined more closely. After all, did not Schliemann find the golden treasures of Troy, accomplishing the materalistic portion of his objectives, the day before the planned termination of his expedition (Ludwig 1964: 120–122)? This archaeological tradition – that the most significant finds are always made near the end of the project – raises some doubts concerning this kind of decision-making. Is this tradition merely an accident of discovery? Or does it indicate faulty decision-making? The spirit of this book is that the use of sampling can improve field decisions and possibly avoid these poorly timed accidents.

This book is primarily methodological in nature and focuses on sampling strategies for conducting archaeological research. Sampling may answer the question of selecting a survey location or excavation unit better than traditional decision-making. The outcome of this comparison is unknown in 1974, and this collection of writings will probably serve as a basis for the comparison. On the other hand, the comparison may be futile because probabilistic sampling and traditional decision-making can and do supplement each other. The ultimate test of any kind of sampling is its contribution to the solution of archaeological problems – for example: chronology building, behavioral reconstruction, community organization, settlement patterns, and culture process.

Sampling is viewed as a tool to aid the archaeologist in selecting units of investigation and in generalizing to larger entities. Because sampling is a methodological tool, sampling concerns do not and should not dominate the discipline. This tool may be useful in certain situations only to accomplish specific theoretical objectives. Hence, the methodological nature of these essays cannot be divorced from theoretical matters; method and theory are inextricably interwoven. This is not a hueristic handbook of cookbook methods. The case studies in this book are particularistic reports of ongoing real-world archaeological research projects in which the theoretical goals and objectives are explicitly stated by each author. The efficacy of various sampling methods can then be specifically evaluated in light of these stated theoretical concerns. A future consequence of this evaluation may be that one can question the oft-repeated motto of scientific relativism—that the choice of field and laboratory methods and relevancy of data are determined by research objectives. It may be time to doff the permissive relativism of the 1960s in favor of increased specification between strategy and objectives.

The anthropological and archaeological tradition of borrowing related concepts from other scientific disciplines is manifest in this collection. Sampling concepts are borrowed from statistics and from plant ecology. One resulting problem is the application and modification of these concepts to the special concerns of archaeology. The transition between sampling theory and archaeological practice is facilitated by the extensive field experience of each anthropological archaeologist contributing to this volume.

The financial and empirical demands of archaeological research increased significantly beginning in the late 1960s, for several interrelated reasons. These factors include; (1) the increasing costs of performing fieldwork, (2) the decreasing availability of research funds, (3) the huge amounts of artifactual and nonartifactual data that can be recovered, and (4) the immensity of regions, sites, and assemblages. The former two financial factors, based on wage, salary, and rental schedules, as well as the redistribution of governmental monies, are usually beyond the control of the archaeologist. The latter two factors refer primarily to the increasing alliance of archaeology with the natural and life sciences as environmental, systemic, and adaptational problems have become popular. The amounts of data and kinds of scientific competencies necessary to process and analyze these naturalistic data which were once considered ancillary have placed new demands on archaeology. These four factors have mitigated against the total survey of a region, the total excavation of a site, and the total analysis of an assemblage. Since the early 1960s, the conscious and explicit use of sampling theory has been advocated when total survey, excavation, or analysis cannot be achieved.

These four factors, combined with a quantitative orientation that was crystalizing at the University of Michigan, led to the appearance of several seminal and classical articles (Vescelius 1960; Spaulding 1953, 1960b; and Binford 1964). These statements encouraged some field trials of probabilistic sampling in the early and middle 1960s, particularly at Carter Ranch (Longacre 1970), Broken K (Hill 1970), and Grasshopper (Wilcox n.d.b), in east central Arizona. In addition to sampling trials, innovative analytical techniques were employed in a laudable attempt to write a paleoethnography of each site. These new and exciting interpretations of the archaeological record created a revolution (Martin 1971; Leone 1971), which resulted in the formation of processual archaeology. The probabilistic sampling methods became associated with the exciting analyses. Therefore, it seems that the interest in sampling was popularized in the discipline not because of its own merits but because it was associated with the substantive conclusions of processual archaeology. Thus, it can be said that sampling was swept into archaeology on the crest of the processual wave.

The responses and reactions have been varied — categorical rejection, blind acceptance, and skeptical positivism. The former two dipolar reactions were more common in the 1960s when the revolution was still in progress (Leone 1971: 222), and when sampling was one of many contentious issues that were being evaluated by archaeologists. Some made the sampling decision independently, while other archaeologists were evaluating the substantive conclusions of the processual approach and let sampling sneak in or out of the door. During the less passionate 1970s, sampling is being evaluated on its own merits and independently from the processual conclusions. As a result, skeptical positivism seems to be the general mood of archaeologists toward sampling in the mid-1970s. This book may be regarded as a compendium of answers to these legitimate questions raised by skeptics: "How does one do probabilistic sampling in the field?"; "What benefits derive from probabilistic sampling designs?"; and "What is the relationship between probabilistic sampling and traditional decision-making?"

This volume was developed from papers presented at a symposium entitled "Sampling in Archaeology" for the Thirty-eighth Annual Meeting of the Society for American Archaeology, in San Francisco, in 1973. I extend to all of the authors my sincere appreciation for their cooperation and tolerance both during my organization of the symposium and afterward during the preparation of this book.

Rebecca Davidson assisted in the preparation of the bibliography and the final editorial changes in the manuscript. Dorothy Baines and Carol Wright graciously translated my confusing drafts of edited manuscript and produced the final copy for the publisher; they also prepared my many letters to the authors. Joanne Cassulo's indexing assistance also is greatly appreciated.

Sandi, my wife, encouraged me to pursue both my idea of the symposium and the resulting book. Our daughter, Alyssa, made us both smile as approaching deadlines made the going rough.

Finally, I am grateful to Marshall Townsend, Director of the University of Arizona Press, who provided me with sound guidance concerning this entire book project. His professionalism is responsible for the positive characteristics of the volume.

James W. Mueller

PART ONE

An Overview of Sampling

One goal of archaeology is the reconstruction of extinct cultures and past human behavior. This behavior is reflected in the artifacts and their relative distribution which the archaeologist perceives in the ground as the archaeological record. As a behavioral science, palaeoanthropology must relate to the behavior that produced the archaeological record. The relationship between the prehistoric deposition of artifacts and the archaeological record is the topic of the chapters by Chenhall and Collins. This background concerning the formation of the archaeological record in the light of space, time, and form provides a perspective for the entire book. The general nature of the research process for the discovery and recovery of data is a topic common to these first three papers. The remaining sections of this book provide detailed elaboration of the general research processes presented in this section.

A classical article (Binford 1964) which stimulated an early interest in sampling was equivocally received by some archaeologists due to its programmatic nature. An introduction to sampling would be incomplete without a test of some programs suggested in this seminal article, and therefore Chenhall's experiment is included in this section. Furthermore, Binford's use of certain sampling concepts and terms was innovative in the mid-1960s. In the ensuing decade, archaeologists have continued to realize that these concepts must be controlled and understood in order to sample in a sophisticated manner. Therefore, the essential sampling concepts that are used throughout this book are discussed and illustrated archaeologically in chapters by Chenhall and Mueller.

The concept random sampling has a specific and restricted usage in sampling but has been misused in archaeology. It has been used in a completely nonstatistical sense to refer to a mindless and unthinking choice which is mistakenly intended to avoid the human bias of conscious selection. This usage of random should be avoided completely. The proper term to convey this meaning is haphazard selection or a grab sample (Cochran, Mosteller, and Tukey 1954). The term random also has a second archaeological usage—as a synonym for probabilistic sampling. Random in this sense implies that chance and the laws of probability are properly used by the archaeologist to avoid human bias. The term probabilistic should be reserved for this major genre of sampling. Random has also been used as part of the phrase, simple random sampling, to refer to one specific technique within the probabilistic genre. Other contrasting techniques within this genre are systematic, stratified, and cluster sampling. The term random should be considered as a synonym for simple random sampling and restricted only to this specific usage. The authors in this volume employ the second and third meanings; context should clarify the author's intention.

J. W. M.

1. A Rationale for Archaeological Sampling

Robert G. Chenhall

Robert G. Chenhall (Ph.D., Arizona State University, 1971) has had an interesting career as executive, student, archaeologist, and museologist in both business and academia. His multifarious interests can be reduced to the archaeological applications of computers and to museum data banks. In pursuit of the former, he originated and edited the *Newsletter of Computer Archaeology* for its first six years, in addition to an IBM-published volume entitled *Computers in Anthropology and Archaeology*. The latter interest eventuated in a position as Executive Director, Museum Data Bank Coordinating Committee, and in the book, *Computerized Museum Catalogs*. This work was supported by grants from the National Museum Act and the National Science Foundation.

SAMPLING THEORY AND THE ARCHAEOLOGICAL RECORD

Archaeologists have long recognized that inferences about past human behavior are in fact based upon small and sometimes inadequate samples. Both Kroeber (1916) and Spier (1917), in their Zuni-area survey reports, reviewed the methods of sampling used to collect surface artifacts; and a "representative sampling" technique was early proposed by Gladwin (1928: 1) as a method to eliminate "bias" in the collection of sherds from the surface of a site. Somewhat later, in both the Viru Valley survey (Ford and Willey 1949) and the survey of the Lower Mississippi Alluvial Valley (Phillips, Ford, and Griffin 1951), Ford discussed sampling procedures in detail. As Ragir (1967: 182) and others have pointed out, however, these early workers, though concerned about the validity of their samples, did not understand the principles of statistical random sampling. It was not until the 1950s under the influence of people such as Vescelius (1960) and particularly Spaulding (1960b) that archaeologists began to equate the word *sampling* with the mathematically derived technique known generally as *random sampling*.

Since 1960 a number of archaeologists (e.g., Binford 1964; Cowgill 1964; Hill 1967; F. Plog 1968; Ragir 1967; Redman 1973; Redman and Watson 1970; Rootenberg 1964) have proposed the use of random sampling as the best means of obtaining "representative and reliable data within the bounds of . . . restricted time and monetary resources" (Binford 1964: 427), and at least two of these (Binford 1964; Redman 1973) have included random sampling as an integral part of comprehensive theoretical research designs.

If random sampling is as effective as claimed by its proponents, it probably should be considered in every archaeological research design. However, the enthusiasm is not universal. For example, both Hill (1967) and Redman and Watson (1970) recommend random sampling of surface evidence at a site as a means of selecting the portion to be excavated, but Hole and Heizer (1969: 140) state that

From our own experience, we believe that the presence of artifacts on the surface is dependent upon so many variables, both natural and cultural, that it is unwise to use surface indications as more than a rough guide to a site's contents. Even preliminary test examination of a refuse deposit *may not yield a sample that is representative*. [Italics added]

A suggestion as to why archaeologists have sampling problems may be contained in Hole and Heizer's last sentence. A test of a refuse deposit may or may not be representative of the *material culture remains* which are buried beneath the surface of the ground, but such a sample is certainly representative of *something* and it is possible to make *some* kinds of valid inferences from samples.

A random sampling formula is, in a sense, a mathematical model of a selected portion of the real world. The theoretical formulations of mathematicians do, in fact, conform to empirical reality when the correlates for the various terms in the model are black and white marbles. The homogeneity of the population and the randomness (i.e., the freedom from bias) in any sample taken are assured in laboratory tests, and attention can be directed to ascertaining the sample sizes necessary to produce a given probability that the sample represents the total population. Archaeologists, however, do not deal with black and white marbles. It would be great to be able to state, in mathematical terms, the probability that archaeological samples represent defined archaeological populations, but this is seldom possible, and the reason this is so is because homogeneity and randomness (the basic premises of statisticians) are never self-evident and are seldom demonstrable in archaeological investigations. Nevertheless, the random sampling *model* is important to archaeologists, for it establishes a framework within which to evaluate the reasonableness of samples whether or not that reasonableness can properly be stated in relative-frequency-probability terms.

Confusion in assessing the appropriateness of random sampling in particular archaeological research designs appears to be primarily the result of (1) a lack of clarity concerning the meanings of some of the terms in a random sampling formula, and (2) a lack of clarity concerning the things in the real world (the empirical correlates) that the formula terms are supposed to represent.

Random Sampling Terminology

Most of the terms in a sampling formula—words such as *population, sample unit, sample frame, sample* and *stratum*—are explained adequately in statistics texts (e.g., Dixon and Massey 1969; Mood and Graybill 1963; Wallis and Roberts 1956), and will not be redefined here. However, the difference between a *target population* and a *sampled population* is often ignored in practice, and the present author believes there is a need for the concept of a statistical *universe* separate from the *population,* even though statisticians are not concerned about the distinction and often consider the words to be interchangeable (e.g., Dixon and Massey 1969: 38; Wallis and Roberts 1956: 31).

A *target population* is defined by Mood and Graybill (1963: 141) as the totality of elements which are under discussion and about which information is desired. A target population may be all the Navajo blankets on dealers' shelves in the Southwest on a certain date, or the prices of bread in New York City on a certain date or the hypothetical sequence of heads and tails obtained by tossing a certain coin an infinite number of times, and so forth. The important thing is that the target population *must be capable of being precisely defined,* although it may be either real or hypothetical.

The problem of inductive inference is to find out something about a target population, even though it is generally impossible or impractical to select a random sample from the entire population. In such cases, a random sample may be selected from some related, smaller population. The related population is then called the *sampled population* to distinguish it from the target population. Valid probability statements can be made about sampled populations on the basis of random samples, but statements about the target population are not valid in a relative-frequency-probability sense unless the target population is also the sampled population.

Suppose that a sociologist desires to study the religious habits of twenty-year-old males. He draws a sample from the twenty-year-old males in a large city to make his study. If he considers his target population to be the twenty-year-old males in that city, then the target population and the sampled population are the same, and valid probability statements can be made about that population on the basis of a random sample. However, if the real interest—the target population—is the religious habits of twenty-year-old males in the United States, and the twenty-year-old males in the one large city comprise only a population that is sampled as a basis for extrapolating to the larger, target population, then there is a quantitative (though presumably not a qualitative) difference between the sampled population and the target population. In such cases, the sample may be a random sample, in the sense that every individual in the sampled population has an equal and independent chance of being chosen, but valid probabilistic conclusions can only be drawn about the sampled population. The sociologist must use his personal judgment to extrapolate to the target population, and the reliability of the extrapolation cannot be measured in statistical terms.

As stated above, the term *universe* is often considered to be synonymous with *population.* In theoretical statistics, this perhaps is satisfactory, but archaeologists are often in the position of being required to make inferences from a sampled population to a class of empirical phenomena quite different than that which is sampled. These differences are not just quantitative (as from a sampled population to a target population) but qualitative as well.

In our illustration, for example, the sociologist may *really* be trying to assess the likelihood that young men will claim conscientious objection status under a proposed armed forces conscription law, and he has evidence from other studies that will enable him to *infer* (note the distinction between this word and *extrapolate* as used above) this from the religious behavior of twenty-year-old males. Here a distinction must be made from both the sampled population and the target population, and, for this purpose, I would follow Binford (1964: 427) and suggest the term *universe* for this isolated field of study, even though this usage is not well-established among statisticians. A universe *may* be the same as a target population, and both *may* be the same as a sampled population. Where they are different, though, the universe is distinguished in that it is qualitatively, not just quantitatively, different from a population, and it is inferred on the basis of an outside correlational study of some kind rather than being determined by extrapolation from the sampled and/or target population.

Empirical Correlates for Sampling Terms

Once the possible terminology in a sampling design is clearly established, it is not too difficult to select the appropriate terms, and thus the available formulae and methodologies, for the things in the real world which are the empirical correlates for the terms. For example, if one is dealing with a population of 500,000 sherds and decides in the interest of time to analyze only a sample, there is no universe or target population that is in any way different from the sampled population. A valid probability statement concerning the population can be made from a random sample. However, if one is doing a survey of an area for the purpose of locating sites, the universe of interest is the totality of the prehistoric cultural manifestations in the area. This can never be directly sampled by random sampling methods, but it can perhaps be inferred from a target population which represents a given segment of geography in the real world and in turn consists of the aggregate of individual areas which have a distribution in space, not culturally (Duncan et al. 1961: 21). Hill (1967: 149) points out the fact that random sampling yields a random selection of the sample units chosen, *not* a random selection of all culturally relevant material. This statement is true most of the time, of course, because it is based upon the assumption that the empirical correlates for the sampled population will be different from the empirical correlates for the universe, as I have used these terms. However, where the sample units do in fact represent homogeneous cultural units such as sites, room outlines, depressions, or sherds, random sampling does provide a random selection of culturally relevant material. The difference is in the terminology of the sampling formula and the empirical correlates for the terms in the formula.

In this paper an attempt will be made to construct a hierarchy of archaeological populations-universes. As indicated above, the main difference between the two hyphenated words is in the empirical correlates that are substituted for the words in a particular research design. This hierarchy perhaps is not a true random sampling hierarchy in the sense that each lower level is a clearly definable subset of the level above. Rather, it considers the data of archaeology as a cube (see Fig. 1.1), with one axis each for time, space, and cultural content. The shape of this hierarchy in space could just as well be visualized some other way. Viewed as a cube, "today" is a plane

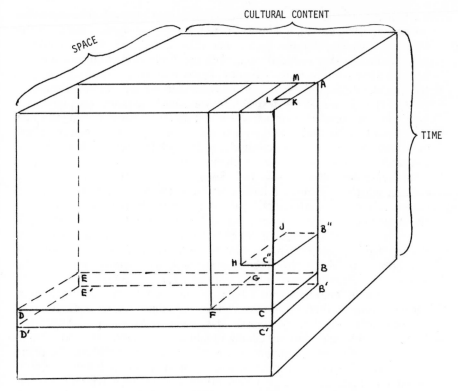

Fig. 1.1.　Data of archaeology represented as a cube
with one axis each for time, space, and cultural content.

across the top which can be divided into geographic areas across one dimension and into cultural traits across the other.

If archaeology is considered to be a part of anthropology, as it customarily is in the United States, then the objective of all archaeological research can be considered as the providing of a diachronic time-depth to the study of human societies and/or human cultures. Beginning from this premise, the hierarchy of populations-universes which archaeologists sample might be stated as:

1. The total behavior pattern of a human society or culture as it once existed. Beginning at point A on Figure 1.1 and moving back through time to point B the universe of interest is the cube bounded by the letters B, C, D, E, and B', C', D', and E'. The people who once formed this society ceased to exist at time-depth B, though, thus eliminating nonmaterial culture. Any inference which is to be made regarding the total behavior pattern (i.e., the universe) must be made from a population consisting of:
2. The artifactual and natural material remains which were left when the society vanished. This may be envisioned by the plane B-C-F-G. How-

ever, many of these material remains consisted of foodstuffs and other perishable objects which would disintegrate in a very short time. Therefore, the only population which conceivably could be sampled would be a population further reduced along both the dimension of cultural content and the dimension of time. This population may be called:

3. Nonperishable materials: It can be visualized by the yet smaller plane, B''-C''-H-J. It would be desirable if we could envision this plane as a nonchanging population of nonperishable materials slowly rising through time from time-depth B'' to the present or time-depth A. However, several factors, both natural and cultural, are at work to cause both a quantitative reduction and a qualitative change through time in the population or universe defined as B''-C''-H-J. Some of these factors are: (a) natural erosion which may move a large portion of the nonperishable materials completely out of the defined space dimension; (b) new construction at the same site which can either erode or add to the cultural content within the given spatial dimension; (c) a burial of the original occupation so deeply that the sampling pattern in the lower strata is more a product of decisions as to where to dig the upper strata than decisions concerning the lower. [See Brown, chap. 9, this volume.] For these and other reasons nonperishable materials can never be assumed to remain unchanged through time. Rather, by the time an archaeologist begins work at a site, the possible population-universe has been reduced to:

4. Nonperishable materials remaining in situ and available. It is possible to conceive of this small remnant of the original behavior pattern, the plane A-K-L-M, as either a nonrandom sample of the target population of nonperishable materials or as a target population in itself which is further sampled by either random or nonrandom methods. Even at this point, though, there are still a number of ways in which the remaining population-universe is further reduced. These may be considered as the aggregate of the decisions that are made by the archaeologist himself, first, in perceiving what is man-made or associated in some way with the prehistoric occupation and, second, in his techniques of collecting and classifying what is considered to be important. Gardin (n.d.) has placed these activities of perception, identification, and classification in a framework of multiple-stage decision-making. At each of these stages in the process of doing archaeology, decisions are constantly made to "keep" some objects and/or data and to "refuse" other objects or data. These stages cannot be readily displayed on the illustration (Fig. 1.1), but each of the paragraphs below describe a part of the total sampling hierarchy in the sense that either the spatial or cultural content dimensions on Figure 1.1 are further reduced and thus any population-universe that might be a basis for inferences at a higher level in the hierarchy is correspondingly reduced.

5. Both the spatial and cultural content dimensions may be modified as a result of the geographic area or areas perceived by the archaeologist to be a site.

6. The cultural content of the site will vary depending upon the areas and the methods used for the selection of surface samples.

7. The cultural content and perhaps even the spatial dimension will vary depending upon the areas that are selected for testing and/or excavation. Even within an area that is excavated, though, the population of artifacts and thus the cultural content dimension is a result of decisions concerning:
8. Artifacts and other objects thought to be significant in terms of current theory, the archaeologist's orientation, and so on. Beyond the decision as to what artifacts will be kept at time of excavation, however, even further keep-refuse decisions are made at every stage in the processes of washing, processing, recording, classifying, and photographing for publication. The decision to weigh and dispose of fire-cracked rock, for example, leaves a different population of artifacts for sampling or analysis than that which results from retaining everything.

Gardin has an interesting theory on this decision-making process. His opinion is that the decision to keep or refuse information and/or artifacts at each stage in the process of doing archaeology should be made independently and on the grounds of the amount of incremental information which is produced, with the word *incremental* presumably defined in terms of our original universe — that is, the population of living people as it once existed.

From this rough conceptual hierarchy of sampling populations-universes it is possible to state a frame of reference for archaeological sampling which eliminates much of the confusion about whether or not sampling is appropriate in a particular research design, and, if it is appropriate, what type of sampling strategy will accomplish the desired results.

The point of beginning is to ask (1) what kinds or classes of empirical objects are available and (2) what kind or class of data are we attempting to describe. The next question is crucial: Can the aggregate of the objects we are really concerned with be sampled directly (i.e., do they comprise the empirical correlate of a sampled population) or can they be determined only by extrapolation from some smaller, perceivable population (i.e., is this the empirical correlate of a target population)? Or, perhaps, are the things we are ultimately interested in directly knowable at all — that is, do they comprise a theoretical universe which at best can be inferred by correlational association with a sampled population or a target population of qualitatively different objects?

Random samples can be taken from any definable population, for the idea of randomness is embedded in the method by which the sample is selected. However, valid probability statements about a random sample can be made only from sampled populations where the total number of items (i.e., the sample frame) is determinable. For archaeology, this means that one cannot make valid probability statements about a random sample unless the sampled population is comprised of extant, perceivable objects: the 500,000 sherds in our previous illustration, the 278 rooms in a PIII Pueblo, the 199 grid squares which represent in total the population of a land surface to be sampled, or the 2,123 cubic feet of soil-sand-shell-artifact mixture in a shell mound. Note that these are all populations which are perceivable at time-depth zero. No population or universe that existed in the past is directly perceivable. Therefore, those described in paragraphs 1 through 4 on our hierarchy must be recognized as being at best target populations which are extrapolated from a perceived sampled population or at worst universes which must be inferred.

The total number of items in a target population may or may not be known. If the number is not known, random samples which can be measured in relative-frequency-probability terms can still be taken from a sampled population that is known and a target population can be extrapolated from this sample. Personal judgment, however, must be used to extrapolate to a target population and the reliability of the extrapolation cannot be measured in statistical terms. This is most often the situation in which the archaeologist is working. The target population, for example, may be the total inventory of nonperishable cultural materials—i.e., paragraph 3 in our hierarchy—at a site such as the 278 room PIII Pueblo. Twenty rooms may have been selected for excavation (the method of selection is not important at the moment) and the nonperishable cultural objects collected during this excavation, washed, classified, and cataloged, may be considered as the sample. In a case such as this, the target population is defined as such because it presumably consists of the same kinds of objects that are contained in the sample. However, several steps in the hierarchy have been jumped in the process of making the extrapolation to the target population, the target population has not and could not have been determined, and the sampling method has not been random. When the empirical correlates for the sampling terms are carefully defined in this way, it is apparent that a sample has been taken in order to determine a target population but that random sampling methods have not been used.

It would have been possible in the illustration above to have applied random sampling techniques but to do so would mean redefining the empirical correlates for several of the terms in this sampling design. One way random sampling might be applied to a situation such as this is to assume a homogeneity among the 278 rooms in the Pueblo and to apply random methodology in the selection of the twenty rooms that are to be excavated. When this is done, though, the sampled population and thus the samples become qualitatively different or different in kind from the originally defined target population. By definition, this cannot happen and the total inventory of nonperishable cultural objects, previously considered as the target population, thus has become the empirical correlate for an inferred *universe* rather than a *target population*. The sampled population and the target population in this case are the same: the aggregate of the 278 rooms per se, not the nonperishable cultural objects in those rooms. This population can be sampled by random methods and probability statements can be made about the validity of the sample. Such statements tend to lose their force, however, for they are removed both quantitatively and qualitatively from the universe which is the real object of interest in the study. Archaeological expertise becomes so important in a situation such as this that one tends to question whether the sampling methodology was worthwhile at all or whether that expertise might not provide a better method for the selection of the rooms to be excavated than any kind of random sampling.

The validity of a universe inferred from a population which in turn is determined at some lower level in the sampling hierarchy is not something which can be evaluated by statistical methods. If there is outside evidence to indicate that the population and the inferred universe do in fact covary, then an inference of this type is immensely strengthened. If there is merely an assumption of covariance the inference is very likely to be questioned. In the illustration above, the assumption that the rooms in the pueblo are culturally homogeneous as well as more or less spatially the same (an assumption which is necessary to such a sampling strategy) may be more than offset by the thought that the skilled archaeologist could probably select rooms which would be more truly representative of the total universe of interest, using nonrandom and perhaps intuitive methods. In another circumstance, however, involving similar *sampling* problems, the conclusion might be quite different. For example, when a person samples a shell mound rather than excavating it completely he does so on the premise that there is sufficient homogeneity in the distribution of cultural remains within shell mounds so that he is relatively safe in inferring what is in this shell mound on the basis of a small sample. Again, the sampled population and the target population are the same – the aggregate of the 2,123 cubic feet of soil-sand-shell-artifacts in the mound – and the sample is determined by random methods from a frame consisting of units of cubic measure of the mixture. In this case, however, there is outside evidence to support homogeneity of culture materials throughout the mound – that is, to support the fact that the total inventory of nonperishable material culture objects in the mound can be reliably inferred from a sample. Treganza and Cook (1948; see also remarks by Cook 1960: 85; and Ascher 1959) long ago made a study demonstrating to their satisfaction that the cultural content of shell mounds is in fact reasonably homogeneous.

AN EXAMPLE FROM THE SOUTHWEST

Rather than to provide additional illustrations of a hypothetical nature, I would like to describe in more detail a sampling project that was designed to test that portion of Binford's (1964) treatise on "A Consideration of Archaeological Research Design" which is devoted to sampling for the selection of archaeological sites. Binford was the first person to apply the principles of random sampling to the location of archaeological sites, and so far as I have been able to determine, every archaeologist who has considered the use of random sampling in an archaeological survey since 1964 has based his work on Binford's research design. A few persons (e.g., Thomas 1973; S. Plog n.d.; Peters 1970) have modified the design by employing alternate techniques for the selection of the sample areas. However, no one has critically questioned or tested the design itself. The objectives of the research described here were to analyze Binford's design and, where possible, to test it by empirical methods to determine whether it is, in fact, a valid technique for the location of archaeological sites in a previously unexplored area.

The region used to test Binford's techniques was the drainage limits of the headwaters of Walnut Creek, near Young, Arizona. This drainage — also known as the Vosberg District (Dittert n.d.) — covers approximately four square miles of land surface where the Arizona State University Archaeological Field School was conducted during the summers of 1967 through 1970. As a part of the Field School activity, the entire region was subjected to an intensive archaeological survey, as this term is defined by Ruppé (1966: 315).

Theoretical Background

The research design which Binford (1964: 432–34) proposes as a means of locating archaeological sites is stated as follows:

Ecofact is the term applied to all culturally relevant nonartifactual data. . . . All those elements which represent or inform about the points of articulation between the cultural system and other natural systems must be sampled. . . . The general class of ecofacts can be broken down into many subclasses representing different populations, such as pollen, soil, and animal bone. . . .

Populations of sites must be investigated within a universe defined in spatial terms, the region. . . .

The initial problem is the location of the various loci of past cultural activity within the region. This phase of the work should be directed toward determining the density and distribution of activity loci with respect to classes of ecofactual phenomena, such as plant communities, physiographic features, and soil types. In order to accomplish this task there is only one appropriate procedure short of complete coverage, a procedure rooted in some form of probability sampling. One suggested approach is to stratify the regional universe on the basis of ecofactual criteria judged desirable to control, such as soil types . . . impose a grid system over the areas of the various soil types [and select the sampling units to be surveyed] by use of a table of random numbers. The sampling units within each frame will then be *completely* surveyed for purposes of locating sites.

Although Binford states that "populations of sites must be investigated within a universe defined in spatial terms . . . ," in the terminology used in this paper the empirical correlate for the universe of interest actually is the aggregate of the sites in the area, and this universe is inferred from a population that is spatially defined.

Any research design may be viewed as a series of steps to be followed in carrying out that particular type of research. From a slightly different point of view, any research design may be looked upon as the logical summation of a series of hypotheses. In order to test the validity of the design, it is necessary to delineate as clearly as possible the hypotheses upon which it is based and then to seek evidence that will lead to acceptance or rejection of each hypothesis. The evidence may be in the form of authoritative statements which are adequate to convince the reader that the hypothesis has been confirmed or rejected by someone else or in the form of experiments designed explicitly to test the hypothesis.

Binford (1964: 432) defines ecofacts as culturally relevant nonartifactual data; and says that "All those elements which represent or inform about the points of articulation between the cultural system and other natural systems must be sampled." Further on (Binford 1964: 434), he suggests that the regional universe should be stratified " . . . on the basis of ecofactual criteria judged desirable to control."

Probably the most significant premise underlying these statements is the undemonstrated assumption that culturally relevant nonartifactual data can be determined by observation and sampling and can be classified as a basis for stratifying a given geographic region. It is important to recognize this explicitly, for it is an assumption that is based upon the further premise that nonhuman natural phenomena are correlated in some dependable manner with human artifactual remains. To many archaeologists (e.g., Binford 1962: 218; 1964: 440; 1965: 205; 1968c: 323–24; Longacre 1968: 91) culture is conceived as primarily, if not solely, an adaptive system or mechanism which enables man to exist within his environment. Environment is sometimes defined in terms of both its noncultural and cultural dimensions, but the cultural aspect is often ignored, and culture is assumed to be a response to habitat.

If culture were entirely a response to the natural environment, it would be possible (theoretically, at least) to predict the precise types of cultural phenomena that would be found in any given environmental situation. No one in recent years has carried environmental determinism to this extreme. However, it is still true that sampling on the basis of ecofactual criteria will produce reliable cultural statements only if the distribution of cultural phenomena is significantly correlated with the distribution of some nonhuman natural phenomena. This may be expressed in the form of a hypothesis as follows:

H_1 – Environmental data that are culturally relevant can be determined by observation and sampling, and can be classified in a consistent and objective manner.

There does not appear to be any way in which this hypothesis, in its present form, can be subjected to an empirical test. However, if the two premises contained within H_1 are separated, it is possible to formulate two testable hypotheses:

H_2 – Environmental data that *may* be culturally relevant can be determined by observation and sampling, and can be classified in a consistent and objective manner; and

H_3 – Some environmental data are culturally relevant – i.e., the distribution of some cultural phenomena are significantly correlated with the distribution of some nonhuman environmental phenomena.

It is possible to confirm H_2 merely by observing, sampling and, classifying the nonhuman natural systems in a given region in the form of subareas or microenvironments. To test H_3, the microenvironments must be compared with the distribution of some human artifact in the same region. In the Vosberg District, settlement patterns were considered as artifacts (see Willey 1968: 225) and, thus, as man's response to some combination of habitat, society and ideology. Binford (1962) classifies artifacts in terms of three functional categories: technomic, sociotechnic and ideotechnic. By this classification he implies that any given class of artifacts is predominately a response or adaptation to one or another of the factors of habitat, society or ideology, rather than to a diffuse and undefinable combination of all of them. Technomic artifacts — the class of concern here — are defined as those which have a "primary functional context in coping directly with the physical environment" (Binford 1962: 219). If settlement patterns are considered as technomic artifacts, H_3 may be restated, in operational terms, as follows:

H_{3a} — There is a significant correlation between settlement patterns and microenvironments.

Another hypothesis embedded in Binford's hypothetical research design is concerned with the mathematical and empirical proof of random sampling theory:

H_4 — Reliable statistical methods are available by means of which relatively small proportions (random samples) of a total number of items (a population) may be considered to be representative of the total.

The testing of this hypothesis is beyond the scope of the present investigation. However, a sufficient proof for the acceptance of the hypothesis has been demonstrated by numerous statisticians. In fact, probability theory — the basis for all random sampling — is the foundation for the science of statistics, and a major section of every elementary statistics test is devoted to this subject. Because of this, it is believed that both the hypothesis and the methodology implicit in the hypothesis may be accepted and used without presenting additional mathematical or empirical proof.

Finally, there is one more hypothesis which I believe to be important to the use of environmental data to stratify a regional universe, even though it is not discussed as a part of Binford's hypothetical research design:

H_5 — Culturally relevant environmental data in the locality under consideration either (a) have remained substantially unchanged since the time horizon with which the investigation is concerned or (b) have changed during the intervening time span in such a way that the bounds of each taxon remain approximately the same as they were during the period of interest.

Nonhuman natural systems have differing rates of change through time. For example, subsurface geological characterizations (excluding ground water) usually may be assumed to be the same today as they were during any prehistoric human occupation of an area. With floral characterizations, though, major changes can occur in the span of a few hundred years. Attempts have been made to determine the extent of environmental change through time by techniques such as palynology (e.g., Schoenwetter and Dittert 1968), dendroclimatology (Fritts 1965), and ethnohistoric reconstruction (e.g., Zawacki and Hausfater 1969); and these techniques should be considered as a part of any research design where the cultural relevance of environmental data may be important.

In the Vosberg District, palynological samples were taken as a part of the intensive survey. However, the study of these samples has not produced sufficient evidence to either confirm or deny the assumption of a substantially unchanged environment since the first human occupation of the area. If H_5 were completely false, Binford's research design could be declared invalid. However, the fact that there is no evidence available to suggest that substantial change *has* occurred in the Vosberg District since the first human occupation permits the assumption that the hypothesis is largely true. Nevertheless, it is recognized here as primarily an assumption to be accepted a priori.

If the four hypotheses (H_2 through H_5) adequately express the underlying premises in Binford's research design, and if H_4 and H_5 are accepted without additional confirming evidence, it should be possible to perform empirical tests of H_2 and H_3, and then to determine the overall validity of the design by sampling an area and comparing the settlement patterns determinable from the sampled data with settlement patterns developed from an intensive survey of the same area.

Microenvironments in the Vosberg District

Microenvironments in the Vosberg District were delineated in order to test the hypothesis (H_2) that environmental data which might be culturally relevant can be determined by observation and sampling. In Binford's research design there is an unstated implication that the investigator will somehow have a basis for selecting one particular environmental criterion as the most reliable basis for stratifying an area to locate archaeological sites. Soil types are given as an example of "ecofactual criteria judged desirable to control" (Binford 1964: 434). The reason for this selection is not stated, though, and in an unknown area (i.e., where there is no way of knowing in advance which environmental phenomena might be ecofacts) the best procedure would seem to be to establish microenvironments by zonation of every possible controllable environmental criterion and to use all of these microenvironmental sets to stratify the universe into populations.

The information that is available concerning the environment is likely to be quite different from one region to another. In the Vosberg District, the only resources available were: a 15-minute quad map; a county geologic map; stereoscopic aerial photographs taken for the United States Forest Service to a scale of 1:15,000; and ground observations made primarily during an eight-week period during the summer of 1969 and nine days during the summer of 1970. From this limited information, it was possible to develop a large-scale (1:6,180) topographic map of the area and microenvironments for six environmental criteria, as shown in Table 1.1. Microenvironments for canopies, understories, and soils were determined entirely from field observations. Prevailing wind types were based upon a combination of field observations, a hydraulic model which simulated wind flow in the area and meteorological theory. Slope angles and slope directions were derived from the large scale topographic map. Several of the techniques used were developed by the author for this project. They are described in detail elsewhere (Chenhall 1971).

In a research design for the sampling of a geographically defined universe, the number of populations to be sampled is equal to the number of microenvironments recognized within that universe (see Binford 1964: 434). If a single environmental criterion, such as soil types, is used for this purpose, a grid can be placed over the areas of each soil type, and sample areas to be intensively surveyed can be determined without too much difficulty — i.e., by numbering each grid square and selecting the sample areas from a list of random numbers. However, if more than one environmental criterion is employed to stratify the universe, the number of strata created is equal to the product of the microenvironments for each criterion. In the Vosberg District, for example, if translucent maps showing soil types, canopy modes and understory modes had been overlaid upon each other and a new map prepared to show every possible combination, there would have been 168 separate zones or strata, each of which would set forth one microenvironmental set of areas to be sampled by random methods — that is, by superimposing a grid and selecting the sample by means of random numbers. If all six criteria in the Vosberg District had been used in this manner the number of sample frames involved would have been 16,368, and each would have had to be considered as a separate population to be sampled. The work necessary to carry out this procedure would be far more time consuming than that required to do an intensive survey.

TABLE 1.1

**Information for Development
of Topographic Map**

| Environmental
Criterion | Number of
Microenvironments |
|---|---|
| Canopy Modes | 6 |
| Understory Modes | 7 |
| Slope Angles | 4 |
| Slope Directions | 8 |
| Prevailing Winds | 3 |
| Soil Types | 4 |

In summary, it is possible, by observation, sampling and analysis, to create microenvironments which might be culturally relevant. H_2 was confirmed by this experiment. But it is not practicable to create usable strata by combining all determinable microenvironments. The cultural relevance of particular environmental phenomena must either be demonstrated or hypothesized in advance if they are to be used as a basis for stratifying a region for purposes of locating archaeological sites.

Correlation Between Settlement Patterns
and Microenvironments in the Vosberg District

Two different means were employed in the Vosberg District to test the hypothesis (H_3) that there is a significant correlation between settlement patterns and microenvironments: (1) translucent map overlays were used, somewhat in the manner described by McHarg (1969), to portray apparent zonal similarities, and (2) appropriate statistics were used to express relationships at specific locations. The first step in the procedure was to place a translucent map showing the location of all sites in the district over maps showing the microenvironments for each environmental criterion in order to determine the microenvironments coincident with each archaeological site. The data for each site were then coded for computer entry, and a lengthy series of relatively simple chi square calculations were made in order to determine the significance of the relationship between particular site types and different microenvironments, either alone or in combination. By means of a header card, placed at the front of the keypunched data deck for each run, a particular site type and microenvironmental criterion (or combination of criteria) were selected. The program then calculated the probability that this correlation was the result of chance alone.

Some of the results of running this computer program with the data from the Vosberg District are shown in Table 1.2. Run numbers 1 and 3 indicate a near perfect correlation between site type 7 (small masonry field houses usually associated with agricultural structures) and the microenvironments defined as the pinyon-oak-juniper canopy and the manzanita-catclaw understory. Run numbers 2 and 4 indicate a somewhat ambiguous relationship of site type 4 (pithouse villages) and these same vegetation zones. Run numbers 5 and 6 show a high probability that both types of sites will be found on slopes of less than 10%; run numbers 7 and 8 suggest that these site types will be found on slopes facing somewhere between southeast and west; and run number 9 indicates an acceptable probability that site type 7 will be found on colluvial soils.

Beginning with run number 10, additive or cumulative comparisons were made. This run indicates that the probability of field houses (site type 7) appearing in the pinyon-oak-juniper/manzanita-catclaw zones on southeast to west-facing slopes of 10% or less is no greater than would occur as a result of chance in 25% of the cases. When this is compared to run number 11, however, eliminating slope angle, the probability is increased to the point that this would be likely to occur as a result of chance in only two cases out of one thousand.

After these runs had been made, a new set of data cards was prepared (mechanically) in which site type 15 was substituted for site types 1 through 14. This is somewhat the same as saying what would have happened if we had ignored all temporal and functional distinctions between sites and determined relationships with microenvironments purely on the presence or absence of sites. The total population is, thus, the total 74 sites and site components in the district, and the probability of these sites appearing in the pinyon-oak-juniper/manzanita-catclaw zone on slopes that face between southeast and west is extremely high.

On the basis of the data in Table 1.2, it would appear as though there is a significant relationship between settlement patterns and some of the microenvironments in the Vosberg District. Both for site type 7 and for all sites in the Vosberg District there is a definite tendency for sites to be located in the microenvironmental zones defined as: the pinyon-oak-juniper canopy; the manzanita-catclaw understory; and a slope direction falling somewhere between southeast and west. A stratification of this regional universe so as to sample only those areas falling in all three of these zones would probably result in a survey which would include most of the type 7 field houses and a large majority of all sites in the district.

TABLE 1.2

Chi Square Probabilities for Various Site Types and Environmental Domains

Run No.	Data	N	F_e	F_o Cell 1	F_o Cell 2	x^2	p
1	Site type 7 and canopy type 3	28	14	28	0	28.000	0.0000
2	Site type 4 and canopy type 3	13	7	10	3	3.769	0.0522
3	Site type 7 and understory type 3	28	14	27	1	24.143	0.0000
4	Site type 4 and understory type 3	13	7	9	4	1.923	0.1655
5	Site type 7 and slope angle 2	28	14	23	5	11.571	0.0007
6	Site type 4 and slope angle 2	13	7	13	0	13.000	0.0000
7	Site type 7 and slope direction 4	28	14	23	5	11.571	0.0007
8	Site type 4 and slope direction 4	13	7	10	3	3.769	0.0522
9	Site type 7 and soil type 2	28	14	20	8	5.143	0.0233
10	Site type 7, canopy type 3, understory type 3, slope angle 2, and slope direction 4	28	14	17	11	1.286	0.2568
11	Site type 7, canopy type 3, understory type 3, and slope direction 4	28	14	22	6	9.143	0.0025
12	Site type 15, canopy type 3, understory type 3, and slope direction 4	74	37	53	21	13.838	0.0002

Samples to Locate Archaeological Sites*

In the Vosberg District, both the settlement patterns and the culturally relevant nonartifactual data (ecofacts) were determined from an intensive survey of the entire area. Assuming that the ecofacts could have been determined by some other method (such as, perhaps, some form of sampling), the district was sampled using the techniques of stratification proposed by Binford (1964: 432–34)—that is, the selected microenvironments determined previously to be ecofacts were delineated on a map of the area, a frame of sample units of approximately equal size was established within that stratum, samples were selected within the sample frame using a table of random numbers, and a determination was made of the settlement patterns which would have resulted from the sample data only. The hypothesis for this portion of the research is that the archaeological sites in the sampled area adequately represent the total population of sites in the district. Hypotheses of this type can be tested, statistically, in terms of the proportion of each site type included in the sample and in the total population; and they can be evaluated by other means to determine the site types which would have been delineated from the samples only, either with or without limited excavations.

In order to delineate the stratum most likely to produce a representative selection of sites in the district, translucent maps showing canopy modes, understory modes and slope directions were superimposed upon each other on a light table, and a sheet of tracing paper was placed over the maps. On the tracing paper, all areas were outlined where the pinyon-oak-juniper canopy, the manzanita-catclaw understory and slopes facing southeast through west were all present. This stratum can be considered as a single, geographically defined population for sampling purposes.

To establish a frame of sample units for this population, consideration must be given to the most desirable size of each unit, as well as to the number of sample units that are created. These are interdependent questions; and, in practice, there is no formula available to answer them easily. For example Binford (1964: 434) says only that:

The actual size of a given unit in the frame would be determined by considerations of survey logistics and the need to have multiple but also practicable units for investigation. For purposes of presentation, it is assumed that the grid is composed of squares equaling one-half square mile. . . . The next methodological considera-

---

*George Cowgill was gracious enough to send me his comments in advance of publication so that, if I wanted to do so, I could change this section to overcome his criticism of my chi square calculations. After much thought, I have decided to leave the paper as it is, even though I now agree (after much correspondence) that his criticism is valid. My reasons for this are several: (1) No change in the chi square calculations would in any way change the conclusion that both of us reached—namely, that for the population defined here something more than a 30% sample is badly needed. (2) After reading Cowgill's discussion carefully I am not convinced that *any* chi square calculation (or any other statistical test) would be an adequate way of appraising a *sampling* strategy when, to use Cowgill's words [chap. 15, this volume], some form of *probing* would be more appropriate. (3) Numerous people, including several of the contributors to this volume, have read this study, yet no one previously has noticed this seemingly obvious error. Perhaps, his critique in Chapter 15 and this note will ultimately prove more enlightening to the reader than could any change in the original manuscript.

tion is arriving at a "sample size." This can be quite complicated. For purposes of argument, it will be dismissed and we will assume that a 20% area coverage within each sampling stratum has been judged sufficient.

In the present research, a trial grid was drawn over the area of the selected stratum with each sample unit equaling a two-inch square on the map. This size unit was selected somewhat arbitrarily, but it was thought that it would probably produce a frame with enough squares in the grid so that significant samples could be taken. Since this did, in fact, produce 95 sample units, a further breakdown of the grid into smaller squares was not felt to be necessary.

The sample units in this frame were not all of equal size. In practice this equality of sample unit size is extremely difficult to achieve when one is dealing with irregular geographic areas. Here, the assumption was made that a sample unit would encompass only that portion of any two-inch square which fell within the boundaries of the ecofactually defined stratum.

In order to avoid having to deal with the problem of small samples, an initial sample of 30 units was selected. By reference to a table of random numbers, the numbers corresponding to 30 of the two-inch squares were chosen. The translucent work map was then placed over the map showing the known archaeological sites in the district to determine those sites which would have been recorded if only the sampled areas had been intensively surveyed. The result was 17 of the 74 known sites and site components in the valley. The distribution of the 17 sites by site type is shown in column 4 of Table 1.3.

All sampling is based upon the premise that the sample adequately represents the total population. In the case of random sampling techniques the adequacy of the sample representation is expressed as a formal hypothesis which is tested in terms of the proportion of each cell (each site type) included in the sample and in the total population. The appropriate statistical test in such cases is the chi square one-sample test (Siegel 1956: 42–47). In the application of the test, the null hypothesis (H_0) states the proportion of the sites falling in each of the categories in the total population. The technique tests whether the observed frequencies (the sample frequencies) are sufficiently close to the expected ones to be likely to have occurred under H_0. If the probability associated with the occurrence is equal to or less than a previously determined level of significance (say 0.05), then H_0 must be rejected. If the probability is higher than .05 then H_0 can be accepted—i.e., the sample can be said to represent the expected frequency distribution (the total population) at the .05 significance level.

From the calculations shown in Table 1.3 it can be seen that chi square calculated from the initial sample of thirty units equals 98.64. According to the table of standard chi square distributions (Siegel 1956: Table C), the probability that a figure this high would occur with 13 degrees of freedom (degrees of freedom are determined as the number of categories or cells, in this case the number of site types, less one) is less than .001. Since this is considerably less than .05, the previously determined level of significance, H_0 must be rejected. In other words, the sample is *not* an adequate representation of the total site distribution.

TABLE 1.3

Calculation of Chi Square With a 30-Unit Sample

Site type	Archaeological sites in the Vosberg District		Archaeological sites in the sample		$(o - e)$	$(o - e)^2$	$\dfrac{(o - e)^2}{e}$
	N	$\%(F_e)$	N	$\%(F_o)$			
1	1	1.3	1	5.9	−4.6	21.16	16.3
2	1	1.3			1.3	1.69	1.3
3	5	6.5			6.5	42.25	6.5
4	13	17.1	3	17.6	− .5	.25	.01
5	2	2.7	2	11.8	−9.1	82.81	30.6
6	8	10.5	2	11.8	−1.3	1.69	.16
7	28	36.9	6	35.2	1.7	2.89	.07
8	1	1.3			1.3	1.69	1.3
9	7	9.2	1	5.9	3.3	10.89	1.2
10	2	2.7	2	11.8	−9.1	82.81	30.6
11	3	4.0			4.0	16.00	4.0
12	1	1.3			1.3	1.69	1.3
13	1	1.3			1.3	1.69	1.3
14	3	4.0			4.0	16.00	4.0
Totals	76	100.0	17	100.0			**98.64**

TABLE 1.4

Calculation of Chi Square With a 48-Unit Sample

Site type	Archaeological sites in the Vosberg District		Archaeological sites in the sample		$(o - e)$	$(o - e)^2$	$\dfrac{(o - e)^2}{e}$
	N	$\%(F_e)$	N	$\%(F_o)$			
1	1	1.3	1	3.0	1.7	2.89	2.2
2	1	1.3			−1.3	1.69	1.3
3	5	6.5	1	3.0	−3.5	12.25	1.9
4	13	17.1	6	18.2	1.1	1.21	.07
5	2	2.7	2	6.1	3.4	11.56	4.3
6	8	10.5	3	9.1	−1.4	1.96	.18
7	28	36.9	12	36.4	− .5	.25	.00
8	1	1.3	1	3.0	1.7	2.89	2.2
9	7	9.2	2	6.1	−3.1	9.61	1.0
10	2	2.7	2	6.1	3.4	11.56	4.3
11	3	4.0	1	3.0	−1.0	1.00	.25
12	1	1.3			−1.3	1.69	1.3
13	1	1.3			−1.3	1.69	1.3
14	3	4.0	2	6.0	2.0	4.00	1.0
Totals	76	100.0	33	100.0			**21.30**

In an effort to determine the sample size probably necessary to represent adequately the total population of sites in the Vosberg District, a second sample of 48 units (50% of the total) was selected from the ecofactually stratified frame and tested in the same manner as previously described. Once again, the table of random numbers was consulted, and the numbers corresponding to 48 of the squares were chosen.

Application of the same statistical procedure used with the initial sample results in a calculated chi square of 21.30 for the 48-unit sample (see Table 1.4). The probability that a calculated chi square of this magnitude would occur with 13 degrees of freedom is somewhat greater than the previously selected significance level of .05. According to the table of chi square distributions (Siegel 1956: Table C), the probability of this occurrence is $0.10 > p > 0.05$, which means that the null hypothesis cannot be rejected. Instead we must *fail to reject* (at the 5% level) and conclude that the variation between the 48-unit sample and the total population is reasonably accounted for by sampling variation.

CONCLUSIONS

The conclusions to be drawn from this study are of two types. First, there are the more obvious conclusions that relate to sampling considerations. Secondly and much more important, there are the conclusions that relate to the theoretical structure created in the first part of this paper.

On the basis of the research conducted in the Vosberg District, it would appear that Binford's (1964) proposed hypothetical research design includes valid and workable techniques for the establishment of sample frames and for the selection of samples from a geographically defined population. The size of the sample that was found to be necessary in order to produce a statistically significant representation of the settlement patterns in the Vosberg District (50% of the sample units) is substantially larger than that customarily encountered in random sampling designs; and it is much larger than either that suggested by Binford (1964: 434) or that employed in the few surveys where his design has actually been used (Thomas 1971, 1973; Matson n.d.). However, even a 50% sample would be a worthwhile saving in the time required to do a survey if the work necessary to delineate the areas to be sampled is not too great and the results are sufficiently reliable.

The major problem which became apparent in carrying out this research concerns the selection of environmental data which might have cultural relevance—i.e., the delineation of a spatially defined population which could reliably be used to infer a cultural universe. It is possible to observe and classify many of the nonhuman environmental systems in an area, and, if one assumes that these systems were substantially the same in prehistoric times as they are today, it is possible to determine which of them are culturally relevant, but: (1) It is not practical to use all available microenvironments to stratify a region; to do so would have meant sampling over 16,000 separate populations in the Vosberg District. (2) It does not appear to be possible to determine by random sampling methods those microenvironments which are culturally relevant. In order to stratify a region on the basis of ecofactual data, it is first necessary to delineate substantially all of the activity loci and the environmental situation in which each is located. This defeats the purpose of sampling, since the entire region would already be known by then and a sample would be unnecessary (cf. Hill 1967: 149; Rootenberg 1964: 182). In the research described here, random samples were selected from ecofactually defined strata, but these strata could only be delineated because culturally relevant environmental data (ecofacts) in the Vosberg District had been determined previously from the intensive survey. In other words, there was found to be a definite correlation between the sampled populations (i.e., the several strata), and the universe of cultural materials inferred from these populations, but neither of these were determined by random sampling techniques alone.

In the Vosberg experiment the empirical correlates for the sampled population and the target population were the same — namely, a definable segment of geography known as the Vosberg District. This population was subdivided into artificially created sample frames in which the sample units consisted of more or less equal sized land areas. The fact that this population was further stratified on the basis of environmental criteria in order to produce a series of populations that were actually used for sampling purposes was simply a matter of convenience in testing the hypothesis that there was, in the Vosberg District, a significant correlation between settlement patterns and microenvironments. If the word *microenvironment* had been expanded to include some larger environmental concept, the entire Vosberg District could just as well have been considered as a single population to be sampled through the use of more or less equal sized land areas.

The important point, however, is the fact that in the Vosberg District and in all situations where sampling is used as a part of an archaeological survey, the populations (of sampled land areas) and the universe (of cultural remains) are not mathematically connected. Because of this, there are no appropriate statistics that can be used to determine the proportion of the universe that has probably been found as a result of the sampling stratagem used. There is no way that the universe of interest to the archaeologist qua anthropologist is either perceivable (see Fig. 1.1) or theoretically definable because there is no way of even approximating a sample frame.

It is a temptation to think about the total corpus of knowledge concerning the prehistory of a given area as if it were in fact the universe of interest. Such things as the statistical tests shown in Tables 1.2 and 1.3, however, are in reality nothing more than a comparison of two different methods of sampling — one derived by techniques spelled out in this paper and the other by the technique known as "an intensive survey." Both of these are still only samples and it must never be forgotten that the inferential linkage from the sampled population to the universe of interest (the total inventory of cultural remains within a given area) is not something that can be subjected to statistical analysis.

The conclusion to be drawn from the Vosberg District study is essentially negative — that is, given the information available it is not possible to go into an unknown area and, using random sampling techniques, to determine both the ecofacts in that area and, on the basis of these, an inventory of cultural remains. However, the reasons for this are not that random sampling is invalid or even that random sampling does not have a place in archaeological research. Rather, it is due to the fact that the inferences which connect any kind of statistical population and a universe (as that term has been defined here) can only be connected by (1) an undemonstrated assumption that a relationship exists between the two phenomena or (2) some type of correlational study, perhaps conducted elsewhere, which is sufficient to convince a reader that there is, in fact, a connection between this kind of population and this universe.

The most important contribution of the Vosberg District study is not what it has proved or disproved concerning the validity of sampling in an archaeological survey. Rather, it is the fact that included within the study was a correlational analysis which demonstrated rather convincingly that ecofacts do exist. Within the Upper Sonoran lifezone of the southwestern United States another archaeologist, faced with the ubiquitous time and money limitations that are a part of every archaeological survey, would be justified in stratifying his region on the basis of environmental criteria corresponding approximately with those in the Vosberg District. This procedure entails his sampling the various environmental zones by whatever sampling stratagem appeared most appropriate, and, on the basis of those samples his making some statement concerning the likelihood (note that the word *probability* is not used here) that he had obtained a good nonrandom sample of the cultural universe. Once a study of this type is conducted it would appear to be valid as a basis for inferring the connection between environmentally defined populations and cultural universes anywhere within the broad region that is roughly definable as being contiguous with and having the same general characteristics as the region under study. However, it would be incumbent upon anyone using a study such as this to demonstrate both the environmental and the cultural similarity between his area and the Vosberg District. Both of these could be done on a test basis, though, and it should be possible to use the *correlational* aspects of this study to justify the validity of a random sampling design elsewhere in the Upper Sonoran life zone. The correlation between environmentally defined populations and cultural universes in other areas remains to be demonstrated.

In the final analysis, the determination of whether or not random sampling is valid, significant, and worth the effort in any archaeological research design can only be made when there is a clear understanding of the relationship between the population that is being sampled and the universe that is being inferred. If there is some basis for hypothesizing that a population actually consists of homogeneous cultural units such as sites, room outlines, depressions, or projectile points, then there is no question about the use of random sampling, for the sampled population and target population will often be the same or the target population can be convincingly extrapolated from the sample population. In either case, the term *universe* becomes unnecessary. However, where the populations are merely said to represent or inform about "the points of articulation between the cultural system and other natural systems. . . ." (Binford 1964: 432), then it is incumbent upon the archaeologist qua archaeologist, not statistician, to demonstrate the correlation of the natural systems (populations) and the cultural system (universe) that is inferred from the sampled populations. This type of correlation ordinarily cannot be demonstrated from sample evidence alone.

2. Sources of Bias in Processual Data: An Appraisal

Michael B. Collins

Michael B. Collins (Ph.D., University of Arizona, 1974) combined archaeological field experience with training in physical anthropology to lead to a dual specialization in lithic analysis and prehistoric demography. These two topics have been the subject of numerous primary and coauthored articles based on his fieldwork in Texas. Between the latter experience and his position as Assistant Professor of Anthropology at the University of Kentucky he did fieldwork in the Near East and the American Southwest as well as analyses of French Paleolithic materials.

INTRODUCTION

A fundamental premise in processual archaeological research holds that human behavior is a patterned part of a system with cultural, social, political, and environmental components. This patterned behavior is reflected in a patterning of material culture. Often it is possible to identify aspects of material culture patterning with specific components in the system. This position has been most explicitly articulated by Lewis Binford (1962; 1964), and has formed the point of departure for several provocative studies, most notably those by Longacre (1970) and Hill (1970). In spite of the very positive contribution to the science of archaeology provided by these studies, the troublesome question of reliable sampling has not been adequately resolved. Basically, this is because it has not been demonstrated that all crucial dimensions of the universe can be covered by a single sampling procedure and because account has not always been taken of the sources of bias which may intervene between the fact of patterned behavior and the discernment of pattern by the archaeologist. It is toward the latter issue that I wish to draw attention.

Cowgill (1970: 161–163) has expressed very eloquently his reservations concerning this basic sampling problem and has suggested that we must examine our quality of sampling in three distinct "populations." Ultimately, according to Cowgill, we often are interested in understanding a finite population of very substantial magnitude, or even an infinite population, to the extent that our understanding of that population could be said to contribute to the general understanding of human behavior. The variables that constitute this population are all of the variables that are found within the domain of the ethnographer. Of course, many of these variables are lost to

[26]

the archaeologist, and he must deal with two residual populations: the *physical consequences* population and the *physical finds* population (Cowgill 1970: 162–163). The former may be described as

The physical consequences of the events constituting elements of the first kind of population . . . (such as) objects and physical structures produced or acquired; wear, damage, and alteration of these objects and structures due to use; effects on plants, animals, natural features, and climate as a result of human activity; and the spatial and contextual relationships between all these manifestations (Cowgill 1970: 162).

Whereas the latter is the population "of all those physical consequences of human behavior which are still present and detectable (by means at our disposal) in a site or in some distinct contextual unit" (Cowgill 1970: 163).

Schiffer (1972) has addressed himself to the dynamics of the formation of archaeological context. Schiffer identifies a "systemic context" as the "condition of an element which is participating in a behavioral system," which would be roughly equivalent to the materials in the first population considered by Cowgill. The principal contribution of Schiffer's statement is explicit recognition of the fact that although refuse items produced at different stages of their systemic context "life cycle" potentially retain identifying attributes, they are subject to relocation. Therefore, although such items may be identifiable as resulting from a particular activity, their locus of discovery may not be the same as their locus of production.

Finally, paleontologists have developed a perspective which views collections of fossils as representing only those individuals in a past biological population whose remains have survived a *sequence* of contingencies. This perspective is best expressed as follows: not all categories of age, sex, health, etc., present in a living population of animals will be equally represented among those individuals dying in a particular time and place; of those dying, not all will die where there is an opportunity for fossilization; of those dying where fossilization is possible, not all will be fossilized; of those initially fossilized, not all will endure; of those enduring, not all will be exposed where the paleontologist may discover them; and of those exposed, not all will be discovered (E. L. Lundelius Jr., personal communication, 1967).

Patterns of material culture may be viewed in precisely this same perspective. Identification of the sequence of contingencies to which these patterns are subject provides a structure for evaluating our control of sources of bias. In actuality, each of these possible contingencies becomes another dimension which must be controlled, at least to some degree, in the sampling procedure.

The present paper may be considered an attempt to develop further the notions of Cowgill (1970) by addition of the contingency sequence perspective and identification of the specific sources of bias that operate *within* the systemic context of Schiffer, *between* that context and the archaeological context from which our samples are drawn, *within* that archaeological context, and *within* our sampling procedures. In examining sampling procedures from this perspective, only generalized problems will be discussed. Specific kinds of bias introduced by archaeological sampling procedures are the topic of several of the accompanying papers, and suggestions for improvement are made which are applicable to the broader issues raised here.

NATURE OF ARCHAEOLOGICAL DATA PATTERNING

Most archaeological interpretation is based on one or more of three kinds of relationships among material evidence. The first are the relationships of attributes in items of material culture. "Attributes" in this sense is used broadly to include all observable and measurable properties, such as state of radioactive decay, kind of material, or evidence of human modification (parallel striations on a sandstone rock; crushed shell tempering in pottery). The second are the spatial relationships among items of material culture and between these and various aspects of the natural environment (charcoal in a pit; pit dug into culturally sterile clay). And the third are the quantitative relationships, either relative or absolute, among these materials (number of serving bowls per hearth; number of notches on a piece of stone or bone).

It is inconsistent with the premise of patterned behavior to base any interpretation on assumed randomness in these relationships. Rather, the notion that random distributions prevail in any or all of these relationships becomes the null hypothesis of archaeological sampling.

Archaeological sampling has long been oriented toward the most valid means of rejecting the null hypothesis with extant materials—the physical finds population of Cowgill (Rootenberg 1964; Hill 1967; Vescelius 1960; Binford 1964). In the present discussion, attention is turned to an appraisal of the degree to which those extant materials are representative of the human activities by which they were produced or modified.

Thus, when Hill (1970: 15) investigated Broken K Pueblo in east central Arizona for the presence of nonrandom distributions of data which could be interpreted as "reflecting parts of a social system," his sampling strategy was to draw a random sample—in this case of rooms—for excavation with the expectation of finding nonrandom distributions of various items. This was successful, and the null hypothesis could be rejected based upon valid sampling procedure. However, it does not follow from this procedure that

after the sample has been excavated and all the artifacts counted, it is a simple matter to predict approximately the total number of any given item at the site—even though all the rooms are not excavated. For example . . . two surface room-type kivas were discovered in the 50 percent sample. . . . Since the unexcavated half of the site also constituted a random sample, we can expect that there are two more such kivas not yet found. This same kind of prediction can be made for any other category or item, and the accuracy of prediction increases when dealing with items that occur in relatively large numbers (Hill 1970: 21).

This is not a serious matter in Hill's Broken K study because he does not attempt interpretations based on estimated total quantities and because, in the case of this site, doubling the quantities of the various data classes noted in the 50 percent sample would apparently yield fairly accurate predictions of the total quantities for the site. As a general practice, though, assuming that the proportional representation of data classes obtained in an initial random sample will hold for the universe cannot be justified. Verification of proportional relationships by further sampling is imperative (Binford 1964; see also Redman 1973; Dorwin 1971: 354–366).

BIASES

Whether the target population of archaeological research is human behavior in general or a restricted range of that behavior, we are confronted with numerous potential discontinuities that separate that behavior from our tangible evidence for it. We may view these discontinuities as sampling biases in the sense that what we recover and observe does not proportionately represent each aspect of the antecedent behavior.

Seven sources of bias which intervene between human action and the archaeologist's perception of that action may be identified as follows: (1) Not all behavior patterns result in patterned material culture. (2) Of those which do, not all will occur where there is an opportunity for inclusion in archaeological context. (3) Of those so occurring, not all will be included in such context. (4) Of those which are included, not all will be preserved. (5) Of those which are preserved initially, not all will survive. (6) Of those surviving, not all will be exposed to, or by, the archaeologist. (7) Among patterns exposed to the archaeologist, not all will be perceived or properly identified.

Archaeologists cannot observe directly the intangible aspects of culture (language, social organization, achievement quotients, values, etc.) but, as thoughtful inquiry has shown, because these are patterned behavior sets which impart patterning to material culture which may survive to be observed, they are subject to at least partial description and understanding (Deetz 1965; Whallon 1968; Hill 1970; Clark 1966: 226; Davies 1969). There remain, none the less, aspects of behavior involving material items which, by their nature, impart no pattern to material culture discernable apart from the actions in which they are involved. We may identify this as the first source of bias. Principally this involves patterned short term shifts in the significance of cultural elements strongly patterned by a prevailing behavioral structure. For example, in significant parts of Western culture clothing involved in daily use is patterned in terms of style, storage, deterioration, disposal, or whatever, by its function as daily clothing. However, on every March 17 a temporary additional significance is attached to the wearing of otherwise undifferentiated items of a particular color. On this same day additional items may be worn which are styled, stored, and maintained specifically for use on March 17. But this does not detract from the fact that only by observing the actors throughout an annual cycle would one perceive this supplemental pattern in the use of daily apparel.

Similarly, the dominant pattern of crop rotation among farmers in Sirkanda, northern India, follows the sequence: barley followed in turn by janghora, then dry rice, then wheat, then khoda, and then barley again. But there are ethnographically observed exceptions to this sequence (Berreman 1972: 47). The behavior, then, is repeated plowing and planting of the same field usually, but not always, following a specific sequence of plant species in rotation. This complete behavior set results in a field area characterized by broken soil containing the residue from a variety of plants (perhaps chemical as well as seeds and pollens). With each plowing, species specific residues would be mixed with the result that only their presence, not their sequence would be discernible. From material evidence, then, only rotation can be inferred, not patterns of species sequencing.

The frequency and severity of this kind of discontinuity are in need of close scrutiny in ethnographic data, and the magnitude of the bias which it introduces into archaeological samples should be appraised.

Of behavioral patterns which clearly result in one or more of the kinds of patterned relationships of materials required for archaeological interpretation, not all occur where there is an opportunity for inclusion in archaeological context. Primarily this discontinuity derives from the scheduling or locating of activities under conditions which preclude any possibility of the material consequences surviving. Perishable food refuse cast in a moving stream or left on an open, stable surface may include strongly patterned attributes which are quickly destroyed by natural forces. There simply is no opportunity for these items to be buried, burned, mineralized, desiccated, or otherwise preserved. For example, pitfalls dug into the snow by Eskimo are distinctive artifacts which will not survive the first thaw (Driver and Massey 1957: 194). Campbell (1968: 15–19) has discussed one specific instance of how quickly and thoroughly archaeological evidence may be lost under certain circumstances. Upon visiting localities in northern Alaska utilized only five years earlier, Campbell could observe virtually no tangible evidence of utilization. Archaeologists are well aware of this source of bias, although it is usually subsumed under the broader category "lack of preservation," or more accurately, "differential preservation." By viewing "differential preservation" as a series of contingencies, as proposed here, the archaeologist is more likely to be aware of the potential bias deriving from the nonrandom patterning of activities in respect to conditions for preservation. That is, activities customarily scheduled for times or systematically conducted at localities, corresponding to better than, or poorer than, average conditions for the preservation of attribute patterning, spatial relationships, or representative quantities among items introduce a bias different from one resulting from a more random conduct of activities relative to opportunities for preservation.

Archaeologists also subsume under "lack of preservation" the discontinuity that results from the failure of material to be buried, desiccated, burned, or otherwise conditioned for preservation even though the necessary conditions may be present. Items deposited where burial by natural processes occurs will not always be buried quickly enough to escape destruction, dislocation, or reduction in numbers. Incomplete burning or dessication of a perishable item may result in its loss while adjacent and identical materials are thoroughly modified to a less perishable state. This is probably a more nearly random phenomenon than those discussed previously, and therefore does not constitute as serious a bias as less random conditions do.

Frequently materials, patterns, or quantities which are initially preserved will not survive. Patterned material consequences of behavior may be preserved under conditions which later change. Dry deposits become moist; buried materials are exposed and/or moved or destroyed by geological forces; subsequent human activity may disturb previously preserved evidence of earlier activities; or chemical and physical aspects of the setting may alter. This is an important source of bias, and archaeologists are constantly facing its consequences. The investigation of the building sequence at Grasshopper Pueblo, Arizona, for example, was dependent upon the investigator's ability to locate the intersections of masonry walls and determine if two walls were bonded by overlapping stones or if they were abutted and separated by a seam (Wilcox n.d.a). In many cases, settling and warping of walls under the weight of the overlying fill, which was responsible for the preservation of the walls, had pulled corners apart or otherwise altered their relative positions to the point that it was impossible to confidently infer their structural relationship. Archaeologists are well aware of this source of bias and are generally in a position to recognize and appraise its effects (e.g. Kenyon 1957: 44–46). We should also include here the very selective destruction of evidence occasioned by the antiquities trade (cf. Robertson 1972).

At the time that any interpretations are being made, not all of the relevant evidence that has survived up to that point is likely to have been exposed to, or by, the archaeologist. Remains that are inconspicuous, deeply buried, or located outside of the sampled area may constitute a nonrandom segment of the patterned behavior which produced them. Thus, agricultural fields of the Pueblo III period (in the American Southwest) are far less conspicuous than are the associated villages; those early neolithic villages in the Near East which were located where centuries of permanent occupations followed (e.g. Jehrico) are less accessible to the archaeologist than those, like Jarmo, that are not buried beneath great tells. The former, as the remains of early colonies in favored localities, are probably distinct as a set from the latter whose locations did not long attract permanent settlers. Many of the sampling issues discussed in the accompanying papers address themselves to problems of this sort.

Finally, even patterned arrays of data which are exposed to the archaeologist are not always perceived. As Benfer (personal communication) has put it, part of the paradox is that sometimes you must know the pattern you are seeking before you can find it; it also involves the asking of the right questions (Watson, LeBlanc, and Redman 1971: 172). Patterns are also subject to misinterpretation even when they are properly perceived.

CONCLUSIONS

There are several aspects of archaeology in its present state which are encouraging. Archaeologists have taken the pains to achieve better understanding of scientific procedures and to integrate their research activities toward specific, well defined goals. Archaeologists are using ethnographic data not only as a source of analogies, but as a source of hypotheses and as a laboratory in which to understand more fully the articulation between behavior and its tangible consequences. Also, they are making ever greater use of technical experts from other disciplines as well as sophisticated techniques for data acquisition and analysis. Perhaps, as Watson, LeBlanc, and Redman (1971: 113) have suggested, the most encouraging aspect of archaeology is its positivism. From this positivist point of view, the sampling biases discussed above should be viewed as challenges.

As Cowgill (1970) has said, we are on firmer ground when we sample at the level of what he calls the *physical finds population* (in other words, when our universe is that which has survived) than when we wish to sample either the *physical* consequences or the original *behavioral* populations. But this begs the question when it is the behavioral population that we seek to understand. We must, therefore, direct our attention to the *discontinuities* between behavior and our record of it, and we must develop sampling procedures to cope with those discontinuities.

As pointed out earlier, there is a *sequence* of potential discontinuities which may intervene between the patterned actions of people in the past and the tangible evidence of that behavior ultimately perceived by the archaeologist. The first of these, the fact that all patterned human behavior may not result in patterns in material culture, is an aspect of what Schiffer (1972) has called the *systemic context* of material culture. Also within the *systemic context* is the bias that may result from activities being scheduled or located where there is little opportunity for inclusion in *archaeological context*. There is at this level the potential for strongly nonrandom bias. It is suggested that ethnographic data may hold the potential for clearer insight into these two discontinuities. Operating *between* what Schiffer calls the *systemic context* and the *archaeological context* are the next two discontinuities—the fact that not all material will be included in the latter and that not all which is initially included will be preserved. These discontinuities, which contribute to the commonly recognized fact of "differential preservation," are well known to the archaeologist. *Within* the archaeological context further differential loss of data occurs with the disturbance or destruction of evidence which was originally preserved. The archaeologist has at his disposal a number of specialized techniques, such as soil chemistry (see, for example, van der Merwe and Stein 1972) with which to deal with the biases created by these last three discontinuities. Finally, in the two areas of exposing and interpreting surviving materials, the discipline is daily making conceptual and technical advances of which the archaeologist may avail himself.

The challenge is to be aware of the discontinuities that exist between the fact of patterned behavior and the surviving evidence of that behavior with which we must work. The advances in sampling procedures directed toward the recovery of surviving materials (the *physical finds population*) in recent years show promise for coping with the broader sampling problem of appraising the effect of the intervening discontinuities.

3. Archaeological Research as Cluster Sampling

James W. Mueller

James W. Mueller (Ph.D., University of Arizona, 1972) has had field experience in the American Southwest and Eastern Woodlands including the Koster Site in Illinois. One publication, "The Use of Sampling in Archaeological Survey," is an example of his special interest in experimental sampling. He has been serving as Assistant Professor of Anthropology at Bridgewater (Massachusetts) State College.

INTRODUCTION: SPACE IN ARCHAEOLOGY

The salient fact of life for archaeologists has always been that prehistoric cultural data have a spatial referent. Space is considered one of the major axes within which archaeological research is performed (Willey and Phillips 1958, Spaulding 1971, and Rouse 1962). The importance of space in archaeology has been mentioned repeatedly in introductory textbooks (Deetz 1967, Chang 1967, Hole and Heizer 1969, Rouse 1972, and Jennings 1968). Despite the primary importance of space (Mueller 1974), " . . . there does not seem to be any elaborate theoretical discussion in abstract terms on time and/or space in archaeological writings" (Chang 1967: 18).

Space is normally conceived of as one of the three axes forming the cuboid of archaeological knowledge; time and form constitute the remaining two (Rouse 1972: 2). When examined by itself, this single axis can be seen to consist of the three familiar dimensions: length, width, and depth. As Spaulding has noted, "It (the locating of artifacts) means no more than the application of a yardstick in the three ordinary directions to produce the latitude, longitude, and depth measurements which define a point uniquely" (Spaulding 1971: 31). In those cases when the depth dimension is reduced to zero, the spatial axis consists of only two dimensions.

Willey and Phillips (1958: 18–21) have discussed archaeological subdivisions of space; their maximal spatial entity is the culture area, and the site is the minimal unit. Intermediate spatial entities are the subarea, the region, and the locality in decreasing order of size, and probably of cultural variability. The site, as a basic unit of analysis may be conceptualized in two ways: (1) an indivisible point and (2) a three-dimensional unit. I have previously discussed each perspective in the following manner:

Within the locale [which is my environmentally-oriented reinterpretation of Willey and Phillips' (1958) concept of locality], the site is the next smaller unit of archaeological analysis. From a regional perspective, the site may be considered as a point in space. In other words, when examining the distribution of sites within a region a site appears as a single indivisible point on a map. When tallied as frequencies, artifacts found at a site are considered to be variables that describe the site. This conceptualization of archaeological space conforms to the regional perspective that is usually employed during the survey phase of archaeological research. On the other hand, the site may be considered a three-dimensional, divisible, spatial unit within the locality. In this case, artifacts are found at points within the site and can be plotted by reference to the three dimensions. The smallest, indivisible unit of space is the point at which artifacts are located. This conceptualization of archaeological space conforms to the site perspective that is usually employed during the excavational phase of research.

Ideally, these two perspectives have been complimentary, and the combination of perspectives is desirable in archaeological analysis. The site perspective is quite narrow for a proper analysis of excavated artifacts. Excavated artifacts from one site are commonly compared to those of other sites in the region. This method of analysis is referred to as the comparative approach. It is an expression of the principle of archaeological context in that the site is analyzed in terms of its artifactual associations with other sites in the region, instead of being considered as an isolated point in space (Mueller 1974).

ARCHAEOLOGICAL RESEARCH FROM A SPATIAL PERSPECTIVE

This section is intended to be a generalized description of archaeological research as it is presently performed. It is intended to be neither programmatic nor critical.

Fieldwork

The purpose of fieldwork is to discover the kinds and the frequency of target populations of data that exist within a given research area. The area may be an unknown region, an unknown tertiary drainage, or the unknown part of site. Discovery entails the perception, recording, and collection of various classes of unknown information by a professionally trained archaeologist. The discovery process may be hastened in two ways: (1) library research concerning the archaeological or environmental knowledge of the area to be investigated or (2) by the adoption of exploratory, first-stage fieldwork (Redman 1973). Either alternative will assist in the qualitative prediction of data populations, that is, whether certain data classes are present or absent. However, neither alternative will do much to help predict the frequencies of occurrence of each population.

The specific kinds of data that are discovered depend on the nature of the research objective. This oft-repeated statement has become a cliche by now and is an expression of the general scientific relativism that prevails in American archaeology in the early 1970s. However, it would seem desirable to be able to specify more precisely the relationships between data and objectives. What follows is obviously a trial formulation at further specification.

In general three classes of primary archaeological data are recognized: (1) cultural, (2) environmental (past and present), and (3) spatial. Four kinds of archaeological objectives are also recognized; these objectives entail (1) the building of a basic chronology, (2) the reconstruction of community patterns, (3) the reconstruction of settlement patterns, and (4) the process of man's adaption to the environment. The data classes are related to the objectives in a polymorphic manner. For purposes of creating a chronology of an unknown area, cultural data are necessary and sufficient information. The second objective of recreating community patterning requires cultural and spatial data. All three kinds of data are necessary in order to accomplish either of the latter two objectives.

The discovery process occurs within a spatial framework that includes several dimensions depending on the phase of fieldwork. During the survey phase, archaeologists are investigating spatial units such as a quadrat, a section, or the area between two streams for the presence of sites and artifacts. These spatial units are generally conceptualized (perhaps unconsciously) as two-dimensional in nature. Survey teams look for sites on the *surface* of the landscape and make *surface* collections of artifacts at each site. The location of artifacts recovered during survey is described only with respect to the two horizontal dimensions; the vertical dimension is a commonly ignored piece of data for artifact location. However, the complete description of a site recorded during survey does include reference to the third dimension—elevation.

During excavation, the spatial framework is always three-dimensional in nature. An archaeologist, when recording the location of a previously undiscovered site, feature, or artifact is defining one point in a huge volume of space. The set of coordinates (e.g., 3.2 m. east, 1.7 m. south, and −2.9 m. from a given datum) that defines the point in space at which a prehistoric specimen has been found is called the quantitative spatial attributes (Spaulding 1971: 32). This kind of attribute is referred to as the provenience of a specimen.

The quantitative spatial attributes may be transformed to qualitative spatial attributes which define a *unit* of space. This kind of attribute actually entails a double set of coordinates, e.g., from 3.2 m. to 3.7 m. east, from 1.7 m. to 2.2 m. south, and from −2.90 m. to −2.95 m. from a given datum. Each unit of space so defined is referred to as a provenience unit, rather than as the provenience. During fieldwork, the modification of quantitative to qualitative attributes implicitly occurs when sites are dug by natural stratigraphic or arbitrary excavation units and when artifacts are bagged by provenience units. An example of a qualitative spatial attribute is the eighth three-inch arbitrary level below surface in test pit 7. The transformation may also occur in the laboratory at the discretion of the archaeologist for ease of manipulation. Alternatively, the quantitative spatial attributes may be retained throughout the analysis " . . . if it is judged that the expected gain in precision justifies the additional work" (Spaulding 1971: 33).

Laboratory Work

The previous discussion of spatial attributes is related to the two kinds of basic calculations used during laboratory work. Spatial and nonspatial calculations are two basic statistical manipulations used for summary and inference. Spatial calculations include those that directly measure the frequency occurrence of data per unit of space. The unit of space corresponds to the provenience unit (not the provenience) of fieldwork, e.g., an arbitrary level in a stratigraphic control pit, or a prehistorically meaningful cultural unit, such as an ash lens in a fire pit. The provenience unit may be either two- or three-dimensional in nature and is designated by the qualitative spatial attributes. Examples of this kind of calculation include the number of sites per square mile (two-dimensional space), the number of lithic waste flakes in a trash pit (a three-dimensional unit of space), and the number of potsherds in floor fill (three dimensions). Such descriptive statistics may be subclassified as volumetric or density statistics when the unit of space is three-dimensional and as surficial or areal with two-dimensional space. Only volumetric statistics result from excavation, while areal calculations derive from survey in most cases.

The second kind of calculation includes data frequencies that are not measured with respect to space. Examples include the proportion of debitage to completed stone tools, the percentage of various pottery types, or the occurrence of various architectural attributes. These descriptive statistics are neither volumetric nor areal because of the absence of a spatial referent. It is realized, however, that nonspatial statistics may be convertible to spatial statistics if the provenience unit can be both determined and quantitatively expressed. Research objectives and the nature of the data collected will influence the necessity for each kind of calculation. Certain kinds of analyses may demand spatial statistics, while the nonspatial variety may be useful for other purposes.

It is also realized that the above scheme serves to classify basic descriptive statistical manipulations. These rudimentary statistics may become the basis for more complex manipulations that are directly useful for quantitative inference. Thus, chi square, correlation coefficients, factor analyses, etc. may build on the quantitative base established by these two kinds of calculations.

Conclusions

The logical flow of research activities and analysis in a comprehensive research program is from larger and more inclusive units to smaller, less inclusive units. We begin, during survey, with a large spatial unit, the region, and proceed to subdivide it in various ways into more manageable and researchable units, such as drainages or quadrats. Finally, the site becomes the focus of analysis which is also subdivided into smaller excavation units. Within these three-dimensional units are found artifacts and features, each of which consists of attributes which are the minimal units of analyses. This characteristic of data to be nested within higher, more inclusive, levels of analysis raises suspicions concerning the clustering analogy which will be pursued in the following section.

SAMPLING THEORY

The use of sampling has always been a means of operating within the immense spatial matrix that archaeologists have been confronting for many generations. The definitions used in this section are a blending of basic sampling concepts given by Kish (1965), Cochran (1963), and Blalock (1960).

Concepts

The relevant sampling concepts include population, frame, sampling unit, and element. These concepts are arranged in decreasing order of "size" and are quite flexible so that their actual application will vary with the research objectives. The element is the basic entity for which information is sought (Kish 1965: 67) and is one of the minimal units in a certain discipline. For example, sociologists refer to an individual, a household, or a dwelling unit as this basic unit of analysis. Archaeological examples include attributes, artifacts, features, and sites. The element is substantive, and its precise nature will be determined by the specific objectives of research. On the other hand, the sampling unit is methodological in nature. The concept refers to the unit that is selected for investigation and observation during fieldwork or laboratory work. The sampling unit is a means to attaining the objective; it is a methodological construct intervening between the element and the population. It is not a unit of analysis, but a convenient unit that can easily be investigated. This dichotomy between element and sampling unit is crucial for the thesis of this paper and for the proper employment of sampling.

The third concept, the population, refers to the collection of all elements or all sampling units and is the maximal empirical entity related to the objective. There are as many different kinds of populations as there are classes of data to collect. The list of elements or sampling units in a given population is also called a frame. The frame and the population are coterminous, but differ slightly in emphasis. The former concept emphasizes the individual elements, while the population focuses upon the totality of elements. [See Chenhall's chap. 1 in this volume for the distinction between target and sampled population.]

In order to execute a successful sampling program, these concepts must be operationalized in terms of the archaeological record. In other words, the researcher must decide whether the elements are attributes, artifacts, or architectural units. For example, a pueblo room may be both an element and a sampling unit. An artifact may also be a sampling unit if one is primarily interested in an attribute analysis.

Procedures

The proper use of sampling requires certain knowledge of the data that must be known prior to the selection of an actual sample. First, one must define the nature of the population(s) that is being sampled. Secondly, one must be able to delimit this population by establishing boundaries that distinguish it from other population(s). Thirdly, the elements or sampling units that constitute the population must be equivalent units that have an equal probability of being selected. Inadequate knowledge of at least one of these factors prevents the employment of true probabilistic sampling. The need to have knowledge of these population characteristics prior to fieldwork is logically inconsistent with the purpose of fieldwork – to discover the nature of cultural populations. This inconsistency is frequently referred to as the sampling paradox.

There are several levels of decision-making in implementing a successful sampling program. These decisions involve the choice of (1) a sampling technique, (2) a sampling scheme, (3) a sampling unit, and (4) a sampling fraction (or sample size). Only the level of sampling technique is germane to the thesis of this paper; therefore, the remaining choices will not be discussed presently—cf. Mueller (1974) for a discussion of these remaining levels.

The two alternative choices at the level of what I have called sampling technique are element and cluster sampling. The former occurs when the frame is a list of the elements to be observed. The elements themselves are selected for investigation and observation from the frame; the element and the sampling unit are one and the same. For example, an archaeologist who wants to measure 70 attributes per lithic artifact and has excavated a larger number of artifacts than can be analyzed may choose to list all artifacts and then select x number for analysis. This situation is element sampling because the elements (that is, the artifacts) to be measured are listed individually and comprise the frame. The lithic artifacts also conform to the definition of the sampling unit, since they are being drawn and selected from the frame. The element technique includes most of the commonly used sampling schemes, such as stratified, systematic, and simple random sampling. A description of each scheme and the comparative advantages is presented elsewhere (Mueller 1974; Ragir 1967).

Cluster sampling, the alternative technique, occurs when the frame is a list of clusters, not a list of elements. A cluster is defined as a group of elements and hence is a larger and more inclusive entity. The cluster is also a sampling unit that can be selected for investigation. Therefore, the cluster technique can also be defined as the situation that exists when the frame is a list of sampling units, rather than a list of elements. To continue the previous example, the archaeologist may not choose to list individual lithic specimens, but instead may list provenience units (either cultural or arbitrary). The frame consists of provenience units, each of which includes clusters of lithic artifacts. Therefore, a list of clusters of elements would be shorter than a list of elements for the same population.

Conclusions

The flow of logic in sampling theory, like archaeological research, is from larger to smaller units. The population and the frame are the largest units and must be defined prior to fieldwork. Ideally, the frame should consist of elements if they are known. Alternatively, it may consist of sampling units which are clusters of elements; in this case the archaeologist is actually cluster sampling.

SUMMARY AND CONCLUSIONS

Spatial, rather than cultural or environmental, information is the only kind of data for which the population is reasonably well known prior to fieldwork. The archaeologist must use this spatial population as the basis for sampling and as a means of circumventing the sampling paradox. The archaeologist chooses for excavation or survey certain spatial units that are used methodologically to help discover cultural and paleoenvironmental data as well as to be incorporated substantively during laboratory analysis. Therefore, the spatial units are actually sampling units. The elements of a research program consist of paleoenvironmental and cultural data that the archaeologist is trying to discover, observe, and record. The uniqueness of archaeological research and discovery lies in the fact that the units of investigation (spatial units) do not correspond to the units of measurement (elements). Each element is found at a unique point (the element's quantitative spatial attribute) within a spatial unit (the element's qualitative spatial attribute). Because each spatial unit contains a varying number of elements, the spatial units may be considered as clusters. Thus, spatial units are both sampling units and clusters during the field aspect of research.

It seems that spatial calculations derived during laboratory analysis do not conform to the thesis of archaeological research as cluster sampling. Spatial calculations result in the combining of both cultural and spatial populations into a single ratio, e.g., the number of sherds per room. Thus, the spatial units lose the methodological qualities and become substantive in nature. In other words, the spatial units become elements in this kind of analysis. Spatial calculations measure the frequency of occurrence of cultural and paleoenvironmental populations relative to the spatial population. On the other hand, the well-known fact that prehistoric data may be grouped nonrandomly in space argues for the extension of this thesis to spatial calculations. This fact seems so obvious that the argument becomes circular.

The use of nonspatial statistics during laboratory work does not conform to the definition of cluster sampling for two reasons. First, for this kind of calculation, the cultural and paleoenvironmental data lose their spatial referent and attributes. (The data can also be considered to be free-floating within the research area; thus, they retain a spatial attribute—the research area—that is so general as to be meaningless.) Secondly (and following from the first) the spatial unit ceases to exist as a sampling unit after the discovery process. Because of the absence of sampling units in this kind of calculation, the population to be analyzed is a list of elements. Since the cluster technique is defined in terms of sampling units, the calculation of nonspatial statistics cannot conform to cluster sampling.

In summary, the field process of discovering prehistoric data conforms precisely to the process of cluster sampling. (Several results of an experiment that I performed [Mueller 1974: 62–63] empirically reinforce this thesis.) However, the spatial and nonspatial calculations of laboratory analysis do not conform to this thesis.

The archaeological process of discovery necessarily involves inspection of spatial units to recover and discover prehistoric data. Archaeologists are constantly sampling space during survey and excavation. This is a methodological fact of life that is inescapable and irrefutable. Each spatial unit contains a cluster of cultural and/or paleoenvironmental data that are the elements of study. Each spatial unit actually conforms to the definition of a cluster and of a sampling unit. In this way, archaeologists engaged in first-stage fieldwork, the discovery of previously unknown data, are actually cluster sampling.

Space is seen as one bright alternative to the unknowability of the target prehistoric populations. Spatial units comprise one population that can be most readily known prior to fieldwork. The spatial limits of a region or a site can be drawn with a minimum of fieldwork during first-stage exploration. The area can be subdivided into equally sized units that have an equal probability of selection. (One field tactic for accomplishing this is outlined in Mueller 1974.) Thus, a spatial population can be conveniently formulated, subdivided, and enumerated to constitute the frame from which a probabilistic sample can be drawn. Thus, the identification of archaeological discovery as cluster sampling offers a viable alternative to the onerous sampling paradox.

The probabilistic sampling of spatial units is related to the use of statistics in archaeology. If a sample is properly drawn in accordance with one of the sampling strictures, then inferential statistics can be employed. A sample of spatial units does conform to the outlines of cluster sampling and, thus, is one acceptable form of quantitative sampling. The interpretation of archaeological research as cluster sampling means that archaeologists are conforming to sampling theory. Archaeologists can therefore use statistical theory to estimate parameters of prehistoric populations. These target populations are the basis for many substantive statements and tested hypotheses concerning culture history and process. These items of substance constitute archaeological theory and knowledge of the human record.

Cluster sampling, therefore, is the conceptual link between contemporary method and theory. It bridges the gap between the "how-to" concerns of archaeological methodology and the "accepted truths" of archaeological knowledge. Methodologically, the unit of investigation used to discover archaeological data is a spatial unit. The only elements that constitute the target populations are the cultural and paleoenvironmental data that are clustered within the methodological sampling unit. In making this statistical leap from sampled clusters to population parameters, a certain amount of caution, as recommended in the following paragraphs, is necessary.

The statistical consequences of this thesis are important in quantitative inference and in the testing of paleoanthropological hypotheses. If archaeological research conforms to cluster sampling in the manner outlined in this paper, then formulas for estimating population characteristics via simple random sampling should not be applied to clustered data. The reason for this lies in the difference of significance levels between formulas based on simple random and cluster sampling. Blalock (1960: 409) notes that "Instead of having significance at the 0.05 level, the true level (as obtained by correct cluster sampling formulas) may be as high as 0.50. . . . "

The meaning and explanation of this changed level of significance is apparent:

Thus, a level of probability that is chosen because it is conservative and "tight" is probably in reality quite liberal and "loose." The effect of this actual laxity is that hypotheses that should be rejected are in fact being accepted. Thus, some statements that are currently accepted as true are false statements of prehistoric cultural reality.

The reason for this is " . . . that cluster samples are less efficient [not to be confused with economical] than simple random samples of the same size" (Blalock 1960: 409). He postulates that the efficiency of a cluster sample with $N = 800$ may be similar to a simple random sample with N = 500. "If simple random sample formulas are used with an N of 800, therefore, we are more likely to obtain significance than if the correct procedures were used" (Blalock 1960: 409). Many formulas, such as Student's t-test, chi square, use N as the denominator of a fractional index. In these formulas, the use of the incorrect N (equal to 800 in this hypothetical case) as a divisor will produce a smaller result than if the denominator, corrected to N = 500, were divided into the same numerator. That is, the incorrect N produces values of the statistical test smaller than does the adjusted N, allowing for greater probability that the statistic will be less than the listed value by which significance is determined. Consequently, it is more likely that significance will be attained with the unadjusted, incorrect N than [with] cluster sampling results [that] are tested with simple random sampling formulas (Mueller 1974: 63).

There seem to be two options available to reconcile this situation. First, the archaeo-statistician may turn to the proper formulas for cluster sampling. Secondly, he may adjust the formulas used for simple random sampling in the manner suggested by Blalock. Although more experimental work is needed to refine both alternatives additional considerations are beyond the scope of this paper.

PART TWO

Sampling Within the Region

Sampling of the largest unit within which archaeologists operate presents quite simplified problems because the units of investigation are treated essentially as two-dimensional entities. Each quadrat, transect, or section has an equal probability of selection in the two-dimensional space of archaeological survey. Thus, probabilistic sampling and statistical theory can be readily applied to spatial, environmental, and cultural data derived from survey.

In Part Two a general chapter introduces the subject of regional sample survey. The three following chapters discuss three case studies involving regional research designs. The focal point of each chapter is the regional approach in spite of the necessary discussions of included sites, variables, artifacts, and features within the region. The general chapter, by Read, outlines the archaeostatistical theory that is necessary for the proper execution of a regional research design. Read also addresses his discussion to certain rudimentary, quasi-philosophical questions concerning truth, reality, and accuracy in statistical hypothesis testing.

The three case studies are critical summaries of sampling experiences encountered in the American Southwest and the Great Basin. Each author discusses the weaknesses in his sampling strategy and suggests improvements for other archaeologists. A second characteristic common to all chapters in Part Two is that sampling decisions are heavily influenced by the kind of statistics selected for analytical purposes. The conclusion is that sampling is a methodological tool subordinate to analytical statistics in a well-conceived research program.

A final characteristic common to these case studies is the use of experimental simulation to resolve problems resulting from the application of sampling theory to archaeological data. In this approach various sampling alternatives are simulated and then compared to a mathematical universe by inferential statistics or to an actual known population. Hill's (1967: 157) statement justifies this experimental approach: "It is evident that a number of archaeologists will not be willing to accept the application of probability sampling in archaeology until several such experiments are made. For this reason, they will be worth the effort."

J.W.M.

4. Regional Sampling

Dwight W. Read

Dwight W. Read (Ph.D., University of California at Los Angeles, 1970), a general anthropologist, has maintained multiple interests in archaeological uses of mathematical models, hominid phylogeny, kinship analysis, and the ethnography of fishing. He has prepared and published numerous articles relating to these topics since 1970 when he assumed a position as Assistant Professor of Anthropology at the University of California at Los Angeles. He also has been serving as Faculty Associate to the Chevelon Archaeological Research Project which is supported by the National Science Foundation.

Archaeology, by its very nature, involves sampling. The archaeologist chooses to dig one site instead of another, to excavate one portion of a site and not the remainder. The criteria for such decisions are generally not explicitly given, but presumably are based on a sense of which site or section of a site will provide more information. Not all sites in a locality have had the same cultural and depositional history and not all portions of a site are equal with respect to distribution of artifacts, structures, and other cultural remains. Sites, and portions of sites, differ in terms of both kind and amount of information obtainable. If pressed, the archaeologist could probably give cogent reasons why a particular choice was made. One site may be felt to represent a transitional period not yet documented, or a particular region of a site may be thought to contain the refuse. To the extent that the archaeologist is interested in a particular site in a descriptive sense, this type of sampling, which can be called *intuitive* sampling, may be quite adequate. But as the interest of archaeologists as individuals, and of archaeology as a science, shifts from description and historical reconstruction as a main focus of interest to an emphasis on explanation, the adequacy of data obtained from intuitive sampling must be considered. Clearly, there are many shortcomings with data collected in this fashion, and nowhere is this more apparent than when such data are utilized in attempts to account for and explain the cultural patterns or mode of adaptation of a now vanished group of individuals, as are used to test models and theories of social organization.

GENERAL ARCHAEO-STATISTICAL CONSIDERATIONS

The problem with an intuitive procedure is not so much that wrong decisions are made about which sites to excavate—in fact they may in many cases be the best choices—but in extrapolating from the known to the unknown. Ideally, the archaeologist would like complete information on all material objects that existed in a site at the time of its abandonment. In fact, such will never be the case. Not all material aspects of a culture preserve through time, nor can the archaeologist recover all material from all sites. [See Chenhall, chap. 1, and Collins, chap. 2, herein.] Inevitably, inferences must be made and, in fact, are made by all archaeologists. These inferences range in credibility from the trivially obvious to the source of major disagreement. The assumptions necessary for their validity accordingly range from straightforward to fundamental and nonobvious assumptions about the manner in which the cultural milieu of a group of individuals influences the decisions that are made with respect to alternative possibilities in the procurement, manufacture, and use of material objects.

An example of the latter is the set of assumptions that would be needed to verify Bordes' much disputed inference that the existence of four different types of Mousterian assemblages implies the existence of four cultures, or "tribes" in the Dordogne region of France (Bordes 1953, 1961, 1968). Whether Bordes' claim is correct or not is only part of the issue. Certainly, knowing the veracity of the claim that the Mousterian assemblages do represent four tribes is of extreme interest in reconstructing man's prehistory. But what is of far greater consequence in this and other issues in archaeology are the criteria that are accepted as validating such an inference. Trivially, a necessary condition is that the inference be consistent with the data. But is this a sufficient condition? Obviously, the answer is no. There are alternative hypotheses that also are consistent with the same data. At a minimum, the specific implicit assumptions that are a part of each inference must be justified. All inferential procedures assume the validity of certain assumptions, or auxiliary hypotheses. These auxiliary hypotheses may, or may not, be explicitly given. Most often they are not and seldom are they verified. They are assumed to be valid. But is it valid to argue, for example, as Bordes (1972: 149) has, and must, that decisions about the form of tools are cultural decisions and effectively independent of their use? The answer to this, and similar questions, is dependent on developing models that relate forms of social organization, human behavior, and material remains in a site. Such models will clearly have far-reaching consequences for archaeological theory and methodology.

Social organization by the word *organization* implies nonrandom behavior. Nonrandom behavior must involve patterning in material objects associated with that behavior, whether it be in terms of formal properties or in terms of spatial and temporal properties (cf. Binford 1962; Deetz 1968). Such patterning can be, and is, recovered by the archaeologist (Binford 1962, 1964; Binford et al. 1970). What is lacking are substantiated hypotheses of the particular form of patterning that should be associated with a given kind or aspect of social organization (but see Williams [1968] for a partial answer). What are the differences in the material objects or features at a site at the time of its occupation if, for instance, matrilocal rather than patrilocal residence is the rule, or if there are matrilineal rather than patrilineal descent groups? What part of this patterning will be preserved through time and hence exist in the site at the time of its excavation? Hypotheses have been made about such questions (Deetz 1965; Longacre 1968, 1970) but lack substantiation (cf. criticism of Longacre [1970] by Stanislawski

[1973]. However, Ember [1973] includes an empirical example of matrilocal/ patrilocal residence differences). Certainly, the answers to such questions will imply that the needed data will be in one of many forms: (1) measurements such as ratios of the number of one kind of artifact to another, (2) change through time in amounts of artifacts, (3) spatial distribution of artifact types based on function, (4) spatial distribution of artifact types based on style, (5) formal properties of features in a site, (6) spatial distribution of features, and (7) temporal sequences. All of these measurements are dependent on having accurate data to be useful.

If models that relate archaeological data to the variables or concepts of interest are known, sampling to obtain the needed information is relatively straightforward. The necessary data are dictated by the model so that the form the sampling should take is determined by efficiency. Nonprobabilistic, or purposeful, sampling may be the most efficient. But such models are few in number, especially when the problem is inference of social organization. Even for the far simpler problem of predicting site location, relatively few verified models exist (Southwestern Anthropological Research Group Research Design, Plog & Hill [1971]). In their absence, it is necessary instead to obtain the kind and form of data that will allow development and testing of hypothesized models.

When intuitive procedures are used to select sites for excavation to obtain such data, the implicit assumption is being made that the unexcavated sites provide no information different in kind from the excavated sites. Or at least this assumption must be made if it is to be claimed that the excavated sites are an accurate representation of the totality of cultural material in these sites. If such an assumption is demonstrable, then no difficulties arise in using such data for hypothesis testing. Most frequently, this is not the case simply because the determinants of site location and cultural content are poorly understood. To use probability sampling in such a case is tantamount to acknowledging that there *is* a lack of sufficient information to predict location and content of sites. To reject probability sampling is to assert either that the determinants are known or that the potential bias can be measured and controlled. But if this is not true, intuitive sampling of necessity introduces uncontrolled bias into the set of excavated data. Contrary to this, probability sampling does not introduce bias or at least it does not introduce bias for which control cannot be made. But more important than this is that it forces an evaluation of what is known and what is unknown. Probability sampling is not a blind application of random sampling for choosing sites to excavate. Rather, it is a judgment of where data are needed and where they are not. It requires assessment of the present state of knowledge in archaeology and requires the realization that in some domains, such as sites to be selected for excavation or regions to be surveyed, a random choice of units can be the most rational and most informative procedure. To say that nothing is known about a region, in terms of location of sites, is equivalent to saying a priori that all parts of the region are as likely to contain sites as not. In such a situation, random choice of units to be surveyed will provide the most information. If it is known that not all parts of the region are equally likely to contain sites, probability sampling requires that this knowledge be converted into a precise delineation of the region according to varying density of sites and that the region be sampled accordingly. Efficient probability sampling depends on the intuitive notions of the archaeologist being stated explicitly, tested as to their veracity, and utilized in formulating the sampling procedure.

Sources of Statistical Bias

The validity of inferences based on archaeological data are inextricably tied to the quality of that data. If they are biased, then without correction, all inferences based on that data must be biased. There are two major sources of bias in archaeological data. The first is the processes by which the material objects of a culture have come to be present in the site at the time of its excavation. The second is the procedure by which the archaeologist obtains those material objects and determines their properties. The first can be made the subject of inquiry, with the degree and kind of bias determined. Correction can be made for such bias. The second, to the extent that the archaeologist uses intuitive procedures that are not made explicit, introduces bias that cannot be precisely delineated. It is idiosyncratic bias and not subject to rational inquiry. Its existence can be noted, but correction cannot be made. The aim and interest of probability sampling is to eliminate this latter form of bias, precisely because if it is not eliminated, it becomes an indelible part of the archaeological record. Without probability sampling there is no way to know the degree and kind of bias present in the excavated material and in its classification.

Since all archaeologists agree that bias must be minimized, it is useful to discuss regional sampling, and in particular probability sampling from the perspective of bias. The statistician defines the bias of an estimation procedure, or *estimator*, for short, by measuring the difference between the average inferred value that would be obtained if the procedure were used repeatedly to estimate a particular quantity, and the true value of that quantity. If on the average the estimator yields the true value, it is said to be an *unbiased* estimator. If the estimator on the average yields a value differing from the true value, the absolute difference between the true value and the average of the estimates is said to be the *bias* of the estimator. The simplest example of this is computing the mean of a randomly chosen sample as an estimate of the population mean. Any particular sample mean may differ from the population mean, but on the average such sample means are equal to the population mean. The process of computing the sample mean is an unbiased estimator for the population mean and the sample mean to an unbiased estimate.

This is a convenient definition of bias, even in nonstatistical contexts. Bias can be thought of as the average deviation from reality by an inferential procedure. The only problem with this definition is that it would appear to be the case that the true value needs to be known before the bias can be measured. However, this is not strictly true. Just as the statistician theoretically determines whether a given estimation procedure will yield a true value, the same can be done for inferential procedures in archaeology. The question can be asked, does selection of a site according to criteria such as "it is the largest site in the region"; or "it promises to yield a large amount of material"; yield biased inferences, on the average? Note that what is of interest here is not whether in a specific instance one happens to obtain an estimate equal to the true value, but whether the estimation procedure yields biased or unbiased estimates. In the same way that the statistician is not interested in the fact that for one sample the estimate is equal to the true value, but rather what will happen on the average, the interest here is not in the fact that for a particular case the inferred value is the same as the true value, but what happens on the average. Obviously, if the particular case is to be used, one wants to know something about the bias present in these data, but that is a separate issue from deciding if a particular inferential procedure is biased.

To determine if there is bias in an inferential procedure, the relationship of the site in question to the purpose of the excavation must be explicitly stated. Bias is not an absolute, but a relative property. If the purpose of the excavation is simply to describe the site itself, then trivially the procedure by which the site is chosen will be an unbiased estimator of the site, no matter what the selection procedure. If the purpose is to describe the set of interrelationships among a series of sites, the way the site was chosen may induce a high degree of bias.

There is no need to belabor the point that inferences drawn from data based on intuitive sampling may be biased. The question that is of more interest to both the archaeologist and the statistician is how to reduce bias, not to demonstrate that it exists. A general answer to this question cannot be given in the abstract, however, for there is no unique answer. For this reason, the distinction between probability sampling and other kinds of sampling is a false dichotomy—the issue is one of reducing bias, not of using one procedure instead of another. In a given context, a specific probability sampling procedure may be highly biased. That does not argue against probability sampling. It only argues against that particular sampling procedure, in that particular context, for that particular question.

Archaeological Data Requirements

While a definitive answer cannot be given to the problem of reducing bias, it is of considerable interest to consider some of the ways it can be reduced for fairly general questions. Without being too definite or specific, a question of general interest is describing and defining the set of parameters affecting and possibly accounting for the features of a site. It may be possible, on the basis of the site itself, to infer many of its features, but any attempt to account for their presence necessitates knowing the relationship of the site in question to the group of interrelated sites of which it is a part. To all intents and purposes, no single group of individuals lives in complete isolation. Any group is affected by other groups and affects them in turn. The range of decisions that will be made and executed is bounded by the set of relations that exists with other groups of individuals.

This case implies that in general no satisfactory explanation for the features of a site can be made without considering its relationship to other sites. This in turn may imply that information is needed from a number of sites over a relatively large area that forms a network of interrelated sites.

This network may be extensive, or it may be limited. The size is irrelevant (except in terms of feasibility of obtaining sufficient information). What is relevant is knowing the properties of this network.

Now the precise data needed are not always clear. In fact, this is certainly one of the main questions facing archaeologists and is inextricably linked with models of social organization. But what is clear is that the success of any endeavor to understand the features of a site at this level of analysis depends heavily on the accuracy of the information available for such an analysis. [See Cowgill's chap. 15 for a contrasting view.]

By accuracy of information is meant two things. First, the degree of bias, and second, the *precision* of the data. The precision of an estimator may be measured by how closely estimates approach the true value. The standard procedure for measuring precision is by the variance of the estimates for the parameter in question. It is perfectly possible to have an unbiased estimator but have the values of the estimates vary widely from case to case. That is, the estimator, on the average, may give the true value, but any one estimate may deviate considerably from the true value. Obviously, estimates that have less variability have more precision.

Now consider some of the methods used by archaeologists to estimate values for certain quantities, or parameters. For instance, if a portion of a site is excavated and it is inferred that this portion is typical of the entire site, then implicitly the archaeologist is using the process of excavating a portion of a site as an estimator for the entire site, and that portion of the site excavated is the estimate. Is it unbiased? Obviously, the answer is almost certainly no. Is it precise? Again, the answer is no. Further, there is no way to estimate the degree of bias or lack of precision. This is critical for it may well be the case that bias, or lack of precision, up to a specified degree, can be tolerated. In some cases the only information needed may be whether a class of objects is present or absent. If the excavation procedures guarantee that it is highly unlikely that the class of objects in question is present, that may be sufficient information. What is not acceptable is having no information on degree of bias or lack of precision.

As archaeologists place greater emphasis on questions that are more highly dependent on accurate data, this problem becomes critical. The point being made is not that probability sampling, or some modified version thereof, is precise and unbiased and other sampling techniques are not, but rather that given *any* technique of sampling, it is necessary to be able to specify the precision and bias that are engendered by that technique. With such information, a rational decision can be made about the worth and usefulness of any given piece of data. Without it, archaeologists are playing a guessing game.

THE REGIONAL APPROACH

Regional surveys are one aspect of archaeological methodology where this question is especially critical. Regional survey usually precludes complete investigation. Since the focus of regional surveys is on understanding inter-relationships among sites, the question of bias and precision is extremely important. To give an extreme example, if only large sites are recorded, the implications about the system of adaptation may be completely contradictory to what would be inferred should it be the case that, say, 90% of the sites are small and only 10% are large.

The reason probability sampling is advocated is that, all other things being equal, probability sampling *does* provide the capability of estimating degree of bias and precision. Indeed, this is precisely its virtue over the intuitively selected sample. The latter sampling technique provides no information that allows the accuracy of the data to be estimated.

Debates over the virtues of 100%, 50%, or 10% sampling are, in the abstract, uninformative. Without question, there may be cases where a 100% sample will yield an intolerably biased impression of the system of social organization, settlement pattern, or whatever is of interest. If the degree of bias, in the form of rare sites missed, is intolerable, then obviously the sample size must be increased. There is no magic figure. In one case a 10% sample may be sufficiently large and in another an 80% sample too small. For instance, a sample of 1% has been sufficiently large to demonstrate that in the Chevelon drainage of Northeastern Arizona, site frequency differs considerably in the three ecological zones defined by desert-grassland, juniper-piñon forest, and ponderosa pine forest. If the sample were 50%, the conclusions would be unchanged. This is not a guess, but a demonstrable proposition. It is demonstrable only because probability sampling allows estimates of bias and precision. Conversely, that 1% sample is not large enough to obtain the kind of information necessary to describe, let alone explain, the system of adaptation used by prehistoric Indians in this region in the time period from roughly A.D. 900 to about A.D. 1300.

Sampling Decisions

There are two basic levels of decision that must be made in constructing a sampling design. The first is the type and size of unit to be used. For a regional survey this precludes using the site itself as a unit as it is the purpose of the survey to locate and classify sites. There are three basic types of units — point, line, and quadrat. The first two need no definition, the third will be used for all cases where the unit of sampling is some area of space. By a quadrat will be meant transects, squares, circles, etc.

The second level of decision is the type of sampling procedure and fraction of population to be sampled. Under the former rubric come simple random sampling, stratified random sampling, systematic sampling, cluster sampling, systematic unaligned sampling, and stratified cluster sampling, to name a few of the possible sample designs. Compound sampling procedures may also be devised, such as two- or three-stage sampling — quadrats are chosen by one sampling procedure and units (other quadrats or sites) are then chosen within these quadrats, possibly by a different procedure. This latter technique, multistage sampling, is in effect what much of archaeological sampling involves. Quadrats are chosen, all sites in these quadrats are recorded, some of the sites are excavated, and in the sites excavated, a sampling procedure may be used. It should be noted that the classification of a sampling procedure is in terms of the population that has been defined. If the population is the collection of sites in the region, then quadrats chosen randomly represent a form of cluster sampling, but if the quadrats are the population, the same sampling procedure would be simple random sampling.

The basic statistical concept is that of a population, and it is to the population that inferences are made. For the archaeologist there are two concepts of a population that need to be distinguished. One is that of a population in the statistical sense — the collection of sites and cultural material that actually exist in a region at the time of survey or excavation. This is the population that is to be sampled. A second population is that of the collection of cultural material at the time of occupation of the site or region. It is for this latter population that the archaeologist desires information and it is the former that is sampled. These may be distinguished by referring to them as *target population* (population of cultural material at time of occupation) and *sampled population* (population of cultural material at time of excavation). The latter is not necessarily, and almost certainly is never, a random sample of the former. The sampled population is a biased representation of the target population and the link between the two is provided by inferential procedures, not sampling (except in an indirect sense). One infers from the properties of the sampled population the characteristics of the target population. Thus the purpose of sampling is to obtain accurate information about the sampled population so as to provide a basis for making valid inferences about the target population. Henceforth in this paper, the word *population* will be used in the sense of *sampled population*.

For the statistician, the purpose of choosing a particular sampling procedure is to increase precision and decrease the bias involved in using a sample to estimate a population parameter. For the archaeologist, there may be two interests. One is to divide the population into subpopulations and the second is to estimate parameters for each of these subpopulations. In the Chevelon Archaeological Research Project, the region was subdivided into ecological zones to determine the effect these zones had on location of sites. Thus the region was stratified to define subpopulations. [See Thomas, chap. 5, herein, for the contrasting view that each zone represents an independent population.] If the interest were to accurately estimate the total number of sites in the total drainage, the stratification would be done to increase the accuracy of that estimate. This may, or may not, correspond to a division into subpopulations. This distinction is important, for it affects the statistical computations that will be made. If the region is stratified into subpopulations and in each subpopulation the units are chosen randomly, the specific procedure for estimating the precision of the values of the parameters for each of the subpopulations is not the same as for estimating the precision of the parameters for the region as a whole.

The subdivision of a region into subpopulations is an archaeological question, not a statistical one. It may be the case that the same stratification has more than one use, but it is within the context of a fixed population that bias and precision of a sampling procedure must be discussed. Stratification for increasing precision must be distinguished from stratification for defining subpopulations.

As has been mentioned, one of the basic purposes of probability sampling is to reduce bias and increase precision, as well as to provide estimates for these two quantities. In general, with the exception of maximum likelihood estimators, most estimators based on probability sampling are unbiased, so that the main distinction between different sampling techniques is in terms of precision. One of the difficulties that arises, though, is that generally procedures which increase precision only do so with increased cost in obtaining samples. For instance, generally speaking, the smaller the quadrat the greater the precision. But for regional surveys, there is usually a high cost per unit surveyed, in terms of man-hours. For a fixed amount of time, decrease in number of small units that can be surveyed with respect to the number of large units that could have been surveyed in the same time period may offset any increase in precision that the smaller units provide. The problem is to find a balance between these two considerations. For those cases where the costs, or at least relative costs, may be reasonably estimated, exact solutions to this problem may be obtained (cf. Cochran 1963; Hanson et al., 1953; Sukhatme 1954; Mueller 1974).

An associated difficulty with small quadrat size is that the number of errors in deciding whether a site belongs to a quadrat increases with the perimeter of the quadrat. This implies that square quadrats are less error prone than are rectangular quadrats for the same surface, and a few large quadrats will have fewer errors than many small quadrats. But long narrow quadrats tend to be easier to survey and involve less error in terms of staying within the prescribed boundaries and covering the entire quadrat. There is no simple answer to this problem. Point sampling, which does not have this source of error, is not a solution as the cost of locating a large number of points is prohibitively expensive. Line surveys are generally more useful for fairly dense, uniform distributions where the interest is in locating boundaries, than for surveying sparsely distributed sites. A line survey is a rapid way to find boundaries of a plant community, but inefficient for finding boundaries of a cluster of sites for which the density is low.

The effectiveness of any sampling procedure for regional surveys is affected by the distribution of sites in space. (Unfortunately this implies that attempts to determine a universally best sampling technique by considering a known distribution of sites — from a complete survey — and testing the efficiency of various sampling procedures on that distribution are only providing information about that distribution. The results cannot be generalized to different distributions.) What is an effective procedure for a random distribution of sites may not be efficient for a clustered or a dispersed distribution. If range of variability in sites is desired, how that variability is distributed in space becomes important. If sites that are alike tend to be in the same locality, a sampling procedure effective for that distribution may be inefficient for a different distribution. Again, if the distribution can be specified, it is possible to determine the most efficient sampling procedure. Since this is generally not known in advance, it may be efficient to use one sampling design to determine the distribution of sites and a second design to obtain the desired precision, based on the first-stage distributional information.

Simple Random and Cluster Sampling

The most straightforward kind of probability sampling is *simple random sampling,* where n units out of a total number N are to be chosen. The ratio n/N is the sampling ratio. Any selection procedure in which the n units are chosen in such a fashion that all possible combinations of n units are equally likely to be drawn is called simple random sampling.

While simple random sampling is conceptually the easiest, it is generally the least precise, if any a priori information is available about the distribution of the sites in question. Most regional sampling, though, is not simple random sampling, even if the units surveyed are chosen in the above fashion. Rather, it is *cluster sampling.* [See Mueller, chap. 3 in this volume.] By cluster sampling is meant that the elements of interest, in this case sites, are first placed in groups, or units, and it is the groups that are sampled, with all elements in the groups, or some subsample therefrom, selected for analysis. By its very nature, dividing a region into quadrats clusters sites, unless quadrats are sufficiently small that the probability of more than one site being in a quadrat is essentially zero. It is the quadrats that form the units of regional sampling, hence regional sampling is, perforce, cluster sampling if the site is the element of interest. Simple random sampling refers explicitly to the case where the sampling unit is itself to be measured or classified.

This introduces certain complications, especially for estimating the precision of an estimate for a parameter. For instance, suppose that the parameter of interest is the ratio of sites in the population of all sites that fall into a specified category, such as having structures present, to the total number of sites. The precision of the estimate is given by the variance of the estimator for this ratio. For simple random sampling of sites, the estimate of the ratio for the population is simply the value of the ratio for the sample, and is an unbiased estimate. For large populations, where the sampling ratio $n/N < 5\%$, the estimated variance s^2 based on the sample of n sites is given by

$$s^2 = pq/n, \tag{1}$$

where p is the ratio in the sample and $q = 1 - p$. For small populations with $n/N > 5\%$, a correction factor, the *finite population correction* (fpc), must be introduced and s^2 now becomes

$$s^2 = \frac{N - n}{N - 1} \frac{pq}{n}, \tag{2}$$

where $\frac{N - n}{N - 1}$ is the fpc. The effect of ignoring the correction factor $(N - n)/(N - 1)$ for small populations is to inflate the variance of the ratio estimate. Now for simple cluster sampling, where n clusters out of a total number N are chosen in a random fashion, p, the estimate for the ratio in the population, is given by

$$p = \frac{\Sigma y_i}{\Sigma x_i} = \frac{y}{x}, \tag{3}$$

where x_i is the number of sites sampled in the ith cluster and y_i is the number of sampled sites in the ith cluster falling into the category of interest. But now

$$s^2 = \frac{N^2}{n(n-1)x^2} \Sigma (y_i - px_i)^2 \tag{4}$$

$$= \frac{1}{n(n-1)\bar{x}^2}(\Sigma y_i^2 + p^2\Sigma x_i^2 - 2p\Sigma x_i y_i) \tag{4'}$$

for large populations and

$$s^2 = \frac{N(n-n)}{n(n-1)x^2} \Sigma (y_i - px_i)^2 \tag{5}$$

$$= \frac{N-n}{Nn(n-1)\bar{x}^2} (\Sigma y_i^2 + p^2\Sigma x_i^2 - 2p\Sigma x_i y_i) \tag{5'}$$

for small populations (see Cochran 1963 for derivations).

Note that the term px_i in (4) is the estimated expected value of y_i for the ith cluster. (It is an estimate since p is an estimate for the true ratio P.) Hence the size of the term

$$\Sigma(y_i - px_i)^2 \tag{6}$$

depends on the degree to which the ratio y_i/x_i varies around p. For archaeological data in which the sites belonging to the category of interest are distributed randomly among the clusters in proportion to the size of the clusters, the value of y_i/x_i for each cluster will be close to p and (6) will be small. If on the contrary these sites are distributed in a clustered fashion, (6) will be large. This implies that as the degree of dispersion in the sites that belong to the category of interest decreases, then so does the precision of cluster sampling. Observe that what is critical is not the distribution of *all* sites, but only those that belong to a given category.

If cluster sampling is compared to simple random sampling, it can be shown that the precision of cluster sampling varies from being more precise than simple random sampling to being less precise, as the distribution of sites of interest varies from being dispersed to clustered. This can be expressed more exactly in terms of *relative efficiency*.

Efficiency, Precision, and Cost

The relative efficiency for two sampling procedures is given by the inverse ratio of the respective variances for each sampling procedure for a particular estimator:

$$E = S_{p_2}^2/S_{p_1}^2, \tag{7}$$

where $S_{p_1}^2$ is the (true) variance for an estimator based on one procedure and

$S_{p_2}^2$ is the (true) variance for the same estimator based on the other procedure. To compare simple random sampling to cluster sampling, assume each cluster contains M elements, for simplicity, and n out of N clusters are to be chosen. All told nM elements will be selected by either technique. For a simple random sample of size nM, if P is the population ratio and $Q = 1 - P$,

$$S_{p_1}^2 = \frac{NM - nM}{NM - 1} \frac{PQ}{nM} \tag{8}$$

$$\simeq \frac{N - n}{N} \frac{PQ}{nM} . \tag{8'}$$

For cluster sampling,

$$S_{p_2}^2 = \frac{N - n}{nN} \frac{\Sigma(p_i - P)^2}{N - 1} \tag{9}$$

$$\simeq \frac{N - n}{N^2 n} \Sigma(p_i - P)^2, \tag{9'}$$

where p_i is the true ratio for the cluster. Equation (8) is equivalent to (5) with true values substituted for the estimates, since the assumption that all clusters are of the same size implies that $x_i = x$ for all i. Then the relative efficiency of simple random sampling in comparison to cluster sampling is given by

$$E = S_{p_2}^2/S_{p_1}^2 = \frac{M\Sigma(p_i - P)^2}{NPQ} \tag{10}$$

$$= \frac{M^2\Sigma(p_i - P)^2}{TPQ}, \tag{10'}$$

where T is the total number of elements in the population. Thus E is proportional to the size of the term

$$\Sigma(p_i - P)^2, \tag{11}$$

which, as noted above, depends on the distribution of the sites that belong to the category of interest. For fixed M, E will be smallest for a uniform, or dispersed, distribution and largest for a clustered distribution. It can be shown that as the distribution varies from dispersed to clustered, E will vary from being less than 1 to greater than 1. Hence simple random sampling is more efficient for clustered distributions and cluster sampling is more efficient for dispersed distributions. Observe that for a given distribution, since (11) tends to increase as M decreases, no universally valid conclusion may be reached about the change in E as M varies. The relative efficiency of cluster sampling tends to be proportional, in most cases, to the square root of the cluster size (cf. Sukhatme 1954). Thus sampling with large clusters tends to be less efficient than sampling with small clusters. (See Mueller 1974 for a contrasting view based on economy.)

As an example, consider the following hypothetical case. Suppose that the total number of sites in a region is 300 and the proportion of sites with structures is the variable of interest. Suppose that in fact this proportion is three-fourths ($P = 3/4$) and a 10% sample (of the total number of sites) is to be selected.

For simple random sampling, $N = 300$ and $n = 30$. For a site selected at random, the probability of it containing a structure is 3/4. A sample of size 30 (with no repetitions) may be drawn from a table of random numbers, with a value between 1 and 225 representing a site with a structure and a number between 226 and 300 representing a site without a structure. This was done, and it was found that there were 21 sites with structures in the sample. Thus $p = 21/30 = 0.7$. Hence s^2, without the fpc, is given by

$$s^2 = pq/n = \frac{(0.7)\,(0.3)}{30} = 0.007 \tag{12}$$

and with the fpc.

$$s^2 = \frac{N-n}{N-1}\frac{pq}{n} = 0.0063 \tag{13}$$

The fpc decreases the variance estimate by a factor of 0.9. When for the same data the sample of size 30 was divided into 6 clusters of size 5, corresponding to cluster sampling with 5 sites per cluster, it was found that $y_1 = 3$, $y_2 = 4$, $y_3 = 4$, $y_4 = 4$, $y_5 = 3$, and $y_6 = 3$. This yields $\Sigma x_i^2 = 75$, $\Sigma y_i^2 = 150$, and $\Sigma x_i y_i = 105$. Here, $N = 60$ and $n = 5$. Thus s^2, without the fpc, is given by

$$s^2 = \frac{1}{n(n-1)\,\bar{x}^2}(\Sigma y_i^2 + p^2 \Sigma x_i^2 - 2p\Sigma x_i y_i) \tag{14}$$

$$= \frac{1}{(6)\,(5)\,(5^2)}\left(75 + (0.7)^2\,(150) - (2)\,(0.7)\,(105)\right) \tag{14'}$$

$$= 0.002. \tag{14''}$$

With the fpc, $s^2 = 0.0018$, as $N = 60$ and $n = 6$.

When the cluster size was increased to 10, it was found that $y_1 = 7$, $y_2 = 8$, and $y_3 = 6$. For this case $s^2 = 0.0033$ without fpc and $s^2 = 0.003$ with the fpc.

If the sites with structures are clustered, rather than random in their distribution, a different value for s^2 will be obtained. Suppose that $y_1 = 2$, $y_2 = 2$, $y_3 = 2$, $y_4 = 5$, and $y_6 = 5$ represent a cluster sample from a clustered distribution. Then $s^2 = 0.02$ without the fpc and $s^2 = 0.018$ with the fpc.

The simple random sample is more precise than the cluster sample by about a factor of 3 for the clustered distribution; whereas the cluster sample is more precise by about a factor of 3 than the simple random sample for a random distribution. Since the variance estimate is proportional to the sample size, this implies that for the random distribution, a sample size of 30% would be needed for simple random sampling to be as efficient as cluster sampling; whereas for the clustered distribution, the reverse is true. The two sizes of clusters illustrate that large clusters tend to be less efficient than small clusters for the same distribution.

The reason that sampling a large percentage of a region is more precise than sampling a small percentage is due more to the fpc than to the uncorrected variance estimate. The fpc varies from 1 to 0 as the sampling ratio varies from 0% to 100%, whereas the variance estimate is simply a function of sample size. A sample of size 100 that represents a 1% sample engenders the same precision, as measured by the uncorrected variance estimate, as a sample of 100 that represents a 75% sample.

Appropriate modification may be made in (10) for the case where the number of elements per cluster is not constant (cf. Cochran 1963). The estimated relative efficiency can also be computed on the basis of sample data (cf. Sukhatme 1954).

It can be shown (Cochran 1963; Sukhatme 1954) that for the optimal cluster size, that is, the cluster size that minimizes variance, the quantity

$$Cc_1M/c_2^2 \tag{15}$$

is approximately constant; where C is the total amount of time available for the sampling program, c_1 is the time needed for recording information on a site plus travel time between two sites in a quadrat, and c_2 is the time spent in locating a quadrat. The exact value for M can be found explicitly (cf. Cochran 1953) and depends on the variability of the data, C, c_1, and c_2. The general implication is that M should decrease if time available increases, travel time decreases, or time for recording information increases. Since it will be the latter that is most variable for an archaeological survey, this implies that the more information desired per site, the smaller M should be.

Two general points need to be observed. The first point is that for regional surveys with a large portion of the population sampled ($n/N > 5\%$), the usual statistics based on infinite populations must be corrected for the fact that sampling is being done without replacement from a finite population. The second point is that the appropriate procedure for evaluating the precision of an estimate is a function of the particular probability sampling procedure utilized. Equation (2) for the variance is that for a binomial distribution corrected for finite population, while (5) has taken into account that fact that the element of interest, in this case the site, is not the sampling unit.

For other sampling designs, appropriate corrections also exist, but will not be given here (cf. Cochran 1963; Hanson et al., 1953; Sukhatme 1954).

Systematic and Stratified Sampling

If information is available about the spatial distribution of the sites, then *stratified* or *systematic* sampling will greatly increase the precision of an estimate over simple random sampling, or simple cluster sampling. By stratified sampling is meant that the population is broken up into strata and from each of these strata a number of units are selected in a random fashion. Systematic sampling refers to listing all units and then picking every kth unit, k an arbitrary integer that is partly dependent on the sampling fraction, where the first unit is generally chosen as random from among the first k units.

Stratified sampling may also be subdivided into *optimal* and *proportional allocation*. Optimal allocation refers to the case where the number of units from each strata is chosen so as to minimize the variance of the parameter being estimated. It can be shown that the variance will be minimized when the number of units chosen from the ith strata is proportional to the product of the total number of units in the ith strata and the standard deviation of the parameter to be estimated over the ith strata. (See Cochran 1963 for details.) In other words, larger samples should be drawn from strata that are more variable. One implication of this is that sampling efficiency will increase only if the strata are chosen so as to increase homogeneity within strata in comparison to the population as a whole.

Proportional allocation occurs when the number of units n_i chosen from the ith strata is such that

$$n_i/n = N_i/N; \tag{16}$$

where N_i is the total number of units in the ith stratum. Proportional allocation requires no previous knowledge of the distribution in each stratum, whereas optimal allocation requires knowledge about the standard deviation of the parameter for each of the strata (or at least relative standard deviations). The difference in terms of gain in precision tends to be negligible unless the standard deviations among the strata differ by at least a factor of two (Cochran 1963).

The distinction between stratified and systematic sampling depends on the spatial distribution of sites. For some data, systematic sampling is more precise and for other data, stratified sampling is the better choice. One of the advantages of systematic sampling is that it is often much easier to choose a sample, though this is not so true of regional surveys. But one of its major drawbacks is the difficulty in obtaining an unbiased estimate of the variance of a parameter.

More complex sampling designs can be constructed by multistage sampling and appropriate corrections for computing estimates of a parameter and its variance are given by Cochran (1963), Hanson et al. (1953), and Sukhatme (1954). The details will not be given here.

SUMMARY

The necessary sample size can also be specified, but not out of the context of the degree of precision desired, the sampling technique used, the characteristics of the population to be sampled, and the cost of obtaining a sample. If these are known, an exact solution can be given as to sample size needed. Generally speaking, the more homogeneous the population and the greater the frequency of any type of site, the smaller the sample size necessary for a given degree of precision. Stratification is one way to increase homogeneity. For the reverse situation, the sample size will need to be large and may approach a complete survey in order to locate rare sites. For the infrequent situation (at least in archaeology) where a specific hypothesis is to be tested, the size of the sample necessary to reject, or accept, a null hypothesis can be considerably reduced by sequential sampling (cf. Wald 1947). Sequential sampling provides for making a decision as to whether the null hypothesis can be rejected (or accepted) or whether more units need to be sampled, after each unit is sampled. On the average, it reduces considerably the number of units needed for testing a specific hypothesis.

There is no single best sampling procedure for regional surveys. The sampling procedure must take into account at least these important parameters: the information desired, the distribution of that information in space, cost of obtaining samples, and degree of precision needed, etc.

The fact that the sampling unit for an archaeological survey is generally a cluster of sites implies that simple random selection of such units is relatively inefficient, unless these sites are distributed in a uniform fashion. While decreasing cluster size is one way to increase efficiency, it only does so at the cost of increased search time for quadrats to be surveyed and increased number of errors in deciding whether a site does or does not belong to a quadrat being surveyed. Since cluster sampling is efficient for random to uniform distributions, intelligent use of stratification can overcome the inherent drawbacks of cluster sampling.

If the region can be stratified so that the various strata are homogeneous with respect to the variables of interest and the sites are distributed in a relatively uniform fashion, cluster sampling will be efficient within each stratum. Consequently, the more information that is available from prior surveys, or from demonstrable propositions about site location and distribution of cultural material, the more efficient a sampling procedure will be. To design an efficient sampling procedure is a challenge to bring into play all knowledge available about a region and intergrate it in such a way that sampling will then efficiently and accurately provide needed answers to gaps in the archaeological record, provide a firm basis for historical reconstruction, and allow development and testing of theory. It is for this latter reason in particular that probability sampling is so important to archaeological methodology; theory cannot be developed or tested in a meaningful fashion unless accurate data are available, and it is only with probability sampling that estimates can be made of the accuracy of the sampled data from the data themselves.

5. Nonsite Sampling in Archaeology: Up the Creek Without a Site?

David Hurst Thomas

David Hurst Thomas (Ph.D., University of California at Davis, 1971), a productive scholar, has devoted himself to the American West, particularly the Great Basin. In addition to a long list of articles, he has authored a text-book, *Predicting the Past: An Introduction to Anthropological Archaeology.* His background and topical specialty of quantitative analysis have enabled him to serve in various consultant and editorial capacities. He has been serving as Assistant Curator of North American Archaeology at the American Museum of Natural History.

What we call progress is the exchange of one nuisance for another nuisance.

H. Ellis

Let us begin with the truism that all sampling in archaeology is not the same. We all know this, of course, but it seems from time-to-time that some archaeologists (in the quest for the ultimate probability sample?) lose sight of their objectives in sampling. At the risk of oversimplifying an admittedly complex topic, I wish to look at the strategy and analytical procedures engendered by some archaeological probability sampling. Specifically, I wish to distinguish between the two basic varieties of regional random samples current in archaeology today.

The first procedure can be called simply *site sampling,* a phrase which may sound to some self-evident. The site concept seems so ingrained into the conventional wisdom of archaeology that few stop to consider how much we truly rely upon the concept. Willey and Phillips, in their definition of archaeology's unit concepts, state that the "*site* is the smallest unit of space dealt with by archaeologists . . . [it] may be anything from a small camp to a large city . . . it is in effect the minimum operational unit of geographic space" (1958: 18). Certainly in archaeological surveys, whether they be random, systematic, haphazard or intuitive, the site is the primary element of interest. The SARG (Southwestern Anthropological Research Group) research design, for example, was conceived to answer a primary question: "Why did prehistoric populations locate their *sites* where they did?" (Plog and Hill 1971: 8). Binford also based his 1964 discussion on the site concept when he argued that there are only two basic sampling universes in excavation or fieldwork: the region and the site. "Populations of sites must be investigated within a universe defined in spatial terms, the region. Populations of cultural items and features must be investigated within a universe defined by . . . the site" (Binford 1964: 433). In other

[61]

words, regional surveys are really only large samples of sites, since the site is the basic operational unit throughout. In fact, it even seems redundant in archaeology to speak of "site surveys." Is there any other kind?

DEFINITION OF NONSITE ARCHAEOLOGY

It is a mistake to conclude that just because the site concept is almost universally accepted as archaeology's minimal *spatial* unit it is always *archaeology's minimal operational unit*. This is simply not so. There is a mode of archaeological research in which the site concept is not only inessential, but even slightly irrelevant. I specifically refer to regional sampling procedures which take the *cultural item* (the artifact, feature, manuport, individual flake, or whatever) as the minimal unit, and ignore traditional sites altogether.

I call this non-site-oriented archaeology "Easter Egg sampling" in order to underscore graphically the shift in analytical unit. Easter eggs are, as we all know, discrete little entities to be spread about upon the lawn, then eagerly collected *one by one* on a Sunday afternoon. Easter egg hunting in archaeology likewise focuses upon the individual elements (the artifacts, the features, the debitage) rather than upon bundles of these elements (the sites). This is not to deny that artifacts generally occur in well-defined sites — Easter eggs often arrive in baskets — but rather to assert that in some instances, under special research circumstances, discrete clumpings of artifacts (a) either do not occur or (b) are not relevant to the problems immediately at hand.

I must point out, in all candor, that James Ford must be credited with the initial discussion on the relevance of Easter eggs to archaeology. In an exchange with Albert Spaulding, Ford admitted that "I am somewhat more uncertain than Spaulding that nature has provided us with a world filled with packaged facts and truths that may be discovered and digested *like Easter eggs on a lawn*" (Ford 1954: 109). Of course, since Ford's Easter eggs didn't exist — and mine do — we are obviously taking aim at different targets.

It is clear that most archaeologists prefer to hunt Easter egg baskets rather than individual Easter eggs. Hole and Heizer probably speak for the vast majority of archaeologists when they suggest that "The excavation and interpretation of sites is at the core of archaeology and is regarded by many as a goal in itself, for it is in the analysis of a site that brings to bear all the aspects of archaeological theory and technique" (Hole and Heizer 1973: 12).

Can it be that with no sites, there can be no archaeological theory or technique? Archaeology's preoccupation with sites — their location, their stratigraphy, their origin, their preservation — has allowed some important information to pass unnoticed, and I think it worthwhile to discuss just what nonsite archaeology has to tell us, and how we may go about deciphering the message.

The issue turns, of course, on one's definition of site. For Plog and Hill (1971: 8), a site consists of "any locus of cultural material, artifacts or facilities." So in this sense, a site could be as small as a square meter or consist merely of a few sherds or even one chip. This position is unassailable—although there might be some analytical problems—and I do not care to quibble with their intent. But, like a pair of worn suspenders, the site concept can be stretched so far that it fails to carry any weight at all. In the fieldwork at Reese River, a site (in the traditional sense) might consist of merely an isolated flake on a hillside or a scatter of hundreds of artifacts and features. Perhaps we could even define the *entire valley* as a single site, in which case we are really concerned with "within-site sampling." But these positions seem to me strained and constricting. Our concepts must be helpful rather than restrictive, so I have scrapped the site concept altogether in this context. The decision is, of course, dictated by the immediate objectives of the survey, and also by the nature of the archaeological remains.

THE REESE RIVER ECOLOGICAL PROJECT

To contain this discussion within manageable proportions, I will direct my attention to a specific archaeological Easter egg hunt: the Reese River Ecological Project. The work at Reese River was the first to my knowledge—and in many ways the least sophisticated—of several applications of systematic archaeological Easter egg collection on a regional scale (e.g., Matson 1971 and Bettinger n.d.); hence it provides a useful target for critical appraisal. Nonsite archaeology of this sort generally produces a host of material remains such as artifacts, features, debitage, manuports and so on; so I will further narrow this discussion to cover only two commonly recovered categories of remains: debitage and projectile points. I intend to illustrate the analysis of nonsite materials upon these two categories, and a complete listing of the data is available from the author.

The objects themselves—in this case, the individual flakes and projectile points—do not constitute the sample *data* of course; the data are measurements and observations made *upon* the objects recovered. So although all the objects may be recovered from a region (or from a site), the data generation process can continue indefinitely, so long as new observations are made upon the artifacts. This merely reaffirms the stricture that *statistical* populations of any sort do not consist of objects, they consist of measurements of variables (variates).

The research at Reese River was basically an attempt to test an ethnographic theory upon some archaeological facts. Specific aspects of the Reese River Ecological Project have been considered elsewhere (Thomas 1969, 1972, 1973); this paper concentrates upon the sampling and analytical issues raised by that project. The theory in question was Julian Steward's synthesis of ethnographic and, by extension, prehistoric patterns of settlement and subsistence of the Great Basin Shoshoneans. There has been some disagreement as to whether the settlement patterns of the historic period (as described by Steward) were adequate representations of the prehistoric situation, or whether those patterns had been altered by the impact of acculturation. The Reese River project viewed the archaeological record of the prehistoric Shoshoni as a "court of last resort" in which to test the case as presented by Steward.

Basically, Steward's (1938) theory of Shoshonean settlement pattern attempted to explain how members of a single hunter-gatherer society moved themselves across the landscape, in a stable yet flexible pattern of transhumance. The theory states that certain techno-economic activities took place within specific microenvironments. Therefore, as a test, the cultural debris left by these peoples must be collected from each microenvironment independently, so that the assemblages can be compared between biotic communities. That is to say, the research strategy must provide for the total recovery of selected items in a manner which preserves the articulation between the cultural debris and the microenvironments in which it was discarded.

The universe of the sample was a tract of land about 30 miles south of Austin in Lander County, Nevada. The lateral boundaries of the sampling area were chosen as the crests of the Toiyabe and Shoshone mountains, which lie about 15 miles apart. The northern and southern boundaries were arbitrarily selected to provide a suitable sampling area, and a 500-meter grid was then imposed over the entire area (Fig. 5.1). The area was superficially divided into primary biotic communities and a 10% random sample of the 500 meter-square tracts was selected from a table of random permutations.

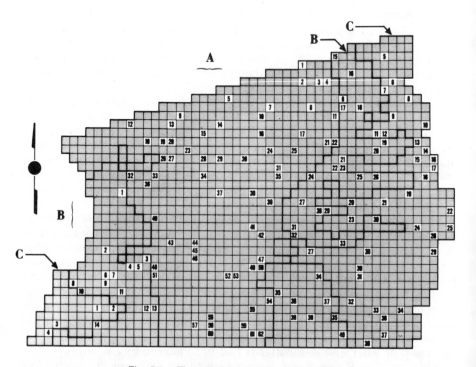

Fig. 5.1. The sampling grid of the Reese River ecological project. Each sampling tract is 500 meters on a side (after Thomas 1973).

Steward's theory was translated from ethnographic descriptions into material culture correlates by means of a computer simulation model, cryptically known as Basin I (see Thomas 1972, 1973). The workings of Basin I are irrelevant to this discussion, but Basin I predictions relating to projectile points and debitage are of direct interest to the analytical techniques discussed here, and an example of these predictions is presented in Thomas (1973, Table 3). To obtain these predictions, the Basin I model asks the following question: If Steward's theory accounts for the prehistoric Reese River settlement pattern, how should the artifacts be distributed on the ground? Artifact distribution was measured in this case by the mean density and the Coefficient of Dispersion; the efficacy of these measures is considered later in this chapter.

This discussion of the Reese River design will differ somewhat from earlier statements. The sampling strategy was described elsewhere (Thomas 1973) as a "stratified random sample of unequal clusters." I now view biotic communities as independent sampling *domains,* rather than as sampling strata within a single domain, since the ecological zones were actually the areas of comparison in this survey. The research design is a simple random sampling from each of three domains, so the sample was not stratified at all.

ELEMENT SAMPLING: DENSITY

Let us now examine exactly how the computer model predictions were tested by the regional sampling design. It has been explained that the archaeological quadrat survey involved a 10% random sampling from 1400 quadrats (each 500 meters on a side); actual random sampling took place within sampling domains defined by extant vegetational communities. But no mention has been made of the *unit of sampling* — is it the attribute, the artifact, the site, the quadrat or the entire valley? Since any definition of the basic sampling element must depend upon the specific questions being asked, it is necessary to return to the Basin I predictions. Two measures were compared between lifezones: density and dispersion. Since both mean density and Coefficient of Dispersion depend upon the number of cultural items per sampling tract, *the basic element of this sample must be taken as the quadrat itself.* The populations consist of each domain of 500 meter-square tracts, and the samples are the sets of randomly selected quadrats.

If artificial grids are the elements of the sample, what then becomes of the artifacts? For the restricted approach considered here — and several other analytical approaches were applied to the same Reese River data — the artifacts are of interest only as they contribute to sample density. All projectile points assume, for example, exactly equal status whether whole or broken, large or small, of basalt, obsidian or rhyolite. This is so because all artifacts are reduced to a single count in the density computation for each tract. Furthermore, in element sampling of this kind, *attributes* of artifacts are of absolutely no interest, except to define categories such as "projectile point" in an operational manner. In addition, archaeological *sites* are of interest only in so far as they contribute artifact and debitage *counts* to the overall density statistics. Element sampling of quadrats considers artifact and debitage counts as observations *about* the tracts, without concrete referents beyond the numbers themselves. For this reason, element sampling at Reese River involves an Easter egg hunting rather than a site survey.

Sampling of this sort is new in archaeology and many questions arise about analytical procedures: When do the data involve simple random sampling and when are they clustered? When are parametric procedures permissible, and when are nonparametric methods useful? What formulas apply to which kinds of survey? How can the data be most meaningfully compared to answer archaeological inquiries? I believe questions can be clarified somewhat by a brief consideration of the Reese River data. These topics have only rarely been considered with relationship to archaeological data, and a dialogue on such analytical techniques can only serve to improve the quality of archaeological sampling procedures.

An initial step in analyzing the Reese River data involves combining the raw variates into meaningful summary statistics. Where possible, notation follows that of Kish (1965). The sample mean of a simple random sample (SRS) of elements is given by

$$\bar{y}_h = \frac{1}{n} \sum y_j$$

where h refers to the hth domain, y_j is the element density per quadrat and n denotes the number of quadrats. The sample mean is an unbiased estimator of the population (domain) mean, μ_h.

The *variance of the sample elements* in a simple random sample of the hth domain is given by

$$S_h^2 = \frac{1}{n-1} \sum (y_j - \bar{y}_h)^2$$

The sample variance is an unbiased estimator of the population element variance, σ_h^2.

The *variance of the SRS mean* is given by

$$\text{var}(\bar{y}_h) = (1 - f) \frac{S_h^2}{n}$$

where f is the sampling fraction $\left(f = \frac{n}{N}\right)$ and the quantity $(1 - f)$ is the *finite population correction,* fpc. While fpc can generally be eliminated in most social science surveys, where extremely large populations are involved, the Reese River design involved a uniform sampling fraction of $f = .10$, so the fpc $= .90$, too large a fraction to be ignored. The effect of a substantial fpc, of course, is to lower the variance of the SRS mean.

To illustrate how these SRS formulas apply to the Reese River data, the mean density of projectile points recovered in the piñon-juniper (B) zone is given by

$$\bar{y}_h = \frac{1}{40}(234) = 5.85 \text{ points per quadrat}$$

with an element variance of

$$S_h{}^2 = \frac{1}{39}(8880.69) = 227.71 \text{ points per quadrat.}$$

The variance of the mean is

$$\text{var}(\bar{y}_h) = (1 - .10)\frac{227.71}{40} = 5.12 \text{ points per quadrat.}$$

The means and appropriate variances are given for projectile points and chippage in Table 5.1.

TABLE 5.1

Summary Statistics From the Reese River Random Sample

	Projectile Points			
Domain = h	A1	A2	B	C
Number of tracts = n	10	52	40	38
Sample mean = $\bar{y}_h$	27.00	1.38	5.85	1.74
Element variance = $S_h{}^2$	1094.95	5.66	227.71	13.84
Variance of the mean = var $(\bar{y}_h)$	98.55	0.10	5.12	0.33
Coefficient of Dispersion = CD	40.55	4.10	38.93	7.95
Standard error of CD = se_{CD}	0.471	0.198	0.227	0.232
	Waste Flakes			
Domain = h	A1	A2	B	C
Number of tracts = n	10	52	40	38
Sample mean = $\bar{y}_h$	6579.90	49.75	171.75	9.16
Element variance = $S_h{}^2$	2.70×10^8	1.87×10^4	1.59×10^5	1161.45
Variance of the mean = var $(\bar{y}_h)$	2.43×10^7	324.14	3.57×10^3	27.50
Coefficient of Dispersion = CD	4.11×10^4	376.44	923.27	126.80
Standard error of CD = se_{CD}	0.471	0.198	0.227	0.232

The Problem of Normality

The question next arises as to how best to compare these descriptive statistics—figures derived from field data—to the expected frequencies from the Basin I computer model. A central concern in planning an appropriate analytical strategy involves the concept of normality: Do the Reese River data presented here violate the assumption of normality? Since most sampling manuals proceed almost exclusively under the normality assumption (e.g. Cochran 1963; Kish 1965); it is wise to consider the applicability of this critical assumption upon real archaeological data.

First of all, exactly what does normality mean? In Figure 5.2, several element distributions are presented. The distributions are obviously not normal. This fact alone does not require us to reject the normality assumption, however, since there are not *one,* but *three* distributions involved here, any one of which may or may not be normal: (1) the distribution of *elements within the population;* (2) the distribution of *elements within the sample* (Fig. 5.2); and (3) the distribution of *statistics* ($\bar{y}_h$, S_h^2 and so on) which characterize the sample. Which of these three distributions must be assumed to be normal before we can apply a large sample theory of errors?

The answer to this important question is given in part by the Central Limit Theorem (CLT) which states, in effect, that sample means of random variates drawn from a population (with finite μ and σ) tend to distribute normally under repeated sampling. Nowhere does the CLT specify the *element* distribution. In fact, so long as n is suitably large, the distribution of sample means will be normal, regardless of the distribution of elements. The sample can be rather small (sometimes even $n = 1$) when elements are distributed in nearly normal fashion. But when the elements are distributed in markedly nonnormal fashion, n will often need to be quite large in order for the CLT to apply.

Most social science surveys produce very large samples and in such cases the CLT can generally be assumed to produce a normal distribution of sample means. But even in such surveys, departures from normality are known to occur. These departures can often be transformed into a normal distribution (so that a smaller n will be required by the CLT) or sometimes nonparametric statistics can be used. But as we shall see, there can be pitfalls with these remedies also.

All of the element distributions in Figure 5.2 are positively skewed, a situation caused by a high proportion of empty tracts and a few extremely high variates. It is probably safe to assume that although these graphs represent sample totals rather than the domains themselves, the domain distributions are at least as asymmetrical as are the sample distributions. Sampling from a highly skewed population can severely strain the assumption of normality of sample means, since a very large n is required for the CLT to hold (see Kish 1965: 410 for suggestions on dealing with skew distributions).

So the real question in this case concerns just how large a sample is required in order to vitiate the skew element distributions? Cochran (1963: 41) suggests the following crude rule for populations of skew elements:

$$n > 25 \ G_1^2$$

where G_1 is Fisher's measure of skewness

$$G_1 = \frac{1}{n \ \sigma^3} \sum (y_j - \bar{y}_h)^3$$

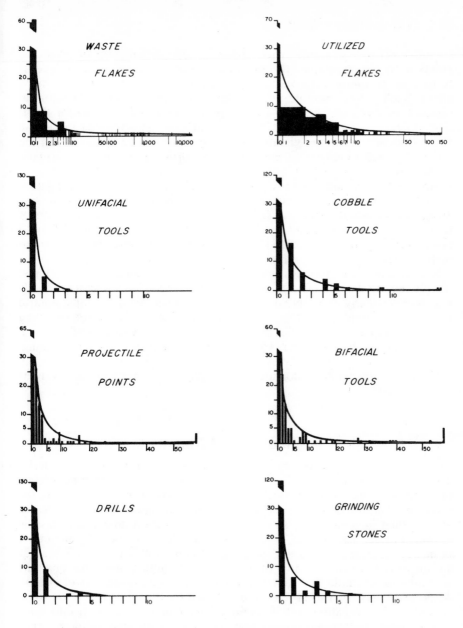

Fig. 5.2. Distribution of cultural debris by sampling quadrat (all domains pooled). The x-axis represents the number of items recovered; the y-axis represents the number of tracts involved. In all cases n = 140.

This rule is designed so that the 95% confidence statements will not be incorrect more than 6% of the time.

By applying Cochran's rule to the Reese River data, it is possible to determine the sample size that would be required to justify the assumption of normality (assuming the samples adequately represent the domain distributions). Cochran's rule when applied to the distribution of projectile points in the piñon-juniper (B) domain shows that a sample size of *at least 623 elements (quadrats) would be required* for the CLT to vitiate the skew effect. Such a large sample size is clearly out of line for archaeological research of this sort (the Reese River project used only n = 40 for the B domain). These results suggest that the statistics characterizing the Reese River data are in serious violation of the normality assumption, given the relatively small sample sizes employed. So normality will not be assumed in this case.

Archaeological data often violate the CLT, and several investigators correctly advocate nonparametric (sometimes also called distribution-free) means of statistical analysis. However, the fact that the assumption of normality is apparently violated by no means entitles one immediately to resort to nonparametric methods. We must not assume that "nonparametric" means "assumption-free."

Specifically, nonparametric methods, like most parametric tests, almost always require the assumption that observations have been drawn *randomly* and *independently* from previous draws. In other words, nonparametric tests require samples resulting from SRS. Since the more complex sampling strategies, especially cluster sampling, do not satisfy SRS procedures, the assumptions of the nonparametric tests are violated (see cluster sampling, this chapter). The Reese River data discussed to this point involve only SRS of elements within a domain, and nonparametric methods can correctly be applied.

Statistical Implications of Density Measures

But caution is still necessary to assure such tests are applied properly. The propositions immediately under examination here involve comparisons of sampling domains in terms of density. The Basin I model predicted, for instance, that projectile points in the habitation areas would be "more dense" than in areas used strictly for seed collection, and chippage was expected to be "less dense" in areas used only for artiodactyl hunting than in quarry localities. The basic sampling element in all cases is the quadrat so *raw density* consists simply of the number of cultural items per quadrat; we know for example that sampling tract A-22 has a raw density of exactly 46 projectile points. But problems arise when these raw densities are to be combined into an expression of *average domain density*, since this measure is a variable, rather than a variate. "Average" is an amorphous concept which can be operationally defined in several ways, each definition producing different results when applied to the archaeological record.

Probably the most common conception of average density refers to the *arithmetic mean* of the cultural items per sampling tract. The Basin I predictions were expressed in terms of domain mean, and we have already considered computation of the sample mean from raw data. The t-test is generally applicable when two sample means are to be compared, and the following statistical hypotheses are tested:

$$H_0: \mu_1 \leq \mu_2$$

$$H_1: \mu_1 > \mu_2$$

These propositions adequately reflect the output of the Basin I model, but since the sample sizes are insufficient to permit the assumption of a normal distribution, the t-test is not applicable.

The most common nonparametric alternative to the t-test is the Wilcoxon (or Mann-Whitney U) test for independent samples (Conover 1971a: 223–237). The Wilcoxon test examines the same statistical hypotheses as the t-test so long as two symmetrical populations are to be compared. But in highly asymmetrical populations, the mean is no longer a suitable measure of central tendency. In the piñon-juniper domain, for example, only 20% of the observations are above the mean, while almost 80% fall below the sample mean. Therefore, in this case a direct comparison of sample means fails to provide a suitable test for difference in cultural density.

The Wilcoxon test does more than simply compare sample means. When asymmetrical populations are involved, the Wilcoxon test operates under a different definition of "average density," thereby sidestepping the problem of measuring central tendency. The null and alternative hypotheses are recast in a new form

$$H_0: P\,(X < Y) \geq 1/2$$

$$H_1: P\,(X < Y) < 1/2$$

where X denotes the number of artifacts in a quadrat of domain 1, and Y the corresponding number in domain 2. These hypotheses ask: If we randomly select a single tract from domain 1 and another tract from domain 2, how likely is it that the second tract will have a larger number of cultural items than the first? These hypotheses seem to fall closer to our intuitive concept of archaeological density than do standard definitions of central tendency.

The U values for the Wilcoxon two-sample test have been computed by the large sample formula given in Siegel (1956: 120–126), and tied scores were converted to midranks. Table 5.2 presents the z-scores associated with the various values of U for all the projectile point and debitage comparisons between domains. Of these eight tests upon the Basin I hypotheses, the Wilcoxon tests confirm only three predictions (chippage: A1 > A2, A1 > C, B > C). In all of the other comparisons, the Wilcoxon tests tells us that more often than not, there is little difference between the two domains. The Basin I model does not fare well at all against the Wilcoxon test of density.

The common assumption accompanying the Wilcoxon test is that both samples consist of *continuous* random variables (Siegel 1956: 123–124; Conover 1971a: 224), so that all ties are viewed as resulting from errors of imprecise measurement rather than from truly identical variates. Because the Reese River data contain so many ties — sometimes over half of one sam-

TABLE 5.2

Results of the Wilcoxon Two-Sample and Chi-Square Tests

Predicted Relationship	z-score	P	Proposition Confirmed	χ^2	df	P	Proposition Confirmed
Projectile Points							
$\mu_B > \mu_{A2}$	0.33	<.87	No	9.97	2	<.01	Yes
$\mu_C > \mu_{A2}$	0.60	<.77	No	0.028	1	<.90	No
$\mu_B > \mu_C$	0.33	<.87	No	17.62	2	<.005	Yes
Waste Flakes							
$\mu_{A1} > \mu_{A2}$	4.76	<.000001	Yes	16.45	1	<.005	Yes
$\mu_{A1} > \mu_C$	5.52	<.000001	Yes	30.77	1	<.005	Yes
$\mu_B > \mu_{A2}$	0.40	<.40	No	7.82	3	<.05	Yes
$\mu_{A2} \cong \mu_C$	4.69	<.000002	No	26.04	2	<.005	No
$\mu_B > \mu_C$	3.69	<.0002	Yes	11.52	2	<.005	Yes

ple is tied at zero density—this assumption is clearly violated. Such will also be the case in many archaeological samples. Recent research on this problem, however, indicates that the continuity assumption can be safely ignored for discrete variates, provided the correction for ties is applied (Conover 1971b; Noether 1972).

But can these procedures be accepted as adequate tests of archaeological density? Let us examine yet another operational definition of density by defining three events: A = absent, R = rare, and F = frequent. When relating these outcomes to archaeological data, the operational definitions of the ordinal categories will vary with the numbers at hand. Suppose we define "rare" as the occurrence of between 1 and 3 artifacts in any particular quadrat and further let P_{A2} be defined as the probability that a quadrat in domain 2 contains between 1 and 3 artifacts (or however "rare" may be defined). A new concept of density emerges when we test the following null hypothesis

$$H_0: P_{A1} = P_{A2}; P_{R1} = P_{R2}; P_{F1} = P_{F2}$$

against the completely general alternative that some (or possibly all) of the above equalities are incorrect. The chi square test for two independent samples is appropriate for testing this definition of density, and the results of these tests are also plotted in Table 5.2.

These various concepts of density can best be illustrated by considering a single application upon the archaeological data from Reese River. The Basin I model predicted that projectile point density should be significantly greater in the piñon-juniper (B) zone than in the lower sagebrush-grass (A2) zone. From Table 5.1, we see that the mean density for B is $\bar{y}_B = 5.85$, while $\bar{y}_{A2} = 1.38$. Obviously the trend is in the proper direction, but difficulty arises when we attempt to determine whether this trend is significant in light of the large variance associated with each mean. The Wilcoxon test indicated that these two domains do not differ significantly with respect to projectile point density (p < 0.87). But these rank order relations of the Wilcoxon test can then be reduced into a contingency table, Table 5.3. Table 5.3 produces a value of $\chi^2 = 9.97$, which is highly significant with p < 0.01 (see Table 5.2 for the remainder of the chi square computations). Hence by one definition of density we have no difference, while another definition of density produces a highly significant difference. Is the Basin I density prediction accepted or rejected?

TABLE 5.3

**Contigency Table of the
Rank Order Results of the Wilson Test**

	A2	B
Absent	24	21
Rare	25	9
Frequent	3	10

The difficulty lies with the initial computer model which clearly over-simplified the concept of artifact density. Basin I projected only that domain B should have a greater average density of projectile points than domain A2. While this statement is probably correct in some sense, it oversimplifies the situation so much that the statistical tests provide ambiguous results. The actual fieldwork showed that 46% of the tracts in domain A2 and 52% of the tracts in domain B contained no projectile points at all. In this respect, the domains are rather similar, with domain B actually pointing in the *opposite* direction of the prediction by Basin I (and also in the opposite direction from the sample means). The Wilcoxon test looked at the data from these two domains and observed — quite correctly — that more often than not, there is little difference between A2 and B. This is to be expected in archaeological terms, even under the Steward model. The initial sampling domains were selected upon operational criteria which were easy to recognize in the field, and to some extent these zones probably do reflect prehistoric differences in subsistence practices (as the chi square subsequently confirmed). But it is unrealistic to assume, as did the primitive Basin I modeling, that each bit of land would equally reflect the subsistence significance of that lifezone. In fact, the prehistoric economies were doubtlessly geared to very specific aspects of each domain. The bulk of the land in each domain remained unexploited. Piñon camps, for instance, occur only in a certain characteristic microtopographic setting. A second sampling stage later disclosed data on the exact variables which associated with the piñon villages. These variables were plotted on aerial photographs and the locations of 65 previously unknown sites were predicted with better than 85% accuracy (Williams, Thomas, and Bettinger 1973). These variables could also be used in the future to construct sets of sampling domains which would reflect subtle density differences. The initial computer modeling and random sampling lacked these detailed insights, and the gross categorization of the environment created so much noise (in the form of unutilized land) that the true differences between domains were obscured. This is what the Wilcoxon test tells us.

The chi square tests, on the other hand, verify that there are far-reaching and significant differences between the domains when the noise is minimized. Once the empty tracts are excluded, the B zone obviously contains more habitation sites than the A2 zone. So the chi square tests verify the Basin I predictions in this case. In yet another approach, the Wilcoxon test could be recast by ignoring the "absent" category, a perfectly legitimate procedure so long as it is made explicit. The resulting Wilcoxon results would produce higher z-values, thereby reflecting differences between domains and likewise confirming the Basin I projections. Taken together, both the chi square and Wilcoxon tests probably can be said to support the following statement: If we restrict ourselves to areas which were utilized aboriginally (i.e., areas which produce at least a minimal amount of cultural debris), domain B tends to have greater density of occupation than does domain A2 (as indicated by projectile points). Similar statements follow for other artifacts and features.

ELEMENT SAMPLING: PATTERN

The Basin I model predicted archaeological outcomes in terms of artifact, feature, and debitage patterning. For the purposes of modeling, pattern was operationally defined by the Coefficient of Dispersion,

$$CD = \frac{S_h^2}{\bar{y}_h} .$$

The variance:mean ratio is little more than an initial attempt to apply the Poisson distribution to grid sampling data. Discrete variables must satisfy two critical conditions to qualify as a Poisson distribution: (1) the mean density must be small relative to the maximum possible value and (2) each event must be independent of prior occurrences within the same grid sample. In other words, Poisson distributions describe discrete events which are both "rare and random" (Sokal and Rohlf 1969: 85).

Given these conditions, how do the Reese River survey data compare to the Poisson distribution? Rareness has been defined by comparing the observed counts with the maximum possible number of items. In quantitative plant ecology, for instance, maximum number is taken to be the number of that species which can physically grow within a sampling quadrat of a fixed size. A similar rationale can be easily applied to archaeological artifacts (as well as features and debitage). Assuming that the artifacts lie flat and that they are not superimposed (or stratified), the theoretically maximum number of items is

$$\frac{\text{Grid area}}{\text{Average item area}} .$$

To determine whether the Reese River artifacts are "rare" in this sense, we must first define the maximum number of projectile points possible within a quadrat. The grid area is a constant of 250,000 square meters (the area of a 500-m. quadrat), discounting surveying errors. Since the average length of Reese River projectile points is about 5 cm., and the average width is about 2 cm., the average surface area (for one side) must be about 5 cm.^{2} or so (since projectile points are triangular). Hence we can approximate the maximum theoretical density to be

$$\frac{250,000 \text{ m}^2}{5 \text{ cm}^2} = \frac{2.50 \times 10^9 \text{ cm}^2}{5 \text{ cm}^2} = 5.0 \times 10^8 \text{ projectile points.}$$

It is proper to conclude, therefore, that the observed density of projectile points recovered in the Reese River fieldwork is suitably below the theoretical total capacity of 500 million, and the actual archaeological find can be operationally considered as "rare."

The question of randomness, however, is not so easily resolved. It is common statistical procedure to a priori posit an expected distribution — the Poisson, in this case — as the null hypothesis. If the observed values are in significant deviation from the expected, the null hypothesis can be re-

TABLE 5.4

**Comparisons of Observed Frequencies
With Theoretically Expected Poisson Frequencies**

Number of Projectile Points per Tract	Observed Frequency f	Expected Frequency Under Poisson Distribution $\hat{f}$	Deviation $(f - \hat{f})$
0	24	13.2	+
1	11	18.2	−
2	9	12.6	−
3 +	8	8.0	−
	$\chi^2 = 12.713$, df $= 3$; p $< .01$		

jected, with the statistical conclusion that the rare individuals are not distributed in Poisson fashion, and hence are termed nonrandom. (There are other distributions which can be applied to rare events such as Neyman's, Thomas' Double Poisson, and Negative Binomial which are not considered in this chapter.)

Since the Poisson is of some interest in considering the rare quadrat data, the observed data can be statistically compared to the frequencies expected under the Poisson distribution (computed by the procedure of Sokal and Rohlf 1969: 86–87). Taking the projectile points from substratum A2 as an example (Table 5.4), a chi square test for goodness of fit indicates a highly significant discrepancy between the observed values and the theoretically expected Poisson values. By rejecting the null hypothesis in this case, one concludes that the projectile points within domain A2 are nonrandomly distributed. In fact, similar comparisons indicate that *none* of the domains contained random distributions of projectile points (or any other artifact type).

That nonrandomness can be clearly established, however, is something less than astounding. In reality, few artifacts or features can be expected to distribute absolutely randomly within archaeological random samples such as that carried out at Reese River. Every artifact found in a primary archaeological context is there as a result of a specified human activity. It is too much to expect that every given particle of land had an equal probability of receiving an artifact during the occupation of the area. Hunters (and game animals) usually follow habit patterns. Gatherers are known to return to very specially defined areas (determined by slope, drainage, soil conditions, precipitation, elevation, etc.), campers rarely settle on steep hillsides, people need water, and dozens of other conditions conspire to pattern prehistoric cultural remains. Absolute randomness did not occur in this portion of the Reese River Valley; nor was it expected. This is not to deny absolutely that randomness can occur in other archaeological contexts in other areas but rather to reiterate that absolute randomness is itself a rather rare event.

The point here is that the initial hypotheses were concerned more with *relative degrees of randomness* rather than with the condition of *absolute randomness;* artifacts were predicted to occur in differing degrees of clumping or dispersion. Projectile points broken in manufacture for instance, should tend to be more clumped than would projectile points broken in the pursuit of artiodactyls. It is this relative degree of dispersal which is of interest in the Reese River work and this is why the Coefficient of Dispersion is a useful tool.

In a perfectly Poisson situation, the mean is exactly equal to the variance, and hence their ratio is 1.00. As the artifacts become more clumped (for whatever reason), the quadrats will tend to become more heterogeneous, and the variances will inflate with respect to the mean (CD > 1). For this reason, the original predictions were expressed in terms of CD rather than absolute frequencies. The standard error of the variance:mean ratio (after Greig-Smith 1964: 62) is given by

$$se_{CD} = \sqrt{\frac{2}{(n-1)}} \, .$$

The standard error of CD is independent of the density of items and depends strictly upon the number of samples, so the standard error of CD is constant for each domain. These figures have been included in Table 5.1. With the standard errors known, the t-statistic can be computed to determine whether the observed variance:mean ratio differs significantly from the random value of 1.00 (with df $= n - 1$). The results of the t-tests performed on the CDs of Table 5.1 indicate that all of the ratios are significantly different from 1.00 at greater than $p < .01$. This is simply another method of confirming that absolute randomness did not exist in the Reese River survey results.

Because of the marked asymmetry of the element distributions in the Reese River sample, the elemental variances — and hence the Coefficients of Dispersion — were rather badly inflated. In fact, a linear transformation of some sort would probably provide more suitable measures of central tendency and dispersion, since these inflated values can impair our judgment as to the degree of randomness, clustering, or dispersion. But so long as concern is only with relative degrees of randomness, the Basin I propositions can be adequately tested through the use of Coefficients of Dispersion computed directly from the raw densities.

CLUSTER SAMPLING

The primary objectives of the Reese River survey were to test some predictions expressed in terms of item density and dispersion. Because of these rather circumscribed aims, the elements of the sample were taken to be artificial sampling quadrats, and the research design was framed in terms of comparing randomly selected domains by SRS. But regional sampling can also answer dozens of additional questions: (1) Are the houses of the winter sites larger than those of the summer dwelling areas? (2) Does the total size of habitation sites change through time? (3) Do the projectile points recovered on the flats tend to be larger than those found in the high altitude hunting areas? (4) Are the vessels from the habitation sites larger in volume than those of the temporary task sites?

However the sampling design must change from the earlier SRS design before these propositions can be tested. So long as the elements in the sample are the sampling quadrats, the design is SRS and rather elementary formulas can be used in analysis of the data. But comparing specific qualities (such as size, shape, sharpness, etc.) requires a basic redefinition of the sampling unit. No longer is the element the sampling quadrat; *the element is now the cultural item itself.*

This shift in research design radically changes the statistical interpretation in a number of ways. Let us assume that a particular theory predicts that since most of the primary tool manufacture (namely working down cores) took place in the winter villages, the amount of waste debitage in these village areas should be significantly greater than in the strictly hunting areas, where chippage should result only from minor tool repair and resharpening. Specifically

$$H_1: \mu_{\text{habitation}} > \mu_{\text{hunting}}$$

where μ is the average chip size, as measured by weight. The null hypothesis holds that the chips should be similar with respect to average weight between the two areas (or conversely, the hunting area should actually have larger flakes).

Because part of the Reese River fieldwork involved collecting a random sample of chippage within all biotic communities, the data at hand should be sufficient to test this proposition. Here is where the nature of the research design must be taken into account. The conflict is that now the individual chips are the *elements* of the sample, and each flake possesses a particular state (a measurement) of the attribute "weight." But these chips were not collected independently, as is required under SRS. The chips were collected by randomly selected quadrat, and hence the data are not independent. In order to collect chippage by SRS, one would first have to construct a frame [This term is defined by Mueller in this volume.] in which the entire population of chips in the Reese River is enumerated. Each chip could then be numbered, and an SRS could be selected such that every flake has an equal and independent chance of selection. But the difficulty and expense in constructing this list makes such a project manifestly impossible in archaeological fieldwork. To know the number and location of every flake is to have already conducted a complete survey of the entire valley, in which case sampling is not involved at all. In order to avoid such a ridiculous situation, the valley was gridded (clustered) and only those chips falling into the randomly selected quadrats were chosen, so that the randomness of the sample was by sampling tract, not by individual flake. Furthermore, since the number of chips (the elements) varies from tract to tract, the clusters are of unequal size. When attention is shifted in this manner from artifact *quantity* to artifact *quality,* the research design likewise shifts from SRS of domains to an unequal cluster sampling design.

Some new formulas are required in this new sampling design. The element mean of an SRS sample was given earlier in this chapter; the aggregate of the variates was summed and then divided by the total frequency of elements, with the sample size directly under the control of the investigator. But the sample size itself becomes subject to error in the case of cluster sampling, and the relationship of sample size to the variable under study becomes complex. The sample mean in cluster sampling is in fact the ratio between two random variables, each varying from sample to sample. In the example at hand, the population value of average chip weight is estimated by (Kish 1965: 186):

$$r = \frac{\Sigma\ y_j}{\Sigma\ x_j} = \frac{\text{total chippage weight}}{\text{total chippage frequency}}.$$

This new statistic, r, is termed the *ratio mean,* and commonly serves as the proper measure of central tendency when interest is upon *population mean per element.* The sampling distribution of r is rather more complex than that of $\bar{y}$, since both the numerator (Σy_j) and the denominator (Σx_j) tend to vary randomly from cluster to cluster.

The variance of the sample ratio mean is given by Kish (1965: 187):

$$\text{var}\ (r) = \frac{1}{x^2}\ [\text{var}\ (y) + r^2\ \text{var}\ (x) - 2r\ \text{cov}\ (y,\ x)].$$

The raw variates from the Reese River sample can be used to illustrate the computation of the ratio means and variances.

$$r_{A2} = \frac{6042.2}{2587} = 2.34 \text{ grams per flake}$$

$$\text{var}\ (r_{A2}) = .50 \text{ grams}$$

$$r_B = \frac{12032.5}{6870} = 1.75 \text{ grams per flake}$$

$$\text{var}\ (r_B) = .05 \text{ grams}$$

Provided that the two domains were sampled independently, the standard error of the difference between the ratio means ($r_{A2} - r_B$) is merely the sum of the two ratio standard errors. In this case, the computed value of t is found to be only 0.796, with 59 degrees of freedom. We can conclude there is no significant difference in chip size between the piñon-juniper lifezone and the lower sagebrush-grass flats in the Reese River survey data.

The ratio mean and its variance are not always unbiased estimators of their respective parameters, however, and an adequate number of clusters should be maintained in order to minimize this bias, because the number of *clusters* (n) rather than the total number of *elements* (x_j) determines sample size in cluster sampling. Sample size is critical here because the ratio estimate only approaches normality as n becomes large. Furthermore, the formula for the var (r) is only an estimate, which becomes more valid as n increases. Cochran (1963: 157) suggests that as a working rule, the sample size (i.e., the number of clusters) should always exceed 30. One of the four domain samples was less than 30 ($n_{A1} = 10$) and this shortcoming should be avoided wherever possible in future designs of this sort.

The cluster *size* must also be considered in addition to the number of clusters. The Coefficient of Variation (CV) should be kept small in order to minimize the bias of the ratio mean. Kish (1965: 187) recommends that, in general, the Coefficient of Variation should be less than .20. In the previous example

$$CV_{A2} = \frac{se_x}{x} = \frac{25.40}{68.08} = .37$$

$$CV_B = \frac{102.70}{298.70} = .34 .$$

Although both these coefficients exceed Kish's standards, they do not appear to be grossly out of line, and probably indicate that the ratio mean and its variance are not unduly biased in the Reese River samples. Kish (1965, esp. chapter 7) makes several suggestions which could help keep cluster size more constant in future sampling.

Cluster sampling, and specifically the use of the ratio mean, thus presents some difficulties not encountered in SRS. For one thing, cluster sampling restricts somewhat the subsequent statistical analysis of the results. The common significance tests cannot generally be applied to clustered samples because most textbook formulas assume SRS. The standard error of the mean under SRS, for instance, is usually taken to be

$$se_{\bar{y}} = \frac{S_y}{\sqrt{n}} .$$

But this commonplace equivalence, used in most statistical inference, cannot be applied to the more complex sampling designs.

A common error in analyzing sampling data is the application of inappropriate statistical tests to data resulting from complex sampling designs, and some of these errors have already appeared in archaeologists' attempts at probability sampling. The incorrect use of parametric formulas assuming SRS, for instance, results in a serious underestimation of the true standard errors, and a correspondingly undesirable conservatism in rejecting the null hypothesis. Also, as noted above, cluster sampling violates the assumptions of nonparametric methods of statistical inference (Kish 1957), and the common textbook nonparametric tests simply do not apply to cluster samples (Blalock 1972: 527). One must be most skeptical of statistical comparisons of clustered data, unless specific measures have been taken to account for the lack of independence between elements within the same sample. The errors resulting from the misapplications range from mild to serious, depending upon several factors—especially the degree of intra-cluster homogeneity—but the effects cannot be ignored (Kish and Frankel 1970: 1072).

These difficulties should not be allowed to overshadow the true necessity of cluster sampling in archaeology. As we saw with the Reese River survey element sampling of artifacts and features was not only difficult and expensive, it was impossible (short of a complete pilot survey which would have vitiated the need for sampling at all). Although cluster sampling is less efficient (in terms of sample error) than is SRS, the cost is also markedly less.

Cluster sampling also allows the use of the normal approximation, generally untenable for element sampling.

CONCLUSIONS AND SUGGESTIONS

This paper has examined the sampling design of the Reese River project in some detail. In many ways, the Reese River design is not typical of modern archaeological sampling, since traditional archaeological sites were not of paramount interest. This paper distinguishes between a *site survey* which comprises most archaeological sampling at the regional level, and *nonsite sampling* which ignores the "site" concept. There were sites at Reese River, of course, and these were located, recorded, and collected in the traditional manner. But the analytical propositions under consideration predicted occurrence of cultural items per se rather than prediction of site occurrence (in the initial sampling phase). I suspect that nonsite sampling will be more important to archaeologists dealing with nonsedentary peoples, who often leave only scanty, widely scattered evidence of their lifeway. In these cases, areas of hunting, seed collecting, quarrying, etc. may be of primary interest and yet not involve "sites" in the conventional sense of the term.

The distinction was also made between element sampling and cluster sampling strategies. The nature of analysis at Reese River was dictated in large measure by the nature of the propositions under examination. When density and dispersion of cultural items was the main concern, the sample design was reduced to an SRS of elements within several domains; stratification, in the strict sense, was not applied, since the domains themselves were the primary sampling universes. But when interest shifted from quantity to quality of the cultural items, the design became an unequal cluster sample (even though the fieldwork was identical). This reorientation complicated the analytical procedure in a number of ways. The computational and analytical steps were explained in terms of a small portion of the actual Reese River data in order to illustrate which specifics apply to which sampling situations.

This paper in no way pretends to be a definitive statement about the proper handling of all archaeological survey data—there can be no such universal statements. Furthermore, progress will undoubtedly be made toward more efficient analytical methods which can be applied to specific sampling strategies. Archaeologists may have spent an inordinate amount of time discussing the various permutations of sampling designs (quadrats, transects, irregular units, etc.) and altogether too little time discussing how the data are to be analyzed after they are collected. Archaeologists sometimes become overly concerned with the superfluous details of sophisticated experimental designs, missing the objective altogether.

ACKNOWLEDGMENTS

I gratefully acknowledge Gottfried E. Noether and Martin R. Frankel for statistical and sampling consultation. Errors remain the responsibility of the author.

6. Sampling in Regional Archaeological Survey

W. James Judge, James I. Ebert, and Robert K. Hitchcock

W. James Judge (Ph.D., University of New Mexico, 1970) has been very active in university-funded and contract fieldwork in the American Southwest. The earliest occupation of this area is the subject of his book, *The Paleo-Indian Occupation of the Central Rio Grande Valley, New Mexico,* while other papers emphasize the intermediate and historical periods. In addition to his position as Associate Professor of Anthropology at the University of New Mexico, he has served as staff archaeologist with the National Park Service at the Chaw Center.

James I. Ebert (A.B., Michigan State University, 1971) has had fieldwork experience in North America and East Africa. He has collaborated with Hitchcock in the authorship and performance of remote sensing in Southwestern regional archaeology. As a doctoral student at the University of New Mexico, he also has been working for the Chaco Center, National Park Service, while holding a National Geographic Society Grant for the investigation of the prehistoric road system of Chaco Canyon.

Robert K. Hitchcock (A.B., University of California at Santa Barbara, 1971) has had most of his field experience in the American Southwest and California. His speciality has been the use of remote sensing, and he has had several papers published related to the topic. As a doctoral student at the University of New Mexico, he also has been serving as archaeological consultant and has been working with the National Park Service at the Chaco Center.

THE TECHNIQUE OF SAMPLING

The changing goals and aims of the science of archaeology make adherence to rigorous inductive-deductive method a necessity. All assumptions, including that of the faithfulness of data, must be tested under such a paradigm; and such an assessment can be made of data only through the technique of probability sampling. Archaeologists have paid little attention to sampling in the past, but guiding studies have been advanced by geographers, ecologists, and other areal scientists. Although archaeologists expressed an interest in statistical techniques two decades ago (Brainerd 1951; Robinson 1951; Spaulding 1953), the consideration of sampling procedures as an adjunct to such techniques did not come under close scrutiny until Vescelius (1960) stressed the importance of controlled data collection methods.

In recent years the theoretical dimensions of archaeology have grown and

[82]

changed rapidly. Culture is no longer an agglomeration of norms and values drifting fortuitously here and there; it is, rather, an organizational system by which men interact with other cultural and natural systems in their environment (Binford 1962; Struever 1971; Odum 1971).

Some archaeologists (for example, Chang 1967) have urged a shift in attention from the artifact as a unit of analysis to a consideration, instead, of the "settlement." Ever since Willey's (1953) pioneering study of settlement patterning in the Viru Valley of Peru, archaeologists have been turning to "settlement archaeology" (Willey 1953, 1956, 1968; Chang 1962, 1967, 1968; Trigger 1967, 1968; Tringham 1972). Binford (1964) has gone a step further, contending that the region is the analytical unit most appropriate to current anthropological inquiry. The concept of the region and techniques for studying regions have been developed largely by geographers (Berry 1964, 1968; Grigg 1967) and "regional scientists" (Isard 1956).

Increasing emphasis on the region as a unit of analysis has considerably increased the physical scope of both anthropology (Skinner 1964–65; Smith 1972) and archaeology (Binford 1964; Struever 1968, 1971; Adams 1968; Plog and Hill 1971). Archaeological sites represent the activity loci of cultural systems. Activities are differentiated spatially; a single archaeological site cannot be expected to reflect all of the activities of a particular cultural system. Sites are merely components of larger and more inclusive settlement systems. Research with the goal of explanation of cultural systems and processes must, then, be framed in such a way that the total range of types of component sites is examined. Whereas previous archaeological problems by their nature limited field activity to comparatively small single sites, the scope of current research may be thousands of square miles. Coherent generalizations about the nature and variability of cultural systems within such immense areas can be induced and tested only through the agency of inductive statistics and data derived by strictly prescribed probability sampling.

Inductive statistics is a way of saying something about the various characteristics of a population on the basis of known facts about a sample drawn from that population. Statistics, the characteristics of samples, reflect—to a certain (and in part knowable) extent—fixed but unknown characteristics of a population, called parameters. The logical status of a single sample is precarious, for statistics vary from sample to sample; it is, rather, the population which is of interest. Samples provide the data by which hypotheses pertaining to the whole population are tested.

Why Sample?

Economy, which is traditionally cited as the primary reason for sampling rather than collection of "all the data," is hardly a realistic justification. It could more logically be argued that a complete inventory of any large population about which little is known can never be taken. One's data thus only partially represent the population, and a sample derived in a known and controlled manner is far more compatible with the overall scientific paradigm than one taken in a whimsical or unstated way.

Natural and social scientists who concern themselves with the explanation of behavioral process are constrained to the use of a rigorous logical framework which entails inductive and innovative formulation of testable hypotheses, strict deductive appraisal of the relevance of available data to these hypotheses, and subsequent testing of hypotheses with these data (Binford 1972). The role of testing in the total scientific process dictates that no hypothesis can ever be completely and satisfactorily proved or disproved; instead, such hypotheses can only be affirmed or rejected with a certain probability of certainty.

The major advantage of the employment of statistical method over intuition in the scientific testing process is that a quantitative knowledge of the risks of error can be derived from statistics. The level of the inductive/ deductive process at which inconsistencies are most likely to lead to error is in the assumption stage; all assumptions must therefore be examined for validity. A sample is an assumption with a logical status as critical as any other, and must be proved to give an unbiased (or biased in a known manner) estimation of the overall body from which data are drawn. A statistically drawn sample can be tested for bias; a "grab sample," chosen intuitively, cannot.

Sample Mechanics

When probabilities are associated with each outcome of an experiment, as in the social sciences, the resulting probability distribution is referred to as the sampling distribution, which suggests the number of times certain outcomes would be expected to occur in a very large number of experiments (Blalock 1960). The sampling distribution is, then, taken as a reflection of the distribution of the concrete but unknown population distribution, the frequency with which all units (or possible outcomes) in a population would be assigned or expected in each category or point on a scale of measurement or taxonomy (Williams 1968). The sampling distribution is in turn inferred from sample distributions, which are the frequencies of observations in a number of samples.

As repeated random samples are drawn from any population, the sampling distribution of sample means approaches a normal distribution, allowing the use of normal curve area tables in the calculation of statistical significance. Significance, a critical concept in the acceptance or rejection of postulated hypotheses, is an assessment of whether or not certain sample differences would occur purely by chance if there were no differences whatsoever in the population.

A sampling distribution has several properties which facilitate an estimation of its utility in the scientific process. If a series of samples is wholly unbiased, the mean of the sampling distribution will be equivalent to the parameter mean. In practice, samples are rarely unbiased; *accuracy* is an expression of the closeness of the sampling mean to the parameter mean. A property of any scalar distribution is variance, which is an expression of the concentration of the distribution about its mean. The closeness of the distribution of sample means about its average compared to the population variance is an indication of *precision*, and is measured in units of standard deviation.

The relation of sampling variance to population variance is expressed by

$$\text{sampling variance} = \text{population variance} \times \frac{1}{n}\left(\frac{N-n}{N-1}\right)$$

where

$$n = \text{sample size}$$

$$N = \text{population size.}$$

It can be seen that, when sampling from a large population with a small sample size, precision is almost wholly dependent upon the sample size. Thus, sample size is not by any means arbitrary in the application of statistical methods, but is dependent upon the confidence level acceptable in each deductive case.

Variation and Error in Sample Distribution

No natural population in which social scientists have an interest is uniform; samples and sampling distributions drawn from them are valuable because they mirror the nature and range of variation in the parent population. Variation in samples of likely interest to archaeology may be due to (1) functional variation within or between parent populations, (2) temporal variation within or between parent populations, and (3) sampling error (Brown and Freeman 1964). As has been illustrated, sampling error is to some extent a function of sample size. The Law of Large Numbers implies that as a sample size grows large in relation to the parent population, such a sample gives an increasingly more accurate representation of the population. In simple random sampling, sampling error decreases in proportion to the square root of the number of observations taken; one reaches a point, then, where increase in sample size has little effect upon accuracy.

Problem Orientation

It should be necessary at this point only to mention the absolute necessity of a problem orientation in any serious research. Although distinctions between "hunch" or problem sampling and "general probability sampling," are often at least implicitly couched (see, for example, Berry and Baker 1968; Rootenberg 1964; Haggett 1965) it is here argued that no such distinction is possible. All research, even if wholly inductive, assumes a problem. Prior to the selection of any finite population from the confusingly subdivided totality which surrounds us, some idea of what questions bear productive examination must, and always does, exist in the researcher's mind. The field of archaeology itself assumes certain broad orientations; no archaeologist is without a problem of sorts. The proper inductive and deductive use of statistical method requires that the orientation be stated, and that such a statement must consider the nature of the possible range of variability within the population prior to its examination. Only with reference to a problem and its specified parameters can choices of proper sampling fraction, confidence limits, and shape, size, and orientation of sampling units be made.

Cluster Sampling

At a very basic level, the nature of most archaeological parameters and the exigencies of practical research dictate a departure from simple random point sampling. This is true because a universe must be totally accessible in order to be sampled randomly (Binford 1964). In exploratory first-stage locational sampling, which is still the primary aim of most archaeological survey and excavation, this is not possible. The archaeologist must instead turn to cluster (after Blalock 1960) or area (Holmes 1967) sampling, a procedure in which samples consist not of elements but of units of plane or 3-dimensional space within which all recovery and recording efforts are concentrated [see Mueller, this volume].

Until the final cluster-recovery stage the selection of a sample of spatial units can be discussed in the same terms as the selection of a point sample of single objects or attributes. It must be remembered, however, that multiple-stage cluster samples are in no means testable in the same manner as point samples. What is more, the goals toward which cluster samples are best applied are rarely the same as for point samples; for instance, patterning of association (which is not revealed by simple noncluster samples) can be approached through cluster samples.

Nor can cluster samples be expected to produce exactly the same results as would point samples. Clusters of sample data, when used as the basis of sampling distributions, lead to a loss in precision arising from an increased probability of dissimilarities in each cluster. Thus, to insure precision (and economic efficiency as well), clusters should be arranged to be as homogeneous as possible, an end that can be accomplished in a number of ways. Most importantly, losses in precision of a cluster over a point-random sample are proportional to the size and spacing of area parcels or cells (Holmes 1967); as clusters approach an infinitely small size, the variance of the sample distribution decreases. If only an unbiased and precise estimation of population parameters is desired, cluster size becomes a question of effort and cost per cluster compared to effort and cost per unit area sampled.

Regular Clusters

Sample clusters can be delineated in a number of ways. Most current plane sampling employs an arbitrary and easily laid grid of equal-area clusters as a basis for definition. Quadrats (square clusters) and transects (rectangular clusters) are common cluster shapes. Clusters of equal size and identical shape are practical in the field; what is more, the use in first-stage sampling of such arbitrary units is no less informed (if the population is relatively unknown) than any other.

Regular clusters can be located and oriented in either a random or a systematic manner in one, two, or three dimensions (Quenouille 1949). Quadrats randomized in two dimensions and transects randomized in one dimension are often recommended and employed for first-stage locational sampling. Random cluster sampling should give accurate and precise estimates of population parameters provided that the population is homogenous at the "grain size," or spatial scale of variability, selected for by the size of the sampling units.

In practice, rarely do either social or natural populations fulfill any such requirements of homogeneity. Systematic sampling, in which an initial grid unit is randomly fixed and subsequent units are spaced according to a pre-determined regular interval, is more appropriate to the realities of areal sampling. This is true because much of the data required by scientists are of a recurrent or cyclical nature, which is probably due largely to the monitoring of unrecognized causal thresholds (Binford n.d.a.). This poses a danger if the spacing of the sampling frame happens (by chance) to coincide with the cycle of regularities within on-the-ground data, bias is introduced. Depending on whether the frame is in or out of phase with the data, statistics will indicate values far too large or small for parameters, and may totally include maximum values or miss the data altogether. The primary advantages of systematic over random cluster sampling are (1) comparative ease of delineating the sample in the field and (2) assurance of samples widely dispersed over the research area. Practically, systematic sampling seems to result in parameter estimates of accuracy similar to those obtained with random sampling, but with significantly greater precision (Sukhatme 1947; Raj 1958).

Stratified Systematic Unaligned Samples

A variation of systematic cluster sampling that transcends many of the phase-coincidence problems of usual systematic designs has been recommended for archaeologists by Binford (1964) and discussed in detail by Haggett (1965), Berry and Baker (1968), and Holmes (1967). Called stratified systematic unaligned sampling, this design entails a two-stage location process in which the area to be sampled is first gridded into arbitrary and equal units. From each of these units, a number of clusters are drawn in such a way that there is no cluster alignment in either of two dimensions. A less commonly encountered arbitrarily stratified areal sample design is the stratified random areal sample, in which each stratum is randomly sampled (Berry and Baker 1968). Both of these designs combine the advantages of sample unit dispersal with insured unalignment and consequent freedom from phase-coincidence problems.

While coincidence of systematic sampling frames with real parameters has been discussed here as a problem, it could be argued that the manipulation of such phenomena in an informed way could lead to a greater knowledge of the target population. It is possible that recurrent regularities in a systematic sample, at any rate, are the product of sampling a cyclically occurring parameter.

Cluster Size, Shape, and Orientation

The determination of cluster size, orientation and shape must depend upon (1) basic statistical laws, (2) economics of funding and time, and (3) a knowledge of the nature or probable nature of the population to be sampled. The selection of units in a totally unknown population is contingent upon the fact that smaller clusters yield more accurate and precise results than do larger clusters. [For an admittedly tested opinion to the contrary, see Mueller (1974).] Large units, however, are more easily located and delimited and are usually cheaper per unit area to sample. A happy medium must be reached by the researcher according to his needs and limitations.

Any scheme of stratification in sampling depends, for advances in accuracy and precision, on a presampling knowledge of the population to be sampled. Often such information is available, and in fact has served as the basis for inductive hypothesis formation. Many sampling efforts, especially those involving mailed questionnaires or censuses, employ a preliminary and small-scale "pilot survey" upon which subsequent stratification is based (Gray 1957; Deming 1960; Hanson, Hurwitz, and Madow 1953).

Clusters, which are simply strata of a more-or-less arbitrary and regular nature, can be manipulated within certain limits on the basis of preknowledge of the target population. The size of quadrats (Harvey 1966) and the width of transects are very important; not only must they be sufficient to include complete patterns, but they may be manipulated to gain information about the scale and nature of the patterns being investigated (Haggett 1965; Getis 1964).

Transects are easy to delimit and follow in the field, and are thus of interest to the archaeologist. Orientation of transects can profitably be designed with reference to the nature of a population. Laid across the grain of variability they inform to a great extent about the variability range (Wood 1955). Unfortunately, transects cannot tell us about the distribution of variability, and are thus of limited utility to geographical problems such as those approached with network analysis. It has been determined by researchers that parallel, systematically spaced transects are more efficient than other transect designs (Osborne 1942; Wood 1955; Haggett and Board 1964; Proudfoot 1942).

While quadrats and transects are easily delimited cluster shapes, other types of cluster would be feasible. A simple field method would be the location of points about which circles of a known diameter could be drawn, thus delimiting each cluster locus. Robinson, Lindberg, and Brinkman (1968) suggest that the most economical means to subdivide an area geometrically is through the use of hexagonal sampling units.

Nonarbitrary Stratification

Simple or cluster sampling of any kind assumes a population in which the parameters to be estimated are distributed in a normal and homogeneous manner. This situation rarely occurs with social data and Poisson distributions attest to the operation, in many cases, of "hidden" thresholds. In fact, if the distribution of a parameter is entirely uniform, it is of little interest to social scientists, whose methods are based upon analysis in terms of departures from randomness (i.e., patterns) over time (Getis 1964).

The sampling of nonrandom parameters is enhanced by informed stratification. Such stratification entails the presampling division of a population on the basis of supplementary information so that the parameter observed is more uniform within a stratum (Sampford 1962). Not only does informed stratification reduce necessary sample size, but it allows the "oversampling" of more variable strata which results in an increase in sample precision. For maximum precision, the sampling fraction within each stratum should be proportional to the square root of the variance within that stratum (Stuart 1962).

The effect of the gain in precision from stratified sampling depends on the magnitude of variation between stratum averages; strata should be constructed so that their averages are as different as possible and their internal variance as small as possible. The researcher, it should be emphasized, must know which stratum is most diverse, for undersampling rather than oversampling of the most variable stratum can seriously affect precision.

Stratification can be arranged with reference to either tested data derived from a prior sampling stage, or inferred or suspected correlates of parameter variability such as ecological zones, drainage pattern class, or altitude.

Multistage Sampling

The almost paradoxical necessity of knowing a population before sampling and stratification encourages the employment of a multistage sampling design in which each prior stage informs the researcher about the advantageous manipulation of the next. Early stages of the sampling of a comparatively unknown population are most properly arbitrarily stratified and unaligned (Redman 1973); comparisons between analogous units within the sample can serve as a check of sample consistency and the basis of preliminary nonarbitrary stratification (Stephan 1934; Goodman 1961; Goodman and Kish 1950). Such stratification is an assumption, and must be tested for validity as must any link in the scientific process. It has been suggested that this can be accomplished by the replication of regional studies over a small but statistically representative fraction of the total universe (Blaut 1962). Subpopulations indicated as grossly abnormal by such a testing procedure should be isolated and, in cases of great variation, sampled separately.

It has been asserted in the last decade that not only hypothesis testing, but in fact all assumptive stages of research, must be planned and organized on a strict inductive-deductive feedback basis (see Redman 1973 for one of the most recent discussions). Successive sampling stages should be designed to amplify information yielded by the former stages, producing an informational cascade effect.

Areal Sampling in the Social and Natural Sciences

Geographers, who are concerned with the spatial arrangement of human variation in the natural world, have been involved in areal and locational probability sampling since the early 1920s. The determination of parameters of geographical/spatial, temporal, and physical/formal variability (as distinguished by Berry and Baker 1968) can only be arrived at through sampling procedures.

Many basic principles of sampling were solidified by geographers while engaged in specific research. During the sampling of cover-types in southern California and Canada, Osborne (1942) experimented with three types of parallel transect spacing: systematic, stratified random, and completely random. He concluded that, while the accuracy of his estimates were nearly identical, the precision of the systematic sample was nearly ten times that of a total random sample. Osborne's assertions were reinforced by Wood (1955) who, during the course of a survey of the distribution of marshes and swamps in Wisconsin, determined that parallel, intervally spaced transects were most efficient in terms of field economy and sample precision. The utility of quadrat sampling units has been discussed by Clark and Evans (1954) who determined that quadrat size manipulation could supply information that transects could not concerning patterning of settlement and resource exploitation.

Geography has supplied much of the methodological direction currently employed by areally oriented social sciences. In an early treatise broaching the subject of the logic of scientific inquiry, Stephan (1934) outlined the inductive-deductive strategy as starting with a knowledge of both dependent and independent variables and entailing the isolation and separate treatment of associated factors. Neprash in the same year warned geographers that the coexistence of phenomena adjacent in space does not necessarily imply causal relationships (Neprash 1934), a caveat that many of today's archaeologists might well take to heart.

With the stated goal of describing the spatial distribution of agricultural production in Maclean Shire, England, Holmes (1967) employed combinations of random, systematic, arbitrarily stratified, and nonarbitrarily stratified samples on both actual known populations and artifically arranged parameters. Holmes' chi square comparisons of the relative accuracy and precision of these designs indicate that, while significant accuracy can result from most designs, nonarbitrarily stratified systematic samples are by far most generally efficient in adjudging spatial distributions.

Probability sampling has received much attention from ecologists, especially in the context of quantitative studies of vegetation (Pielou 1969; Kershaw 1964; Grieg-Smith 1964; Patil, Pielou, and Waters 1971). A primary focus of many ecological studies is the patterning of plant and animal communities with respect to one another; accordingly, ecological researchers have dealt in detail with the comparative effects of variation in size, shape, and placement of sampling units.

The majority of sampling in ecology has employed the quadrat method, which was first introduced into the ecological literature by Pound and Clements (1898). Recently, however, serious questions have been raised regarding the relative accuracy and efficiency of quadrat sampling. In 1922 Arrhenius hailed "a new method for the analysis of plant communities" based on the use of lines or narrow belt-shaped sampling clusters called transects. His lead was followed by Clapham (1932) who showed that in at least one particular instance the variance between strips was markedly less than that between squares. According to Clapham long, narrow plots were both more efficient and more informative than were square plots.

Lindsey, Barton, and Miles (1956), in testing the efficiency of various sampling methods in forests, found that rectangular sampling units were more efficient than either squares or circles. Bauer (1936, 1943) pointed out that a transect can be run and desired data recorded in a fraction of the time it takes to locate a quadrat and record the data. Strong (1966) also stressed the speed and convenience of the line-transect method. Perhaps, as Clapham (1932: 194) concluded, the quadrat is not the most efficient sampling unit in ecology after all.

In a series of experimental tests on simulated plant communities, Bauer (1943) compared the accuracy and efficiency of quadrats and transects. He found that the two methods were equally accurate in estimating frequency and numerical abundance of species, but that transects were decidedly more accurate when it came to estimating the distribution of plant species. He also found that in sampling chaparral vegetation in the San Dimas Experimental Forest in southern California, transects were much more economical than quadrats.

Random versus systematic placement of sample units has also received attention from ecologists. Gleason (1920), in studying the location of quadrats, found that errors were much higher when contiguous quadrats were employed; consequently, he advocated the use of intervally spaced quadrats. Haig (1929) also advocated the use of quadrats and strips at intervals. Hasel (1938), working in the Blacks Mountain Experimental Forest in northeastern California, concluded that "systematic cruises" gave closer estimates of volume than did "random cruises." Westman (1971) compared the results of random and systematic transects and found that systematic transects were most accurate. A possible reason for the superiority of systematic over random designs is that they provide more dispersed and uniform areal coverage.

Transects are decidely better-suited to some ecological problems than to others. A number of ecologists (e.g., Jolly 1954; Arrhenius 1922; Clapham 1932; Kershaw 1964) argued that the transect is the best sampling unit for studying zonations or gradients. The transect also lends itself to the graphical representation of vegetation (Jolly 1954, Clapham 1932). Hasel (1938, 1941) feels transects are better for map-making than quadrats. Bauer (1936) asserts that the transect method has an advantage over quadrats in certain kinds of vegetation, such as dense scrub or forest.

Orientation of sample units has been another concern of ecologists. Clapham (1932) stated that the variance between samples was least if the strips were oriented at right angles to the observable strata of the area being sampled; this conclusion has been confirmed in subsequent research. Hasel (1938) found that the accuracy of sampling was enhanced when the sample units cut across ecological zones. Bormann (1953), who worked in an oak-hickory forest in the North Carolina piedmont, found that rectangular plots should be arranged so that the longest axis crosses contour lines.

Ecologists, then, have found both quadrats and transects to yield desired information, but that the sampling method varies with the problem being investigated. For this reason, McIntyre (1953), in discussing the use of line-transects in vegetation studies, says that quadrats and transects can profitably be employed together in sampling heterogeneous stands of vegetation.

Our short summary of the sampling literature has dealt thus far primarily with the approaches of the two applied sciences, geography and ecology, to the problems of gathering data representative of a total study population. We have very deliberately skirted any discussion of the voluminous body of "formal" mathematical sampling literature on the grounds that sampling is a methodological tool the utility of which can only be evaluated in the context of a body of stated theory and a specific research orientation. To "do science" is to operate within a logical evaluative system, the parts of which depend for their validity upon each other unit within that system. When viewed in the light of such a framework, *in vacuuo* logical discussion about best methods is fruitless. In its most reduced form, this argument becomes apparently destructive of any need for a summary of past experiences – by any science – with sampling. We feel, however, that given a small number of practical general sampling methods or designs, some statement of the appropriateness of each to likewise general orientations can be made. Statements of this sort will be explored in terms of both very broad as well as rather specific archaeological orientations in the sections to follow.

Regional Survey Sampling in Archaeology

The most commonly advanced rationale for archaeological survey is that it provides archaeologists with the data needed to determine which of a large population of sites merits excavation (Binford 1964; Ruppé 1966; Plog 1968). We would argue additionally that archaeological survey can in and of itself provide data which are of use in the suggestion and testing of hypotheses relating to culture process.

Although survey is an important part of archaeology, it has been dealt with only in a cursory manner in the literature (exceptions include Ruppé 1966; F. Plog 1968; Judge 1973). Both questions and endorsements can be raised regarding the reliability of interpretations made on the basis of data derived from survey alone. Some of the questions involve problems of (1) the relationship between surface and subsurface exposure and preservation, (2) the difference between regional and site-specific sample collection, and (3) the standardization of data collection on both an intersurvey and intrasurvey basis. The existence of such difficulties only serves to reemphasize that a strict logical paradigm, in which assumptions and statements are repeatedly scrutinized for validity and research-specific appropriateness, must be employed in all social inquiry.

Robert McC. Adams has stated that "in spite of widespread acceptance in theory of regional-ecological models that should depend on rigorous statistical sampling, the predominant focus of research for most investigators remains the arbitrarily chosen slice of a particular ancient site that is excavated" (1968: 1192). An examination of the archaeological literature supports Adams' contention. There are few regional archaeological surveys that have been carried out using probability sampling; even fewer archaeologists have attempted to undertake tests of various sampling designs using archaeological data. Most archaeological researchers have uncritically applied sampling designs without attempting to discern whether or not they were appropriate to the problem at hand.

Possibly the most forceful statement of the need for probability sampling in archaeology is provided by Binford (1964), who advocates a research design that is (1) regional in scope and (2) based on probability sampling. He advances a hypothetical research design which illustrates, among other things, the implementation of problem-oriented sampling. An attempt to test the surveying portion of Binford's hypothetical research design has been made by Robert Chenhall (1971). [A summary of this experiment is part of Chenhall's paper in this volume.] Mueller (1974) also attempted to test the use of sampling in regional archaeological survey, using data collected during an intensive survey of the Paria Plateau in north-central Arizona. Various kinds of simulated samples of real data were selected on paper and then compared to one another and to the parent population. Five basic probabilistic schemes were investigated using three classes of sampling units: a square unit one mile on a side, which Mueller termed a "section," a square "quarter-section" one-half mile on a side, and a rectangular unit 0.0666 mile wide and one-half mile long. Mueller determined that the most economical sampling unit was the section, chosen by the cluster scheme.

Regional sampling schemes have actually been implemented in the Reese River Ecological Project in central Nevada (Thomas 1969), in the Cedar Mesa survey in southeast Utah (Lipe and Matson 1971), and in the Chaco Canyon survey in northwestern New Mexico (Judge 1972). In the Reese River project Thomas employed a sampling strategy in which the region was stratified according to biotic community, and a 10% sample of quadrats five hundred meters on a side was taken within each stratum. Lipe and Matson (1971) likewise favored quadrats five hundred meters on a side. They employed a multistage design in which "clusters" or drainage units were stratified physiographically, a random sample being drawn from each of the strata within the "clusters" (Lipe and Matson 1971: 142). The Chaco Canyon survey will be discussed further below.

Steve Plog (n.d.), in an informative but unfortunately unpublished paper, examines the practicability and precision of a number of spatially clustered samples of archaeological data derived under various sampling designs from three populations in the Valley of Oaxaca, Mexico. In these tests both quadrats and transects were considered as sampling units. Plog found that in varying the size of the sampling units, the largest and most consistent gains in precision resulted from a decrease in the size of those sampling units. Further, the size of archaeological sites and their pattern of distribution had an effect on the estimation precision of the various sampling strategies. The outcome of statistical tests performed on these samples indicated that, for Plog's distributions, arbitrarily stratified, systematic unaligned samples were less efficient than systematic or stratified random samples, and that transects were more efficient than quadrats. While these results are at variance with the speculations of some geographers (cf. Berry and Baker 1968), their derivation from actual sampled archaeological data cannot be ignored. Practical archaeologists may, in fact, be interested in different kinds of data than are theoretical geographers.

An approach to the archaeological investigation of regions has recently been suggested by the Southwestern Anthropological Research Group (SARG) (see Gumerman 1971, 1972). This group, founded in 1971, is composed of a number of Southwestern archaeologists who wish to address themselves to a common problem: explaining spatial and temporal variability in the distribution of sites. In order to accomplish this objective it was ascertained that a common research design should be employed to insure comparability in the kinds of cultural and environmental information recorded. A theoretical basis of the SARG research design is the minimax "hypothesis," which is actually a warranted assumption: sites are located so as to minimize effort expended in resource acquisition and maximize resources acquired. This research design specifies the variables to be recorded and also contains a section on sampling strategy which advocates the use of random strip transects in regional archaeological survey (Plog and Hill 1971).

THE SAMPLING EXPERIMENT

Sample Versus Population: An Archaeological Test

As noted previously, a sample must be designed with reference to specific research problems; this necessarily limits the final formulation of any sampling design to the individual researcher. Nonetheless, an examination of some of the current trends in archaeological sampling in light of broad problem orientations of a regional nature may be informative at both the inductive and deductive stages of the process of inquiry.

The area selected for this research was Chaco Canyon National Monument (Fig. 6.1), located in the semiarid San Juan Basin of northwestern New Mexico. The monument consists of a portion of Chaco Canyon, a topographically distinct feature cut into sedimentary rock. The canyon, which is twenty miles long and varies between one-half and three-quarters of a mile wide, lies in a region of cold desert with rainfall varying from six to fifteen inches annually (Brand et al. 1937: 44–45). The area is especially suited to the testing of archaeological sampling designs because an intensive archaeological survey of the entire monument has recently been completed. Multidisciplinary research in the canyon, including studies in geology, physical geography, ecology, and aerial remote sensing, conducted under the auspices of the Chaco Center at the University of New Mexico, has yielded data on independent nonsocial variables. Perhaps most importantly, a great deal of background information exists as a result of many years of archaeological research in the canyon. This permits the recognition and the explanation for any significant deviation from expected sampling results.

A number of archaeological surveys have been conducted in the Chaco Canyon region. The earliest of the surveys was carried out in 1930 under the direction of Reginald Fisher, but the complete data were never published (Fisher 1930, 1934; Pierson n.d.). Another survey was conducted in 1947 by Lloyd Pierson (Pierson 1949). Both of these surveys concentrated on easily identifiable (usually late) sites and were limited in extent. The 1971 survey, under the direction of W. James Judge, was a problem oriented survey which was inductively oriented toward gaining a thorough under-

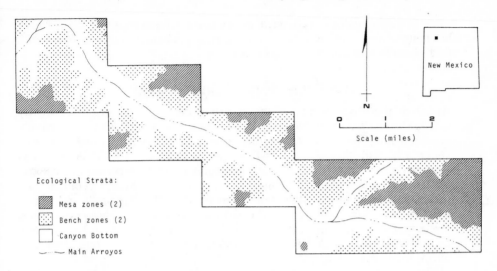

Fig. 6.1.   Sampled portion of Chaco
Canyon National Monument

standing of the range of environmental variation in the survey area and of
how sites were located with respect to that variation. In addition, the survey
was designed in such a way that it could serve as a test for the random strip
transect sampling method endorsed by SARG. Transects were oriented in a
north-south direction, perpendicular to the known environmental zones in
the canyon; as they were surveyed, changes in landform, vegetation, and
drainage were recorded (Judge n.d.; Witter n.d.). The 1972 survey, under
the direction of Alden C. Hayes, was an "inventory survey" designed to
assess the archaeological resources in the Chaco region. This survey was
organized along the same lines as the Wetherill Mesa survey in southwestern
Colorado (Hayes 1964). The primary difference between the two Chaco
surveys was not so much in the kinds of archaeological information recorded
as it was in the collection of detailed ecological information on the part of
the 1971 survey. Also, the 1971 survey was based on a sampling strategy
whereas the 1972 survey covered the entire area.

The vegetation of Chaco Canyon can be broadly classified as Upper
Sonoran (Bailey 1913). Recent ecological work in the area (Jones 1970,
n.d.; Witter n.d.) has shown that there is marked variability in the distribution of vegetation, due primarily to differences in precipitation, soil, slope,
exposure, and ground water availability. The mesa tops exhibit a mixed
grassland association while the canyon bottomlands have a riparian association consisting of shrubs and small trees (Jones n.d.). Vivian (1970) notes
a difference in kinds and density of vegetation between the northern and
southern portions of the canyon, the south mesa boasting a pinyon-juniper
association unlike the north mesa. In addition Vivian notes a vegetational
difference between mesa tops and talus slopes (benches). It is possible,

then, to distinguish five ecological zones in the Chaco region, each of which has distinctive vegetation: the south mesa, south bench, canyon bottomland, north bench, and north mesa (Fig. 6.1).

The Prehistory of Chaco Canyon

Although there is evidence of man's existence in the Chaco area as early as 10,000 years ago (Judge n.d.), the canyon was probably not intensively occupied until sedentary agricultural populations began to utilize the area about A.D. 500. Anasazi cultural development reached its culmination in Chaco Canyon around A.D. 1050; the remains of this period are characterized by huge miltistory habitation units (one of which, Pueblo Bonito, had 800 rooms and may have housed as many as 1200 people), small habitation sites, limited activity sites (i.e. storage cists, hearths, chipping stations, petroglyphs, etc.), large ceremonial structures (great kivas), elaborate water control systems, and a road system thought to be the only one of its kind north of Mexico.

The occupational history of Chaco Canyon can be divided into three cultural "periods," traditionally differentiated on the basis of lithic, ceramic, and architectural styles. The first, or Presedentary period, characterized by a hunting-gathering mode of adaptation, includes PaleoIndian, Archaic, and Basketmaker II manifestations. The second, or Sedentary period, incorporates the traditional Basketmaker III, and Pueblo I, II, and III divisions. Pueblo III society reached a peak of cultural complexity about A.D. 1050, and yet by A.D. 1175, Chaco was almost completely abandoned. It was not until the sixteenth century, when the canyon was reoccupied by a culturally distinct group of nomadic people, that the third, or Navajo period, began. This period continues to the present time. Evolving technology from one phase to the next was accompanied by distinctive changes not only in social complexity, but also in settlement locations and the nature and location of resources exploited.

Such variation serves to emphasize the unique nature of the Chaco data base. The rich prehistory of the region, plus the fact that it is easily stratified ecologically, and that a sophisticated archaeological survey has been completed, permit the formulation and testing of experimental designs not usually possible in archaeology. It is in recognition of the uniqueness of this data base that the present sampling experiments were undertaken.

Parameters of the Chaco Survey Population

The survey region dealt with here consists of a 20 square mile portion of Chaco Canyon National Monument, containing a total of 1130 sites. Although existing survey data include a wide range of recorded variables for each site, we have limited the number tested here to five variables which adequately represent the range of research problems of specific interest to the Southwestern Anthropological Research Group. These variables were (1) site frequency, (2) site density, (3) site type (habitation vs. limited activity), (4) cultural period (i.e., Archaic, BM-2, BM-3, P-1, P-2, P-3,

Navajo), and (5) site size in square meters. It should be pointed out that all of these variables are based on an assessment of surface evidence alone. For this reason, some information was deemed unreliable and was thus considered as "unknown" or "missing" data. While only three of the 1130 sites were recorded as unknown with respect to site type, a total of 509 (45%) of the sites are considered unknown with respect to cultural period. Forty-two sites (3.7%) were judged to be unreliable in terms of site size and thus coded as missing data.

Population parameters derived from the Chaco survey are presented in Table 6.1; general trends can be summarized briefly here. The canyon bottom is the largest of the five ecologically stratified zones, containing 41% of the total target area. The remaining zones are roughly equal in area, with the exception of the south mesa zone which contains only 4% of the total. The canyon bottom contains over half of the total inventoried archaeological sites (57%), while both north and south mesas contain significantly fewer than the number expected, given their respective sizes. This is reflected in the density figures, as indicated in Table 6.1.

Habitation sites comprise slightly over half (53.4%) and limited activity sites slightly under half (46.4%), of the inventoried population. In the canyon bottom, 67.5% of the sites are habitation sites, whereas on the north and south bench zones the number of limited activity sites exceeds that of habitation sites. In the north mesa zone, the frequency of the two types is approximately equal, while in the south mesa zone limited activity sites predominate. In the case of the latter, however, the total number of sites is not considered large enough to permit generalization. It is apparent, therefore, that a significant variation in site type distribution exists within the Chaco data, with the higher elevations selected for limited activity foci.* Further analysis to isolate the source of this variation will be presented later.

Regarding the distribution of sites per cultural period, significant variation is again present in the population. It is convenient to divide the population into Anasazi and Navajo sites to isolate the source of this variation (the frequency of both Archaic and BM-2 sites was very low — 1.3% of the total — thus these two cultural periods were excluded from further analysis). In each of the Anasazi groups (BM-3 through P-3) over half of the sites are located in the canyon bottom. On the other hand, over half of the Navajo sites (56.5%) are found on the elevated strata — predominantly on the benches — while only 43.5% are located on the canyon bottom. Thus there is a significant variation in distribution between Anasazi and Navajo sites, with the latter tending to select elevated loci. Of the Anasazi sites, BM-3 most closely approaches the Navajo sites in this respect.†

With regard to the parameter of site size, great variation exists both within the population as a whole, and between the five ecological strata. The mean site area for the entire population is 1913.41 square meters. Sites range from 1 to 25,650 square meters, with a standard deviation of 9756.76 square

---

*This distribution is statistically significant. Chi square = 78.024 with 4 degrees of freedom. P < 0.001.
†The frequency of sites of each cultural period per ecological zone varies significantly. Chi square = 160.42 with 23 degrees of freedom. P < 0.001.

meters. A closer examination of the frequency distribution indicates it to be heavily skewed toward small site size. In fact, 350 (31.0%) of the sites contain 25 square meters or less, while only 51 sites are larger than 8000 square meters. Due to the wide range in site size, this parameter was not used in the test of sample design accuracy. Recoding of this variable to an ordinal scale would have been necessary to permit this. However, the mean values of site size, as distributed in the various zones, are given in Table 6.1 to illustrate the significant variation that does exist.

Sampling Designs

Based on these known parameters in the Chaco data, we formulated three sampling experiments which we felt were relevant to modern archaeological research at the regional level. These were (1) a "consistency" test, which attempts to measure the consistency with which a given sampling design predicts site frequency and site attributes in both stratified and unstratified samples, (2) a "significance" test, in which the ability of a given sampling design to accurately monitor significant variation known to exist in the population is assessed, and (3) a "reliability" test, in which the effectiveness of various cluster shapes and sampling designs in predicting site attributes and frequency in an unstratified sample is compared on the basis of a number of trials using the same universe.

Four sampling designs were chosen for experimental comparison of accuracy as estimators of population parameters: random transects, interval transects, random quadrats, and "systematic" quadrats. It was felt that these particular designs would test effectively the variation existing between transect and quadrat sampling, as well as the variation existing between random and systematic schemes. Further, pragmatism was a primary consideration in the experimental testing; each of these designs would be quite simple to implement in an actual field survey. In fact, one design (random transects) was employed in the 1971 Chaco survey.

To facilitate computer processing of the experimental runs, the designs were selected and drawn on a regional site map, and were then coded as actual attributes of the sites themselves. For example, if a particular site was included in the interval transect and random quadrat sampling designs, these were punched as attributes of the site. While facilitating computer programming, this necessarily limited the number of designs that could be tested, due to the time-consuming process of coding sites. The five ecological zones in the canyon constitute "sampling strata" for experimentation.

Transect Designs

The transects selected were each 1/5 mile wide, and ran in a north-south direction along township lines, perpendicular to the general direction of the ecological strata in the Chaco area. As mentioned previously, the sampling universe had been selected specifically to facilitate experimental sample testing, consisting of an irregular block 10 miles long and 2 miles wide (see Fig. 6.1). This block was divided into a total of 50 transects, each 1/5 mile wide and two miles long.

TABLE 6.1

Population Parameters of the Chaco Survey Region

Variables	South Mesa	South Bench	Canyon Bottom	North Bench	North Mesa	Total
			Ecological Strata			
1. Zonal area (miles²)	0.83	3.64	8.15	3.57	3.81	20.00
2. Site frequency	10	167	644	221	88	1130
3. Site density (sites/mile²)	12.06	45.85	79.03	61.89	23.11	56.50[a]
4. Site size (meters²)	594.10	4360.50	1845.45	575.57	1395.95	1913.41[a]
5. Habitation sites	2	81	407	68	45	603
6. Limited activity sites	8	86	234	153	43	524
7. Frequency per cultural period						
A. Archaic	1	0	3	1	0	5
B. BM-2	0	2	1	0	0	3
C. BM-3	0	17	36	8	6	67
D. P-1	0	2	36	0	0	38
E. P-2	1	1	44	0	7	53
F. P-3	0	2	35	2	1	40
G. Navajo	3	73	138	89	14	317
H. Multicomponent	0	9	80	6	3	98
Total[b]	5	106	373	106	31	621

[a] These figures are averages for the entire Chaco survey region and not cumulative totals.

[b] Data on 621 sites only. Of the total survey population, 509 sites could not be reliably assigned to a cultural period on the basis of surface evidence.

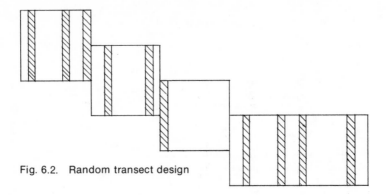

Fig. 6.2.   Random transect design

The *Random Transect* design consisted of a total of ten transects chosen through a random number table. These are shown in Figure 6.2. The total area covered by this design (as in the case of each of the designs tested here) is four miles, yielding a sampling fraction of 1/5. The amount of area *within* each ecological zone varies for each design and is given in line 1 of Tables 6.2–6.5 for each sampling scheme. Table 6.2 presents the statistics of population attributes per ecological zone of those sites located by the random transect design. Each of these frequencies, when compared with the population parameter as adjusted by the sampling fraction, will yield a measure of accuracy of this design for both the stratified and unstratified samples.

The *Systematic* (or *Interval*) *Transect* design combines initial random selection with systematic spacing of the transects. Selection was made from the same 50 transects used in the first design. The initial transect was selected randomly, then nine additional transects were chosen at evenly spaced intervals (i.e. every fifth transect) to complete the design. This resulted in 10 transects, each 1/5 mile wide by 2 miles long, evenly spaced 1 mile apart for the 10-mile width of the sampling region (Fig. 6.3). Again, the sampling fraction was 1/5. The statistics of the sites contained in the interval transect design are presented in Table 6.3. The sampling fractions within ecological

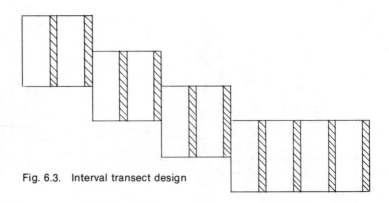

Fig. 6.3.   Interval transect design

TABLE 6.2
Random Transect Design – Sample Frequencies

Variables	Ecological Strata					
	South Mesa	South Bench	Canyon Bottom	North Bench	North Mesa	Total
1. Zonal area (miles^2)	0.093	0.796	1.773	0.661	0.676	4.000
2. Sampling fraction	0.112	0.219	0.218	0.185	0.178	0.200[a]
3. Site frequency	0	25	148	28	17	218
4. Site density (sites/mile^2)	0.00	31.41	83.47	42.36	25.15	54.50[a]
5. Habitation sites	0	12	96	9	9	126
6. Limited activity sites	0	13	52	19	8	92
7. Frequency per cultural period						
A. Archaic	0	0	2	0	0	2
B. BM-2	0	0	0	0	0	0
C. BM-3	0	2	7	0	3	12
D. P-1	0	0	5	0	0	5
E. P-2	0	0	10	0	2	12
F. P-3	0	0	5	0	0	5
G. Navajo	0	13	37	11	3	64
H. Multicomponent	0	1	11	2	1	15
Total	0	16	77	13	9	115

[a]These figures are averages for the entire Chaco survey region and not cumulative totals.

TABLE 6.3

Interval Transect Design – Sample Frequencies

Variables	Ecological Strata					
	South Mesa	South Bench	Canyon Bottom	North Bench	North Mesa	Total
1. Zonal area (miles²)	0.177	0.611	1.434	0.851	0.928	4.000
2. Sampling fraction	0.213	0.168	0.176	0.238	0.244	0.200[a]
3. Site frequency	2	33	122	49	21	227
4. Site density (sites/mile²)	11.30	54.01	85.08	57.58	22.63	56.75[a]
5. Habitation sites	0	11	85	9	10	115
6. Limited activity sites	2	22	36	40	11	111
7. Frequency per cultural period						
A. Archaic	0	0	0	0	0	0
B. BM-2	0	1	0	0	0	1
C. BM-3	0	3	7	2	0	12
D. P-1	0	1	5	0	0	6
E. P-2	0	0	10	0	2	12
F. P-3	0	1	10	0	0	11
G. Navajo	1	12	32	18	6	69
H. Multicomponent	0	2	17	3	0	22
Total	1	20	81	23	8	133

[a]These figures are averages for the entire Chaco survey region and not cumulative totals.

zones are shown also, and it can be seen that these vary somewhat from the stratum subsampling fractions of the random transect design.

Quadrat Designs

Quadrats were established in the region by dividing each of the 50 transects into 10 equal parts. This resulted in a total of 500 quadrats, each 1/25 of a mile square. Each of these were numbered, and the appropriate quadrat number was coded as a site attribute for computer processing.

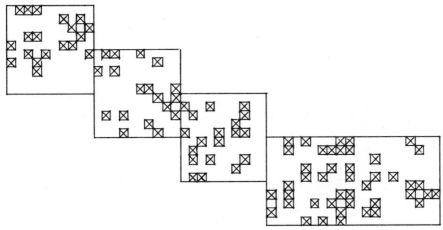

Fig. 6.4. Random quadrat design

The *Random Quadrat* design was chosen by selecting 100 quadrats from a table of random numbers. This resulted in a total area sampled of 4 square miles, or a sampling fraction of 1/5 (Fig. 6.4). Again, the amount of area covered within each ecological zone varied with the design, and was calculated separately with a polar planimeter. These stratum subsampling fractions, along with the statistics of the sites contained in the random quadrat design, are shown in Table 6.4.

The *Systematic Quadrat* design combined the unbiased features of random selection with the insured area coverage of a systematic sample. The mechanics of selection were similar to that described by Haggett (1965: 197) and modified for quadrat selection by S. Plog (n.d.). In this case, the sampling universe was stratified into two sampling rows of 50 columns each, corresponding to the 50 transects previously described. The bottom row was dealt with first, and one quadrat was randomly selected from each column. After the first 50 quadrats were selected, their "mirror" counterparts were selected from the top row. This resulted in 100 quadrats (1/5 sampling fraction) comprising a relatively systematic coverage of the sampling region (Fig. 6.5). The zonal area covered, as well as the site statistics, of the systematic quadrat design are presented in Table 6.5.

TABLE 6.4

Random Quadrat Design—Sample Frequencies

			Ecological Strata			
Variables	South Mesa	South Bench	Canyon Bottom	North Bench	North Mesa	Total
1. Zonal area (miles²)	0.113	0.570	1.793	0.870	0.654	4.000
2. Sampling fraction	0.136	0.156	0.220	0.244	0.172	0.200[a]
3. Site frequency	4	29	119	53	9	214
4. Site density (sites/mile²)	35.40	50.88	66.37	60.92	13.76	53.50[a]
5. Habitation sites	0	10	83	14	4	111
6. Limited activity sites	4	19	35	39	5	102
7. Frequency per cultural period						
A. Archaic	0	0	2	0	0	2
B. BM-2	0	1	0	0	0	1
C. BM-3	0	1	3	3	1	8
D. P-1	0	1	9	0	0	10
E. P-2	0	0	6	0	0	6
F. P-3	0	1	15	1	1	18
G. Navajo	1	15	27	22	1	66
H. Multicomponent	0	1	11	1	0	13
Total	1	20	73	27	3	124

[a]These figures are averages for the entire Chaco survey region and not cumulative totals.

TABLE 6.5

Systematic Quadrat Design – Sample Frequencies

Variables	South Mesa	South Bench	Canyon Bottom	North Bench	North Mesa	Total
1. Zonal area (miles^2)	0.103	0.898	1.558	0.782	0.660	4.000
2. Sampling fraction	0.124	0.247	0.191	0.219	0.173	0.200[a]
3. Site frequency	2	53	115	43	9	222
4. Site density (sites/mile^2)	19.42	59.02	73.81	54.99	13.64	55.50[a]
5. Habitation sites	0	23	68	13	3	107
6. Limited activity sites	2	30	47	30	6	115
7. Frequency per cultural period						
A. Archaic	0	0	2	0	0	2
B. BM-2	0	0	1	0	0	1
C. BM-3	0	2	11	3	1	17
D. P-1	0	2	9	0	0	11
E. P-2	0	0	10	0	0	10
F. P-3	0	0	2	0	0	2
G. Navajo	0	26	23	18	0	67
H. Multicomponent	0	3	12	0	1	16
Total	0	33	70	21	2*	126

Ecological Strata

[a]These figures are average for the entire Chaco survey region and not cumulative totals.

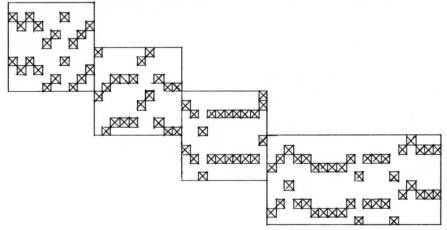

Fig. 6.5. Systematic quadrat design

Consistency Test

Only one computer run of each design was made in the consistency experiment. This was a result of the fact that for each design, a different sampling fraction had to be calculated due to variation in the ecological zonal area covered. The lengthy process of calculating area with a polar planimeter thus prohibited repetitions of each sampling design within the ecological zones. However, repetitive experiments were conducted for the unstratified samples in the reliability test, and these are discussed later.

To test the accuracy of each sample design in the consistency experiment, the raw data (site and attribute frequencies) generated by each sampling design were compared to the corresponding population parameters adjusted by appropriate sampling fractions. The sample frequency was recorded as the "observed" variable, while the corresponding population parameter was considered the "expected" variable. The basic chi square statistic, $(O - E)^2/E$, was then calculated and used as a relative basis of comparison of accuracy of sampling designs (cf. Mueller 1974). This statistic is effective only as a relative basis of comparison, and in fact is referred to here as an "accuracy index" rather than a chi square value. No statistical significance can be attached to these indices, since minimum rather than maximum values represent the more accurate sampling designs. Further, the question of whether or not a particular sampling scheme estimates parameters within significant limits must be a function of the nature of each specific research problem, since limits of acceptability vary accordingly.

It should be reemphasized that since repetitions of sampling designs are not possible here, we cannot generalize about the relative effectiveness of one specific design over another. Again, the purpose of this particular experiment is to assess the consistency of the sampling designs in their ability to predict attributes both within and between ecological zones with equal reliability.

In order to measure consistency between stratified and unstratified samples, accuracy indices were calculated for each sampling design. The data tabulated by variables in Table 6.6 represent averages of accuracy indices of each individual sampling design, as well as compiled indices for the transect and quadrat designs, and the random and systematic designs. A discussion of the results of the experiment for each of the major population parameters follows. The supporting data for all parameters in this consistency test are presented in Table 6.6.

Zonal Area

Although the experiment was designed so that each unstratified sampling scheme had an equal sampling fraction, it was noted previously that the amount of area *within* each ecological zone varied with the sampling design. Thus the designs themselves vary in their accuracy of estimating the total area in each ecological stratum. However, as indicated by the low values in Table 6.6, all four sampling designs are good estimators of zonal area. Although differences between designs are minimal, transect designs appear slightly better than quadrats, and random designs hold the edge over systematic.

Site Frequency

The accuracy index of each sampling design was calculated for its estimation of site frequency without regard for ecological zone (unstratified sample) as well as the site frequencies within each ecological zone (nonarbitrarily stratified sample). The results of the unstratified and stratified samples will be presented as each parameter is discussed.

Unstratified: Here the interval transect design is the best estimator of site frequency. Taken together, the two transect designs are, in general, better estimators than the two quadrat designs. By the same token, the two systematic designs exhibit greater accuracy of estimation than do the two random designs.

Stratified: Here the averages for the five zones yield the same results obtained in the unstratified sample—interval transects are best, with transects better than quadrat designs, and systematic better than random.

Again, it should be noted that although accuracy can only be measured on a relative scale, the sample designs all estimate site frequency very closely. The best estimator (interval transects) is off by only one site. Projected to the regional level, this design would have predicted 1135 sites, compared to an actual total of 1130. Even the poorest predictor (in this case, random quadrats) would have estimated 1170 sites, an error of only 5.75%.

Site Density

The results in estimating site density are identical to those of predicting site frequency, as one would expect. Interval transects are most accurate in both the unstratified and stratified samples. In general, transects are better than quadrats, and systematic better than random designs.

TABLE 6.6

Comparative Accuracy Indices of Tested Sample Designs

Variable	Random Transects	Interval Transects	Random Quadrats	Systematic Quadrats	Both Transects	Both Quadrats	Both Random	Both Systematic
1. Zonal area								
a. Stratified	0.013	0.021	0.023	0.017	0.017	0.020	0.018	0.019
2. Site frequency								
a. Stratified	1.87	0.36	1.64	1.46	1.11	1.55	1.75	0.91
b. Unstratified	0.28	0.00	0.64	0.07	0.14	0.36	0.46	0.04
3. Site density								
a. Stratified	4.64	0.45	10.31	2.65	2.54	6.48	7.47	1.55
b. Unstratified	0.07	0.00	0.16	0.02	0.04	0.09	0.12	0.01
4. Habitation sites								
a. Stratified	0.76	1.34	0.70	1.02	1.05	0.86	0.73	1.18
b. Unstratified	0.24	0.26	0.76	1.53	0.25	1.15	0.50	0.90
5. Limited activity sites								
a. Stratified	1.16	1.00	3.24	1.08	1.08	2.16	2.20	1.04
b. Unstratified	1.56	0.37	0.07	0.99	0.97	0.53	0.82	0.68
6. BM-3 sites								
a. Stratified	1.46	0.38	1.16	1.12	0.92	1.14	1.31	0.75
b. Unstratified	0.15	0.15	2.18	0.97	0.15	1.58	1.17	0.56
7. Pueblo sites								
a. Stratified	0.57	0.68	0.71	0.49	0.62	0.60	0.64	0.58
b. Unstratified	0.67	0.30	2.32	0.39	0.49	1.36	1.50	0.35
8. Navajo sites								
a. Stratified	0.88	1.01	0.63	1.37	0.94	1.00	0.75	1.19
b. Unstratified	0.01	0.49	0.11	0.20	0.25	0.16	0.06	0.35
9. All Cultural variables summarized								
a. Stratified	1.42	0.66	2.30	1.15	1.04	1.73	1.86	0.91
b. Unstratified	0.43	0.22	0.87	0.59	0.32	0.73	0.65	0.40

Note. Accuracy indices shown are averages of chi square values of all ecological strata.

The accuracy of estimation is very high. The interval transect design estimated a density figure of 56.75 sites per square mile, compared to the actual value of 56.50 sites per mile. Within the stratified zones, however, accuracy is reduced somewhat, especially when the site frequency of the population is very low, as in the case of the south mesa (10 sites total). Due to this low frequency, it is doubtful that any of the sampling designs can be accurately tested in the south mesa zone. The random quadrat design, for example, predicted a site density of 35.40 on the south mesa, almost three times the actual value of 12.06. In testing the designs, therefore, the south mesa data must be examined with caution.

Site Type

It is in the testing of attributes of sites, rather than their frequencies, that considerable variation in effectiveness of the designs appears. This increase in variation is possibly a function of the reduction in site frequency which results from subdividing the population on the basis of specific attributes.

Habitation Sites. In the case of the unstratified sample (ecological zones ignored), the random transect design emerged as the most accurate, estimating 630 sites as opposed to the actual value of 603. In general, transects were better estimators than quadrats, and the random designs better than systematic.

In the stratified sample, however, the results were quite different. Here the average values show the random quadrat design to be the most effective, and quadrats generally more accurate than transects. As in the case of the unstratified sample, random designs are better than systematic. These rather divergent results between the stratified and unstratified samples merit further investigation and will be reexamined later.

Limited Activity Sites. In the case of the unstratified sample, the random quadrat design yielded the best results, estimating 510 sites of an actual 524. In general, quadrats were better than transects, and the systematic design better than random.

With respect to the stratified sample, the situation is reversed, as in the case of the habitation sites. Here, the average values show the interval transect design to be most accurate, and, in general, transects are better than quadrats. Again the systematic designs are better than random.

While the implications of conflicting sampling-scheme comparison between limited activity and habitation sites will not be fully explored at this point, the discrepancy may be informative as to functional or locational differences between the two site types. Such an indication, evaluated in terms of a higher body of theory and assumptions, can result in a total reevaluation of the relevance of variables or the boundaries beyond which new variables become important. This is the essence of a "feedback" research design.

Cultural Period

In order to simplify testing of sample design effectiveness in estimating frequency of sites by cultural period, the population was divided into three cultural units exhibiting distinctive adaptations: Basketmaker III, Pueblo (including P-1, P-2, and P-3) and Navajo. The results of each of these tests are examined separately.

Basketmaker. In the unstratified sample, both the random and interval transect designs yielded equally accurate results, estimating 60 of an actual 67 sites. Transects were generally better than quadrats, and systematic better than random designs.

In the stratified sample, the results were similar. Interval transects were the best, but were followed by systematic quadrats rather than random transects. The remainder was the same as in the unstratified sample.

Pueblo. In the sampling of Pueblo cultural period categories a situation quite similar to that encountered in testing the habitation parameter appears. In the case of the unstratified sample, interval transects yielded the best results, estimating 145 sites, compared to an actual 131. In general, transects were better than quadrats, and the systematic better than random designs.

With respect to the stratified sample, however, the systematic quadrat design yielded the best average accuracy index. In general, quadrats were slightly better than transects, and systematic designs better than random.

Navajo. In the unstratified sample, the random transect design was by far the best, estimating 320 sites compared with an actual 317. However, quadrat designs were better in general, and random better than systematic.

In the stratified case, random quadrats were the most accurate, although the two transect designs were better in general. Again, random designs were better than systematic.

To summarize, in the case of the unstratified samples (ecozones ignored), the interval transect design emerges as the best overall estimator of population parameters. In comparing the designs, the two transect designs average better than the quadrats, and the two systematic designs better than the random. Exceptions to the general superiority of transects occur in the case of limited activity sites and partially in the case of Navajo sites, where quadrats are better estimators.

Where the region was stratified into the 5 ecozones, and within-zone estimations made, similar results emerged. Again, the interval transect design was the best estimator, and transect and systematic designs were better than quadrat and random designs, respectively. The exceptions to transect superiority in the stratified samples occurred in the cases of habitation sites and Pueblo-period sites, where quadrats were generally better estimators.

This suggests, then, that while transects are the best overall estimators, under certain conditions quadrats are superior; specifically, quadrat designs are better estimators of limited activity sites in the unstratified samples, and of habitation sites in the stratified samples.

We may conclude that sampling designs vary in their effectiveness in predicting attributes between stratified and unstratified samples. Thus a specific design which estimates an attribute best in the unstratified sample may not be equally reliable in estimating that same attribute within the ecologically stratified zones.

A possible explanation of this phenomenon might involve coincidence between the sampling frame and on-the-ground data patterning. The primary distinction between transect and quadrat sampling is that the former contains a linear bias, in this case purposely oriented perpendicular to the ecological strata. A skewed sample of limited activity sites within each zone, presumably located near resources being exploited, might well be favored by such a linear bias. On the other hand, habitation sites within each zone would more likely be spaced with a bias in the direction of the strata rather than perpendicular to it. The linear bias of transects would not favor the accurate prediction of habitation sites, then, and quadrats would be better predictors as the test results indicated.

It will be recalled that just the opposite results were obtained in the tests of unstratified samples. Here the relationship of limited activity sites *between* ecological zones is being sampled and no between-zone linear bias necessarily exists. The between-zone resource relationships might thus be more accurately monitored by quadrats, as the data would indicate.

The interpretation of the results of these tests suggests strongly that no single sampling design can be expected to yield equally accurate results in both intra- and interzonal predictions of site characteristics. For this reason we suggest that a two-phase sampling scheme may be most appropriate to regional survey and we will recommend specific designs in the conclusions of this chapter.

Significance Test

As mentioned earlier, the chi square "accuracy indices" calculated here can be used only as relative, rather than absolute, measures of the accuracy of a particular sampling design. Whether or not a given design estimates population parameters within acceptable limits depends entirely on the degree of tolerance set by the research problem under investigation. As such, we felt that experimental testing of the various sampling designs with respect to an actual research problem might be profitable, in order to determine whether variation known to be significant in terms of the problem would be accurately monitored.

An initial examination of the data suggested that significant variation in the distribution of sites by time period existed in the Chaco survey population. To simplify analysis, the categories of cultural period were reduced to the three with most frequent site occurrences: BM-3, Pueblo, and Navajo. From other studies in the Southwest, these three cultural units are known to have exhibited distinctive adaptations in the past. A cross-tabulation of the distribution of these three kinds of sites within the five ecological zones indicates that significant variation does exist in the Chaco region. In this case, chi square equals 91.98 with 8 degrees of freedom, which is significant at the 0.001 level (Table 6.7).

The source of this variation lies in the similarity between BM-3 and Navajo site distributions, and the distinction between these two and the Pueblo sites. Pueblo sites are concentrated in the canyon bottom, while BM-3 and

TABLE 6.7

Sample Design Prediction of Significant Variation

Part A: Population Data

Ecological Strata

Variables	South Mesa	South Bench	Canyon Bottom	North Bench	North Mesa
1. Habitation sites					
a. BM-3	0	11	17	4	4
b. Pueblo	1	5	102	0	7
c. Navajo	1	49	101	45	6
2. Limited activity sites					
a. BM-3	0	6	19	4	2
b. Pueblo	0	0	13	2	1
c. Navajo	2	24	37	44	8
3. Total habitation & limited activity					
a. BM-3	0	17	36	8	6
b. Pueblo	1	5	115	2	8
c. Navajo	3	73	138	89	14

Part B: Chi square Values

| | | | Sample Designs | | |
Variables	Population	Random Transects	Interval Transects	Random Quadrats	Systematic Quadrats
1. Habitation sites					
a. Chi square value	69.66	23.50	7.65	16.52	16.00
b. Degrees of freedom	8	6	6	6	4
c. Significance level	<.001	<.001	<.30	<.02	<.01
2. Limited activity sites					
a. Chi square value	22.27	3.55	8.78	15.96	12.82
b. Degrees of freedom	8	3	8	8	6
c. Significance level	<.01	<.50	<.50	<.05	<.05
3. Total habitation and limited activity					
a. Chi square value	91.98	18.26	17.14	26.46	30.59
b. Degrees of freedom	8	6	8	8	6
c. Significance level	<.001	<.01	<.05	<.001	<.001

Navajo sites frequent the north and south benches as well. In the case of Navajo, less than half the sites are found in the canyon bottom.

This variation was defined further by examining habitation and limited activity sites of each cultural period separately (Table 6.7). Again, the distinctiveness of the Pueblo site distribution compared to the other two is apparent. Further, it can be seen that the primary difference between the BM-3 and Navajo distributions lies in BM-3's dominant use of the canyon bottom for limited activity. Chi square values indicate that both the habitation and limited activity site distributions of the three cultural periods vary significantly between the ecological zones (0.001 and 0.01 levels of significance, respectively).

This variation in site distribution in the survey population is one which poses a research problem suitable to the paradigm upon which the Southwestern Anthropological Research Group is based. The hypothesis that efficiency in resource acquisition is a prime determinant of site location is certainly relevant to the site distribution manifest by the Chaco survey population and could presumably be tested here. For this reason, we felt it appropriate to determine the degree to which the various sampling designs discerned the significance of such variations in site distribution. An estimate of each of the four sampling designs of the site type distribution within the five ecological zones was attained for the BM-3, Pueblo, and Navajo periods. The significance level of the chi square statistic was examined in each case to determine whether a significant variation was predicted (Table 6.7). We assumed that the 0.05 level would be considered significant by an archaeologist examining the data from a survey sample. Thus, in this experiment, sampling designs were not ranked with respect to relative chi square values. Instead, they were scaled on the basis of whether or not they estimated significance at the 0.05 level or greater.

The results of the experiment indicate that when the criteria of site type (i.e., habitation versus limited activity) was ignored, all sample designs estimated significant variation in the distribution of BM-3, Pueblo, and Navajo sites between the five ecological zones. In general, the quadrat designs predicted higher significance levels than the transects. In fact, the random transect design estimated no Basketmaker sites on the north bench, when actually 12% of the BM-3 sites are located in this particular zone. Since this is one of the features which illustrates the intriguing similarity of BM-3 and Navajo adaptations, its omission by the random transect design is unfortunate.

When the habitation sites were treated separately, however, not all designs predicted significant variation. In the case of the interval transect design, the chi square level of significance was between .30 and .20, and thus probably would have been ignored by an archaeologist analyzing such a survey sample. Another design (random quadrat), while predicting significance, was quite disparate in its estimation of the BM-3 distinction. Still, quadrats were generally more successful in predicting significant variations than were transects.

When the limited activity sites were examined separately, neither transect design predicted significant variation, while both quadrat designs did. The random transect design missed the Pueblo sites entirely (approximately 10% of the sample).

Undoubtedly, a good deal of the error here can be attributed to a reduction in site frequency as a function of an increase in selective criteria; nevertheless, the results of these experimental sampling runs dictate that caution be exercised in the kinds of generalizations made on the basis of survey data attained through formal sampling techniques. The experiments suggest further that in using sample data for the generation of hypotheses, significant variation in the population attributes might well be overlooked. Actual testing of hypotheses on the basis of sample-derived data such as these would be even more tenuous. Again, a multistage sampling design is advised. Judging from the results of the experiments conducted here, we would suggest an initial systematic transect design, followed by quadrat sampling within ecological zones to confirm significant variation in site type distribution.

Reliability Test

The purpose of this experiment is to compare the effectiveness of one sampling design against another in estimating site frequency and selected site attributes. In this case, however, comparative measurements are based on several repetitions of each of the four sampling designs. For this reason, it was possible to deal only with the unstratified region. Stratification by ecological zone could not be effected due to the necessity of calculating a different sampling fraction with a polar planimeter for each repetition of each sampling design. Only five repetitions of each sampling design were run. More than five runs would have resulted in redundancy for the interval transect design, due to its 1/5 sampling fraction and systematic nature. Remaining sampling designs were limited to five repetitions also to permit standardization in comparison of results.

Measurement in this test was effected by calculating accuracy indices in the same manner as before, except here the *mean values* of five repetitions were used as observed frequencies. In addition, an index of "precision," measured by calculating the standard error of each series of repetitions, was also used (cf. Plog, n.d., for a discussion of the concept of precision in sampling experiments). These indices, as well as the data from which they were derived, are presented in Table 6.8.

As interpreted from the averaged accuracy indices, interval transects are the best general estimators of those variables considered, followed by random transects, random quadrats, and systematic quadrats, in that order. Transects are better general predictors than quadrats, and systematic designs slightly better than random. Thus the results of the repetitive experiment tend to confirm those noted earlier in the consistency test. Here, however, broader generalization is permitted about the effectiveness of the designs, due to the repetitive trials.

The precision measurements yielded somewhat different results. Here minimal deviation, as measured by averaged standard errors, was exhibited

TABLE 6.8

Accuracy and Precision Indices of Sampling Designs Based on Five Repetitions

Variable	Actual Parameter	Prediction Mean	Accuracy Index	Accuracy Rank	Standard Error	Precision Rank
1. Site frequency						
a. Random transects	226	224.40	0.011	2	5.819	3
b. Interval transects	226	226.00	0.000	1	2.828	1
c. Random quadrats	226	215.60	0.478	4	3.855	2
d. Systematic quadrats	226	233.40	0.242	3	6.772	4
2. Habitation sites						
a. Random transects	121	124.00	0.206	3	7.120	4
b. Interval transects	121	120.60	0.003	1	3.894	2
c. Random quadrats	121	115.20	0.278	4	3.680	1
d. Systematic quadrats	121	122.40	0.016	2	4.308	3
3. Limited activity sites						
a. Random transects	105	100.20	0.219	2	3.216	2
b. Interval transects	105	104.80	0.000	1	3.878	3
c. Random quadrats	105	99.60	0.277	3	2.821	1
d. Systematic quadrats	105	110.60	0.299	4	5.972	4
4. Basketmaker-III sites						
a. Random transects	13	12.60	0.012	1	0.980	1
b. Interval transects	13	13.40	0.012	2	2.135	4
c. Random quadrats	13	11.20	0.249	3	1.020	2
d. Systematic quadrats	13	16.00	0.692	4	1.483	3
5. Pueblo sites						
a. Random transects	27	30.20	0.379	4	4.176	4
b. Interval transects	27	26.20	0.024	1	2.223	1
c. Random quadrats	27	29.20	0.179	2	2.437	2
d. Systematic quadrats	27	29.40	0.213	3	3.140	3
6. Navajo sites						
a. Random transects	63	64.00	0.016	2	0.837	1
b. Interval transects	63	63.40	0.003	1	2.379	3
c. Random quadrats	63	62.00	0.016	3	3.536	4
d. Systematic quadrats	63	66.80	0.229	4	1.393	2

TABLE 6.9

Mean Rank Evaluation of Sampling Designs

Sampling Design	Variables						Mean Rank
	Site Frequency	Habitation	Limited Activity	BM-III	Pueblo	Navajo	
1. Random transects							
a. Accuracy rank	2	3	2	1	4	2	
b. Precision rank	3	4	2	1	4	1	
c. Mean rank	2.5	3.5	2.0	1.0	4.0	1.5	2.416
2. Interval transects							
a. Accuracy rank	1	1	1	2	1	1	
b. Precision rank	1	2	3	4	1	3	
c. Mean rank	1.0	1.5	2.0	2.5	1.0	2.0	1.750
3. Random quadrats							
a. Accuracy rank	4	4	3	3	2	3	
b. Precision rank	2	1	1	2	2	4	
c. Mean rank	3.0	2.5	2.0	2.5	2.0	3.5	2.583
4. Systematic quadrats							
a. Accuracy rank	3	2	4	4	3	4	
b. Precision rank	4	3	4	3	3	2	
c. Mean rank	3.5	2.5	4.0	3.5	3.0	3.0	3.250

virtually equally by the interval transect and random quadrat designs, followed by random transects and systematic quadrats in that order. Precision was especially high in the random quadrat measurement of site type (habitation vs. limited activity). It must be pointed out, however, that in both of these cases where precision was high, accuracy was quite low. In other words, the random quadrat repetitive designs yielded predictions with relatively little deviation, but relatively inaccurate means; not exactly an optimal situation.

Obviously what is sought by archaeologists is a sample design which is both accurate and precise. The selection of such a design would of course be a function of the area to be sampled and the particular research problem in question. However, it is possible at this point to suggest a tentative order of reliability of those sampling designs tested herein, based on a combination of accuracy and precision measurements. This hierarchy can be established by ranking the sampling designs in order of accuracy and precision indices for each variable tested. The indices and their associated ranks are provided in Table 6.9. The precision and accuracy ranks can then be averaged, and these values themselves averaged for each sample design. The result is a hierarchy of sample design reliability, based on the combined accuracy and precision of each in estimating the Chaco survey variables. As indicated by the mean values expressed in Table 6.9, interval transects again emerge as best, followed by random transects and random quadrats (closely associated), and finally systematic quadrats. This hierarchy can be viewed as establishing preference for use in first-stage sampling of a region such as Chaco Canyon.

SUMMARY AND CONCLUSIONS

Summary

The viewpoints expressed in this study are predicated upon a number of assumptions, the most fundamental of which is the importance of the regional approach to archaeological research. Although the regional approach in archaeology was by no means initiated by "processual" archaeologists, there is little doubt about the critical role it plays in the modern archaeological paradigm. Recent emphases on the systemic perspective, the settlement as a unit of analysis, the social environment as an independent variable and resource utilization at the macroenvironmental scale, have illustrated the necessity of a formal regional strategy.

Two very important considerations emerge from emphasis on a regional approach. First, such archaeology cannot be undertaken in the absence of problem-oriented regional survey which precedes excavation and in fact dictates the character of the research problems to be followed during excavation. Secondly, regional archaeology cannot be undertaken in the absence of formalized probability sampling methods, incorporated as an integral part of survey. Archaeologists have devoted little time or attention to formal sampling techniques in the past, but an attempt to undertake research of a regional scope without a rigorous approach to sampling is no longer admissible.

A frequently neglected assumption of archaeological research, whether it is of an intersite or intrasite nature, is the assumption of validity of the sample design employed. Yet it is no less important to validate this assumption than it is to validate others which are often dealt with in detail; it may indeed be more important since the validity of the sampling affects the reliability of the data upon which interpretations are based. Attaining a reliable sample is not always easy, however. Most of those who have attempted to implement formal sampling techniques are aware of the paradox which exists in their implementation; specifically, one needs reliable information about the parameters of a population before one can select the appropriate sampling design. By the same token, if one had the desired information at his disposal, there would be little need to sample.

The inherent problems of sampling are of course not limited to archaeology, and researchers in other disciplines have refined their techniques by utilizing multistage sampling approaches. The results of sampling at one stage serve to inform the researcher how to sample most effectively during the next stage. Such multistage designs, profiting by continual feedback at each stage, have been advocated recently by archaeologists (cf. Redman 1973).

Sampling designs can be refined in other ways, however. Again prehistorians can profit from work done in other disciplines, particularly geography and ecology, which have suggested and practiced sampling techniques quite appropriate to archaeological survey. The question of the comparative advantages of systematic versus random sampling techniques has been dealt with experimentally, as has that of transect versus quadrat designs. The inportance of informed stratification of a survey region has been emphasized, and this is of particular significance to the social scientist dealing with population elements which are rarely distributed in a homogeneous fashion.

Formal sampling methods are important in at least one recent experiment in regional archaeology, undertaken by the members of the Southwest Anthropological Research Group (cf. Gumerman 1971). The SARG design calls for the coordination of data collection at the regional level in terms of a shared research problem: the explanation of site location in the Southwestern United States.

The general model advanced toward the resolution of this problem is that sites are located so that access to critical resources is maximized, implying a minimization of effort or "cost." Those fieldworkers in the Southwest who endorse the SARG design have agreed on standardized field collection techniques which hopefully will result in a body of data upon which site-locational hypotheses can be tested. The importance of such an approach to anthropological research cannot be overemphasized, for here is an excellent opportunity to do processual archaeology at the regional level.

Formal sampling techniques are fundamental to the SARG research design. At the survey stage, random transects employed in conjunction with informed stratification on the basis of geomorphological and ecological criteria have been recommended (cf. Plog and Hill 1971). It was in the context of the SARG regional approach, and its recommended sampling techniques, that the present study was undertaken. The Chaco Canyon area was selected specifically because of its location in the Southwestern region, and because of the fact that an "inventory" survey of Chaco Canyon National Monument has been carried out recently, thus facilitating the testing of various experimental sampling designs. It is important to point out that we are not testing the validity of sampling in general here. We see no alternative to formal sampling techniques in regional archaeology, and thus cannot question the necessity of sampling; sufficient work has been carried out in analogous situations in ancillary disciplines to prove the effectiveness and reliability of probability sampling when implemented properly. Our aim instead is to test several sampling techniques and to gauge their effectiveness in serving the needs of the SARG research problems in particular, and regional survey archaeology in general.

For the purposes of this study, a 20 square mile portion of Chaco Canyon National Monument was selected as the sampling region. Intensive surface survey had revealed 1130 sites in this region; their locations and several selected attributes served as population parameters. Four sampling designs were selected for experimentation in predicting the parameters: random transects, interval transects, random quadrats, and systematic quadrats. The transects selected were 1/5 mile on each side. A 20% sampling fraction was selected for each design. The region was stratified ecologically into five zones, and both unstratified and stratified samples were tested.

Three types of sampling experiments were selected for testing the sampling designs: (1) a test of the consistency with which each design predicted attributes for the stratified vs. the unstratified samples; (2) a test of the degree to which each sampling design monitored the significance of variation in site distribution in the population; and (3) an assessment of the relative effectiveness of each sampling design, based on measurements of accuracy and precision in repetitive trials. In the first two tests, only one repetition was used, since the time involved in calculating the stratified sampling fraction for successive repetitions of each design would have been prohibitive. For the same reason, only unstratified samples were dealt with in the third test, involving repetitive trials.

The results of the first test indicated intervally spaced transects to be the best overall predictors of population parameters in investigating the region, both as an unstratified entity and as stratified into ecological zones. When estimating site attributes within ecological zones, as opposed to estimating site frequency, it is possible that the linear bias of transects may affect their reliability, and in such cases quadrats may be better estimators. In any case, there seems little doubt that systematic designs are as effective as random designs. This is significant, since interval transects are much more practical to implement in the field than other sampling designs. It should also be noted that transects are effective in providing data to test the validity of the criteria employed in the initial stratification of the region, by accurately predicting variations in site density between zones. In attempting to isolate the source of this variation by analyzing specific site attributes, however, the quadrat designs may well be more effective.

The purpose of the second test was to determine whether the sampling designs would predict significant variations that were known to exist in the population on the basis of the inventory survey. Variation significant to the research aims of SARG was selected specifically for this test case, i.e., the differing location of limited activity versus habitation sites of the Basketmaker, Pueblo, and Navajo time periods. All sampling designs tested in this phase predicted population variability with at least a .05 level of significance; such results could be productively used by a survey archaeologist to set the stage for further research. However, it was noted that when a combination of selective criteria (e.g., BM-3 limited activity sites within a specific zone) served to reduce the number of sites in the samples to very low frequencies, it is doubtful whether the significant variation known to exist would have been accurately monitored by the single-stage sample design.

The third test involved a comparative assessment of the four sampling designs, based on an evaluation of the accuracy and precision with which each design monitored the unstratified region. Five repetitions of each design were run (more than five trials would have resulted in redundancy for the interval transect design) and mean frequencies of the results were compiled for accuracy and precision calculations. The results of the accuracy tests indicated that interval transects were best, followed by random transects, random quadrats, and systematic quadrats. In the precision tests, interval transects yielded least deviation, followed very closely by random quadrats, and then random transects, and systematic quadrats. A tendency to cluster around an erroneous mean was indicated by the random quadrat values, however.

It was noted that the ideal sampling design would be one which maximized both accuracy and precision. A method of determining this for the four designs tested here was effected by ranking the precision and accuracy indices, then averaging the rank values. In this final, and probably most reliable, evaluation, interval transects emerged as the best overall estimator, followed by random transects, random quadrats, and systematic quadrats.

Conclusions

On the basis of the research undertaken in this study, several conclusions and recommendations can be offered. First, we can assume that regional archaeology is here to stay and that formalized probability sampling designs must become an integral part of the field techniques of every archaeologist interested in providing answers to meaningful regional problems. Second, as suggested by researchers in archaeology as well as other disciplines, and as confirmed by experiments with the Chaco data, a multistage approach to sampling is virtually mandatory. We would offer the following guidelines concerning regional sampling to those survey archaeologists planning regional research in the future:

Stratification

Since it is unlikely that cultural sites will be evenly distributed throughout the survey region, sampling results will be enhanced by stratification. In the absence of prior knowledge about the distribution of the sites, we recommend that the region be stratified with respect to ecological and geomorphological

criteria derived through aerial remote sensing techniques. The survey archaeologist must remember that initially these criteria are arbitrary, and that
their validity must be confirmed by the statistics obtained from the survey
itself.

First Sampling Stage

We recommend that for the first sampling stage, a system of interval or
evenly spaced transects be selected. The sample unit size and the sampling
fraction will both be a function of the general problem orientation of the
researcher, as well as the nature of the region and the exigencies of funding.
Transects should be arranged counter to the grain of the ecological strata,
and should then be field surveyed intensively for all archaeological sites.
Locations must be plotted accurately, and selected attributes relevant to
the research problem in question recorded.

Data Analysis and Interpretation (first stage)

Interpretation of the data derived from the first stage of sampling should be
oriented toward a number of specific objectives which will vary with the
particular research design. We suggest that at least the following be derived:
(a) a confirmation of the significance of the criteria used for initial stratification of the region; (b) the definition of significant variation (patterning) in
the survey population as manifested by the sample data; and (c) the generation of specific hypotheses, relevant to the research problem, to be tested
with additional survey data collected during the second sampling stage.

Second Sampling Stage

Second-stage sample design, as well as sampling fraction and unit size, will
be dictated by the results of the first sampling stage; such feedback is instru-
mental to an increase in sample reliability. On the basis of the results of
experiments with the Chaco data, we suggest that a reasonable approach
would be the implementation of a system of random quadrats within each of
the previously selected, and now deductively confirmed, strata. The mor-
phology of the various ecological zones would indicate the most effective
and practical unit size of quadrats for each stratum. The variability within
each of the zones would suggest the sampling fraction for each stratum.
Once plotted, quadrats should be surveyed intensively, and site location
and attributes (perhaps further augmented by feedback from the first stage)
recorded.

Data Analysis and Interpretation (second stage)

At least the following should be derived from review of the second-stage
data: (a) the actual testing of hypotheses generated from the first stage,
and (b) the formulation of a general research design — regionally oriented —
which will serve to direct priorities in the selection of sites for excavation,
as well as to individually problem-orient the excavation of each of the
sites selected.
    Although only the first two of these five recommended guidelines were
tested in the present study, it should be apparent that the remaining sugges-

tions are also logical and appropriate components of the process of explanation. In a day when social scientists experience difficulty in expressing their goals and needs to the general public and especially to funding agencies, it is hoped that the implementation of coherently designed sampling methods will at least help to establish the validity of the archaeologist's techniques and conclusions in his own mind.

ACKNOWLEDGMENTS

Support for the archaeological surveys of Chaco Canyon was provided by the United States Department of the Interior, National Park Service, through its Chaco Center at the University of New Mexico. We wish especially to thank Alden Hayes and Thomas Windes of that office for their helpful contributions, without which this paper could not have been written. Also we would like to thank Henry Harpending for his sound statistical advice; Steve Plog for so unhesitatingly sending us his excellent sampling paper; and, especially, Marge Judge and Melinda Ebert for putting up with us while this paper was being written.

This chapter is also inventoried as Contribution No. 8 of the Chaco Center, National Park Service and the University of New Mexico, for purposes of bibliographic control of research relating to Chaco Canyon.

7. Regional Sampling:
A Case Study of Cedar Mesa, Utah

Richard G. Matson and William D. Lipe

Richard G. Matson (Ph.D., University of California at Davis, 1971) has had field experience in the American Southwest, the Northwest, and California. He has published several articles concerning regional human ecology and quantitative analysis. He has been serving as an Assistant Professor of Anthropology at the University of British Columbia.

William D. Lipe (Ph.D., Yale University, 1966) has devoted his research energies to the American Southwest and to the Eastern Woodlands. His work in the Glen Canyon project was partially responsible for the revitalization of the standards of salvage archaeology in the late 1950s and resulted in several published monographs, in addition to more recent Southwestern articles and reviews. His primary focus has been regional analysis investigations on Cedar Mesa, Utah, under a National Science Foundation grant. His positions as Assistant Director, Museum of Northern Arizona, and Chairman, Southwestern Anthropological Research Group, have furthered his earlier interests in archaeological resource conservation and research administration.

INTRODUCTION

The Cedar Mesa Project has three main goals: (1) to reconstruct the adaptive strategies of prehistoric cultures, (2) to identify the environmental limits of these adaptations, and (3) to attempt to account for stability and change in the cultural strategies. Since we are involved in generating and testing ideas about adaptive patterns of the last two thousand years, the variables of interest are many and complex. We require data on many small-scale as well as large-scale archaeological and environmental phenomena. For example, variables of interest include densities and locations of specific artifact and botanical classes as well as densities and locations of general site types and environmental zones. Because Cedar Mesa, the area under consideration, encompasses over 500 square kilometers, the detailed information required by the project cannot be obtained by intensive survey of the entire region. Thus, survey sampling or regional sampling is an integral part of the project.

We include in this chapter an outline of the rationale for our sampling design and of the procedures being used to carry it out. We also discuss some of the problems involved in constructing and carrying out the design, and make suggestions for further work. Decisions made in formulating a sampling design are necessarily dependent on what is known beforehand

Note: The Cedar Mesa Project is supported by National Science Foundation Grant GS 33413-X to the Museum of Northern Arizona.

about the populations to be sampled. Since the Cedar Mesa Project is involved in delimiting relations between archaeology and environment, we have provided a brief introduction to both the area environment and its archaeology so the reader may better follow the succeeding discussion of the sampling design.

We discuss the general question of the utility of the parametric assumptions found in sampling textbooks and suggest some partial alternatives to these assumptions. The question of the reliability or precision of the Cedar Mesa variables sampled so far is discussed and tested through sampling simulation. We have shown that for certain variables (not for all), other designs would be much more efficient. We conclude with a statement on the state of the area of regional sampling in archaeology as we have found it.

THE AREA

Cedar Mesa is located just north of the San Juan River in western San Juan County, Utah. It has natural physiographic boundaries (Gregory 1938) and contrasts with much of the surrounding country in geology, elevation, vegetation, and climate. The region is over 99 percent public land, and is administered by the U.S. Bureau of Land Management. A network of dirt roads makes most of the mesa top and a few of the canyon areas accessible by car or pickup.

The divide between eastward and westward flowing drainages runs approximately north-south down the mesa. This divide, which forms the highest part of the mesa, slopes gradually from about 6900 or 7000 feet at the mesa's north end to about 6400 feet at the south end. From this divide, the mesa top gradually slopes to the east and west; the 5600 foot contour fairly well delimits the edge of the mesa top. Because most of the streams draining the highland have deeply entrenched themselves in their lower courses in canyons of up to 1000 feet in depth, most edges of the mesa have a ragged or fringed appearance when viewed from above.

Cedar Mesa has been sculptured almost entirely out of the Cedar Mesa sandstone, a cross-bedded formation of Permian age (Thaden et al. 1964). In a few of the deeper canyons, the underlying Permian Halgaito and Rico formations are exposed. The Cedar Mesa sandstone is horizontal and not deformed over most of the mesa, but dips gradually to the east along its eastern edge, as part of the Comb monocline.

Annual rainfall ranges from about 10 inches on the southern tip of the mesa to between 12 and 13 inches on the northern margin. The main sources of precipitation are late winter and late summer storms; 30 to 40 percent of the annual rainfall comes during the May-September growing season (U.S. Bureau of Land Management n.d.a; n.d.b). The Cedar Mesa sandstone is a good aquifer, and there generally are good springs in the canyons, both at the point near the middle reaches of the drainage where the stream first begins to entrench, and in the canyon bottoms after full entrenchment.

Potholes on the mesa top and in the canyons also hold water for up to several weeks after storms. Because of the abundant canyon-head springs, water is fairly easy to obtain on the mesa top, even in dry seasons.

A mantle of fine sandy loam of probably aeolian derivation covers most of the mesa top, reaching depths of more than ten feet on some of the relatively level divide areas, but thinning rapidly near the canyon rims. The soil has a limy zone at varying depths below the surface, and in many places, shows a well-developed caliche horizon.

Many of the watercourses on the mesa have upper reaches that consist of broad, shallow valleys with substantial alluvial fills. Most of these watercourses undergo a marked steepening of gradient as they entrench themselves into the Cedar Mesa sandstone near the edge of the mesa; these sections are usually barren of alluvial soils, although they may have deposits of colluvium resting in steep slopes against the canyon sides. After full entrenchment, the stream gradients again flatten out, and the larger fully entrenched canyons often have substantial deposits of alluvium on their floors. The present cycle of arroyo cutting is rapidly removing the thick but generally narrow alluvial fills from the entrenched canyons. Arroyos have also begun in most of the shallow upper valleys of the watercourses, but have made less headway in removing the alluvial bodies there.

The growing season on Cedar Mesa ranges from about 129 days at 6,950 feet elevation on the north end of the mesa to about 144 days at 6,240 feet elevation near the south end (U.S. Bureau of Land Management n.d.b). North of the mesa, the land rises rapidly to over 8,000 feet. Hack (1942) estimates that Hopi maize crops require a growing season of about 130 days; if these figures are applicable to the prehistoric period, it would appear that the highest parts of Cedar Mesa are about at the margin for aboriginal maize cultivation. There is currently one farm on the mesa, near its center, at an elevation of about 6,500 feet. Using dry farming techniques, the farmer has been able to raise pinto beans, and in 1970 planted small crops of maize and melons. This farm does not appear to be a success commercially, but it demonstrates that subsistence dry farming would have been possible on the deeper soils on Cedar Mesa, under climatic conditions like those prevailing now. Sheet floods also sweep down the shallow upper parts of the major drainages; floodwater farming in these locations should have been possible in prehistoric times. Prior to the current cycle of arroyo-cutting, floodwater farming would probably have been feasible in the entrenched canyons. Springs and seeps in these locations also would have made small-scale irrigation possible, although there is no definite evidence that this technique was used.

The mesa top vegetation is dominated by dense stands of pinyon and juniper, with occasional parks covered predominantly with sagebrush (*Artemisia tridentata*) and grasses located in the shallow valleys formed by the main watercourses before they entrench. Some sagebrush parks also occur on the divide areas in places where the soil is deep but caliche layers are not well-developed. On the rimrock areas and canyon wall ledges, pinyon and juniper become sparsely distributed, but there are stands of mountain mahogany, cliffrose, and gambel oak. The deeper canyons, after full entrenchment, have cottonwood, willow, tamarix, and big squawbush in the arroyos, and sage, prickly pear, and yucca on the alluvial remnants.

Plants that could have been important food sources for prehistoric peoples include the pinyon, which has a good crop of nuts every few years, and wild grasses, especially Indian rice grass (*Oryzopsis hymenoides*). The sego lily is also abundant, as are both narrow and broad-leaved yuccas, saltbush, and prickly pear. The juxtaposition of the mesa top and deep canyon environments makes a large number of plant species available in any given part of the area.

Thus the dominant vegetation on Cedar Mesa is pinyon-juniper interspersed with sagebrush flats. In the southern portion of the mesa blackbrush (*Coleogyne ramosissima*) communities also exist. While the canyon bottoms are very important with respect to human habitation they make up only a very small fraction of the area involved. The main thrust of our work so far has been an attempt to obtain a representative sample from the non-canyon areas.

ARCHAEOLOGICAL BACKGROUND

Grand Gulch, which drains the western portion of Cedar Mesa, was the scene of considerable archaeological activity in the 1890s, due largely to the well-preserved perishable artifacts and burials that at that time could be found abundantly in its numerous dry caves. The best known work of this period was by Richard Wetherill (McNitt 1957). Several unpublished surveys were carried out in Grand Gulch and environs between 1920 and 1960, and in the 1960s, Sharrock (1964) and Schroeder (1965) excavated several small sites in the northern part of the mesa (see Lipe and Matson 1971 for a thorough review of this earlier work). In 1969 and 1970, Lipe excavated several Basketmaker II and III sites, intensively surveyed an approximately 1 by 4 mile mesa top transect in the central part of the mesa, and did extensive survey in Grand Gulch and several smaller canyons.* Fieldwork for the present study of prehistoric adaptation—The Cedar Mesa Project— was begun by Lipe and Matson in the summer of 1972.

Although a few traces of Archaic occupation have been found, virtually all prehistoric occupation on the mesa can be assigned to the San Juan Anasazi tradition, and appears to be confined to the period ca. A.D. 1–1250. Within this time frame, there appear to be substantial changes in population and in general settlement pattern. Using the units of the Pecos classification as a shorthand notation for time periods, the following brief outline seems sound: Basketmaker II sites are abundant, both in the sheltered sites in the canyons, and on the mesa top. Basketmaker III sites also occur, but not so abundant as those of the preceding period. They appear to occur predominantly on the mesa top. In the Pueblo I and early Pueblo II periods, there appears to be a near lack of occupation in the region. By late Pueblo II and early Pueblo III, a strong occupation is again evident, occurring

*This work was supported by a grant from the National Geographic Society and by grants from the Research Foundation of the State University of New York.

largely on the mesa top. By mid-Pueblo III, the canyons are again heavily occupied. During late Pueblo III, the region is abandoned.

At all periods, habitation sites tend to be small by southwestern standards, and there are many small activity areas detached from habitation areas. The localization of the bulk of activities within the confines of large community habitation sites seems not to have occurred in the Cedar Mesa region at any period. Most sites appear to have only thin deposits of cultural debris, and to be single component, at least in terms of the general periodization given above. Significant exceptions occur in some of the larger alluvium-filled canyons. Most of the sites in the Cedar Mesa region appear, however, to have been occupied briefly.

The intensive surveys by Lipe in 1969 and 1970 and by Matson and Lipe in 1972 have revealed site densities ranging from about 25 per square mile near some of the canyon rims to upwards of 100 per square mile in some locations near the main mesa divide. The term "site" in our usage means simply a conveniently mappable concentration of artifacts and/or features, ordinarily separated from other such concentrations by areas in which features and artifacts are absent or occur in extremely low densities. In some cases, numerous overlapping small activity areas may extend over very large areas, making the notion of "site" as a spatially bounded concentration difficult to apply. In other cases, separate sites can easily be distinguished. In any case, the "sites" we discuss later in the paper are largely field designations — i.e., convenient mapping units. As the project progresses, analytical work will sort out units of relative cultural and temporal homogeneity which in many cases will divide or even subdivide the sites distinguished in the field. Because so much of our current activity is going into fieldwork and because analysis has not progressed very far, we have been forced to work with rough and preliminary data.

THE SAMPLING DESIGN

At the outset of the Cedar Mesa Project, a series of decisions was made as to the structure of the research design. These decisions were based on the characteristics of the environment and archaeology of the region, insofar as they were already known, on the data requirements of the research questions being asked, and on considerations of general sampling theory. Basically, we decided (1) to do our intensive survey within 400-meter square quadrats, (2) to select such quadrats at random within naturally defined clusters, in this case, drainage basins, (3) within a selected cluster, to stratify the sample of quadrats into canyon and noncanyon portions, (4) to select only certain drainages, or clusters, for study, and (5) to select these at random within a stratification of the region as a whole into north and south portions.

Cluster Sampling

Involved in the goal of reconstructing adaptive strategies is the problem of estimating the characteristics of settlement patterns throughout the history of occupation in the region. Settlement pattern here refers to the spatial relationships of various kinds of sites/activity loci to one another and to environmental features and resources. Gaining information about this kind of spatial structuring of the cultural and environmental data would require sampling at a fairly high rate. If, for example, settlement was organized around a single primary center, several secondary centers, and an abundance of satellite hamlets, a low sampling rate might fail to recover anything but hamlets. Furthermore, since the intensive survey unit on the ground was to be 400 meter-square quadrats, a number of such quadrats would have to be surveyed in any given area to permit valid comparisons of subareas within the region.

Unfortunately, considerations of time and money precluded sampling the entire region at a high rate, yet we still wished to maintain a focus on the Cedar Mesa region as a whole, that is, to make reliable statements about the archaeology and environment of the whole area, not just a part of it. Therefore, some sort of reduction had to be made in the amount of area actually sampled. When the population elements (in this case, 400 meter-square quadrats) occur in some kind of unit or cluster, the selection of such units as primary sample units is said to be cluster sampling (Cochran 1963: 235). Within our universe, potential units of this sort occur in the form of drainage systems. The watersheds of the tributaries to the main streams draining Cedar Mesa are of approximately equal size, if one subdivides a few of the Comb Wash tributaries. We therefore decided to focus our study on a sample of such drainage basins, or clusters.

There are several rationales for believing that such drainage areas are natural units with respect to the archaeological variables. Perhaps the most important is that the only springs in the area are in the canyons or at the points where the drainages begin to entrench. If a nearby source of water was important, habitation sites should be located with respect to springs and hence to drainages. Sagebrush flats also tend to occur in the middle portions of drainages, before they entrench; if these were important farming areas, and there is some evidence they were at some times, then drainages rather than divides would have been the foci of occupation. Likewise, if floodwater farming was an important technique, then the middle reaches of drainages on the mesa top and the entrenched canyons would have been focal. In terms of many environmental characteristics, drainage areas are natural units. We recognize that all the factors cited above may have varied through time with environmental and adaptive strategy changes. Nevertheless, we believe that on present evidence clusters can most reasonably be defined in this way. They appear better than other physiographically defined units and are to be preferred over arbitrary clusters.

An alternative approach to the above would be to draw a simple random sample of quadrats from Cedar Mesa at large. With this approach there would be no problem about different parts of the mesa being represented; surely all sectors would be sampled. Because our time and budget allows us to survey only a limited number of quadrats, this means an average of about four units per drainage could be sampled. This size sample would be too small to compare drainages or to obtain settlement pattern data. Thus to compare portions of the mesa, large areas would have to be lumped together and details about the drainages would be obscured. Finally, our belief that drainages are natural units would not be exploited. In short, while the over-all simple random sample might be an efficient way of making generalizations about the mesa as a whole, the sample in one area would be too sparse to give us the local information we desire.

Since cost efficiency is a central aspect of sampling (inexpensive way to make inferences about the whole) the economic aspect also has validity here. That is, a great deal of time would be spent locating the widely dis-persed quadrats, finding roads, and moving camp, if the simple random sam-ple approach was used. In terms of amount of time spent surveying versus amount of total time spent in the field this design would be inefficient. The advantage that the simple random sample design does have is its simplicity.

Stratification of the Cluster Sample

From previous work on the mesa, substantial differences between the north-ern and southern portions were known to exist. While the entire mesa is dominated by pinyon-juniper with sagebrush flats there are significant differences within this class. In general the relative amount and size of pinyon-juniper increases as one goes north. The relative importance of the sagebrush flats conversely increases as one goes south. Further, the blackbrush communities are found primarily in the south. A physiographic variable is also correlated with the above observations; areas of loose aeo-lian soil are much more common in the southern end of Cedar Mesa than in the north. As mentioned above, the precipitation pattern seems to vary along a north-south axis, with lesser amounts found in the south and greater amounts in the north.

The known environmental variables would therefore suggest that if the cluster sample were to be stratified it should be done on a north-south basis. Impressions from previous sketchy archaeological reconnaissance also indicated that archaeological differences existed on a north-south basis. Kayenta style late Pueblo II ceramics seemed to be more frequent in the south, with Basketmaker III and PII-III Mesa Verde ceramics more fre-quent in the north. Because of the trends of both archaeological and environ-mental data we chose to stratify the sample of drainages on a north-south basis, mainly to ensure that areas from both ends of the continuum were sampled, enabling north-south differences to be tested and inspected in detail. Since we knew we could only select a few clusters, and that we would be choosing them at random, this stratification would ensure that all our clusters would not fall in the north, or south, purely by chance.

While most of the basic decisions for selecting the drainages have been recounted, there were many details needed to implement the above plan. Details such as mesa boundaries were drawn on the basis of drainages and elevations. The drainages were delineated and subdivided into relatively equal portions. A relatively arbitrary point was picked in the center of the mesa to separate the drainages into a north and a south stratum. Of the drainages, 12 were in the north and 8 in the south. Sampling the drainages at a 25% rate would mean the selection of two from the south and three from the north.

The decision to use natural drainage units instead of artificial units as clusters poses the problem of unequal size. This can be alleviated by assigning probability of being chosen as a cluster to drainage units on the basis of their size. By making the probability of being selected proportional to the amount of area within a drainage any given area has an equal probability of being sampled (Cochran 1963: 251). Thus, even with unequal sizes of clusters, the basic concept of equal probability sampling (and simpler formulas) can be used (Cochran 1963: 297).

The approximate area of each drainage was calculated, as well as that of each stratum. Then each drainage was assigned a list of consecutive numbers proportional in length to the proportion of the total stratum area contained in that drainage. In other words, if the first drainage contained five percent of the area in the stratum, and the second drainage contained ten percent, the first would be assigned numbers one through five, and the second, numbers six through fifteen. A random number table was then used to select the five drainages—two from the south and three from the north. That is, when a randomly selected number matched any number in the list for a particular drainage, that drainage was selected.

Other ways of selecting drainages might have been as appropriate. For instance, some sort of systematic sampling, such as randomizing a beginning point and then picking every fifth drainage, might be as unbiased and more straightforward. The only obvious drawback would be the chance of hidden periodicity in the drainages. On first glance such a patterning in the data would seem unlikely. On the other hand, Hudson's theory of colonization (Hudson 1969) suggests that in a developed settlement system competition between settlement centers develops and that this leads to relative equal spacing between centers. This sort of factor could create the sort of "periodicity" that would make problems for a systematic sample (Cochran 1963: 230). There might even be a reason to suspect something of this sort in late Pueblo times. So there are some clear benefits to using the stratified random approach, even though it may well be inefficient in some circumstances; it is safer if periodicities occur.

Quadrat Sampling

Although the area enclosed by the five selected drainages is small relative to Cedar Mesa as a whole, it is still much too large to completely survey in an intensive way. Thus we had to subsample or use a two-stage design. A series of decisions was made concerning the kind of unit to be used and whether this subsample should itself be stratified.

There are two choices in the question of the shape of the sampling unit—a square quadrat or narrow transect. While Binford (1964) in his pioneering paper on research design suggested quadrats, some recent suggestions have favored transects (Plog and Hill 1971; S. Plog n.d.). S. Plog showed in experiments based on a survey in Oaxaca that transect samples were more efficient than quadrats in 14 out of 16 trials for estimating population (number of sites), as measured by the standard squared error (S. Plog n.d.). In plant ecology, the transect has been shown to be the most efficient shape for obtaining population parameter estimates (Daubenmire 1968: 87–88).

The very reason for the efficiency of transects is, however, a drawback for our project. To quote Daubenmire "Since the individuals representing each species tend to be grouped into isodimetric clusters, an elongate plot has a high probability of intercepting parts of several clusters at once without falling entirely into one" (Daubenmire 1968: 88). This statement might be translated into archaeological terms as "since a transect plot will crosscut more sites and environmental areas than a quadrat of equal size, it thus will be more representative of an area." Since, however, we are not only interested in population estimates but also in associations, we would prefer to minimize the environmental change within each unit and maximize the area surrounding each site within each sampling unit. Another disadvantage with a transect is that it has more margin per area and thus the problem of sites located on unit edges is magnified. For the above reasons, transects were rejected and quadrats were used.

The size of the quadrat used is also important. One effect that has to do with size is the "grab" sample effect. That is, items found in any grab sample tend to be more like each other than items in the population at large. This effect becomes more evident if quadrats are larger in size and smaller in number than if they are smaller in size and larger in number. Thus reducing the size of quadrats increases the precision of the sample for any given sampled area (S. Plog n.d.). Another effect has to do with the size of quadrat and size of stratum. If the strata are small and quadrats large, error will be introduced because of quadrats overlapping into different strata. Also, the larger the quadrats, the larger will be the percentage of the stratum area that will have to be sampled in order to get a sufficient number of sampling units to run comparisons. Thus, the maximum useful size of a quadrat is dependent on characteristics of the population to be sampled including the nature of stratification, if any.

Although the above problems will tend to decrease with the size of the quadrat, there are economic problems which are inversely related to quadrat size. For surveying any given area, decreasing the quadrat size also decreases the proportion of time actually spent surveying and increases the proportion of time spent getting to the quadrat, locating and marking its boundaries, etc. The problem of sites being located on borders also increases with decreasing size. Quadrats must also be large enough to completely include, on the average, the sites being surveyed.

The efficiency of the quadrat size being used depends also on the distribution of the variables involved. Since a large number of variables are being studied in our project, the best size must by definition be a compromise. Since the distribution of the variables was unknown, any exact calculations were impossible.

Binford (1964) suggested the use of quadrats one-half mile on a side, while Matson (1971 n.d.) and Thomas (1969) both used quadrats 500 meters on a side. In past usage of 500 meter-square quadrats, Matson and Thomas found that sufficient information was recovered for their projects, which were somewhat similar in objectives to ours. On Cedar Mesa, site and artifact densities are much higher than in the areas surveyed by Matson and Thomas; therefore, a smaller size should be feasible. Moreover, most analysis of variance type statistics are dependent on number of sampling units rather than size of sample units, so that for a given length of time in the field, reducing the size of the quadrat will increase the sensitivity and reliability of this sort of statistic. Taking all these factors into account, then, we settled on square quadrats 400 meters on a side.

In practice the 400 meter quadrat has proven satisfactory in most respects. Only a single quadrat has not included at least one "site" and even then a fair amount of material was found. On the other hand other quadrats had up to a dozen "sites" which might suggest the usage of a smaller quadrat size. Besides the problem of sites located on the edge of a quadrat a few sites clearly have maximum dimensions greater than 400 meters. We will return to effects of quadrat size later.

Once the size and shape of quadrats is established the method of selection yet remains. Again referring to the botany literature we find that:

Systematic sampling . . . is . . . more advantageous if interest centres on variability within the area. . . . Of the two it is clear that, in most circumstances random sampling is the better if overall information on the composition is desired . . . (Greig-Smith 1964: 23).

It would appear, then, that random sampling is more generally useful for our purposes. Cochran in a discussion of systematic sampling asserts it can safely be recommended under four conditions.

The first is where the ordering of the population is essentially random, the second where a stratified design with numerous strata is used, the third is for subsampling the unit, and the fourth is for sampling populations of a continuous type (Cochran 1963: 230).

The first two cases are obviously inappropriate for the Cedar Mesa project. The third case of subsampling might be appropriate. However considering the drainages as units and quadrats as subsampling units does not seem to be in accord with the examples given of this case. Thus the subsampling condition does not seem appropriate for these circumstances. Although the fourth case may hold for some situations in plant ecology, we do not think that archaeological material is continuously variable.

Besides the above nonarchaeologically orientated reasons for not using systematic sampling there is one study which indicates the inefficiency of this sort of approach with archaeological data (S. Plog n.d.). Using data from Oaxaca, systematic samples were shown to be inferior to stratified random samples in terms of standard errors of estimating the number of sites in the population. Furthermore "the range in the precision of the systematic samples was greater than the range for any other design. This suggests that even though systematic samples may provide very precise estimates at times, they should be avoided" (S. Plog n.d.). As noted above none of the recommended conditions for systematic sampling occurs. Thus theoretical and empirical evidence combine to eliminate this approach from our consideration.

Another approach suggested recently is that of the systematic-unaligned sample in which one coordinate remains fixed and one random for each interval row (Berry and Baker 1968; Redman and Watson 1970). This procedure was also tested by Plog and was found to be the least efficient of the tested designs (S. Plog n.d.). It should be noted that the situations where this design was shown to be superior to random sampling (Berry and Baker 1968) land use or land type was the variable under consideration which has nearly continuous variation while sites or artifacts do not. Again this type of sampling has both theoretical and pragmatic disadvantages that would seem to make it a poor choice for our purposes.

Both of the above alternatives to random sampling have a further limitation in that the estimate of sampling error is either unobtainable or of questionable validity (Cochran 1963: 230). It seems that these approaches should not be used under other situations than those mentioned above. Only when those conditions are met do these methods have advantages that outweigh the inability to estimate sampling error.

Thus some form of random sampling seemed to be the most appropriate choice for sampling drainages. A further decision to use simple random sampling or a more complicated stratified design had to be made. A stratified design could be justified on the basis of known or suspected homogeneity of some portion of the universe (drainages) under consideration.

From previous work in the area, it appeared that some environmental types were likely to display less archaeological variability than the drainages as a whole. A major difference appeared to be the entrenched canyons and their immediate surroundings versus the mesa top areas. Within the latter, possible contrasting subdivisions include areas along the main interstream divides versus areas between the divides and the entrenched canyons; and sagebrush dominated vegetation versus pinyon-juniper dominated vegetation. The stability of the pinyon-juniper versus sagebrush boundaries is, however, undemonstrated, and the divide versus nondivide dichotomy is difficult to deal with, being a continuous rather than discrete variation. Therefore, of these possible physiographic distinctions, only the entrenched canyon versus mesa top division was used to stratify the sample. Since the area of the canyons is quite small relative to the area of the mesa top, the former is being sampled at a higher rate. The other physiographic contrasts are still being used, but by poststratifying the sample rather than prestratifying it. That is, we assume that our mesa top data will include enough examples of divide and nondivide, pinyon-juniper and sagebrush areas to enable us to meaningfully study the covariation of archaeological characteristic with these environmental variables. After-the-fact stratification will of course have to be used with most of the environmental and archaeological variables we are studying. This is an advantage in that much greater information will be available on environmental variables after the study than before; the danger is that the sample of archaeological associations with particular variables may not be large enough. We did not feel that this possibility warranted the extra complications involved. In fact the poststratification that we have used so far is often based on environmental information that is collected on the quadrats. Thus we have no way of prestratifying the sample for at least some cases.

PRELIMINARY EVALUATION OF THE DESIGN

We spent the 1972 season surveying and collecting quadrats in two drainages following the above design. The quadrats were selected by simple random samples at a 7% rate. The actual procedure used was to prepare a mosaic of aerial photos for the target drainage and to overlay a mylar sheet with the quadrats drawn on it. The drainage borders were then drawn, the quadrats numbered and then selected. The quadrat boundaries were then copied from the overlay onto the aerial photos, which were then used in locating the quadrats.

The field procedure was to locate a corner by reference to the photo and to mark off the sides by compass and measured ropes; then the actual location was drawn on the photo. The quadrats were surveyed by a crew of three to six, walking abreast in a systematic back and forth search pattern. Stray artifacts were collected and their general location noted while surveying, but concentrations of artifacts were usually just noted and flagged at this time. After the quadrat had been surveyed sites would be laid out, usually in 50 meter grids with each grid being mapped on graph paper. Artifacts within such a unit were given a number and placed in a plastic bag. The number was then recorded on the map showing the location. These locations are not points but might include a number of objects within one or two square meters. In areas of high concentrations, small grids of 2 by 2 or 3 by 3 meters were used instead. All features, such as hearths, slab-walled structures, or masonry rooms were assigned letters of the alphabet and were mapped separately. By these means all artifactual material was collected or mapped and the provenience noted.

In addition to artifactual remains other information was collected for each concentration. First hand impressions about temporal position and cultural affinities as well as inferences about functions of structures were coded on forms. Most of the environmental information was recorded on two forms, one of botanical variables and one of physiographic variables. These two forms were completed for all sites and for all quadrats. After removal from the forms of some rare or nonexistent plants we had 72 usable botanical variables. These ranged from placement within a major plant community (pinyon-juniper, sagebrush) to identification of specific plants which were noted for each site. Thus a wide variety of botanical information was collected for each site and quadrat.

The physiographic form included such information as type of surficial deposit, exposure, amount of dissection, and so forth. An important measurement was the depth of caliche zone which limits the effective soil depth at Cedar Mesa. This depth was found by testing excavated soil with HCl. The idea that effective soil depth is highly related to the archaeology has been confirmed in a number of ways including the high correlation of soil depth and certain artifacts found on BM II sites. The depth of soil is also related to the sort of plants found; sagebrush is usually found in deep soil areas, although some interesting exceptions occur.

Thus we focused on detailed examination of small sites, being concerned more with activities related to resource extraction rather than large community centers, which were rare in the area. So far we have not had to subsample many sites, and have been able to collect completely the artifacts from most sites within the sample quadrats. The number of archaeological objects recovered from the quadrats in the two completed drainages varies from a low of 30 to a high of 14497 with a mean of 2027 and a median of 1288. The number of sites found within a quadrat varied from 0 (one quadrat) to 12 with a mean and median of 5. (For more details see Table 7.1.)

TABLE 7.1

**Summary Statistics by Period for Quadrats
Collected During 1972**

	BM II	BM III	P II-III	Total
Site medians[a]	1-2	0	2	5
Site means	1.5	.68	2.5	5.1
Artifact medians	123-151	0	859-1028	1267-1310
Artifact means	323.5	80.6	1623.3	2027.5
Site interquartiles	0, 2	0, 1	2, 3	4, 6
Artifact interquartiles	0, 392	0, 53	379, 1310	714, 2028

[a]Medians, means and interquartiles in Tables 7.1 and 7.3 are for quadrats ranked by numbers of sites and numbers of artifacts, respectively.

In general the analysis of variance results based on poststratification have been satisfactory. We have been using the Wilcoxon-Kruskal-Wallis family of nonparametric tests (Bradley 1968, Conover 1971a) since the distribution of many of the variables can clearly be shown to be unsymmetrical and more closely related to the Poisson and negative binomial distributions than to the normal distribution. It might be noted that the asymptotic relative efficiency of the Wilcoxon-Kruskal-Wallis family, with respect to the familiar t test - f test family against the location alternative, is at a minimum .864 and at a maximum is arbitrarily high. These figures indicate that at a minimum only a 13.6% larger sample is needed for the Wilcoxon family to reject the null hypothesis at the same level of the t - f test. Conversely there are situations when no matter how much larger the sample is made for the t - f test family, they will not reject the null hypothesis at the same level as the Wilcoxon-Kruskal-Wallis tests. Thus one has little to lose and much to gain by using this family of tests.

Using the Wilcoxon-Kruskal-Wallis tests, we have, for example, been able to verify at the .025 level that BM II sites tend to be located in rim areas rather than on the divides, as predicted (Lipe and Matson 1971: 136). Likewise, we have verified, at least in the Bullet drainage, that P II-III sites tend to be located in areas closer to the divides. Thus, even using some of the less frequent variables (sites) the sample size and distribution with respect to the environment seem to be sufficient at the 7 percent sampling rate for poststratification analysis.

Utility of Parametric Assumption

While the distributions of most archaeological variables per unit area in this project do not approximate the normal distribution, much of sampling theory is based on the assumption that the distribution of repeated *estimates* of the population values does approach the normal distribution (Cochran 1963: 11–16). This assumption is easily verified for large samples of normally distributed variables. However, the utility of this approach becomes less as the population values depart more from the normal curve and the sample size becomes smaller. Some sampling texts do discuss this problem in some length (cf. Cochran 1963: 38–44) but nevertheless continue to use the assumption of normality. It may well be that such assumptions are well employed in sociological surveys where the samples are large and population variables may be approximately normally distributed. The utility of this assumption for sampling has, however, recently been questioned (Kempthorne 1969: 674–5). In fact, referring to the accuracy of estimates of standard error, an introductory text states "That is, however, a more difficult problem, about which we shall say only that, under realistic assumptions about the distribution of the measurements X and the population value V, a rather large sample is required to produce satisfactorily precise estimates" (Hodges and Lehman 1964: 250).

In short the assumption of normal distribution of estimates is likely to be incorrect for archaeological survey sampling where the sample size is moderate and the distributions of population variables are nonnormal (as is certainly the case with the Cedar Mesa Project — see also Matson 1971).

Thus two questions arise: what are the effects of improperly using such an assumption and what possible alternatives exist?

Three common uses of the standard error are comparing the precision of sampling methods, estimating the size of a sample needed and estimating the precision attained in a sample (establishing confidence limits) (Cochran 1963: 24). It is quite clear that assuming the " . . . use of the 'normal' formula for appraising the variance of S^2 [standard error] may give a very misleading impression of the stability of S^2" (Cochran 1963: 44). Thus, in the three uses above, the precision of sampling methods would be overestimated; the estimated sample sizes would be too small and the confidence limits would be too narrow.

To see what the effects would be on Cedar Mesa data, a series of samples were drawn from simulated data whose population parameters were similar to those of the Cedar Mesa samples. The mean standard error was calculated and the Student's t distribution was used to calculate 95 percent confidence intervals. (That is, intervals in which the population mean would be included approximately 95 times out of a hundred if the assumption of normality was correct.) While the Student's t distribution is not the normal distribution it is closely related and recommended if the sample size is less than 60 (Cochran 1963: 50). In the run which showed the most deviation from the expected on the basis of normal assumptions, in 7 out of the 20 samples the population mean lay outside of the calculated interval. In another, the mean lay outside of the interval 17 times out of a hundred. Even when the interval seemed about right the intervals were often one-sided, as in one case where only 7 out of 100 times the mean lay outside of the interval, but it was on the lower side in all seven cases (for examples see Table 7.2). Thus with simulated data similar to that found on Cedar Mesa, the use of "normal" (Student) approximation would lead to incorrect inferences in many cases. Presumably this would be the case with other regional sampling projects; not only in establishing confidence intervals, but by extension, sample sizes and comparative precision of sampling methods.

However, there is an alternative to assuming normal distribution of population estimates that works well with nonnormal as well as with normal distributed data, that of the use of Binomial Confidence Limits (Cochran 1963: 58–59, Conover 1971a: 110). Here assumptions are not made about the shape of the distribution of the estimates but the probability of obtaining a set of "successes" or "failures" with only the ranks of the data being used in the calculations. Then the values of the data are used to replace the ranks (see Table 7.3 for examples).

There are several disadvantages of using binomial confidence intervals. As with many nonparametric statistics, the probabilities do not usually fall on the traditional 0.001, 0.01, and 0.05, thus forcing one to use the closest interval (such as 0.97 instead of 0.95 in Table 7.3). The intervals are usually larger than those calculated by normal-theory related techniques. This is to be expected, since the added assumption of symmetry is not used in this technique. Of course this is no disadvantage in conditions when the distribution is not symmetrical. Finally, the measures used are not the familiar ones of mean and variance but those of median and interquartile range. In the absence of other accurate methods, these drawbacks are not substantial.

TABLE 7.2

Comparison of "Normal" Confidence Intervals on Mean With "Binomial" Intervals on Median

Simulated data, sample size = 10, 100 samples			
95% "Student" Intervals		98% "Binomial" Intervals	
Means within	85	Medians within	97
Means outside	15	Medians outside	0
Means low side	15	Medians tied low side	2
Means high side	0	Medians tied high side	1
Simulated Cedar Mesa data, 400 meter quadrats (see Table 7.6) sample size = 21, 100 samples			
95% "Student" Intervals		97% "Binomial" Intervals	
Means within	83	Medians within	99
Means outside	17	Medians outside	1
Means high side	17	Medians high side	1
Means low side	0	Medians low side	0

TABLE 7.3

Bullet Drainage Summary
Site Statistics for Quadrats

	BM II	BM III	P II-III	Total
Site medians	2 (1-3)[a]	0 (0-1)	3 (2-4)	5 (4-6)
Artifacts median	182 (0-391)	0 (0-53)	1043 (383-1310)	1256 (714-1936)
Site means	2.0	.71	2.67	5.0
Artifact means	336.6	44.7	1126.4	1507.4
Site interquartiles	0,3	0,1	1,4	4,8
Artifact interquartiles	0,392	0,74	369,1743	693,1767

[a]Figures in parentheses give 97% confidence intervals.

In the simulation runs detailed above, the binomial confidence intervals seemed to be conservative and showed no tendencies for skewness, as exhibited by the intervals based on standard error (see Table 7.2). Thus the errors introduced by unwarranted assumption of normality can be substantial and at least a partial alternative exists which we have found useful.

Evaluation by Simulation

Since we are dealing with a large number of variables it would be unexpected, using one compromise sampling design, if we had been able to sample all of them satisfactorily. In the Bullet Canyon drainage, sites assigned to the Basketmaker III period are much less common than those of Basketmaker II or Pueblo II-III (see Table 7.3). Some previous ideas about the location of Basketmaker III sites (Lipe and Matson 1971) were not confirmed by our tests, since no significant difference between environmental areas was found. Whether this finding would be confirmed with a sample of more or larger quadrats is unknown, but because of the low numbers of Basketmaker III sites, the present findings are slightly suspect. While most of the variables investigated have been sampled sufficiently for most purposes, a few of the rarer ones such as the Basketmaker III sites in the Bullet Drainage are at most minimally represented. Of course the sort of question asked bears on the sufficiency of the sample and as our questions become more detailed some variables will undoubtedly be shown to be inadequately sampled.

In general, then, our experience has so far indicated that our sampling design has been successful. Estimates of the population parameters of a wide variety of variables have been shown to be easily obtainable for the two completed drainages. Medians, interquartile ranges, and confidence intervals for them based on the binomial distribution are all easily derived (Conover 1971a: 110). We are able to characterize the drainages, at least, by relatively small samples. Furthermore, the data seem to be adequate for the questions we have asked so far about location and relationships with other variables.

It is clear which sort of variables are suspect and which are not. Most types of lithic and ceramic artifact types could be adequately sampled with much smaller quadrats or at a lower sampling rate. On the other end, composite variables such as specific "site" types may only be minimally represented. To explore the reliability of sampling of such composite variables we conducted some sampling experiments based on the samples that have been collected.

From the beginning we considered that very "rare" items such as "defensive" sites would be "sampled" in some other fashion than the above. We hoped, however, that such items as "unit pueblos" (ordinarily, a kiva and several associated room structures), while rare relative to other site varieties, would be common enough to be sampled reliably by the proceeding scheme. As one might expect, after sampling only two drainages, we were unsure of the reliability of our sampling with respect to the "unit pueblos." This problem was more acute in the Bullet drainage where the apparent density of this site type was much lower than in Upper Grand Gulch, the other drainage sampled in 1972. In order to check empirically the reliability of the estimates, the site density that had been observed in the field was assumed to hold for the entire drainage. Then, the total assumed site inventory was repeatedly sampled at the rate that had been used in the field. Thus, a 7 percent sample of 400 meter quadrats was repeatedly simulated. Even though only two unit pueblos were found in the actual Bullet drainage sample, in a simulation of 20 such samples, only one sampling of the area did not have any units and only one sampling had more than three units (see Table 7.4). Even though the item was very rare, found in less than 10 percent of the quadrats sampled, most of the simulated samples were in good agreement with one another and with the assumed "actual" distribution of this type of site. Thus our faith in our sample of unit pueblos from the Bullet drainage was considerably strengthened.

In the Upper Grand Gulch Drainage, this type of site was more frequent, although fewer quadrats were collected because the drainage was smaller. Again, the question of reliability was checked by further sampling simulation, with the field-sampled distribution assumed for the drainage as a whole. Again the reliability was better than expected with only 6 samples out of 100 lacking any unit pueblos and only 5 samples having three or more units more than expected (see Table 7.5).

TABLE 7.4

Comparison of Simulation of 400-Meter Quadrat
Samples of "Unit" Type Sites From Bullet
With 800-Meter Quadrat Sampling Simulation
(20 Samples Each)

	800 Meter	400 Meter
Sample mean (of means)	.122	.129
Sample median (of means)	.12	.14
Interquartile (6,15) (of means)	.95, .143	.10, .14
Low (of means)	.067	0.0
High (of means)	.17	.29

Note: Population Mean = .12 (per 160,000 sq. meters).

TABLE 7.5

Upper Grand Gulch 400-Meter Quadrat "Unit" Type Site Simulation (100 Samples)

Sample mean (of means)	.445	
Sample median (of means)	.375 (.375, .500)	
Interquartile (25, 76)	.25, .75	
Low (of means)	0.0 (6)	(6 samples had mean of .125)
High (of means)	1.0 (1)	(4 samples had mean of .875)

Note: Population Mean = .46. ( ) = 95% confidence intervals of median.

Thus even for site types which are much less common than the great majority of the variables we are interested in, the techniques employed (sampling rate, quadrat size, and collection procedures) give us a reasonably precise estimate of their occurrence, although not of their location within the individual drainages. Clearly if we were only interested in the number of unit pueblos, the present sampling designs and collecting procedures would be woefully inefficient. A much less intensive search of, say, 800 meter quadrats with collection only of unit type sites would be much more efficient, as they could be searched and collected on the same amount of time as the 400 meter quadrats are under the present scheme.

We simulated a comparison of this procedure using the same sample size as used in the project (a sampling rate of 28 percent as compared to 7 percent because the 800 meter quadrats have four times the area). We again based our population on the sampling results and expanded it to fit the new conditions. With a run of 20 samples the means of the 800 meter quadrats ranged from .07 to .16 (mean of population of unit pueblos per 160,000 sq. meters is .12). This is compared to a spread of .0 to .29 (mean of the population .12) for the 400 meter quadrat simulation. Thus, as expected, the 800 meter quadrat scheme would be much more precise for the same or less money in terms of the distribution of unit pueblos in the Bullet drainage.

If some variables of interest were undersampled and could have been sampled more efficiently using some other scheme, the opposite is also true. Some common variables were oversampled and could have been more efficiently sampled by using a larger number of smaller quadrats but with a smaller amount of area being surveyed. Such a variable is amount of Pueblo II–III material. Again assuming the sample artifact density was true for the population we simulated 100 samples of 200 meter quadrats at a 7 percent rate (Table 7.6). We then simulated 100 samples of 200 meter quadrats at a 2.4 percent rate with the population being based on the previous simulated population. As is seen in Table 7.6 the 200 meter quadrat samples are substantially more precise than the 400 meter quadrat samples with a definitely smaller interquartile range (1039 to 1362 compared to 969 to 1365). This increase in precision is probably due to increased sample size (30 as compared to 21) in spite of the decrease in the area sampled.

Thus for many of the variables under consideration much more efficient sampling schemes could be developed. However, since we are concentrating on a wide range of variables, including very common and small scale

TABLE 7.6

**Comparison of Simulation of 7% 400-Meter Quadrat
Samples of Pueblo II-III Material with 2.4%
200-Meter Quadrat Samples (100 Samples Each)**

	400 Meter	200 Meter
Number in sample	21	30
Population mean (per 160,000 sq. meters)	1202.2	1231.3
Population median	970	1010.1
Sample mean (of means)	1172.7	1216.1
Sample median (of means)	1130	1181
Sample interquartile (of means)	969, 1365	1039, 1362
Sample low (of means)	676	748
Sample high (of means)	1957	1967

ones as well as rare and large ones, we wanted a sampling design that offered general usefulness, rather than a high efficiency for one or a limited number of variables. In fact, given our interest in a number of variables, we decided a generalized sampling design would be the most efficient, offering reliable data on a number of variables. The alternative solution, to design a number of different sampling techniques for specific variables, would seem to be unduly complicated and probably unworkable.

However, for variables that have very limited distribution, such specialized sampling schemes might well be used in conjunction with the above. For instance, defensive sites, which are unlikely to be recovered by our sampling procedures, could be sampled in other fashions. Large scale aerial photos might also be examined for the rare large multiroom pueblos in the drainages that were previously "sampled" by the overall scheme. Large areas might also be searched rapidly according to extensive large-site inventory practices rather than with the intensive procedures we have been using.

CONCLUSIONS

Regional sampling in archaeology still has many poorly understood aspects. It would appear that many "survey" ideas based on sociological surveys have questionable utility since archaeological surveys include spatial problems and are usually concerned with a large number of variables, problems which are not usually present in sociological surveys. Furthermore, much of the established sampling literature is heavily dependent on parametric assumptions of questionable utility for many archaeological variables. It appears that the spatial problems are of immediate importance, since the decisions made in this sphere may radically affect the outcome of the sampling (S. Plog n.d.).

One of the major choices is that of sampling design, whether systematic, stratified, or simple equal probability sampling. The decisions made at this point would seem to be dependent on the nature of the variables to be sampled and their spatial setting. Thus, if subregions of homogeneity do exist, stratification may be desired; if continuous variation exists, some sort of systematic sampling may be the most efficient. Prior knowledge, then, about the variables is almost a prerequisite for making decisions about sampling design.

Optimum quadrat size and shape are also closely tied to the goals and the nature of the variables of the sampling design. Thus, for population estimates, transects have a number of advantages; for association studies, we feel quadrats have advantages. The size of the units chosen would seem to be even more closely tied to the distribution of the variables under consideration. For most regional survey probably a wide variety of variables will need to be sampled and the size of the unit selected will be a compromise.

In setting up the Cedar Mesa Project, the selection of quadrat size and shape was one of the most difficult decisions. Other sampling choices either seemed self-evident or optional in that probably only a relatively small amount of "precision" was involved. It seemed to us that quadrat size and shape might be of great importance but there was little relevant literature to consult. Thus, further experimentation and simulation with different sizes and shapes of quadrats would be very valuable for future regional survey workers.

ACKNOWLEDGMENT

We would like to acknowledge the helpful comments of Michel De Virville on earlier versions of this paper.

PART THREE

Sampling Within the Site

Sampling the three-dimensional space within a site is the most difficult kind of sampling. One reason for the comparative difficulty of intrasite excavational sampling is the presence of the vertical dimension; this point is clearly made in Brown's chapter. The depth factor encumbers the process of insuring equal probability of selection of sampling units within a site; as a consequence, probability sampling becomes an unattainable goal in some situations. The chapters — by Redman, Brown, and Asch — discuss the role on nonprobabilistic sampling in excavation. The second difficulty in three-dimensional sampling is that the sampling units do not correspond to the behavioral space of the prehistoric occupants; Brown — as well as Reid, Schiffer, and Neff — emphasizes this incongruity and presents solutions. The strategy outlined by Redman is a general means of minimizing the effects of both of these difficulties.

The chapters in Part Three are arranged from the general to the specific. The introductory chapters by Redman and Brown are programmatic statements outlining methodologies for various excavational situations. Although Brown's chapter is specifically intended for deep-site below-ground situations, the implications can easily be extended to cave and tell situations where depositional history is an important consideration. The remaining three chapters are specific case studies in which solutions to sampling problems are critically examined in the light of certain theoretical objectives. These studies provide illustrations of decision-making at each of the three levels of the sampling procedure — the sampling scheme, fraction (or size), and unit. The case studies involve ongoing research projects at a variety of sites — Eastern Woodland agricultural villages, southwestern pueblos, and a large urban site in the Peruvian Andes. These projects may be used as a yardstick for measuring one's understanding of sampling; anyone who controls the sampling problems and alternative solutions has commendable command of the overall sampling process.

J. W. M.

8. Productive Sampling Strategies for Archaeological Sites

Charles L. Redman

Charles L. Redman (Ph.D., University of Chicago, 1971) has had a very prolific career which includes two volumes — *Explanation in Archaeology: An Explicitly Scientific Approach* (coauthored with P. J. Watson and S. A. LeBlanc) and *Research and Theory in Current Archaeology* (editor). He has published, reviewed, and prepared for publication many articles relating to research strategy and quantitative analysis. This work is based on his extensive field experiences in the American Southwest, Eastern Woodlands, and the Near East (including Morocco, Turkey, and Iran). He has been holding a Smithsonian Foreign Currency Grant for the Moroccan Project and an Associate Professorship at the State University of New York at Binghamton.

During the course of an archaeological research project the investigator is constantly being confronted with situations where he can study only a portion of the total universe of possibilities. This is due in large part to the increasing complexity and abundance of data required to answer questions being investigated. Because of the limited resources of most archaeologists and the increasing requirements of his work, he is forced to select only a portion of the total material available, and to hope that it accurately reflects the parameters of the total population. Sampling is a compromise; it is a means of getting an adequate representation of the total range of information without having to deal with all of the data in that universe. Archaeologists often utilize sampling at various stages of research. The archaeologist is infrequently explicit about the method used in sampling at each of these stages. This may be a reflection of the nonprobabilistic manner in which it has been done.

The most important contribution sampling makes to archaeological research has little to do with statistical theory. Sampling requires careful, well-conceived planning in order to select the most productive sampling design for a project. The researcher must (1) clearly outline the project's goals; (2) determine what data must be collected to satisfy these goals; and (3) assess the adequacy of the proposed procedures for collecting the necessary data. The most productive research strategies and reliable results are promoted by carefully considering whether the goals of the impending work can be achieved and by rigorously justifying the methods to be employed.

Other chapters discuss the necessity of sampling in general or sampling as used in a regional survey. This chapter will emphasize the decisions that must be made while investigating individual sites and give examples of some useful strategies I have employed.

GENERAL CONSIDERATIONS OF REGIONAL, SITE, AND ARTIFACT SAMPLING

Although the actual sampling procedures should vary with the nature of the remains and the exact questions being asked, it is useful to outline some general principles which can be adapted to the specific situation. When a broad range of information is desired from a large site or region I recommend the use of a multistage approach (Redman 1973; Binford 1964). The fundamental concept of this approach is to initially investigate in a generalized manner the entire population of materials, and in each subsequent step more intensively investigate a smaller portion of the universe. Initial work can help direct subsequent research more efficiently and detailed results of later intensive work can refine inferences based on the more general earlier stages.

The sampling procedures followed after a site is located during a regional survey determine the usefulness of the information collected. The general categories of data sought from the investigation of individual sites (either during regional surveys or intensive excavations) include the site's potential for excavation, the chronology of its occupations, its size during each of these occupations, plus a general understanding of the lifeways of each community. Aspects of these lifeways might include activities performed, resources utilized, environmental setting, community plan, and organizational system.

In a program of regional survey it is necessary to perform certain minimal procedures on all sites located. This includes locating the site on an air photo, making a brief controlled surface collection, recording the environmental setting, and mapping any visible features and the distribution of artifacts. A sample of sites from all those located should be selected for more intensive work. These sites should be subjected to complete controlled surface collections, some wall clearing, and detailed mapping of features and artifact scatter. On a sample of these sites test excavations can be conducted. At each stage of research the selection for more intensive work of sites, or areas within sites, should be related to the data required and the overall design of the survey. The criteria for dividing sites into strata or groups of similar sites, can be based on topographic and biotic zones, or on chronological period and site type. A predetermined proportion of the sites in each strata is then selected by probability sampling for further work.

On the basis of these preliminary stages of investigation one or more sites are chosen for extensive excavations. The controlled surface collection and detailed mapping of surface features can aid in the selection of potentially productive areas for excavation (Redman & Watson 1970). Once excavations are begun some scheme should be devised for selecting dirt to be screened and floated. I recommend taking a fixed percentage of the dirt from every level excavated. If the desired proportion is 20% this could be accomplished by sampling every fifth bucketful or every fifth wheelbarrowful. Deposits suspected to be rich can be sampled more intensively (completely if desired), but in all cases the amount and percentage of dirt examined should be recorded.

Once the artifacts are recovered it is frequently decided that there are too many pieces for every one to be studied in full detail. This is especially true of chemical, physical, and microscopic analysis. For these situations I recommend performing a preliminary classification on all of the artifacts recovered, and the more detailed time consuming analyses on only a sample of the pieces from each category. I found that in making simple measurements on obsidian blade fragments from an early village in Turkey, very little precision would have been lost if I had only measured a ten percent sample of the blades (Redman 1973). The mean length of the total population of 1850 blade fragments is 25.2 mm. with a standard deviation of 10.7, while the mean length of the 10% random sample (185 blade fragments) is 25.6 mm. with a standard deviation of 10.3. The close proximity of these results demonstrates how it is possible to characterize the parameters of a large population of artifacts with observations on only a relatively small proportion of them.

ALTERNATIVE SAMPLING PROCEDURES

In designing a research strategy decisions have to be made about the actual sampling procedures to be utilized in order to accomplish the proposed goals with a reasonable amount of effort. There are three general types of sampling that can be employed; judgment (purposeful), haphazard (grab), or probability. Judgment sampling is the conscious selection of units to investigate based on what the researcher considers to be the most productive or most representative examples. In this way past knowledge and experience can be incorporated into the selection (Alcock 1951). The fundamental shortcoming of judgment sampling is that the units selected are according to the investigator's preconceived notions about the nature of the population to be studied. There is the danger of biasing the results and, in a way, creating a self-fulfilling investigation. Haphazard sampling is the response of some archaeologists to the pitfalls of judgment sampling (Ford and Willey 1949). These researchers consider the selection of units to be representative or random if they are chosen in a haphazard or chance manner. It is a basic misconception that a random selection of units is simply one in which there is no obvious order. This is not true. Random sampling is a carefully controlled technique based on probability statistics. What actually happens in a haphazard sample, is that biases are introduced implicitly by the manner in which the sample is chosen (e.g. painted sherds that the surface collector notices first, sites which can be reached easily by jeep, excavation units without tree cover).

The third type of sampling, which I recommend for most situations, is probability sampling. In probability sampling the samples are drawn to conform to rigorous mathematical theory. The effects of explicit or implicit human biases are minimized. Theoretical limits of reliability have been calculated by statisticians to estimate how closely the values derived from the sampled units approximate the parameters of the entire population. Hence, one can assign some measure of reliability to the quantitative trends observed in material, and can evaluate whether these trends are the result of cultural processes or could be due to sampling error alone.

Several different forms of probability sampling are available to the researcher, each with its own advantages and disadvantages (Ragir 1967; Hill 1967). Simple random sampling is often discussed and occasionally utilized on archaeological projects. In this type of procedure the entire population of sampling units is treated in an undifferentiated manner and the likelihood of each unit being selected or any combination of units being selected is equal. The choice of previous units does not affect the selection of subsequent units. The selection is done on the basis of a random numbers table (Arkin and Colton 1963) or by drawing lots (not a perfect technique due to inadequate mixing of the lots). The advantage of simple random sampling is that it requires a minimum of assumptions to be made about the material under study. Only the boundaries of the universe (population), the list of the sampling units (sampling frame), and the proportion to be investigated (sampling fraction) must be decided in advance. Theoretical estimates of the reliability of the sample values have been calculated. A random sample is relatively difficult to lay out and investigate, because by definition there is no regularity to the units selected. In areal sampling there is also the possibility of leaving some areas unsampled while others have clusters of sampling units. This is not a theoretical shortcoming, but may be a practical consideration when one of the research goals is to make inferences about areal patterning.

The sample which is simplest to lay out and most evenly dispersed is a systematic, or geometric design. In this strategy a checkerboard of areas, or a regular interval between units is used as the means of selection. Results of empirical and theoretical tests indicate that a systematic sample is not only simpler to perform, but comes very close to an accurate estimate of the total population values (Osborne 1941; Haggett 1965). The greatest danger in utilizing systematic samples is that, because the arrangement of sampling units is determined by a geometric pattern, it is possible for the periodicity of the material being investigated and that of the sampling strategy to coincide and seriously skew the results.

If the archaeologist has prior knowledge of some aspect of the material to be investigated or is willing to make some assumptions about it, it is possible to incorporate this information by stratifying the population to be sampled into separate groups, or strata. Each of these groups is believed to be internally more homogeneous than the entire population and is sampled separately. These divisions can be made on the basis of environmental zones in a regional survey, visible features on a single site, or simply geometric patterns in order to insure maximum dispersal of sampling units. Each strata can be sampled with equal intensity or can be differentially sampled. The differing proportions can be taken into account when calculating mean values. Stratification is particularly useful in situations where previous research has led to a basic knowledge of the structure of the archaeological remains to be investigated. Although stratification biases the sample, it is in an explicit manner that can be accounted for when making inferences. Stratification is the appropriate procedure for utilizing the knowledge, experience, and intuition of the investigator in structuring the universe into separate populations to be sampled. The most productive research design utilizes both the previous knowledge of the archaeological remains and some form of probability sampling. In this way it is possible to take advantage of available archaeological expertise while guarding against the possibility of "creating" what one seeks.

In situations where previous knowledge is minimal or the investigator is unwilling to make assumptions about his material, one can employ a maximally dispersed, yet nonperiodic sampling strategy. Human geographers have developed a stratified, systematic, unaligned sampling procedure for gathering data on areal problems (Berry 1962; Haggett 1965). The procedure for generating this type of sample produces an even coverage of the entire area being investigated without the sampling units forming a precisely geometric pattern. Another advantage of stratified, systematic, unaligned sampling is that the boundaries of the area to be investigated do not have to be fixed before drawing the sample as in simple random sampling. With this design once the proportion of the population to be selected is determined the sample can be generated for a very large area, any portion of which can be investigated by itself.

Multistage or nested sampling is more a structure for proceeding with sampling than a design itself. With this technique the investigator first chooses a sample of large areas (or numbers of individuals), and then chooses from within these areas samples of smaller areas to be investigated. This has the practical advantage of facilitating the investigation, and produces more detailed information about limited areas within the universe. Archaeological projects are frequently organized in a multistage manner, but do not report the methods of selection. A typical procedure is the preliminary investigation of a region followed by more detailed work on one or more sites, and finishing with limited excavations on one of these sites. The important aspect of multistage sampling is to make the selection of units to be investigated at each stage an explicit decision, based on proper stratification of the universe, probability sampling, and available resources.

Decisions on the proportion of the universe to investigate and the size of each sampling unit are important in all types of sampling procedures. The answers depend on the questions being asked, the nature of the material, and the resources available. The larger the proportion of the universe examined, the more reliable is the estimate of the total population. The greater number of units investigated also increases reliability (see Asch, this volume). Hence, although one can get a good estimate from 20% of a universe split into small units (e.g. 1000 total), to get a reliable estimate from a universe of 50 units it is necessary to sample 50% of it. Therefore, it is preferable to split the universe into very small sampling units. However, this increases the practical difficulty of collecting the data. A balance must be reached between ease of collection, adequate sampling proportions, and size of sampling units.

A probability sample of a region or a site will produce estimates of the total inventory of the site or region which can be assessed as to how accurately they reflect the total values. However, probability sampling does not adequately investigate configurational and associational patterns. By definition, sampling units are most effective if they are small and scattered. Yet, if one is interested in the distribution of artifacts or structures on a site, or the configuration of small settlements around a larger center then probability sampling will not be the proper approach.

SAMPLING PROGRAM OF THE CIBOLA ARCHAEOLOGICAL RESEARCH PROJECT

A series of different sampling procedures are being employed by the Cibola Archaeological Research Project which I have been codirecting. Because the configuration of small sites around the large centers in the El Morro Valley of west Central New Mexico was one of our goals, we conducted a two-part survey (Redman and LeBlanc n.d.). Broad contiguous investigations located on the basis of the initial probability sampling produced associational information to complement the data on total inventory gathered by the probability sample. The archaeologist can always investigate outside the boundaries of the selected units in a probability sample, but this data should be analyzed in a different manner. The primary survey sampling on our New Mexican project was of half section units (1/2 mile by one mile areas) selected by random numbers from each of the four major topographic zones; valley floor, ridges, mesas, and mountain slopes. In addition, contiguous areas 3/4 mile in radius were completely surveyed around five of the largest sites in the valley. The results of this survey will produce a general picture of the nature of settlement in the entire valley, and also the particular pattern of settlement around large sites.

Each site found is investigated with varying degrees of intensity, depending on its size and period. All sites located were subjected to some form of controlled surface collection (Redman and Watson 1970). If the site were small it might be divided into only four quadrants and all artifacts collected. On larger sites the design would be more complex. In the case of sites with traces of visible architecture the sampling was stratified into room blocks, trash mounds, and surrounding areas. Each strata would be sampled by both quantitative and qualitative techniques. Intensive surface collections from very limited areas (circles two meters in radius) were supplemented by collections from much larger areas of diagnostic pieces judged to be important for nonquantitative stylistic or chronological analysis. In this way samples usable in quantitative comparisons and samples usable in qualitative analyses would be collected in a geographically differentiated manner in order to help delineate on the basis of surface data different periods within the site or activity areas within one occupation. Excavations were carried out on a number of sites in order to collect floral, faunal, dendrochronological, architectural, and in situ artifactual information. Rooms and trash mounds were selected from each room block or trash area located during the surface investigation of the chosen sites.

On one large (*ca.* 500 rooms) rectangular thirteenth century pueblo the Cibola Archaeological Research Project spent a limited amount of time wall-clearing. After preliminary wall-clearing had defined the boundaries of the site it was decided that there was only enough time for 25% of the site to be wall-cleared. It was agreed that large blocks of rooms were desirable as well as examples of architecture from all parts of the site. This square site was then stratified into four sides and four corners. Each side was divided into four blocks or sampling units. On the basis of random numbers one of the four corners, plus one block from each of the sides was selected for wall-clearing. This provided for large blocks, and maximal spatial dispersion of areas investigated while determining the ultimate selection of units by a random process. On the basis of this information fourteen rooms were selected for excavation. In order to maximize the variability in room location, size, and building sequence, a pair of rooms was sampled from each side of the pueblo and from one corner, stratifying the universe so as to insure the testing of at least one room from each row of rooms, and from different sizes recorded during wall-clearing.

EVALUATION

A general skepticism or apathy toward sampling is shared by some archaeologists who know little about it and by a few who are well-versed in sampling procedures. For the uninitiated, the reason generally is related to the extra effort involved and the apparent lack of significant substantive results. Sampling obviously has little to offer researchers not concerned with representativeness of their material and reliability of their results. If a researcher is willing to make inferences on the basis of potentially biased data and intuitive feelings then sampling is unnecessary. However, with the rising interest in rigorous justification of results and obtaining the full range of variation in archaeological materials, probability sampling must play a central role.

A few archaeologists who are knowledgeable in the techniques of sampling have adopted this attitude because they claim to recognize the limitations of sampling. The attitude of these archaeologists is based on disproportionate expectations for the use of sampling. *Sampling is not the answer to every problem* and equally important, *sampling is not easy to use!*

It should be clear that most sampling designs produce only a limited sort of information. While probability sampling can yield a reliable estimate of the total inventory of items in a population, it will not provide adequate data on their configurational or associational patterns. There is no doubt that it would be better to investigate the entire population of items rather than a sample before making summary statements about them. However, because of practical limitations this is seldom possible and it is in these situations that sampling is most useful. Even if resources were available for an investigation of some entire population there is a serious question in my mind as to whether it would be an efficient use of these resources. *Sampling is a compromise* forced on archaeologists because there are not enough resources for complete coverage. Where the balance is struck in this compromise depends on the data requirements of the researcher and on his general goals.

I seriously question whether archaeologists using present forms of survey and excavation are able to investigate sufficient numbers of units to attain adequate statistical reliability. The problem is accentuated when the project goals include obtaining configurational data as well as total inventory information. One solution to this problem is for archaeologists to accept lower confidence limits as usable. This is clearly what is being done implicitly by almost every archaeologist with a goal of making statistical statements. Archaeologists should discuss whether or not it would be sufficient to accept results with .10 or even .20 confidence limits at the present stage of development in the field.

My own approach to the problem of confidence limits is — for the present — to accept the lack of statistical precision and emphasize other aspects of sampling as the main rationale for its employment. In addition to the careful planning sampling necessitates, conducting a probability sample of a region or a site gives the researcher a thorough, first-hand acquaintance with the subject of study. The more important consideration is the value of probability sampling in the process of discovery. Either in the case of survey reconnaissance or of site excavation, it forces the researcher to look everywhere, not just where he thinks things will be found. It is a form of insurance against an investigator shaping what he finds according to what is thought to be there beforehand. The value of a probability sample as an exploratory technique as well as a method of obtaining an unbiased sample of material makes it a necessary tool for most archaeological projects.

Another common misconception is the notion that there is no role for archaeological expertise in sampling. As I mention above, this is emphatically not the case. Considerable archaeological expertise and insight are necessary to formulate a sampling design which will produce the required information with a minimum expenditure of resources. When stratifying the population to be sampled one must call upon all one's knowledge of the population and of archaeological remains in general.

Another misconception on this order is that researchers who use probability sampling cannot investigate items outside the sample. It is true that only material selected for the sample should be used in calculating population values. However, if on the basis of surface indications, other reasons, or pure accident, a particularly interesting archaeological situation is encountered, it is possible to investigate it if there are available resources to carry out the work without jeopardizing other aspects of the research. Following this point, if one excavates half of a building in a trench selected by a probability sample, it is permissible to excavate the remainder of the building. The only cautions are to analyze the material from the probability separately from samples deriving from other investigations, and not to let additional jobs absorb so much of one's time and resources that achievement of the original goals are jeopardized (unless a major strategic decision is made to shift priorities).

In summary, probability sampling is a valuable tool in the methodological inventory of archaeologists. I remain optimistic as to its potential and am personally experimenting with different forms of sampling in my own fieldwork. Clearly it has great value as a method of exploration and as a means of obtaining unbiased estimates of total inventories. In planning research archaeologists should consider carefully the advantages of probability sampling in contrast to the bias involved in less rigorous techniques for selecting materials to be investigated.

9. Deep-site Excavation Strategy as a Sampling Problem

James A. Brown

James A. Brown (Ph.D., University of Chicago, 1965) has been involved in computerized data analysis and data management for the Koster site research project. The remainder of his research has been devoted to publications on the Spiro site, the social dimensions of mortuary behavior, and statistical analysis. An areal specialization in the Eastern Woodlands has emerged from excavations at Mound City, Ohio, the boreal forest zone in Saskatchewan, historic sites in Michigan, and various sites in Illinois. He has been serving as Associate Professor of Anthropology at Northwestern University in addition to serving as Editor of the *Illinois Archaeological Survey*.

INTRODUCTION

The traditional strength of archaeology has been its reliance upon stratified cultural deposits to construct cultural-historical sequences. In the future, stratigraphy will continue to constitute an important control in comparative research in spite of the technological modernization of non-Western societies and the redundancy of information from stratified sites. However, some difficult problems lie in the way of the use of stratigraphy for more general research interests. Of these problems the most conspicuous is the difficulty with which the strata from deeply stratified sites are comparable within a single site and between sites with respect to sample size, sample control, and overall scope of the cultural record.

Despite the fact that some of the most important archaeological sequences are based on excavations in multilayered sites with long histories, the deeply stratified site remains a mixed blessing. Because part of its record is sufficiently deep to be masked and hidden by the surface, the data recovered from deeper levels contain inherent limitations that jeopardize the scope of comparability even when the artifact yield is ample. Thus many old-style archaeological soundings have offered good sequences of a few distinctive artifacts and adequate information on their immediate context but are very deficient in information about other aspects of the occupation. Examples include insufficient data on artifactual depositional patterning and on community layout, both of which are essential to interpretation of the site and its socio-cultural organization. A more grievous (and typical) problem of deep soundings is the inadequacy of the information yield caused by culturally undiagnostic artifacts; in these cases, it is hardly possible to infer anything beyond the existence and age of an occupation in a particular horizon.

[155]

Traditional Strategies

The relative inaccessibility of buried layers is implicitly acknowledged because most excavation strategies treat the more accessible uppermost strata differently from the deeply buried strata. The result is scant concern for sampling comparability among the affected strata. There are surprisingly few statements in the archaeological literature that concern themselves specifically with this problem and its implications for excavation strategy. For example, one monograph devoted to methods of village mound excavation does not consider interoccupational comparability at all in the discussions of excavation strategies (Lloyd 1963). However, the problem is at least implicitly recognized in most systematic treatments of archaeological methods and techniques.

The traditional approach to stratified sites of all depths is to place excavations in one of several areas: (1) in opportunistic locations, (2) in locations with the greatest potential depth, and (3) in areas with the maximum or most interesting potential information payoff, such as the area with the greatest expected cultural diversity.

Opportunistic strategies are clearly those that exploit unforeseen aspects of the site that are revealed in the course of excavation. Among the more explicit strategies, the most common is the one that chooses excavation location on the basis of cores and other indicators pointing to the longest or best preserved sequence. One common approach is the practice of placing an excavation in the center of a site or on the summit of the deposits in the expectation that the fullest (and deepest) sequence will be found there.

There are also a substantial number of reports that recognize a strategy of optimization in the yield of selected data classes, the location of which is relatively predictable. This type of strategy was commonly employed in the complex Near Eastern tells. Wheeler writes:

The ultimate goals of a *tell*-excavation should be *(a)* to establish its cultural or chronological range by the marginal sections indicated above, and *(b)* to uncover *completely* a specific phase or phases of its occupation (Wheeler 1956: 112).

And again:

Apart from the marginal bite, as on a "flat" site, the clearance of a gateway is highly desirable, combined with an area-dig in the adjacent interior on a sufficiently large scale to establish firmly the cultural context of successive gateways and fortifications. Further in the interior, an elevation may indicate the position of a citadel or temple and may also be subjected to an area-excavation, which should subsequently be linked up systematically with that adjoining the gateway, and thereafter continued to the designed limits of the enterprise (Wheeler 1956: 112).

In one notable example the strategy of tell excavation centered around the location of the temple which was anticipated to be a reliable producer of texts that could be expected to be located directly above other temples (Woolley 1953). A series of superimposed temples eventually led the excavator down to the first temple on the original ground surface. Other locations were also dug, but despite the fact that Woolley's strategy led to successful achievement of his research objectives, one would suspect the generalizations concerning the various occupation levels based on his biased sample. The problem is not a trivial one since the Near Eastern archaeologist interested in community patterning is left without adequate material for his interests (Adams 1966: 28). The choice of excavation strategy in deep-site excavation obviously cannot be cavalierly ignored.

The most direct approach to the excavation of a deep site would be to treat it as if it were as accessible as a surface site and excavate it completely. This approach entails sinking a large block excavation to the base of the site. However, even under the most favorable excavation conditions deeply buried occupations cannot be as extensively excavated as surface occupations because of the great expense in opening large exposures and because of the inordinate future commitment to pursuing such a vast objective (Kenyon 1957: 41–3). On the other hand, the expedient stripping away of overlying occupations is expensive enough to question whether such a short cut to deep levels would be adopted for the exclusive purpose of treating the deeply buried occupation like a surface exposure. In addition, most stratified sites either do not warrant this expedient treatment or their size and location impose insuperable obstacles to stripping.

Limitations of Small-scale Probes

As an alternative to the impracticality of complete excavation and massive stripping, there remains the time-honored uses of small-scale probes. These can be in centrally located test pits or soundings, in cuts along the exposed margins of a site, and in trenches placed along site transects. Each has its particular utility, but all are alike in their *limited* applicability to site-wide problems. Such small-scale exposures are essentially incapable of predicting the contents of a buried site. This incapacity is because excavation of the lowest strata is a direct projection of the strategy applicable to the overlying strata.

In practice the limitations of small-scale probes are ameliorated by increasing the number of test pits or soundings. However, without the use of sampling controls, the multiplication of test pits results solely in a geometric increase in effort that effectively decreases the logistical efficiency of the strategy. Another shortcoming is the loss of stratigraphic control. Braidwood and Howe (1960) have given us an important case in point in the Jarmo excavation where the advantage of multiple, spaced test pits was compromised by the inability to cross-correlate the stratification of individual pits. The use of multiple test pits is really dependent upon compensatory control over intrasite variability in each of the strata; this control can be attained by preexcavation coring and remote sensing.

Deep soundings also entail an inherent physical disadvantage. As one proceeds to deeper levels, the top of the units must be increasingly stepped back or benched to gain safe access to the bottom. The practical implications of this fact mean that deep excavations are limited to their original locations. Moreover, they represent an expensive investment that effectively limits the investigator's choice of where to dig once the pit is begun. This constraint is, in effect, progressive with descent to greater depths. Under these conditions one would expect that there is an inverse relationship between the flexibility in choice of sample and the expense of excavating at increasingly greater depths.

Concerning the blindness of deep testing, prediction is largely intuitive and its success largely depends upon the application of relevant prior knowledge of cultural behavior. If we discount the contribution of hunches, it can be expected that the probability of actually achieving a sampling objective will roughly vary in inverse proportion to the depth of the deposit; other factors include the nature of the desired feature or deposit, e.g., a dump, a living area, a fortification, or other definable portion of a site.

Unfortunately, the problems entailed in small-scale probes are compounded by the heuristic usefulness of fragmentary data from the deepest portions of stratified sites. It is commonly thought that the effort necessary to extract the data from the deepest levels is sufficient justification for the detailed comparison of admittedly inadequate data to data from better controlled excavations in more accessible locations. It is the opportunistic nature of many deep site explorations that has caused a shift in archaeological attention away from the problems presented by stratified sites and to focus attention instead on explicit, controlled work on surface sites.

SAMPLING AND RESEARCH OBJECTIVES

The excavation of deeply buried occupations appears superficially to be an excavation strategy that contradicts sampling principles. For this reason alone it is not surprising that the challenge of deep-site sampling has largely been ignored in discussion of archaeological site sampling (e.g., Binford 1964; Plog and Hill 1971; Ragir 1967). In most discussions sampling is equated with probability sampling, which assumes that all locations within a sampling universe be truly accessible and that the limits of the occupations composing the site are known. However, most programs incorporate a sequence of investigatory stages in which both probabilistic and nonprobabilistic sampling as well as other controlled procedures are usually brought to bear on a research problem in different phases of research (Redman 1973; Struever 1968). It is clearly justifiable to suppose that sampling begins whenever a choice is made as to the location of a sounding or to the extent of an excavation. Read (this volume) has cogently observed that the necessary precondition for sampling is the presence of independent controls allowing for the extrapolating from the known to the unknown. When intuition is used, the sampling is nonprobabilistic in contrast to the formal probabilistic procedures that have been discussed by sampling theorists. Deep-site excavation strategies do not allow for probabilistic sampling, and there are types of nonprobabilistic sampling that can and need to be developed.

The consequence of continued inadequate sampling of deeply buried occupations is to foster a complacent attitude toward deeply stratified sites and to shift attention to surface sites. Deep-site excavation will continue to remain opportunistic in conception. The archaeologist who capitalizes on unique situations is left with many tangled interpretive problems that are a product of the excavation's scope and not the prehistoric record.

Sampling Criteria in Stratified Sites

The existence of site stratification generates a problem in the creation of cultural stratigraphy. The major vehicles for conversion are the cultural remains included within each stratum, especially common artifacts. Context finds are usually conceived of as indexing the stratigraphy and providing a sequence of cultures. Hence, the purpose of the strata-cut is to index stratigraphy. The example quoted from Wheeler earlier is a typical use of a test to discover the range in stratigraphic depth, the number of distinct strata, and the distinguishing characteristics of each stratum. The most successful use of strata-cuts is in rich sites with large artifact yields and a mixture of artifactual contexts represented in the deposits. Sample size is usually judged by the sufficiency of the artifact yield to provide relatively clear cultural stratigraphy. Although quantity of artifacts, especially pottery, is important in distinguishing strata and in establishing sequences of artifacts, qualitative differences are more important. Barring no internal contradictions, small amounts of pottery and stylistically distinctive artifacts can potentially document cultural stratigraphy. Contradictions might be due to mistaken identification or the presence of stratigraphic intrusion. The use of ceramics to document stratigraphy is generally successful because the high information content of ceramic variation is sufficient to insure that distinctive, diagnostic artifacts can be identified.

As long as the indexing functions of ceramics are used to identify cultural content of stratigraphy, complications due to sampling biases will be relatively rare. However, once attention is switched to a concern for cultural behavior in an occupation, then variability in artifact occurrence and style which is largely ignored in strata-cuts is important (Brown and Freeman 1964). Thus the difficulties in making minimal extrapolation from the strata-cut to the total occupation are sampling problems that are partially independent of the cultural chronology based on the stratigraphic position of ceramic remains.

However, artifacts with low or little stylistic variability, such as many chipped stone utility tools, are also used in indexing stratigraphy. In this case, the occurrence of "diagnostic" items should be more heavily dependent upon functional contexts. Although the finds in strata-cuts are commonly treated as "representative samples" of the cultural inventories, there are components of variability in almost all excavations that are unexplained by the chronological model of interphase similarities and differences (Binford 1965, 1968a, 1972).

There are many examples of strata-cut interpretations that fail to attribute the differences in artifact frequency to the areal distribution of associated activities. Fluctuation of artifact frequencies can be due to the conjunction of particular activity areas within the strata-cuts rather than to site-wide progressive change. Willey and McGimsey's (1954) treatment of cultural stratification of a shell mound, for example, explicitly assumes the latter interpretation without adequate control of activity area differences. It is unjustified to employ most artifacts for chronology construction without adequate control of activity dependent distributions. Even more misleading are the generalizations made from the successes of ceramic chronology in strata-cuts that are applied to all artifacts. Binford (1972) has demonstrated the fallacy of this logic.

A more conservative approach to strata-cuts is to use the results of its chronological record as a guide to the temporal order of other sites, most of which are unstratified or dominated by one specific cultural period (e.g., MacNeish 1958: 52–3). The obvious working assumption to this strategy is that the strengths of the strata-cut can be used to chronologically order single component, unstratified sites. Because such sites are parts of organized settlement systems, this application of the strata-cut strategy introduces sampling errors. That is, artifacts may have the appearance of chronological change when in fact the "change" is a product of sampling error in a single-component system with different activity loci than the same system super-imposed in the strata-cut. Yet, even with sound chronological control this strategy neglects potentially salvageable information in the soundings of the buried strata. Thus, this application of the strata-cut strategy does not eliminate the problem of spurious cultural stratigraphy.

The relative inaccessibility of deeply buried strata has been an effective barrier to complete excavation of deep strata and to their controlled sampling. Unlike the surface or shallow site that can be sampled using a repertoire of sampling strategies, the deeply buried occupation imposes extremely difficult problems in the effective use of sampling controls. The fact that in the practical world the size and location of the lowest stratum excavation is largely determined by what is chosen for excavation above it means that a sampling strategy should be designed to mitigate this dependency.

Sampling may be facilitated by the lack of complete independence in the location of activity types among adjacent layers. In many sites the location of the upper strata activity loci are respondent to the same conditions that made for determining the location of underlying activities of the same type. Hence, the locations of whole occupations and functionally significant portions of sites may not be completely independent from layer to layer in a single site.

Activity Areas as a Focus of Sampling

Basically, the excavation of deeply stratified sites has been undertaken to gather information that measures cultural change during the period bridged by the strata. This basic objective is true regardless of the sampling design. However, the treatment of the archaeological findings in these strata differs in distinctly fundamental ways according to theoretical orientation. The traditional research strategy has been to search the data for patterns of change and to attribute as much of the resulting pattern to cultural differences. Such differences automatically become temporal differences due to the order imposed by stratification. In this and closely related research strategies strata-cuts are deemed sufficient sample cuts since it is assumed that cultural similarites can be measured on a single undifferentiated scale. Thus the findings in strata-cuts can provide samples sufficient to demonstrate or measure cultural change irrespective of the variability that may exist within each component layer of a site. As Binford (1972: 262) has observed, this model of cultural change and differentiation has found confirmation in the minds of its adherents by the directional variability within a single class of artifacts representing well-defined and stable cultural traditions. The fact that seriation, the primary ordering technique in unidimensional analysis through time has achieved such widespread use among American archaeologists testifies to the hold that the unidimensional model has. Differences in the respective merits of multiple dimensional scaling and seriation reflect the underlying differences in theoretical paradigms held by the respective adherents. Although the unidimensional model was once widely subscribed to, it has come under increasing attack from those adhering to ecological and systemic models of cultural behavior. It has frequently been known as the normative model, but recently Binford (1972) has more aptly characterized this model as unidimensional in contrast to the multidimensional model, which he and others have found to explain more satisfactorily archaeological patterning as early as the beginnings of tool production by our hominid predecessors (Binford and Binford 1966; Binford 1972; Freeman 1973).

The notion that a site assemblage consists of activity-based sets of artifacts with associated life-maintenance by-products strikes at the assumptions of the unidimensional model (Binford 1972; Struever 1968). The assumptions that lie behind the activity-focus view of archaeological assemblages has been spelled out in several places (cf. Binford and Binford 1966; Freeman 1973; Isaac 1971; Schiffer 1972; Struever 1968), but Binford (1972) has condensed them into the following essentials:

Since tools are the technical aids used in the performance of work, in the literal sense of the word, we should expect that other things being equal, the composition of tool assemblages would vary directly in accordance with the tasks performed. The differential distribution of assemblages in space should exhibit compositional differences in direct relation to the degree of mobility characteristic of the adaptive strategy and the degree that mobility was differentially exercised by task group segments of the larger social unit. It should vary inversely with the degree that tools were multi-functional and/or curated in anticipation of future tasks (Binford 1972: 265).

In effect the multidimensional model recognizes that assemblages are compounds of the variable expression of many independent dimensions. The composition of assemblages is also affected by secondary behavior. That is, the use of multifunctional tools and the curation of artifacts acts to decrease the segregation or compartmentalization that is due to the inherent spatial segregation of specific activities. Conversely, increased spatial segregation is also promoted to the degree that work groups are mobile and individuals participate differentially in specific task groups. An example of the interaction of these factors was made by Freeman (1973) in his observation that constrictions in the available area of shelter or occupation act to merge functionally distinct activity areas.

Interlayer Comparison in Stratified Sites

The payoff in excavating deeply stratified sites is in the efficiency with which information on cultural change can be gathered. If the change is to truly reflect change rather than sampling bias, then it is important that there be as much true comparability between separate strata as possible. Comparability in this sense is not the comparability in artifacts, soils, or another observational phenomenon. Rather, the comparability refers to activities, which are classifications based on informed preliminary analysis of archaeologically derived materials and observations. Comparability in the setting of deep-site analysis amounts to ensuring that the activities that are represented in the archaeological record are as much alike as possible from layer to layer. A unique set of activities represented in a sample from a single layer contributes little to any truly comparative statement. Its contribution decreases as the questions framed by archaeologists become more specific and demand greater precision. As interesting as unique phenomena might intrinsically be, unusual or rare data simply do not lead to comparable comparisons that are necessary to statements of change. Unfortunately, little explicit attention has been directed towards the problem of how sampling incomparability effects statements of cultural process or style change in stratified sites. Even in specialized sites such as a rock-shelter, it is possible (and often empirically demonstrated) that at different times different tasks and activities were performed by participants in the same cultural system (or tradition). The potential heterogeneity of activities performed at different periods of the same site qualifies interpretations of style change in all artifact categories. Successful elicitation of style chronologies has usually depended upon a shrewd assessment of those attributes and modes present that are *least* effected by exclusive dependency on specific activities. And conversely, the more a "functional load" exists on an attribute set the less successful is the chronology erected from them.

The difficulties in drawing inferences about the nature of site organizational change from deep-site samples in spatially limited exposures with unknown or unmeasured bias is illustrated by the case discussed by Movius (1966) at Abri Pataud. He states the distribution of the hearth class of facility in the following way:

Herein it is proposed to discuss the significance and implications of the hearths with respect to the basic structuring of certain early Upper Paleolithic societies, in particular those groups who occupied the site during the time intervals represented by Couches 3, 4, 5, 7, 8, 11, 12, and 14. No true hearths were found in Couche 1, while only dispersed ash layers were encountered in Couches 2, 6, 9, 10, and 13. Doubtless the latter originated from true hearths situated beyond the limits of the excavated area, but no evidence of clearly defined areas of dense ash concentration came to light in these five couches (Movius 1966: 297).

In the first place here we see an example of the classic archaeological situation in which the only evidence of a particular feature is represented by a displaced residue or activity by-product, ash in this case. The inference that Movius draws is that hearths were present but not contained within the limits of the excavation. But in his conclusions regarding the layers with hearths, Movius does not seriously consider the distribution of different hearths in the same light. He classified his hearths into 6 types that happen to be so distributed in the 8 hearth-containing layers that only one layer has examples of two. The other hearths are distributed uniquely. Furthermore, when he identifies the hearth types to 3 or possibly 4 task group types (his communities), the reduction in types does not increase the overlap at all. Hence he is left with the hearth types indicative of the largest social aggregate in the latest group of layers belonging to the Upper Perigordian and the commoner small hearth in the earlier Aurignacian layers. The sampling problems are obvious although this evidence tempts one to generalize from the sequence of hearths in a limited excavation to the whole site or to sites of the entire Upper Perigordian and Aurignacian settlement systems. Movius does not so generalize but nonetheless he is left with a common archaeological problem. How indicative is the sample of activity areas in the series of superimposed strata of the total habitation area in each of the strata? The answer to this question is crucial to the generalizations about the evolution of cultural systems represented by the occupations. The excavation at Abri Pataud presents a record that can be read quite differently depending upon whether one learns later that the sample is unbiased or is biased for the different occupations. Thus, it is quite possible that the activity area represented by the alignment of hearths in the Upper Perigordian layer (couche 3) is truly unrepresented in the underlying layers. There remains the possibility (although unlikely) in this case that this hearth pattern was simply not discovered in the section of occupational samples in underlying layers. Moreover, the site itself may be specialized within the settlement system. The finding of isolated simple basin-shaped hearths indicative of small work groups in the Aurignacian and Upper Perigordian layers may not be an instance of the lack of large communal hearths in the cultural systems involved as much as a case of the sole presence of small work group occupations in the early levels of the excavated portion of the site.

THEORY AND METHOD

The Depositional Model

The primary focus of sampling in archaeology has been to promote more controlled comparison between and within sites through the application of probability sampling. [See Asch and Read, this volume.] The direction of such research is inevitably away from the nonprobabilistic procedures necessary to sample buried layers within a site. The sampling problems associated with an ordered temporal sequence of samples have received little attention (cf. Whallon and Kantman 1969; Asch, this volume), probably because of the impossibility of estimating population parameters. Sampling within buried occupational layers (or strata) in a stratified site is clearly a different problem than sampling over an exposed surface. All probabilistic sampling procedures assume that the total surface of the site is equally accessible (Berry and Baker 1968). But superposition of sample populations imposes difficulties that rule out probabilistic sampling procedures in any realistic research design.

It is one matter to specify a goal of discovering activity areas as a means for controlling intrasite variability in assemblages and quite a different matter to actually achieve the goal. There are several problems that interfere with its easy achievement. First is the major problem of determining the contribution of postdepositional processes of decomposition, soil movement, erosion, soil formation and the like to the actual physical record recovered by the archaeologist. The contribution can result in postdepositional additions (e.g., deflation accumulations) as it can deletions (e.g., decomposition). Fortunately for archaeological research, geomorphic and geochemical disturbances are generally isolable analytically and are likely to exhibit patterns of distribution independent of the archaeological finds. Hence these disturbances are potentially separable from archaeological context where destruction is not great and where excavations are sufficiently large.

The goal of archaeological research is the actual behavior that produced the original physical residue before postdepositional processes have altered that record. This objective implies that we are faced with the more complex problem of discovering the original behavior patterning that is *aggregated* with the geological patterning of deposition and with subsequent alterations at abandonment. As Schiffer (1972) has pointed out we can describe the interrelationship as a complex one-way line of causation. Following his example, the physical residue that is due to human behavior is the *archaeological context* and the actual behavior responsible for the depositional patterning is the *systemic context*. The flow and transformation of materials through systemic context to their archaeological context and ultimately to the physical context of finds is largely temporal and can be represented by a complex linear flow with local feedback loops (Schiffer 1972). This representation of the behavioral and depositional history of a site is particularly fortunate since it allows the linear dependency to be described as a vector. The flow of material through this linear vector is sufficiently complex in itself to rule out simple mapping of categories of systemic context even when geological disturbances are eliminated or controlled (Krause and Thorne 1971; Schiffer 1972). There are more substantial reasons that militate against a simple one-to-one correspondence between systemic context behaviors and patterns in the archaeological context. Since the multidimensional model predicts that several behavioral dimensions potentially enter into any single pattern of archaeological context, all patterns in archaeological context must be regarded as potential aggregates of several discrete activities that happen to be carried out on the same or overlapping plot(s) of ground. The multidimensionality of behavioral determinants of artifact and debris patterning can be visualized clearly in the difference between two basic modes of artifact usage and disposal. In the case where artifacts and material by-products are dropped in place each activity will produce its own independent set of patterns that are clearly definable even though they might coincide completely. In this case there exists a direct relationship between frequency of activity elements and the intensity or duration of the activity. However, where materials that have been "disposed of" are salvaged and recycled for another activity, the later activity can have an effect on the material record of the earlier (Binford n.d.a). If we consider the effect of conservation and curation of objects associated with an activity, it is self-evident that (a) many of the material manifestations of a particular activity might be locally absent or be poorly related to the intensity of that activity, and (b) objects and artifacts might appear out of the primary context or at least out of their original context of utilization. However, the effect of conservation on extended and repeated use of an artifact does not result in spurious clusters of artifacts and debris, since the context of disposal (or accidental loss) is itself patterned and predictable. Rather, empirically observed patterns potentially will be composed of components determined by diverse behavioral patterns. The identification of these determinants is completely beyond direct inference from patterning. The statistical discovery of the antecedent behavioral dimensions through application of a factorial model applied to a series of similar archaeological contexts is far more satisfactory.

Controlled Sampling: The Initial Phases

Sampling among occupation layers in a stratified site is conceived of as a procedure of maximizing the comparability between layers at the sacrifice of reliability in the estimation of the target population. The goal is the recovery of archaeological data sets from each of the layers that belong to the same systemic/archaeological context. The procedure can be likened to a regional surface survey routine that attempts to maximize the distinctions among sampling strata by enlarging the coverage of each strata.

The sampling task amounts to a problem of finding settlement parts or components in archaeological context that are repeated in as many of the buried strata as possible. There are two important aspects to the strategy: (1) categories of settlement use must be capable of identification and isolation, e.g., as activity areas or as areas of social distinction; (2) the number or size of a category must be potentially capable of being increased. For these reasons the sampling procedure that I am describing is one that attempts to *categorize* settlement parts given the available range of archaeological materials and contexts in each of the layers. Simultaneously, excavations are to be directed into parts of each layer that would increase the sample of the categories of settlement use held in common by the greatest number of layers.

This sampling strategy is essentially multiphase in organization and requires in practice continual sifting of information and evaluating of the number and distribution of activity areas. The initial step involves the collecting of information relevant to the number and distribution of subsurface archaeological zones within the site limits. This is the information that would be recoverable prior to excavation from such opportunistically available sources as erosional cuts, topographic/geomorphic information, and intentional sources such as coring. The latter greatly increases the knowledge of the depth and distribution of subsurface strata above what would be available through sections produced by natural erosion. In actual cases a knowledge of subsurface cultural topography would be constructed from whatever sources were available and technically within the means of the investigator. Perhaps most important is the archaeologist's understanding of the principal variables influencing human occupation in the study area. For instance, in the eastern United States, such variables as topography, type of shelter, distance from water, and proximity to other important resources which are known to structure settlement location and organization are the obvious pieces of information that are needed before one can establish the basic sampling units in the subsurface topography.

The preexcavation inventory of data relating to the extent and number of buried occupations allows the archaeologist to set up divisions of the site surface that constitute the initial "sampling strata" (or the first-order sample). The factors that are known to be critical to the organization of settlement work and living space should be used to partition the sampling strata. One of the principal considerations is topographic zonation, and another relevant variable should be distance from water or another important resource locally present. These factors would provide the best prediction for intrasite differences whether the settlement is exposed or buried. Naturally, the first-order partitioning of sample space might require modification and adjustment after the archaeologist is able to observe the buried sequence of occupations. Such an adjustment would constitute a second-order sampling.

A sensitive phase in the sampling procedure lies in the adjustment of the first-order sample. First, there is the matter of how does one recognize that adjustments are required? Second, how can one maximize information and sample control per unit effort while at the same time duly consider wall shoring and all of the other crucial safety and logistic questions that enter into decisions as to where to continue digging and where to cease digging? For the remainder of this paper I will address myself to matters having to do with the problem of recognition. The logistic problem deserves much more extended treatment than is possible here.

Controlled Sampling: The Following Phases

The sampling procedures that will be developed below are dependent upon a multidimensional model of patterning of materials and facilities on the surface of an occupation. From the assumptions stated by Binford (1972) quoted above and others (Freeman 1973; Isaac 1971) I propose that the archaeological context of a site or a component of a site can be empirically represented as a set of components, which are in effect aggregate activity areas. Each of these areas according to Schiffer's representation of the behavioral-archaeological-geological transformational process is defined as a distinct and separable combination of aggregates. These aggregates can further be represented as vectors in a matrix that has the additional capacity of representing either the locations of the cultural components or the vector components that identify the vector. Hence the locational contexts of disposal patterns in a stratified multicomponent site can be represented by a three- or four-dimensional matrix depending on whether occupation alone or occupations and locations are recorded. At least one of the dimensions of the matrix contains the observed characteristics which can be used to extract aggregate activity areas over a set of superimposed settlements and even locations within settlements. These activity areas are members of the total set of activity patterns that contrast in at least one characteristic. Since cultural, archaeological and even geological contexts are represented in the collection of vectors from a site, the population of characteristics that can differentiate an activity set is potentially large. Hence grouping criteria have to be developed to avoid the extreme case in which every collecting unit is a unique vector. However, it is not necessary to be able to identify the components in every vector since the sampling procedure depends on grouping of collecting units into aggregate activity areas irrespective of the problem of identification of their vector components. If identification is required to simplify the number of members in the set of activities, then priority should be placed on simplifying or eliminating geological context in order to clearly expose cultural and archaeological behavior.

The sampling procedure is based on experience with the problems of excavation of a large, deep, stratified site in south-central Illinois – the Koster site (Houart 1971). This is an extensive open-air site along the margin of the Illinois River Valley trench that contains the record of at least 12 occupational layers separated by sterile layers. The strata are distributed through more than 30 feet of deposits in a tract that includes a minimum of 1 1/2 acres (Brown and Struever 1973). The layer-cake stratigraphy at the site constitutes a useful laboratory for the investigation of sampling problems. It is the experience of Stuart Struever, Bruce MacMillan, David Asch, and specialists associated with the project that has brought us face to face with the exigencies of deep-site sampling. Out of our experience a data processing system has evolved that has attempted to manage the materials and observations flowing from the excavation for purposes of on-site decision making (Brown and Struever 1973; Brown and Werner n.d.). Our decisions as to where to excavate and where not to are predicated on a sampling rationale that is outlined below.

The characteristics used to code collecting units as a step to discovering aggregate activity areas are classes of material that include both recognizable artifacts and the material by-products in the artifact processing and life-maintenance systems that Schiffer (1972) labels as refuse. These material debris classes are sufficiently common to be expected in every collecting unit that contained occupation. The most common materials were limestone fragments and chert artifacts and debris. They consisted of limestone weight, chert weight, animal bone weight and counts, and the weights and counts of other debris. Artifacts as a distinct class were not counted because they exist in very low densities in each of the occupations and are not easily identified in the field. Nor do they qualify by being sufficiently common to be found in all units of occupation. In richer sites, artifact classes alone are very useful in defining activity areas, but their utility in sampling is a direct function of the ease of sorting and identification. This limited utility is due to the fact that activity-oriented sampling necessitates quick measures of aggregate activity area variability.

Reliance on debris classes to provide the measures of activity variations rests on a more basic consideration than expediency. First, debris deposition is a simpler process than artifact deposition since the former is more often a product of a single act than is artifact deposition. Secondly, Binford (n.d.) has shown that artifacts are frequently curated, and for the most part are conserved and thereby excluded from the archaeological record, in direct proportion to their use and importance. Hence artifacts can be relatively poor indicators of the primary activity carried on in the area of their depositional context. Debris, on the other hand, is less often tampered with, especially in the smaller size range. Hence, debris will be more reliably a direct reflection of the activity responsible for the depositional record. Moreover, those materials that are connected to the activities pertaining to the most common and ubiquitous energy transfers (burning, digging, shelter construction) and to the production, use, and disposal of common materials have potentially the best discriminable characteristics in defining patterning in a human settlement (cf. Binford and others 1970).

After the different contrast sets are labeled, the sampling strategy becomes one of maximizing the number of similar aggregate activity areas among all occupation layers. It depends for its success on the speed and ease with which the observations on debris classes and other indicators can be made and processed during the excavation. For this reason the sampling procedure advanced here is dependent on computerization.

After observations and collections have been processed on the basis of the first-order sampling in this multiphase strategy, we are in a position to evaluate the degree to which the target sample has been achieved. During excavation, a running assessment can be kept for all occupations. Since it cannot be expected that empirically discovered activity locations should conform to or be congruent with first-order sampling expectations, an assessment of the degree of comparability between occupations during the field excavation program is necessary to define a second-order sample, exploiting unexpected results in all strata. In other words, the second-order sampling is basically opportunistic. The role of the admittedly preliminary first-order sample strata is to set up *expectations* that can be compared to the actual observations and used to define second-order sample strata based on the departures of observed from expected.

The classification procedure itself need not be restricted to any particular statistical treatment. There are several possibilities. Analysis of residuals of least squares approximations is sufficient to recover concentrations of materials that are independent of the intensity of activity. It would be expected that surpluses and deficits of particular materials would covary with feature types in each of the layers, and together the two in poorly structured sites would yield the best indication of aggregate activity areas. An examination of variability between several layers could be pursued with an analysis of covariance. More directly cluster analysis and factor analysis are potentially fruitful techniques for classification over several layers at a time. Factor analysis is especially capable of extracting common aggregate activity areas over a set of layers while eliminating character redundancy (Benfer 1972) but discovering multifactor areas (Binford and Binford 1966; Binford 1972). Other work using factor analysis is represented by Freeman for simple sites (1973) and by Hill (1970) for sites partitioned by formal facilities (e.g., masonry).

It is one matter to be able to assess the first-order sampling after the excavation is completed and be powerless to change the sample, and quite another to be able to use an assessment to plan a second-order sampling while the excavations are in progress. In fact, the sampling potential of the strategy described here is dependent upon rapid assessment of the results of the first-order sample. For this reason the observations chosen as group defining characteristics should be easily acquired and processed and minimally efficient in number.

CONCLUSIONS

One of the difficulties that traditional sampling strategies have in their search for obvious formally defined features is that they are dependent upon intuitive search procedures. In fact, the strategy that searches for obvious features rarely is successful. In the case of Archaic sites in the midwestern U.S. one cannot expect to find clear-cut formally distinct features. The example of the Koster site is a case in point. Here the formal distinctions among features are relatively small in magnitude, even in the instance of two relatively rich occupations (Horizons 6 and 8) which are densely filled with features. Upon detailed inspection some of the features in both horizons have been formed to be house plans. In sites such as Koster it is apparent that a sampling program must make use of the large amount of data that is not incorporated in obvious, formally distinct features.

The problem of deep-site sampling has been framed in terms of the need for discovering a procedure that allows repeated sampling under the control of shifting sampling criteria. The operationalizing of sampling strata identification entails a classification of empirically recovered evidence of activities for each layer in order to search for sets of activities held in common with as many layers as possible.

The general procedures outlined above are (1) the collecting of information relevant to the number, depth and extent of the subsurface archaeological zones within the site limits; (2) the creation of a first-order sample stratification of the site sample space; (3) the excavation of the set of sample excavation units; (4) the classification of sample units for each layer to recover activity categories held in common among the set of layers; and (5) the expansion of excavation as a result of creating a second-order sample to improve on the representation of activity types in each layer.

10. On Sample Size Problems and the Uses of Nonprobabilistic Sampling

David L. Asch

David Asch (M.A., University of Chicago, 1971) has had specialized interests in the quantitative recovery and analysis of cultural ecological data pertaining to prehistoric demography in the Eastern Woodlands. In addition to being a junior author of *Paleoethnobotany of the Koster Site,* he has been serving as a well-respected field consultant to the Archaeological Program of Northwestern University, simultaneously serving as Lecturer in Northwestern's Department of Anthropology.

INTRODUCTION

In bridging the gap between textbook sampling designs in statistics and the data and goals of archaeology, a number of important if prosaic problems are encountered. Indeed, Cowgill (1970: 163) has remarked that currently in archaeology "there may almost be an inverse relationship between elaboration of the formal statistical machinery and sophistication about behavioral interpretation." Sampling conducted as if one were following a cookbook recipe is likely to be inefficient and perhaps even incompatible with the research goals. Good sampling designs will be shaped by the research objectives — translated as explicitly as possible into statements about the kinds, quantities, and priorities for collection of data; they will reflect the complexities of the archaeological record which are specific to the site under investigation; and they will vary with respect to the resources and time available for conducting research.

This paper examines two problems of sampling in archaeology: (1) the adequacy of archaeological sample sizes in relation to descriptive and analytical demands; and (2) the potential and limitations of probabilistic sampling, contrasted with nonprobabilistic alternatives for sample selection.

SMALL SAMPLE PROBLEMS

Research Requirements

Concomitantly with the growth of archaeological method and theory, there has been an increasing disparity between the ability to define interesting archaeological problems and the capability of mobilizing the resources required to solve them (Struever 1968). This has occurred not only because

[170]

the archaeological relevance of more classes of material is now recognized, but also because excavated samples are typically small in relation to the new descriptive and analytical demands made of them. More and more, prehistoric cultures are investigated not merely as inventories of artifact types but as systems whose elements enter into consistently patterned relationships with one another and with the natural environment. For archaeology the crucial assertion is that

the intimate systematic articulation of localities, facilities, and tools with specific tasks performed by social segments results in a structured set of spatial-formal relationships in the archaeological record (Binford 1964: 425).

That is to say, the scope for delineation of prehistoric cultural behavior is greatly enhanced by taking account of the formal and spatial variability of cultural remains and their formal and spatial organization.

Much larger samples are required to document the diversity and organization of cultural materials reliably than to determine their central tendencies. A few examples will suffice to illustrate the magnitude of the sampling problem. First, consider the value of large artifact samples. Not only can they give more reliable estimates of population statistics, but they also yield information not even approximately attainable from small samples. A study of sherds decorated by the same stamp impression (identified by defects in the impression) could be used to assess a minimum level of variability present in a pottery assemblage over a short time span. But in order to sample adequately this subpopulation of sherds, it might be necessary to recover virtually all of the sherds from a site. The value of very large samples of archaeological fauna is illustrated by a recent report on animal utilization at the Apple Creek site located in the lower Illinois River Valley (Parmalee, Paloumpis, and Wilson 1972). The age distribution of deer (ascertained from the stage of tooth eruption and degree of tooth wear in mandibles) can be used as evidence for seasonality in the occupation of a village. However, deer mandibles generally constitute a very small fraction of a faunal assemblage, and at Apple Creek only 58 complete enough for aging were found from among 26,600 excavated mammal bones. Even this sample is marginal since accurate estimates of the proportion of mandibles belonging to different age classes are required. Excluding scales, nearly 100,000 fish bones were excavated at Apple Creek; of this number only 1,756 could be determined to species level. From measurements of bone size for this subset, the size distributions of the catch of different species were inferred. Bones of many species ranged from those of the youngest to the oldest of fish. This pattern is inconsistent with the distributions expected for hook-and-line fishing, spearing, or netting but is explicable as a harvest of entire fish populations from shallow backwater lakes that were drained or which dried up during the summer.

The spatial attributes of archaeological remains may be studied at many scales, ranging from the distribution of materials in a regional population of sites down to the plotting of nearest neighbor statistics for artifacts on living floors. Artifact populations have spatial dimensions not only in the distribution of specific kinds of items but also in the joint variation of artifact classes. The adequacy of a sample of cultural materials must therefore be judged with an understanding that "populations" of spatial relations among materials are being sampled as well as the items themselves. Each test pit at a site is a unit sample of spatial relationships within which the frequencies of various items may be regarded as attributes of the test pits. Thus, for instance, while Meighan (1961: 21) suggests that 1000 pieces each of different materials such as bone, shell, and plant remains is an acceptable sample size, an adequate sample of test pits is likely to result in collection of far more than this number. And since one is usually concerned with the covariability of many subclasses rather than of a few broad categories such as bone, shell, and plant remains, the population of spatial relationships among subclasses will be a more critical determinant of the adequacy of a sample than the broad categories themselves. Sampling requirements are multiplied if, in investigating internal diversity of a site, each activity area and each living surface is treated as a separate population.

Cultural features such as storage pits, hearths, and house floors also serve as units for spatial analysis, and just as formal analysis of artifact classes often requires large samples of artifacts, so also are large samples of features required to establish and to investigate feature types. There will be special interest in features with highly structured contents, which give the best clues to their prehistoric function. The distribution of perishable materials such as bone and carbonized plant remains is often skewed so that a small percentage of features contains a large percentage of these materials. For example, at Loy, another site in the lower Illinois Valley region, the 10 percent of flotation units from features with the highest density of plant remains accounted for more than 40 percent of the total quantity of plant remains in the feature samples (N. Asch, personal communication). More spectacularly, more than 45 percent of the deer bone in 160 Loy site features (house floors excluded) occurred in just six features, and two thirds of all features contained no deer bone at all (K. Farnsworth and R. Rawlins, personal communication). Statistical manipulations of skewed distributions are unreliable even if many units are sampled unless a reasonably large subsample of the infrequent high-density units is taken.

Populations of features also exhibit a spatial structure. There should be patterning in the locations of hearths, houses, pits and classes of artifacts, and food remains at a site, and large areas must be excavated to expose it.

One is drawn to the conclusion therefore that, short of complete and meticulous dissection of sites, no single level of sampling can be adequate for the range of potential archaeological problems. Sites become inaccessible or are destroyed today at a discouraging rate by new roads, reservoirs, homes, industries, and agricultural practices. Thus, for every archaeologist to follow a microscopic program of data recovery would be to doom count-less sites to unrecorded destruction. In other words, for a fixed level of resources, one reduces sample size problems at the level of single sites at the cost of compounding them at the regional level. Site destruction is particularly serious for problems relating to regional settlement structure, for which one samples not just the sites but their relationships with each other as well.

At the other extreme is field research which in the excavation process itself is highly destructive. For example, sampling the population of features from a site and delineating their spatial relationships requires exposure of large areas, but in many instances this is economically feasible only if power equipment is used to strip off midden until a living surface is discerned or pits are observed intruding into sterile soil. Methods that scrape away large quantities of data cannot be condemned for this reason alone if there is no realistic alternative for gaining the information. Every research program involves destruction or loss of data either implicitly or explicitly. Thus, since no absolute criterion exists for judging the adequacy of archaeological samples, a sampling strategy must be evaluated in terms of its appropriateness for solving a particular set of problems. Ultimately, the quality of the problems themselves must come under review.

To state the problem in another way: No one expects a sociologist or historian to collect data about a community which will reveal all that can be known about it. Not only is the necessary quantity too vast but also in the very process of gaining some kinds of information one forecloses the opportunity to collect other kinds. An archaeologist is a social scientist who studies extinct communities. Less information is accessible to him than to a sociologist, but far more exists than was suspected a few years ago.

More explicit and narrow problem orientation is an important means of limiting data requirements, but it cannot be recommended unreservedly. Three opposing considerations are mentioned below. First, over the long run, research strategy developed for a cluster of problems rather than for a sequence of isolated projects may reduce the cost and increase the efficiency of research. Second, most nontrivial problems require many kinds of evidence for solution, especially because tests of archaeological hypotheses are often indirect and weak. Moreover, multiple alternative hypotheses commonly increase data requirements. Third, good contextual information in nonexperimental, explanatory research provides a measure of protection against spurious imputation of causation to observed correlations. In comparison with experimental research, archaeological excavation for analytical purposes is a dubious undertaking, even when it is conducted in a manner which permits objective descriptions in accordance with sampling theory. Many statisticians have low confidence in any explanatory research conducted without experimental controls, as evidenced in the quote from Brownlee:

The justification sometimes advanced that a multiple regression analysis of observational [nonexperimental] data can be relied upon if there is adequate theoretical background is utterly specious and disregards the unlimited capability of the human intellect for producing plausible explanations by the carload lot (Brownlee 1965: 454).

If one adhered strictly to this advice, all attempts at explaining excavated data would cease. Even so, it must not be dismissed lightly. Objective interpretation of experiments is possible because the effects of extraneous variables may be accounted for by exercising control over them or because their effects may be rigorously averaged out by randomizing the explanatory variables (i.e., the independent and dependent variables that are the object of research) with respect to them (Kish 1965: 594). In contrast, the validity of interpretations based on nonexperimental investigations is highly dependent upon the skill of the investigator in identifying and allowing for biases introduced by extraneous variables. In such research the inherent subjective aspect can be reduced but not eliminated by providing better contextual information (Kish 1965: 593–597; Moser and Kalton 1971: 226–230).

Levels of Reliability:
Some Archaeological Examples

The problem of small sample size confronts not only the archaeologist with the ambition of "sampling everything." Some illustrations of the reliability of estimates based on probability sampling will be introduced as evidence of its pervasiveness. They are based on results of excavations at the Macoupin site (Jersey County, Illinois) in 1968, directed by Stuart Struever and Frank Rackerby and for which I designed a sampling procedure. In the probabilistic sampling phase 155 test pits (2 1/2-ft. × 5-ft. rectangles) were excavated—more than the amount of excavation achieved in most archaeological programs. They were divided among 24 horizontal sampling strata (with the sampling intensity permitted to vary between strata).

Consider the problem of estimating the total number of sherds at the site by the product $N\bar{x}$, where $\bar{x}$ is the sample mean weighted to form a combined estimate for the entire population of sampling units and $N = 18,592$ is the number of 2 1/2-ft. × 5-ft. units required for complete excavation of the site. The value of $\bar{x}$ was 50.68 sherds/unit with a standard error of 3.36. Thus the estimated number of sherds at Macoupin site is 942,179 with a standard error of $N \cdot se(\bar{x}) = 62,483$. The (two-sided) 95% confidence limits for the total are 818,000 to 1,066,000 sherds. While this range is sufficiently narrow for most uses, it seemed surprising that a sample of this magnitude did not give better reliability. (The sampling design of disproportionate stratification is not responsible for the rather large standard error, since it is estimated—using Cochran [1963: 98–99]—that a simple random sample of 155 excavation units would have yielded a much larger standard error of 5.00 and that a design of proportionate stratification would have marginally reduced the standard error from 3.36 to 3.30.)

In Table 10.1, estimated sherd frequencies are given for each stratum. The confidence limits are so wide that meaningful comparisons are possible only for strata with the lowest and highest densities and for a few of the larger spatial units of archaeological interest (see tabulations for combinations of strata at bottom of Table 10.1).

Very good estimates had been expected for the Macoupin sherd counts. Pottery is plentiful and widely dispersed across the site, and the sherds from a single vessel are generally distributed over a substantial area. One therefore expects that small sampling strata will be quite homogeneous, a characteristic which contributes to the reliability of sample estimates. Furthermore, on a shallow site like Macoupin, sherd densities at the surface can be, and were, employed in constructing more homogeneous strata.

Results for many other populations at Macoupin are poorer. Some populations are more patchy than sherds, and the sampling strata are less likely to be in alignment with their density distributions; standard errors for statistics of infrequently occurring items commonly are large in proportion to the means. An estimate of the number of features at the site, for example, is highly unreliable. No information about spatial variation in feature density was available when the Macoupin sampling strata were constructed. The 155 excavation units of the probability sample intersected 44 features. Of these only 25 had 50 percent or more of their volume within the test units. Weighting for features fractionally represented in the sample, an estimated .0898 feature per 2 1/2-ft. × 5-ft. grid unit is obtained, or 1669 throughout the entire site. The standard error of the estimate is 466, which gives a 95 percent (two-sided) confidence interval of 751 to 2584 features in all. With a range this large, it is obvious that within-site density comparisons will be meaningless.

Influence of Sample Size and Sampling Fraction on Reliability

Do the poor results relate to the small sampling fraction (defining sampling fraction, f, as the percentage of area excavated) which varied between .16 and 3.9 percent within strata and was an average of .83 percent for the entire site? To answer this it is necessary to examine the formula for standard error of descriptive statistics. For the sake of simplicity, the formula pertaining to simple random samples (without replacement) of excavation units is used:

$$se(\bar{x}) = \sqrt{1 - f}\, s_x / \sqrt{n},$$

where n is the number of units excavated, $\bar{x}$ the sample mean for a variable, and s_x the sample standard deviation between units. The expected value of s_x is independent of sample size, but both $\sqrt{1 - f}$ (termed the "finite population correction factor" or "fpc") and $1/\sqrt{n}$ become smaller as excavations increase. Suppose that the area excavated is quadrupled from 1 percent to 4 percent. Then the fpc decreases only from $\sqrt{1 - .01} = .9950$ to $\sqrt{1 - .04} = .9798$. For sampling fractions less than 20 percent of the site a good approximation is that

$$\sqrt{1 - f} \doteq 1 - 1/2f.$$

Even when one half of the site is excavated $\sqrt{1 - f}$ decreases but modestly to .7071, and 75 percent must be excavated for it to decline to .5. Of course if the entire site is excavated (f = 1), the fpc decreases to zero, meaning that the value of a statistic is obtained without error. These remarks apply only to descriptive statistics. For analytical problems, which are directed toward the underlying causes of the observed statistics, use of the fpc is not appropriate (Deming 1950: 147–261); i.e.,

$$se(\bar{x}) = s_x / \sqrt{n}.$$

For most excavations, percentage of site excavated has little significance

TABLE 10.1

Levels of Reliability for Estimates of Sherd Densities at the Macoupin Site

Sampling Stratum	Area of Stratum (sq. ft.)	Sample Size	Mean Number of Sherds per 2 1/2' × 5' Ex. Unit	Standard Error	95 Percent (Two-sided) Confidence Limits	
					Lower Bound	Upper Bound
1	80,000	10	5.60	2.26	.49	10.71
2	18,000	7	19.57	6.54	3.57	35.58
3a	1,600	5	55.00	13.71	16.95	93.05
3b	7,200	6	27.67	4.15	17.00	38.33
4	4,400	4	60.25	26.80	-25.03	145.53
5	6,800	5	33.00	4.45	20.64	45.36
6	4,800	7	93.86	19.82	47.36	144.36
7	4,400	7	98.71	18.16	54.28	143.15
8	4,000	7	81.71	12.58	50.93	112.50
9	3,600	8	95.75	13.57	63.73	127.77
10	3,600	8	135.37	16.85	95.53	175.22
11	14,800	3	32.33	23.37	-68.22	132.89
12	6,800	4	74.50	28.09	-14.87	163.87
13	4,400	2	141.50	97.22	-1093.81	1376.81
14	4,400	6	146.17	31.38	65.48	226.85
15	6,400	8	128.38	16.53	89.27	167.48
16	10,000	10	96.00	16.96	57.64	134.36

17	2,800	6	98.17	39.66	-3.81	200.14
18	2,800	7	157.00	24.24	97.69	216.31
19	10,000	3	27.00	13.29	-30.19	84.19
20	6,800	13	114.62	10.96	90.74	138.49
21	7,200	9	126.56	24.20	70.74	182.37
22	7,600	4	83.25	15.29	34.59	131.91
23	10,000	6	80.67	20.28	28.54	132.80
1-23	Entire site	155	50.68	3.36	44.02	57.33
2-10	W ridge	64	54.49	3.98	46.46	62.52
9-10	N end	16	115.56	10.81	92.38	138.74
4,6-8	S end	25	84.45	10.14	63.36	105.55
2-3b,5	Periphery	23	25.71	3.78	17.79	33.63
11-23	E ridge	81	86.67	7.70	71.30	102.04
18,20	N end	20	126.98	10.50	104.92	149.03
16-17,22-23	Center	26	87.97	10.17	66.86	109.07
12,14-15,21	S end	27	116.23	12.57	90.23	142.23
11,13,19	Periphery	8	46.96	19.38	-2.87	96.79

per se for sample reliability. What is important is the number of units sampled, n. To illustrate, for samples of 50 and 200 units from a site, the value of $1/\sqrt{n}$ is smaller by 50 percent in the large sample; and in general: to halve the error one must quadruple sample size. Thus, even if f remains very small, reliable statistics may be obtained for a large site provided that the number of units excavated, n, is large. For a variable having the same standard deviation s_x at each of two sites, excavation of the same area at both will give nearly identical error terms even if the sites differ greatly in size.

Note that reduction of standard error becomes increasingly costly as n increases since the denominator of $\sqrt{1-f}\, s_x/\sqrt{n}$ contains the *square root* of sample size; e.g., at Macoupin the sample of 155 units achieves only about twice the reliability that could have been obtained with 40 units.

Reliability for Samples of Subareas

As Table 10.1 illustrates, the reliability of statistics for subareas is generally much poorer than for the entire population even when within-stratum sampling fractions exceed the sampling fraction for the entire site. This is because standard errors are largely a function of sample size, n, rather than sampling fraction, f. If a subarea is as heterogeneous as the site as a whole with respect to a particular population and if a uniform sampling fraction is maintained throughout the site, then the difference in standard errors of the mean between the smaller domain and the whole is attributable entirely to the influence of the factor $1/\sqrt{n}$—e.g., the standard error of the mean for a partition consisting of $1/10$ of the site by area will be $\sqrt{10} = 3.16$ times the size of the standard error for the whole-site estimator. Ordinarily, sampling strata are more homogeneous than the site as a whole, so that the within-stratum standard deviations for the subpopulations are less than the standard deviation for the entire site. But a *stratified* random sample takes advantage of within-stratum homogeneity to reduce standard errors of whole-site estimates, and consequently the effects of smaller sample sizes for subareas usually remain at the order of magnitude suggested above.

The statement that adequacy of sampling is more dependent on sample size than on sampling fraction can be very misleading. Ordinarily, it is true for whole-site estimates. However, equal sample sizes for two sites do not imply equal levels of information in all respects. Consider two sites A and B having areas of .1 and 1.0 acres, respectively, with the same internal heterogeneity per unit area. Let seventy 2 1/2-ft. × 5-ft. test units be selected by simple random sampling from each, i.e., $f_A = 20$ percent of Site A and $f_B = 2$ percent of Site B. Standard errors for the whole site estimates differ negligibly:

$$\frac{se(\bar{x}_A)}{se(\bar{x}_B)} = \frac{\sqrt{1-f_A}\, s_{xA}/\sqrt{n_A}}{\sqrt{1-f_B}\, s_{xB}/\sqrt{n_B}} \doteq \frac{\sqrt{1-.02}}{\sqrt{1-.2}} = .9035.$$

On the average, however, a subregion H within the smaller site contains 10 times as many excavation units as a region K of equal area in the larger site ($n_{hA} = 10n_{kB}$), and the ratio of standard errors for the regions is on the order of

$$\frac{se(\bar{x}_{hA})}{se(\bar{x}_{hB})} = \frac{\sqrt{1-f_A}\ s_{hxA}/\sqrt{n_{hA}}}{\sqrt{1-f_B}\ s_{kxB}/\sqrt{n_{kB}}} \doteq \frac{\sqrt{1-.02}/\sqrt{10n_{kB}}}{\sqrt{1-.2}/\ \sqrt{n_{kB}}} = .2857.$$

To summarize, equal sample sizes among sites having similar heterogeneity per unit area will give whole site statistics whose standard errors differ only in the value of the factor $\sqrt{1-f}$. For small and moderate sampling fractions, this factor varies negligibly. Equal intensities of excavation give roughly equal levels of reliability even when sites vary widely in size. Under the same conditions, however, standard errors for domains of equal area within these sites differ in proportion to the respective values of $1/\sqrt{f}$ or equivalently, in proportion to $\sqrt{\text{total site area}}$. This suggests that equal amounts of excavation do not give equally informative and reliable information about internal site variability when sites differ in size. To achieve equality in this respect, larger sites require larger samples.

Clustering Effects

Another reason why archaeological samples are often statistically small relates to the necessity of using a sampling unit consisting not of the artifacts themselves but rather of a volume of earth in which they are contained. Consequently, excavation of artifact populations is a case of cluster sampling.

In general, locations in a site close to one another are more similar than distant ones. For instance, the two halves of a 5-ft. × 5-ft. excavation are normally more similar than those of two randomly selected 2 1/2-ft. × 5-ft. units — i.e., some of the information from the larger unit is redundant. A simple random sample of 5-ft. × 5-ft. units therefore yields less reliable statistics than a simple random sample of twice as many smaller test pits. Continuing with the logic, the best sampling unit of all — measured in terms of information content about artifact populations per unit area — is a point sample.

For cluster sampling, statisticians distinguish between an "effective sample size" of items and the actual sample size. Effective size is the number of elements (artifacts) that would have to be selected by simple random sampling of elements (rather than excavation units) in order to give reliability equal to that of the cluster sample. For example, in Sampling Stratum #10 at the Macoupin site eight 2 1/2-ft. × 5-ft. units yielded 1,083 sherds of which 90 belong to the White Hall series (see Table 10.2). Formulae for cluster sampling (Kish 1965) predict that the true proportion of White Hall sherds in the stratum is 8.31 percent, with a standard error of 2.51 percent. Now, suppose it were possible to take a simple random sample of *sherds* from the stratum. The standard error of a proportion p obtained in a simple random selection (neglecting the finite population correction factor) is

$$se(p) = \sqrt{p(1-p)/(n-1)},$$

TABLE 10.2

**White Hall Series Sherds
Excavated from Sampling Stratum #10
at the Macoupin Site in the
Probabilistic Sampling Phase**

Excavation Unit #	Number of Sherds	Number of White Hall Series Sherds
1	187	4
2	163	30
3	127	22
4	68	9
5	170	11
6	93	2
7	86	2
8	189	10
	$\Sigma = 1083$	$\Sigma = 90$

or, solving for n,

$$n = \frac{p(1 - p)}{var(p)} + 1.$$

If the true proportion of White Hall sherds is in fact 8.31 percent, then a simple random sample of

$$n = .0831(.9169)/(.0251)^2 + 1 = 122$$

sherds would have given a standard error equal to that of the cluster sample; i.e., the actual cluster sample size is 9.00 times the effective sample size.

This "design effect" depends in part on the variable being sampled, and may even vary for different characteristics of the same class of material. For example, if the proportions of different White Hall pottery decorations are associated with spatially differentiated social groups at a site, then they are likely to have large design effects as a consequence. A technical characteristic such as sherd thickness might well vary independently of location, however, in which case cluster sampling would be as efficient as simple random sampling.

NONPROBABILISTIC SAMPLING TECHNIQUES IN ARCHAEOLOGY

Potential and Limitations of Probability Sampling

Random sampling is widely regarded as the scientific sampling procedure par excellence. However, for several reasons archaeologists use it as just one in a repertoire of sampling techniques. Binford (1964) and Struever

(1968), for instance, propose multiphase sampling designs in which different sampling procedures, including probability sampling, complement each other. The second part of this paper will discuss the relative merits of probabilistic and nonprobabilistic techniques.

Statisticians prefer the use of probabilistic sampling (1) because population characteristics can be estimated with little or no bias (in statistical parlance, a sample estimator of a population statistic is unbiased if its expected value equals that of the population statistic); (2) because measurable (i.e., objective) estimates of the reliability of sample statistics can be made; (3) because if the entire target population is accessible, the reliability of estimates can be controlled at any desired level by taking a sufficiently large sample.

It should be emphasized that probability sampling was developed to give statistics pertaining to *aggregates* of elements—e.g., for central tendencies and for measures of dispersion such as standard deviation, which characterize no element in particular but refer to the population as a whole. Single units selected in a sample have no significance whatsoever from the probabilistic viewpoint.

The statistical theory of sampling is oriented primarily toward descriptive statistics (rather than for analytical, explanatory statistics)—in particular for estimates of central tendencies of finite populations such as means, percentages, ratios, and aggregates—and also for the simple analytical statistic of the difference between means for two populations (Kish 1965: 582). These estimates also can be made using various nonprobabilistic designs; but they will then have indeterminate bias, and objective estimates of their reliability cannot be made. (Systematic unaligned sampling designs—in which a random component is added to a systematic selection procedure—give unbiased statistics and permit statements of reliability which usually *underestimate* the true level of confidence; see Cochran 1963.) In principle, no other sampling methods have comparable potential for objectivity; i.e., they cannot, to a similar extent, detach the theories, techniques, and reputation of the observer from the validity of descriptive statistics.

In archaeology, probability samples give several useful kinds of estimates, including: (a) densities of artifact populations per unit surface area or per unit volume; (b) the size of artifact populations at a site; (c) ratios of frequencies between items; (d) percentages of subclasses and types; and (e) frequencies for discrete attributes of cultural materials and the mean and distribution of metrical attributes of materials. All of these statistics may be computed for populations within an entire site, within its subareas, and within vertical levels. Quantitative comparisons of a variable between different areas of a site or between sites can also be made, as can measures of covariability in the distribution of two or more classes of cultural material.

Although probability samples are designed to provide estimates of population statistics with objectively estimated levels of reliability, it may be misleading to regard this as the primary reason probability sampling is used in archaeology. Archaeologists commonly investigate behavioral implications of the contents and structure of one or a few nearby sampling units, and seldom does this lead to probabilistic statements about the percentage of excavation units with evidence of a particular kind of behavior. Probabilistic and systematic samples disperse excavation through the site giving some chance of selection to every location. Thus, if locations for the performance of various prehistoric activities were spatially differentiated, these strategies afford protection against a spatially unrepresentative sample which gives a highly skewed picture of the range of cultural behavior at the site. Hill (1967: 150), for example, states: "The purpose of random sampling is primarily to show the excavator what kind of things will likely be found (spatial distribution)."

Sampling Spatial Structure

Serious difficulties arise when probability techniques are used to sample the spatial structure of sites. Some of the more promising applications of random methods in this regard are:

(1) Comparing levels in vertically stratified sites.
(2) Comparing horizontal sampling strata. (This will often be limited by small within-stratum sample sizes.)
(3) Investigating measurable or countable spatial relationships which can be defined in element-population terms and which occur on a scale small enough to be observed within a sampling unit; e.g., nearest neighbor distances between sherds.
(4) Investigating the covariation of characteristics of the spatial sampling units (test pits and features), which may be regarded as elements of a population of excavation units—e.g., the ratio of cores to secondary chipping debris considered as an attribute of test pits of a given size and shape.
(5) Determining behavioral implications of the spatial patterning of materials within an excavation unit.
(6) Constructing contour maps of the densities, ratios, etc. of materials across the site.

The first two applications involve standard uses of probabilistic methods. In the third, a fundamental violation of probabilistic sampling requirements occurs because spatial relationships extending outside excavation units are unobservable. Consequently, they are systematically undercounted, and there is bias in favor of observing relationships with smaller spatial dimensions. The problem is minimized if excavation units are very large relative to the size of the spatial relationship. Observations can be brought within the pale of sampling theory, albeit expediently, by redefining the target population to consist only of those relationships lying entirely within the units of a sampling grid.

Applications of the fourth kind are concerned with differences in the contents of spatial sampling units, but in contrast with Application 5, they do not refer to the spatial arrangement of this variability across the site. Sampling theory is not rigorously developed to take account of intercorrelations among spatial units due to their locations with respect to one another. One

important objective of these investigations is to discriminate sets of artifact and debris classes which occur in covarying frequencies as a result of
their association with a specific prehistoric activity. Obviously, a sampling
scheme that gives every unit an equal chance of selection is more likely to
cover the range of activities and to disclose instances in which they occur
in contrastive frequencies than a single trench or block excavation. However, a representative sample (i.e., one with the same selection probability
for all units) is not necessarily the most efficient means of covering this
range. For instance, one might sample a localized activity area more
intensively than its spatial extent would dictate, particularly if relatively
few units can be excavated. It may be desirable to dig fewer but larger units
in low density areas in order to increase the per unit yield of cultural material
and thus to obtain more stable within-unit relative frequencies for the
different kinds of cultural material. Variable selection probabilities for
excavation units may be achieved by a stratified design with constant within-
stratum selection probabilities but with sampling fractions that vary from
one stratum to another. Hence, objective descriptive statistics can still be
obtained. Such designs are incompatible, however, with the rigorous application of statistical theory for analytical purposes because most analytical
statistics rest upon the assumption of simple random sampling (Kish 1965:
582–587).

In the fifth and sixth applications rigorous use of probability sampling
theory is abandoned altogether, since they do not involve inferences about
quantitative characteristics of *populations*. Probabilistic selection is irrelevant to the study of variability within a single sampling unit. However, as
mentioned previously, the resulting dispersion of test units still provides
a sample which collectively gives information about a wide range of spatially
segregated activities. Mapping is just one of many kinds of interpolation
between sampling units which, in presuming that the units are representative
of the region immediately surrounding them, involves nonprobabilistic
reasoning – that is to say, reasoning whose reliability cannot be objectively
assessed. For instance, in observing that several test pits near each other all
contain more than the average number of features, an archaeologist – without
reliance on sampling theory, but probably correctly – will infer the existence
of a high feature density in the vicinity of the test pits. From the point of
view of sampling theory, single excavation units have no statistical significance. Meaning inheres only in the aggregate sample from formally defined
populations or subpopulations. This restriction cannot be circumvented
legitimately by using a sample both to partition the site into homogeneous
subregions on the basis of postulated intercorrelations between spatially
proximal locations and to characterize those subregions (Kish 1965: 487).

A basic difficulty of using probabilistic techniques to sample spatial structure is that the structure must be specified in element-population terms.
Following von Bertalanffy (1968: 54–55), I recognize three kinds of properties of complexes of elements: (1) their number; (2) their species, or individual, characteristics; (3) the relations of elements. The elements of a
statistical population have only the first two properties, or, if relations
between them exist, they are ignored. Consequently, in order to sample

relations probabilistically, the units of the universe under investigation must be redefined so that properties of the third kind become properties of "super-elements" in a new population. For example, for a population of artifacts, the joint spatial variability of chert cores and secondary chipping debris is a relational property and therefore is not amenable to investigation by a simple random sample of artifacts (if such were possible); but for a sample of excavation units, at least part of that spatial variation becomes a species property of test pits. The more organized the system the more difficult it becomes to define a population of sampling units in which all of the significant relationships become species properties. This is evident in particular for archaeological sites which have escaped the disorganization that results from repeated, superimposed prehistoric activities. For instance, what would be the elements and how could one sample a Hopewell burial mound in order to reconstruct the sequence of mortuary activities? How could one define and sample a series of statistical populations at a Paleo-Indian mammoth kill site in order to discover the butchering sequence and spatial arrangement of tasks?

For archaeological sites, two serious problems are (1) that the small, dispersed units of a probability sample cannot reduce all significant relational properties to species properties (e.g., spatial relationships which are at the same scale as the excavation units) and (2) that it may be difficult to define the elements with precision (especially their spatial dimensions) *prior* to excavation (e.g., how to formulate an a priori definition of "a house and its associated storage and cooking pits").

The task of sampling a modern town illustrates some of the problems that attend investigation of site structure by probability sampling. For certain purposes, small randomly placed excavation units would be informative. One might thereby discover a positive correlation, for instance, in the distribution of such items as forks and spoons. However, one would also be interested in sampling complete cultural units, perhaps rooms in buildings. The amount of excavation would have to be expanded to yield a statistically large sample of rooms. Furthermore, samples of clusters of rooms, i.e., buildings, would show correlations which cannot be discovered in a random sample of rooms. In addition, the archaeologist's interests extend beyond describing the typical building. To be sure, some structural details would be common to most buildings, but there would be obvious differences among them. Some building variability might reflect status differentiation in the society. Certain buildings—e.g., ceremonial centers—would be relatively rare, and the archaeologist would probably concentrate his search for such structures in selected areas of the town. The buildings themselves are components of a larger spatial structure. For example, there would be a repetitive structure of blocks, and buildings on corners of blocks might be larger and more elaborate. Finally, it would probably be discovered that building types lie in different activity areas. Only by excavating the greater part of the town could one discover most of the structural details that become obvious as larger and larger areas are exposed. Operating on a modest scale, the archaeologist would be unable to excavate areas large enough to expose many of these details. He might therefore decide to increase his sample of buildings rather than devote equal effort to the surrounding areas of lawn and highway. Or he might limit excavations to two or three apparent food-preparation activity areas of buildings, undertaking the time-consuming task of plotting the location of each artifact in order to obtain distributions that give additional information about behavior patterns.

Clearly, observation of spatial structure depends on the scale of the excavation unit (Whallon 1973). Large blocks can reveal much information about structure on a scale not provided by digging an equal area in small, dispersed test pits (e.g., the location of hearths and storage pits in relation to houses), while at the same time they can give information about small-scale relationships if adequate locational control is exercised within them. For example, it is often impossible to correlate living surfaces observed in widely spaced units. Large blocks are also better suited for many of the statistical pattern analyses utilized by ecologists and geographers (Goodall 1970: 110).

Unfortunately, if large units are sampled, the total number that can be excavated will be small — usually so few that whole-site statistical estimates will have enormous standard errors. Consequently, locating large blocks by judgment will be preferable to a probabilistic selection procedure. Bias is an attribute of selection procedures; representativeness, a characteristic of the sample itself. In unbiased probabilistic sampling there is always some risk that an unrepresentative sample will be selected, and the smaller the sample the greater the risk. For very small samples, judgment selection can provide more representative samples even though it is biased (Hendricks 1956: 12–17, Deming 1950: 23). Kish, a survey statistician, states:

If a research project must be confined to a single city of the United States, I would rather use my judgment to choose a "typical" city than select one at random. Even for a sample of 10 cities, I would rather trust my knowledge of U.S. cities than a random sample (Kish 1965: 29).

Instead of choosing a "typical" sample of blocks by judgment, one might attempt to maximize differences between them. In part, this was the procedure followed in selecting four blocks for excavation at the Macoupin site. An advantage is the assurance of sampling a large range of the variation in spatial relationships even though, from a statistical prespective, the sample is tiny. Furthermore, whole-site statistics are unlikely to be more extreme than the ranges displayed within blocks selected in this manner. At Macoupin some blocks were also placed in locations where preservation of contextual information was thought to be good.

Sampling Disturbed Populations and Their Relationships

Destruction and disturbance of cultural materials and contexts have serious consequences for the objectivity and reliability of probability sampling. The primary objective is to characterize an imperfectly preserved set of target populations and their joint relationships rather than to describe the contents of the site per se (Cowgill 1970). Target populations of cultural materials are reduced by decay, by physical destruction, or by removal by relic collectors. Populations of spatial relationships are subject to additional disturbance by natural processes, by modern human activities such as plowing, and, very, importantly, by the prehistoric occupants themselves (e.g., disturbance of midden by pit construction). Superimposition of prehistoric activities can also mask if not destroy the primary contexts of materials. On multicomponent sites the cultural affiliations of nondiagnostic materials may be undeterminable except in single component areas, in parts of the site where vertical stratigraphy exists, or in pit features. Perhaps only at the site periphery where occupational intensity is lowest will the materials and relationships resulting from a specific kind of prehistoric activity be found with little disturbance.

Given the problems of disturbance and differential preservation, a case can be made—albeit an extreme one—for abandonment of probability sampling altogether. It is rooted in the observation that much of our knowledge of prehistoric behavior is pieced together from deterministic implications of the conjunction of different kinds and quantities of cultural materials and debris in sampling units, along with the spatial arrangement of materials in these units. That is to say, a single unit may give much valid, if possibly unrepresentative, behavioral information. The potential information carried by a sampling unit varies widely in accordance with the degree of preservation of materials and contexts, and in the extreme one may argue that the reconstruction of activities performed at a site will be essentially the sum of behaviors inferred from areas with the best information. From this viewpoint, many sampling units have little to contribute to the study of prehistoric behavior, and little is lost if they are not examined; it is more important to concentrate on areas with highest information content. In effect, it is denied that representative samples of extant populations are especially valuable; rather, investigations should be oriented toward discovery of the special situations which are the keys to the past. One excavation unit located in a favorable area may be worth a hundred other units that sample materials in mediocre contexts. Furthermore, since the context for each unit varies in quality, the behavioral implications of different sampling units must be weighed against one another. Normally, those that arise from better contexts take precedence over conflicting implications from units with weaker contexts. This balancing of the information from sampling units is the antithesis of reasoning from the aggregate characteristics of samples.

From this perspective sampling should be a sifting procedure with the purpose of locating and concentrating quickly on high-yield units. That representativeness is a legitimate sampling objective need not be denied. Rather it is given lower priority than sifting; and since probability sampling is not employed, the representativeness and reliability of the sample must be evaluated informally.

Whatever one's position with respect to the argument above, it is readily seen that destruction and disturbance compromise a probability sample conducted with limited resources. The different populations and relationships that make up a site may vary widely in degree of disturbance and in the reliability of extrapolations from extant populations to their target populations. For instance, depth of storage pits is more susceptible to disturbance than width of the working edge of chert scrapers; and in a partially destroyed site the mean width of scrapers in the target population is probably more reliably extrapolated than the total number of scrapers. A sample that is obtained without prejudice from all areas of a site, disturbed or undisturbed, comes from the largest possible subset of a target population. But this approach to the ideal of sampling from an entire target population is attained at the expense of reduced sample sizes for materials with spatially variable preservation (such as bone), as well as reduction in the sample of areas with good contextual control. On the other hand, restricting excavation to select areas with the highest information return increases the likelihood of biased statistics.

One mixed strategy is first to take a nominal sample from the entire site, then to restrict sampling to favored areas. However, standard errors of statistics based upon the whole-site sample then reflect a huge contribution of uncertainty due to the tiny sampling fraction used in disturbed areas. One could perhaps make whole-site estimates more reliably (though less objectively) by disregarding the small sample from disturbed areas, estimating statistics for the remaining areas, and extrapolating these to the entire site. The advantage of the limited sample from disturbed areas would lie in the possibility of detecting major biases, if they exist, arising from extrapolation of statistics beyond the subpopulations of relatively undisturbed materials.

Some examples of nonprobabilistic strategies that concentrate on less disturbed subpopulations are listed below. (1) Scrape away the plow zone with power equipment or discard it unscreened because of damage to cultural materials and destruction of their contents. (2) On a site with a midden that varies in depth because of a variable history of soil deposition (e.g., as often occurs when soil washes onto a habitation located at the base of a hillslope), choose areas with thinner cultural deposits for preferential excavation. Often the limits of pit features which intrude into earlier midden deposits are impossible to delineate accurately because contrasts in soil color and densities of material between pit fill and midden are subtle. Where the midden is thin, features intrude largely into sterile soil and thus can be discovered and delineated easily. (3) Restrict excavation to single component areas of the site so that nondiagnostic artifacts can be attributed to a specific occupation. In vertically stratified sites, excavate where the separation of occupations is best. (4) If the site contains no single component areas, excavate pit features in preference to midden. (5) Concentrate investigations in parts of the site where occupation was short rather than in "rich" areas, in order to minimize disturbance of primary contexts.

All of the preceding tactics may be complemented with a probabilistic sampling phase.

Feedback in Sampling Designs

Typically, much of the potential and limitations of a site awaits excavation for its discovery. Thus, sampling is often called upon both for the definition of domains within the site that merit separate study and for their investigation. Archaeologists therefore usually favor a flexible research design—one which develops as a series of decisions based in part on the accumulation of information from previous stages—in which there is interaction between problem definition, data collection, time and resources, and the unfolding characteristics of the site.

However, feedback potentially conflicts with the requirements of independent choice and random location of excavation units in probabilistic designs prohibiting use of results from a random test pit to guide the positioning of subsequent units. Partitioning a site into horizontal sampling strata is an important method for creating more flexible sampling designs. This provides freedom to increase the sampling rate within the more interesting strata without violating the sampling rules. Hill (n.d: 5–6, 8) contends that although "the major criticism of the use of probability sampling in archaeology is that it is a blind, mechanical technique that obviates the archaeologist's expertise . . . this criticism results from a misunderstanding of how random sampling can be profitably employed." Stratification, he suggests, permits use of "all previous knowledge the investigator possesses." Then, "given the new evidence provided by the random sample, the archaeologist might be able to subdivide the population of units in accordance with his newly discovered structural differentiation, and . . . select further random samples of the new subdivisions separately."

The latter statement requires extensive qualification. Horizontal sampling strata may serve as domains for the study of within-site variability, provided their boundaries reflect the variability in cultural activities throughout the site. In making probabilistic statements, one may not alter stratum boundaries to exclude the data from "deviant" units. For example, *after* the sample is taken, one may not legitimately construct a culturally unmixed stratum by altering its boundaries to exclude units yielding the "wrong" sherd types. Once a probabilistic sampling phase begins strata can be reformulated only if the criteria for new boundaries are independent of information provided by the sample and of knowledge of the location of excavation units. On this subject Kish (1965: 487) emphasizes:

To avoid selection bias, a keystone of any procedure [for shifting population elements between strata] *must be a guarantee that the sorting of units into new strata is not affected by their having been initially selected.*

If the archaeologist nevertheless changes stratum boundaries on the basis of new information, his choices include (1) accepting the transformation of the design to one of judgment sampling or (2) taking entirely new samples within the reformed strata—i.e., employing a two-phase probabilistic sample. Under the second alternative, previously excavated units must be excluded from the final sample (unless they are selected again without prejudice). For some designs, weighted results from both sampling phases can still be used in calculating the whole-site sample statistics and their reliability.

A mixed strategy may also be proposed: basing whole-site probability estimates on a first-phase probabilistic sample and, for this purpose, retaining the original definition of strata. Next, establishing domains for additional investigation in accordance with the optimal boundaries suggested by excavation but without discarding units excavated in the first stage (that is to say, using judgment sampling to investigate subareas). This would lessen the problem of small sample sizes—a problem which is expected to be severe for statistics computed for partitions of the site. Its rationalization would be that gains in reliability from the larger judgment samples are thought to outweigh the costs of selection bias and subjective estimation of reliability.

It should be noted that the objectivity of a probabilistic sample is not compromised by using results from a prior nonrandom discovery phase to establish stratum boundaries, since for this task *any* information may be used. Controlled surface survey, for example, often can serve this function because it returns information at a rapid rate. In drawing stratum boundaries "neither objectivity nor regularity are needed. . . . In the entire selection procedure this is the area *par excellence* for the exercise of personal judgment . . ." (Kish 1965: 100). Sometimes the resulting strata will be more heterogeneous than desired, and segregation of domains of special interest within single strata may not be satisfactory; but statistics calculated for the random sample are nonetheless obtained objectively.

Sampling Rare and Infrequent Data

Sometimes—at the cost of possible selection bias—nonprobabilistic sampling must be used to increase the collecting rate for rare or infrequent data. Surface survey provides a prime example of such a nonprobabilistic technique (even if surface populations are sampled probabilistically) in the sense that samples are drawn from a restricted domain (surface-exposed material) of the much larger target population consisting of both surface and subsurface remains. Much information is provided efficiently about the kinds and quantities of materials and their large-scale spatial structure. At the Macoupin site no more than one sixth of the summer field season was required to conduct a complete, spatially controlled surface survey and preliminary analysis, but larger samples of many classes of artifacts were recovered during this stage of investigation than during the remainder of the field season. In the vicinity of the site and over much of its surface, densities of cultural materials were so low that only surface survey could provide enough materials for spatial and formal analyses. Defects of surface data are obvious, but they vary in importance from one site to another and with respect to the kinds of questions asked. Often a subjective analysis of the biases can still be made.

As another example, nonprobabilistic techniques may be employed to increase the sample of features. In a small test pit, feature excavation is slow and inefficient because a large proportion of features lie partially outside the arbitrary excavation unit and require its extension. In addition, excavation within the confines of a small unit can be rather unreliable: when lacking the context of soil-color differences over a large area, it is sometimes difficult even to discern feature boundaries. When feature density is low, the sample size may be greatly increased by using power equipment to strip off the midden from part of the site to a level where features are easily discerned. Since only a few large blocks can be treated in this manner, it would usually be preferable to select locations for them on the basis of judgment rather than by random sampling.

SUMMARY AND CONCLUSIONS

Small Samples

Small sample problems are pervasive in archaeological research, especially where information is required on the formal and spatial variability and organization of cultural remains. If there exists a law of diminishing returns for the number and significance of new archaeological opportunities which arise as sampling is augmented, it operates very slowly. No absolute standard for archaeological sample sizes can be established; their adequacy must therefore be evaluated in terms of the research problems set forth by the individual investigators and by the larger archaeological community.

Even when large quantities of cultural materials have been collected, levels of reliability for probability samples can be poor—particularly for statistics of subareas of a site. Discussion of factors influencing reliability included sample size, sampling fraction, and clustering due to use of spatial sampling units.

The enumeration of small sample problems in this paper is by no means comprehensive. One which was not broached concerns use of the sampling theory for normally distributed populations when the population sampled is actually nonnormal, as indeed is usually the case in archaeology (see Hanson, Hurwitz, and Madow 1953: 129–148; Kish 1965: 13–17, 410–412). The Central Limit Theorem of statistics states that sampling distributions for the mean and most other commonly used sample statistics (usually) approach normality for large samples—which permits the use of normal sampling theory. However, statistics computed from very small samples of skewed populations are not only likely to be unreliable, but estimates of the degree of reliability will also be in error.

Another small sample problem worthy of mention is that, for analytical purposes, samples from small *populations* may be inadequate even if every element is selected. The archaeological ("physical finds") population may be considered a sample from a hypothetical infinite population of possibilities, just as the results of 10 throws of a die are elements of an infinite sample space (Deming 1950: 247–252). To illustrate, suppose that the only culturally diagnostic materials from a feature located in a multicomponent site are three sherds, all attributable to one component. For many analytical purposes one requires deterministic assessments of the cultural affiliations of features. But in this case, the statistical run is so short that the possibility of disturbance and admixture of nondiagnostic materials from more than one component is difficult to exclude.

Nonprobabilistic Sampling

The theory of probability sampling was developed largely to provide descriptive statistics and objectively estimated levels of reliability for population variables. It is ideally adapted for estimating the aggregate properties of populations and subpopulations of discrete elements. In archaeology its use is often recommended because the resulting dispersal of sampling units increases chances of discovering the range of spatially restricted behavior patterns at a site. Nonprobabilistic sampling strategies still have functions in archaeological research, however, and in many respects are complementary to probabilistic selection of small excavation units. Some reasons for employing a nonprobabilistic sampling phase are (1) to investigate spatial structure; (2) to select more representative, if biased, samples when only a few sampling units can be excavated; (3) to investigate sites in which preservation of contexts varies widely; (4) to establish feedback between field data and the design employed in collecting them; and (5) to increase the collecting efficiency for rare items.

Discussion of the role of nonprobability sampling in archaeology also needs further exploration. For example, in selecting a working universe, many of the same issues of representativeness and reliability are raised. Except in the most historically oriented archaeological studies, the ultimate range of generalization will extend beyond the universe actually sampled. Thus, results from a special working universe provide a nonrandom sample from an often ill-defined general universe (Sjoberg and Nett 1968: 129–144). Due to resource limitations, intensive excavation from a single site is often assumed to provide representative information about a "site type." The case study approach is employed at the regional level as well; e.g., patterns of resource utilization documented for prehistoric cultures in the lower Illinois River Valley research universe of the Foundation for Illinois Archaeology are often extended, at least as trends if not as quantitatively replicated patterns, to other less intensively investigated regions of the Midwest. Though they are deficient in methodological rigor, such extrapolations are not for that reason alone unscientific. For instance, despite widespread use of probability sampling in sociology, randomized selection has not superseded all of the methodological functions of case analysis (Sjoberg and Nett 1968: 257–264). In chemistry, experiments with water may be replicated (a pseudo-randomizing procedure) to average out measurement error, but the water molecules are not selected randomly because the invariance of their reactions is accepted theory. When theoretical knowledge permits safe restriction of randomization requirements, greater efficiency in scientific research may often be achieved.

ACKNOWLEDGMENTS

In writing this paper I have profited from numerous discussions of sampling strategy with Stuart Struever. The Foundation for Illinois Archaeology has provided financial support for my investigation of sampling problems.

11. Sampling in the Excavation of Urban Sites: The Case at Huánuco Pampa

Craig Morris

Craig Morris (Ph.D., University of Chicago, 1967), Assistant Professor of Anthropology at Brandeis University, has held National Science Foundation and National Defense Education Act fellowships as well as membership in Phi Beta Kappa and other professional societies relevant to his major research interests in Inca civilization. Numerous papers and reviews have resulted from an active field research program in the Peruvian Andes. A National Science Foundation Senior Research Grant has been awarded for his investigations of the processes of Inca urbanism.

Sampling problems connected with the study of urban sites differ more in degree than in kind from the problems involved in smaller sites. First of all the large size of urban sites puts extremely severe demands on limited archaeological resources, and the ideal of a complete study and excavation is essentially never a realistic alternative to some kind of sampling. The proportion of the total site which can be excavated in fact is usually very small. A second characteristic of urban sites is that their internal structure is extremely complicated; the archaeologist is faced with the description and reconstruction of a large number of overlapping activity patterns. This means that internal variability is high, and the combination of large size and high variability makes it extremely difficult to approach a "representative" sample of an urban site which can even come close to portraying its vast internal complexity.

I do not feel that it is necessary for present purposes to define rigidly an "urban" site beyond the above general remarks on size and internal diversity. Many of the same problems and principles apply to any large complex site, regardless of whether it is generally agreed to fall within the domain of an urban society. While most of my general remarks apply to many, if not most, urban sites, they are based mainly on the preliminary sampling strategies employed by the Huánuco Pampa Archaeological Project in excavations in the Inca administrative center at Huánuco Pampa, about 275 km. northeast of Lima in the Peruvian central highlands. We are attempting to investigate a series of specific questions regarding the economic and political expansion of the Inca state, and the interrelationships between the state and various local populations it had recently conquered. At the same time we are trying to reconstruct, as well as the resources and the nature of the data permit, a site ethnography which will give a fairly detailed picture of activities in the city, its internal structure, and the role it played in the empire as a whole. The principal data collection procedures involve the preparation of a complete surface map and the excavation of a sample, initially fairly small, which at least in some sense tries to cover the whole city. The analytical procedures envisioned are aimed mainly at studies of association and distribution patterns of artifacts, features, and architecture which will give us the kind of activity pattern information needed to answer our primary questions.

In spite of the difficult sampling problems we have, and the inescapable fact that we must eventually deal with millions of items of information, Huánuco Pampa poses far fewer sampling problems than most urban sites. It was selected in fact because preliminary survey suggested that, given the questions we are interested in, it posed the fewest methodological problems. Its advantages include: (1) Preservation of surface architecture is unusually good. We have been able to map an estimated 80% of the city's original buildings. This map (see Fig. 11.1) not only provides information on the city's plan, architecture, and possible internal circulation patterns, it is also the basis of much of the sampling strategy for excavation. (2) The size of the site, slightly more than two and one half square kilometers, is not prohibitive for fairly intensive study. (3) Early excavations had demonstrated easily discernible association patterns between architecture, ceramics, and other aspects of the archaeological record. (4) A short occupation, estimated from historical sources at less than 75 years, makes it stratigraphically far less complex than many urban sites.

The relatively special "advantages" of Huánuco Pampa, besides making possible some of the sample stratification procedures outlined in the following sections, have modified our approach to a couple of common sampling problems which other urban site archaeologists are likely to have to face in a much more substantial way. One of these involves the sampling of the region in which a city is set. The other involves the sampling of sites with multiple components or phases. Any study which seeks to reconstruct activity patterns for relatively "synchronic" time units faces problems of chronological measurement and control which frequently are very difficult. Although we have had to cope with a very brief occupation by a small number of Europeans in parts of Huánuco Pampa, the stratigraphic situation on the whole is rather straightforward and simple because of the short occupation of the city. In the majority of urban sites the problems of identifying and separately sampling multiple components will require significantly more complicated sampling strategies than ours. [See chapter by Brown in this volume.]

Somewhat more detailed comments are in order regarding special problems encountered in the sampling of regions controlled by complex societies. (The reader will find much of the material in the regional section of this volume pertinent to urban situations.) Regional considerations are especially important in studying urban societies, since cities are probably never self-sufficient units, but participate in much larger systems.

Coping with the socio-political, economic, ecological, and large spatial dimensions of complex societies involves several special tasks in most

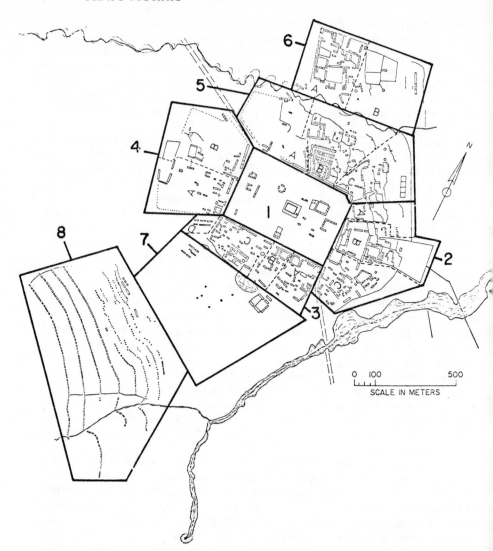

Fig. 11.1. Diagram of Huánuco Pampa showing division of the city into zones and subzones. Based on an aerial photograph; drawn in 1969.

cases. Perhaps the most important of these is that of defining the specific sustaining hinterland on which a particular urban site is dependent for its subsistence goods. The socio-political relationships between the urban center and its hinterlands should be investigated, as should the character of the exchanges in goods and/or services and the ecological diversity of the sustaining area. Second, it is important to determine if the particular urban site is part of a larger political unit containing other urban sites, and if so, what kinds of relationships exist within the larger political system. Third, what is the maximum extent to which the site's external relationships extends? Here I refer to the relatively flexible "trade" linkages, usually in raw materials and luxury goods. Direct political control is not usually implied in these cases, but they may nonetheless be vital to sustaining an urban center and explaining its rise.

All of these levels of a city's external involvement must be taken into account in most cases, but the enormous areas encompassed almost never make it possible to design systematic sampling strategies for adequate coverage – given archaeology's present resources. The broader regions and levels must not be lost sight of, however, and an archaeologist's immediate research strategy can be supplemented from past research. New research designs and sampling plans, whether in the context of a single site or a broader area, have to build upon and compensate for major gaps in what has already been done. A further source of information which is often of major value is documentary evidence. For instance in the Huánuco case much of our information on the broader political and economic system into which the site fits comes from European chroniclers, and parts of the supporting hinterlands were documented in detail (Murra 1962; Thompson 1968; Morris 1972a). Indeed the unusual quality of information on the site's political and economic context was a primary reason for its selection for intensive study. While documentary evidence frequently requires some degree of archaeological testing, on the whole archaeologists have not tended to make maximum use of available documents.

GENERAL CONSIDERATIONS
FOR EXCAVATIONAL SAMPLING

Research in archaeology is a process which requires constant feedback. Specific research strategies should be so arranged that inputs from new findings can be utilized promptly and effectively in planning further work. This is particularly important in large-scale excavation programs where new evidence and unanticipated conditions below the surface frequently require substantial revisions of original sampling plans, including sampling.

Research designs for excavations have to build in the necessary feedbacks and provide sufficient flexibility to meet new conditions, without sacrifices in methodological rigor. These requirements are met by research and sampling designs which separate the work into a number of stages, much as Redman (1973) has outlined for a somewhat different context. Periodic reviews of preliminary results and explicit arrangements for making modifications in strategy based on new information is called for, and this of course means ongoing artifact analysis. Implicitly at least most excavations operate in this manner, but the system of feedbacks should be more formalized than it frequently is. The scale of urban excavations in particular demands that feedback be formalized. Sampling plans also have to avoid the two extremes – a very loose plan with no probabilistic sampling procedures on the one hand, or, on the other hand, using an inflexible design which is resolutely followed through without the constant monitoring required to assure good results and maximum utilization of available resources.

The designs of initial sampling strategies for excavation are based on the aims of the research, what is known and/or expected about the character of the site, the descriptive and analytical procedures which are likely to be used in treating the material produced by the excavations, and the funds and time available for carrying out the work. The aims of the excavation of course are the primary consideration, and the selection of the site and the analytical procedures are largely dependent on those aims. There are, however, frequently some disjunctions between the sampling assumptions of various statistical procedures which may seem useful for a given set of problems and the sampling designs which appear practical for a given set of data or field situation.

As will be reflected in the following sections, our own attempts to cope with the various problems of sampling a large, isolated site, involve a variety of approaches, sometimes dictated by practical considerations rather than scientific ideals. Given our stated objectives, it was necessary to plan the excavations so that as many as possible of the subgroups in the material record, and presumably in the city's activity patterning, can be identified, described, and explained. In translating these broad goals into specific strategies the following guidelines have been very important: (1) To try to take maximum advantage of previous experience and surface data to make excavations more productive and efficient—in practice this mainly means making extensive use of stratified sampling. (2) To reduce unintended biases whenever possible by using randomization procedures. (3) To plan a sample which would cover the entire city spatially so as to minimize the possibility of missing any major activity patterns. (4) To check the digging operations with small-scale analyses so that we could have some ongoing idea of our success. (5) To view the sampling in at least two stages, a "minimum" initial sample which would probably be "expanded" in many areas as field and laboratory suggested necessary.

It will be evident that nonprobability sampling has entered into our procedures—particularly in the case of "expanded" samples. Nonprobability sampling should be kept to a minimum because of the limitations it poses on the statistical manipulations of the data. However, I feel that occasional nonprobability sampling, like the extremely complex probability designs, are almost inevitable in excavating an urban site unless one is willing to ignore certain important data and the usefulness of past experience.

Most of the excavations discussed were carried out in late 1971 and the summer of 1972. As is all too frequently the case we have not accomplished all we had hoped for by this date, partly because of the unexpected richness of the material. Also our "trial analyses" have been much more impressionistic than was originally planned—again largely because of the quantity of the material. We are currently beginning a phase of intensive data analysis on which further excavational sampling will be based. A better evaluation of the usefulness of the various procedures described below will follow the more intensive studies.

The remarks here thus provide a tentative overview, based on work in progress, of some of the sampling problems encountered in an urban site excavation. While each site and each set of questions for investigation will impose somewhat different sampling demands, our experiences hopefully provide some generally useful suggestions. Particularly I feel that our case demonstrates the fruitfulness of designing a sample around surface architecture whenever possible, and the necessity of using several approaches to sampling for different problems within the same site.

THE STRUCTURE AS THE BASIC SAMPLING UNIT

As the architectural plan of Huánuco Pampa (Fig. 11.1) suggests, the site is composed of about 3,500 structures placed in widely varying patterns of distribution which leave a significant amount of open space. The variability and complexity of such a site calls for the use of a variety of sampling designs (for example, those appropriate to areas of dense construction are inappropriate for the distinct cultural and physical nature of large plazas and open spaces). As a later section discusses in detail, our approach to such complex internal diversity is to divide it into a large number of sampling strata based on architecture and other surface characteristics.

The sampling designs for the greater part of the site have utilized the individual structure as the basic unit for excavation and other work. The walls of buildings are clearly related to patterning of activities and in most cases they are the minimal surface unit with clear cultural significance. If structures were characteristically grouped into multiple structure compounds of a relatively few standardized types, more efficient sampling designs could be created using such compounds as the primary units. Only a minority of the structures at Huánuco Pampa are grouped into compound units, and such compounds as are present are highly variable and difficult to classify. We take large clearly defined compounds into consideration in the stratification procedures as indicated below. In sites with agglutinated architecture or numerous multiroom buildings, the room is likely to be a more appropriate sampling unit than the separate structure or building (Hill 1966). Multiroom structures are very rare at Huánuco Pampa, and our present sampling procedures call for the excavation or testing of all rooms of multiroom structures which fall into a sample.

A basic problem involved in using the structure as the sampling unit (as opposed to grid squares or some other arbitrary units) is that a procedure must be worked out that provides for sampling both the interior space as well as the exterior area immediately around a structure and frequently associated with its activities. In particular, care must be taken to design the sample so that large areas outside the buildings are systematically included. At the same time it is important not to waste valuable excavation resources working in exterior areas beyond the limits where any traces of human activities can be recovered.

In some senses the simplest way to sample the interior of buildings would be to lay a grid over them. The great differences in size and shapes of buildings made it very difficult to adopt a satisfactory, standardized square size for all structures; it was thus decided to allow the size of the excavation unit

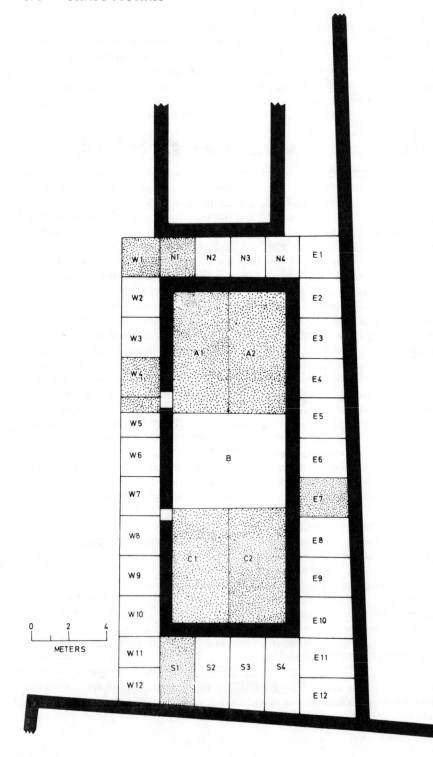

to vary from building to building, clearly requiring some kind of standard-ization of densities of resulting artifacts for certain comparative purposes. Circular structures which in general are small, are divided into pie-shaped quadrants. Rectangular buildings are divided into equal units along their long axes (see Fig. 11.2). Widths of no less than one meter or greater than six meters were established as limits, but the exact number of equal sized sampling units into which a building is divided varies greatly within those limits and is frequently determined by practical considerations, such as the safety of the surrounding walls and the estimated thickness of the upper fill, as well as the length of buildings. Sampling units are usually further subdivided for purposes of recording provenience. In principle it would be preferable to use smaller units better distributed over the structure. This is not practical in most cases at Huánuco Pampa because stone must be re-moved from a large area before any of the cultural material lying on the floor can be excavated.

Once the structure is subdivided into sampling units one or more of these is selected using a table of random numbers so that a minimum of 25 percent of the interior is excavated—except for structures exceeding 100 square meters in area, where the minimum sample is 10 percent. The proportion excavated usually exceeds this minimum. It is little more difficult to ex-cavate a small building entirely than it is to sample it, since the rock fall from the collapsed wall must be removed in any case. Also a deliberate effort was made to excavate at least one structure from each of the sampling strata (described below) in its entirety. The selection of interior sampling *in excess* of the minimum sample is usually, but not always, done randomly. The 10–25 percent minimum random selection of units is held as a check against unwanted biases, but when sampling units completely beyond the minimum are selected, nonrandom factors are sometimes allowed to enter in. For example, extra excavations are frequently placed to clarify certain architectural points, to complete a feature, or to give us a needed profile. The extent to which the excavated sample of a structure is expanded beyond the "minimum" in any given case depends in part on some of the practical field situations just mentioned, but the main guideline is whether it is felt that enough material has been obtained to give a good indication of the kinds and quantities of artifacts and features associated with the structure's in-terior. Here it would be advisable to have actual preliminary studies to determine if this is indeed the case, as part of the monitoring procedure I mentioned above. In fact we have so far had to rely on field impressions of the quantities of material coming from the various excavation units and of the variability in the material. We plan to modify this situation in future work.

←——   Fig. 11.2.   Plan of a structure from Huánuco Pampa's north side (Zone VB) showing the layout of potential excavation units for sampling and areas actually excavated. Note that the internal divisions were adjusted slightly in accordance with the structure's doors. Interior units A1 and A2 were ex-cavated as part of an expanded sample to give a larger artifact sample from the building's interior and to provide a second profile of the debris on the floor. A portion of trench W5 was excavated to complete the uncovering of a concentration of broken jars in front of the door, first revealed in Trench W4. All other excavation units were selected randomly.

Sampling the area's surrounding structures is even more complicated than interior sampling. First, a decision must be made on whether to relate the exterior sample to that of the interior of nearby structures, or to adopt a procedure in which the two are conducted independently. We considered it likely that artifacts would tend to cluster around structures, with densities dropping off as one moves away from a building. Early excavations proved this to be the case virtually every time at Huánuco Pampa. A word of caution must be used here, however. The sampling of outside areas should not be "tied" to buildings the way we have done unless it is quite clear that the outdoor activities also tend to be associated with structures; otherwise there is a risk of obscuring certain outside activities and distorting patterns of association. Even if outside areas are selected with the buildings, as part of a stratified cluster of excavation units, certain safeguards must be built into the recording of provenience so that activities important to streets, passageways and plazas are not missed.

The areas surrounding the Inca buildings are sampled by a series of trenches radiating out from the buildings (see Fig. 11.1). The widths of the trenches vary, depending on the size of the buildings as above. However, narrower excavation units are more feasible on the outside of buildings than on the inside because there is little over burden from fallen walls; they usually range between one and two meters. The minimum length of the trenches is two meters, but as a guideline (and in general practice) they extend either to the wall of the next structure, if it is within ten meters, or until there has been no evidence of cultural material for at least two meters. Long trenches are divided into several horizontal units for controlling provenience, so that degree of association of material with a structure's wall can be measured. This is especially crucial when a trench runs between two buildings, so that material associated with each building may be kept separate.

One starting point for a trench is randomly selected along each wall, except that the long axis is taken not as the building length, but as the building length plus the length of the trenches extending from the two ends (see Fig. 11.2). This is done so that the corners are not automatically eliminated from the sample. The number of trenches along the long axis is increased if the building's length exceeds 20 meters. If the first randomly selected trench for the long axis falls in a corner, another trench is selected at random from those that touch the wall, so that all four wall areas are represented. We have not so far selected trenches nonrandomly beyond the minimum sample, except for small excavations in clearing doors and increasing the excavated areas to completely uncover a feature which extends into an adjoining unit.

It is readily apparent that this manner of sampling the areas surrounding buildings is cumbersome. It is equally apparent, however, that important material is associated with the exteriors of structures. The location of that material cannot be predicted from the surface. A procedure similar to the one presently employed is clearly necessary, and my own main criticism of our procedure to date is that we need to increase the number of exterior units excavated in order to catch the large number of activities which took place just outside of buildings.

In summary, structures are the basic sampling units we are most interested in observing and comparing with other similar units. They are selected individually, in most cases from stratified populations of structures. The structures themselves are then stratified into interior and exterior areas, the five resulting strata (inside plus four sides) are divided into arbitrary units, and a certain number of the units are selected randomly for excavation to provide a "minimum" sample of the artifacts and features associated with the structures. The artifacts and features excavated are thus cluster samples selected from disproportionately stratified clusters of excavation units. The complexity of this design is evident even before we admit the occasional use of nonprobability sampling in expanding the excavations, and proceed to the ways the structures are themselves selected. For many purposes we have clearly built enormous statistical complexity into the artifact samples with the stratification, clustering and rather wide differences in proportions excavated. However, the gain in flexibility, which enables us to adapt our sampling and excavation units to culturally meaningful spatial units and to practical problems in the field, seems at this point to outweigh these problems. In any case we do have a clearly, although complexly, defined probability sample for a set "minimum" of most of the material. We also know when nonprobability factors have entered in. The ultimate test of the procedures is whether they give us the kinds of activity isolates we are interested in. Our tentative studies of parts of the material suggest that in most cases they will.

GUIDELINES FOR STRATIFICATION OF THE SITE

The structures described above are, except in certain special cases in the city's eastern sector, selected randomly from sampling strata defined on the basis of architectural types and distributions. The stratification is done in order to produce relatively homogeneous groups, divided in terms of criteria which hopefully are closely related to the activity and social grouping variables being studied. The division of the site into strata was guided by a hierarchy of criteria which attempted to do the following: (1) isolate groups of buildings or areas within the city which are separated either by walls, streets, or open space, thus forming some sort of "natural" division; (2) provide a relatively complete spatial coverage of the city—though concentrating more excavations in certain areas than others because of their greater pertinence to the problems we are working on or because of higher internal variation; and (3) separately sampling various structure types within the spatially distinct strata.

The site was first divided into eight zones based largely on the city's apparent planning (see Fig. 11.1), with four principal zones (2–5) spaced around a large Plaza (Zone 1); a deep *quebrada* separates Zones 5 and 6; Zone 8 is located on a steep hill, and its function as the city's main storage facility was determined in 1964–65 (Morris 1967); Zone 7, intermediate between Zones 3 and 8, has a somewhat arbitrary feel about it, but it is separated from Zone 3 by a series of small lakes and canals, and its functional distinction from Zone 8 was tested and verified to my satisfaction by excavation in 1965 (Morris 1967). All but three of the primary zones are divided into two or more subzones, largely on the basis of what appear to be streets. Some of the subzones in turn contain walled compounds which are considered separate strata. At present we have defined 21 spatially separate strata, and more intensive studies of walls in three of the subzones where we have not yet excavated may suggest the designation of new strata which seem to make sense in terms of the site's spatial segmentation.

The partition of the site in the manner just described, and the separate sampling of each area, on the one hand satisfies the demand for some sort of areal coverage of the entire city and on the other sets up a series of hypothetically distinct major activity areas within it. The strata are not just criteria for sample selection, they also provide the framework for testing ideas about the city's structure. Do the resultant artifact types and distributions from the excavations confirm our divisions, or do they suggest that our boundaries are meaningless? While we have completed no artifact studies except for the storage zone, preliminary evidence suggests that most of our boundaries are meaningful, and that the combination of artifacts, features and architecture — with a substantial boost from some hypotheses on Inca society borrowed from ethnohistory — will enable us to suggest in some detail what they mean.

The strata created on the basis of distributional considerations are cross-cut by a series of architectural types. The building types are still tentative, and were indeed created for the purposes of sample stratification in planning excavations. The number of types is almost certain to be expanded as refinements are made and plans drawn up for the excavation of areas not yet intensively studied, but we are presently working with 14 building types. These are based primarily on shape and size attributes and do not include such unique architectural features as the giant platform (the *Ushnu*) in the central plaza and the rare buildings of carefully cut and fitted stone masonry thought to have been palaces and temples. The latter buildings have special problems, and to the extent that we have worked in them, we have not used probability sampling procedures (see below). The combination of distributional criteria and architectural form could lead, with the distinctions we now make, to as many as 294 distinct strata. The actual strata so far defined come to less than half that number, since only a few architectural types occur in most zones. The fact that a given building may (and usually does) occur in more than one spatial unit, creating a certain amount of redundancy, is discussed below in relation to sample size.

In general we have been satisfied with the results the above procedures seem to be producing, particularly for areas where the spatial arrangements of the buildings are clear-cut. There is always room for improvement and increased efficiency, however, and we plan to experiment with some modifications in areas where architecture is less homogeneous. In particular we plan to try selecting clusters of buildings within these more irregular areas as an alternative to stratification by building type. In addition to using some clustering procedures in subzones not yet sampled, we hope to try clustering in areas already sampled by the procedures above so that the results of the two can be compared. Different and even more economical procedures than those we have been using are likely to be required for working larger sites or sites with less well preserved architecture, and in spite of some disadvantages, extensive use of cluster sampling would seem to be the answer. Indeed in cases where excavation is required before architecture is uncovered, the investigation of clusters of structures may be the only answer.

GUIDELINES FOR DETERMINING SAMPLE SIZES

In dealing with the question of sample size one has to perform the nearly impossible task of balancing the equation between the ideal and the possible. In the sampling of urban sites with artifact counts sometimes mounting at the rate of a few thousand a day, processing, coding, and analysis costs have to be weighed as carefully as those of excavation.

We are probably not ready yet in archaeology to speak of "optimum allocation" (Blalock 1972: 518–519) in any realistic sense. But certainly the practicality and efficiency of a sampling design ranks just below its adequacy in relative importance. One of the main reasons for using the structure as the principal sampling unit, and for the complicated stratification procedures is to try to take much of the variation into consideration before excavation is begun so the overall sample size can be smaller without undue sacrifices in adequacy. Another economizing step is to keep the initial samples relatively small, expanding them when preliminary analysis suggests that more excavation is necessary.

In deciding how many structures from a given stratum to excavate, our primary concern, as implied above, is with obtaining enough artifacts and features from the excavations to validate or invalidate the distinctions between the strata and to recognize important differences within the strata which are not apparent in the architectural information. In actually arriving at a judgment of whether a sample is sufficient, the main considerations are the number of structures in the stratum and the number and variability in the artifact samples which result from the excavations.

The initial sample of course can take only the architectural evidence into consideration. In doing that we have used a procedure of sampling the strata disproportionately, with the proportion of a given stratum excavated decreasing rather rapidly as the number of buildings it contains increases. The scale of primary sampling fractions ranges from 100% testing of a stratum composed of only one or two structures to only 8% of the structures in a stratum of more than 100. This system prevents rare strata from being under-represented in the artifact and feature samples, and at the same time seems to offer a fair chance of picking up any greater variability in strata with larger numbers of buildings.

The initial or "minimum" sample of a stratum may be expanded if the results seem inadequate and the resources are not needed more urgently elsewhere. It is desirable to excavate more structures from those strata where (a) variation is very high in the artifacts and/or features or (b) the total quantity of excavated material is so low that it is not likely to be very useful in inference. It is theoretically possible to calculate variances for at least some of the pertinent variables in a stratum, but since our artifact samples are clusters drawn from disproportionately sampled strata within other clusters (i.e. the structures) the calculations are well beyond what can ordinarily be undertaken in the field. Some judgments can be based on inspection of rough tabulations for the various artifact and feature classes from the various structures within a stratum to form an estimate of its homogeneity. In the case of our own study, if there is no strong similarity in the proportions of various vessel forms for example, further excavation is indicated.

The sampling problems posed by strata which yield little information in excavation pose even more worrisome problems than those strata which prove to be very heterogeneous. For example rectangular storehouses at Huánuco Pampa contain essentially no ceramics, and screening and flotation of material from the first few examples excavated succeeded in suggesting that the stratum was indeed homogeneous, but with no indication of the buildings' function. As we continued with our sample we excavated 3 (out of 29) structures that had been burned and contained charred remains of root crops carefully stored in bales of straw. The crucial evidence for interpretation may be some rare artifact or condition of preservation which is likely to be found only by a large sampling fraction. The decision on whether to expand a sample which is yielding little evidence is a very difficult one, for on the one hand one runs the risk of missing the rare or seldom preserved data class on which an interpretation might be based, but on the other hand there is the risk of using up valuable resources for only negative results.

Many of the architectural types occur in several different zones, and one of the major questions facing us in the analysis before further excavation concerns adjustments that can be made in the sampling procedure for a zone containing many buildings of a type already explored in some detail elsewhere. Our use of a minimum and expanded sample in selecting buildings is one way of coping with the matter. But obviously if a building type tends to have closely similar artifact constellations associated with it, whatever zone it occurs in, it would only be necessary to establish that with some confidence – not to follow through on sampling that building type as if it were a new one in each zone. A strategy hopefully can be worked out whereby the minimum sample of a given architectural type already extensively excavated elsewhere in the city can be reduced when a new zone is excavated. We already know enough to use caution in this, for some structure types are certainly multifunctional and were adapted to different purposes in different parts of the site.

A final note on sample size has to recognize the fact that samples can seldom be as large as desirable, and we may have to accept confidence levels that are lower than we would like and realize that there is simply much that will be missed. But at least at sites like Huánuco Pampa, where there are ways of increasing sampling efficiency by stratification, and where the record from excavation is quite rich, I feel that an unusually full activity picture can be constructed with the excavation of only 8% to 10% of the city.

SAMPLING LARGE OPEN AREAS

Urban sites frequently contain large plazas or other open areas which were the scenes of activity, even though they may not have utilized architecture. Huánuco Pampa for example has three relatively large plazas (see Fig. 11.1) all of which are central to its plan and presumably to its activities. Obviously the sampling procedure based on architectural remains cannot be applied to these areas. In cases like these we are interested in fairly even coverage, but again want a sampling strategy that avoids bias. A good solution seems to be the stratified, systematic unaligned samples worked out by geographers and frequently used by archaeologists. Since the procedure is well described in the literature (Redman and Watson 1970; Haggett 1965; Berry 1962) I will not go into detail here, other than to suggest its utility where relatively uniform coverage of large, relatively undifferentiated areas is required.

SPECIAL CIRCUMSTANCES
AND PURPOSIVE SAMPLING

The sample stratification of Huánuco Pampa on the basis of surface evidence has brought a systematic use of knowledge about the site and archaeological experience to the research design. It is also apparent that new evidence in the course of work makes it necessary to increase initial samples, and that this occasionally involves an excavation of a particular size in a particular place—rather than one determined by some kind of probabilistic sampling. While we have tried to avoid overuse of purposive sampling because of the built-in problems regarding the quantitative treatment of the data, we have not hesitated to use it when a special question required some particular piece of information. The crucial canon regarding such purposive excavations is that their nonprobability nature be noted so that appropriate operations can be employed when studying the data, and the results interpreted with knowledge of how the sample was made. Also purposive sampling must have a real rationale—not be based on "whim" or "grab" techniques which are not in fact purposive.

Situations in which purposive excavations are likely to be desirable may be illustrated by two common examples from urban sites archaeology. One of these involves the need to find stratified refuse for chronological control. Probabilistic sampling may help in many cases, but frequently surface characteristics are the key to locating such refuse. However located and identified, the size and other aspects of the excavation should not be tied to some sampling procedure which has a different aim—e.g. to provide data on activity patterns. Different objectives often require quite different sampling procedures.

Another common use of purposive sampling is for unique structures or areas of known special importance to particular hypotheses being tested. In our case a unique building would form a stratum composed of only one member and would therefore be tested. But Zone 2, Subzone B is an example of an area which is especially pertinent to questions central to our research; on architectural grounds it appears to have been the seat of administrative activities. We are working on a sample of that area which is unusually large (we hope to test all of its structures) and makes extensive use of purposive sampling. One of the reasons for insisting on some kind of systematic sampling of an entire city is to eliminate the heavy emphasis on temples and palaces so pervasive in early urban sites archaeology. But these constructions cannot be omitted, and because of their special nature and significance they may require purposive strategies designed especially for each case.

Purposive sampling is sometimes done for reasons of economy. If time allows only one or two tests in a site, one is likely to get more information by searching for places which surface evidence suggests are likely to have considerable architectural and artifactual material than by selecting one or two squares at random (assuming there were time to actually grid the site and make a proper random selection). In addition to purposive excavations in which a particular place is selected, sampling designs may deliberately eliminate certain regions of a site. This might be done for areas which yield so little information that they do not seem to justify the expense. It may also be desirable to avoid very rich areas which are not directly pertinent to one's immediate questions—as soon as one is reasonably certain of this.

Like other sampling procedures, purposive sampling has its uses as well as its misuses. When a lot is known about a site or there is a great deal of surface evidence, purposive sampling may be very valuable, and to go out of one's way to avoid purposive sampling may be almost as inappropriate as digging by whim. The caution should always be followed that each case where purposive excavation is made has a specific and clearly stated rationale. In cases where there is little evidence on which such a rationale can be based, some other procedure is called for.

SUMMARY AND RECOMMENDATIONS

I hope this consideration of our sampling procedures at Huánuco Pampa provides some insight into the problems and possibilities of excavating an urban site. In summary, I would like to reiterate the following points:

   1. The aims of urban sites excavations are likely to be related to defining and comparing the various subpopulations of artifacts and features from which we can infer activities and some of the patterns of interrelationships of a site's former occupants. This will require data collection and analytical procedures aimed at reconstructing a complex "horizontal" internal structure (or series of such structures) rather than summary statements about the site as a whole.

   2. Given these aims, the most effective sampling procedures to pursue in most cases are those which take maximum advantage of stratification. The site is divided into relatively homogeneous initial groupings to the maximum extent possible before excavation—using criteria closely related to the problems or variables on which the research focuses. In our case the stratification is based on the forms and distributions of surface architecture, with the individual buildings as the primary units of study. Although our

work is still in progress, preliminary results suggest that surface architecture is an excellent predictor of many of the patterns in the excavated material. I strongly recommend that when substantial architectural remains are preserved they be accurately mapped and carefully studied prior to designing the sampling strategy for excavation. In cases where standing architecture is not present, other surface remains such as pottery may be of help in stratifying the sample. If ceramics are used, however, care must be taken that the ceramic variables employed are related to the kinds of subgroups or "strata" one is interested in. For example we have found size and forms of rims and handles to be crucial indicators of the functions and activities of various zones. Classification schemes designed for chronological measurement sometimes obscure these attributes of shape.

When architecture is not present on the surface, some kind of cluster is likely to be the basic excavation and sampling unit. It may be possible and desirable to stratify architecturally within such clusters. While stressing the usefulness of stratified sampling, we must reemphasize that urban sites present a variety of problems and that the investigator likely will be interested in a wide range of questions. Therefore numerous sampling procedures are required as part of a coordinated set of designs.

3. I have suggested that the excavation of an urban site be constantly checked by ongoing preliminary analyses, and that it may be advantageous to formalize this in terms of a series of stages. We have attempted to do this with the notion of a fairly limited "minimum" sample which may be expanded, sometimes more than once, in areas where the need for additional excavation is especially great. While difficult to set up and administer, this seems the best way to concentrate limited resources where they are most needed and likely to be most productive.

4. It is no surprise that the excavational sampling of a city is an enormously complicated and difficult matter. Besides the sampling problems that all archaeologists must face, the excavator of an urban site must cope with quantities of data so large that sampling schemes necessarily come into play at various steps in the research. But because they are often so very rich in preserved remains of human activities, urban sites offer unusual opportunities for detailed reconstructions of activity patterns and the organizational contexts into which they fit. Our research designs must strive to take advantage of the exceptional richness of urban sites without being overcome by a deluge of information which we cannot use effectively. While I think we can already claim considerable success in this, much hard work lies ahead in developing appropriate sampling, analytical and inferential procedures — all separate parts of the same package — which can allow us to deal more productively with problems on the scale of those posed by an urban site.

ACKNOWLEDGMENTS

Professor George Cowgill, who is adviser on statistical methods and related matters to the Huánuco Pampa Project, has contributed many suggestions in the course of our work which are incorporated here. I am also grateful to him and to Professor Robert Hunt for comments on an earlier draft of this paper. Responsibility for its shortcomings are solely my own. The work is financed by National Science Foundation Grant GS28815 and authorized by Resoluciones Supremas Nos. 015 and 1030, of the year 1972, granted by the Peruvian government.

12. Archaeological Considerations of Intrasite Sampling

J. Jefferson Reid, Michael B. Schiffer, and Jeffrey M. Neff

J. Jefferson Reid (Ph.D., University of Arizona, 1973) has focused his energies on the archaeology of the American Southeast and Southwest. Most of his papers, publications, and manuscripts concern research at the Grasshopper Ruin where he has been serving as Associate Director. Additionally, he has served on various professional committees and has organized several symposia and conferences.

Michael B. Schiffer (Ph.D., University of Arizona, 1973) has performed fieldwork in Arizona, California, and Arkansas. He has held several fellowships and awards, including the Woodrow Wilson Fellowship in 1969–70. His special interests in archaeological epistemology and the formation of the archaeological record are reflected in several published articles and many manuscripts. He has been serving as Assistant Archaeologist in the Arkansas Archaeological Survey at Fayetteville.

Jeffrey M. Neff has been enrolled in the undergraduate anthropology program at the University of Arizona while working as a computer programmer for the Arizona State Museum.

Most persons agree that archaeology is anthropology or it is nothing (Willey and Phillips 1958), and even that archaeology is comparison or it is nothing (Chang 1967). It is not widely acknowledged that archaeology may be sampling or nothing, though a substantial argument can be made to support this position. There are two important senses in which archaeology is sampling or it is nothing. In the first place, because field archaeology is time consuming and expensive, few archaeologists are able to examine every site in a region or to excavate a single site entirely. Even if we had unlimited resources, we would still be faced with a sampling problem. In the second place, no more than a portion of the material components of a past behavioral system is presently available at a site for the archaeologist to recover since the total behavioral system of interest may have encompassed activities at several discrete locations (Binford 1964; Tringham 1972: xxi; Struever 1968; Winters 1969). In addition, even at one site, the entire inventory of material objects used there in the past may not have been discarded or preserved and thus many items would not be encountered by the archaeologist in the present (Collins, this volume). Consequently, the archaeologist always recovers the remains of only a portion of the past behavioral system that he seeks to describe and explain.

Despite the fact that the archaeological record of today contains the remains of just a portion of the behavioral system of the past, there are regular relationships between a past system and the archaeological record it produces that allow archaeologists to recover data relevant to reconstructing what is not directly preserved. The question is not whether to sample, for all archaeological recovery is sampling, but how to secure the sample that best provides data to answer questions about the past behavioral system. The choice, then, of an appropriate sampling strategy is a decision faced in all archaeological research projects and requires urgent attention. The sampling problem will not disappear through benign neglect or haphazard collections, nor will it be resolved through simplistic applications of probability sampling techniques (see also Hill 1967). This discussion focuses on the uniquely archaeological considerations which are logically and methodologically prior to a statistical consideration of intrasite sampling strategies in archaeology. These considerations, which apply as well to other phases of archaeological investigation (Reid n.d.; Schiffer 1973), form the basis of viable sampling programs.

The goals of a "behavioral archaeology" are to describe and explain behavioral variability in socio-cultural systems regardless of spatial or temporal provenience (Reid n.d., 1973; Reid, Rathje, & Schiffer n.d.; 1974; Schiffer 1973). These goals encompass questions of chronology, history, lifeways, adaptations, and process, especially as these questions relate to the explanation of behavioral change. The achievement of these goals requires that material remains and their patterns in the archaeological record be utilized to derive behaviorally meaningful statements about the past. This requirement is made complex by the obvious condition that the archaeological record is not the socio-cultural system to be described and explained, but it is an ambiguous by-product of that system's operation as well as other cultural and noncultural processes.

ARCHAEOLOGICAL CONTEXT AND SYSTEMIC CONTEXT

Archaeologists are not unaware of the problems in mixing levels and artifacts. Just as arbitrary and natural excavation levels should maintain their integrity as partition classes for artifacts, so should the archaeological record maintain its integrity as a structure distinct from the structure of the socio-cultural system by which it was formed (cf. Binford 1968a, 1968b). Conceptualization of this distinction is achieved within the archaeological and systemic contexts of remains (Schiffer 1972). The "systemic context labels the condition of an element which is participating in a behavioral system" while the "archaeological context describes materials which have passed through a cultural system, and which are now the objects of investigation of archaeologists" (Schiffer 1972: 157). By amplifying this distinction, and developing some of its implications, a framework is provided for discussing the formation processes of the archaeological record and, thereby, for indicating solutions to the sampling problem.

The archaeological context includes the structure of the archaeological record as perceived in the formal, spatial, quantitative, and relational properties of cultural and environmental materials. These properties are phenomena of the present inasmuch as they are identified by activities of survey and excavation in the present and are accorded the status of observational units or facts. The present phenomena of the archaeological context exist as they are perceived and described by the investigator. For example, the statement that antelope bone occurs in association with deer bone describes presently observable relationships of the archaeological context.

In contrast, the systemic context of archaeological remains encompasses aspects of the behavioral system of which the remains were once a part. This context is both the living socio-cultural system and our models of that system. For example, the statement that metates were used in habitation rooms pertains to the systemic context of an artifact class. The temporal dimension of past behavioral events is also within the systemic context. The significance of this distinction is intuitively obvious from the statement that all sites (archaeological context) are contemporaneous while all prehistoric communities (systemic context), obviously, were not.

As remains and events can be considered within an archaeological and systemic context, so can space. "Recovery space" describes the spatial units of archaeological activity such as squares, trenches, and levels, which are defined for purposes of recovering and recording archaeological materials. It should be clear that recovery space maintains no necessary isomorphic relationship to "behavioral space" — the analytically defined areas of past human behavior.*

The systemic context is seen to include the items, events, and locations of the past behavior that archaeologists seek to document and explain. Though one might seek merely to describe observations within the archaeological context, rare, indeed, is the archaeologist seeking solely this aim. Instead, highly credible descriptions and explanations about the systemic context are the objectives of most archaeological research. The *general* sampling problem is thus posed: how can we sample the systemic context of remains in order to derive meaningful statements about human behavior? Strictly speaking, we can never sample the systemic context because it is gone. But we can sample in the archaeological context those recovery spaces and debris classes that relate to analytic units containing information relevant to our systemic context objectives. The sampling problem is only partially grasped by many when they fantasize some futuristic gadget to allow observation of the total three-dimensional structure of the archaeological context. Even if we had complete knowledge of this structure as it is today, inert and buried, the question would remain of how to relate that which we perceive in the present to human behavior of the past.

As archaeologists, we necessarily begin sampling in the archaeological context in order to estimate parameters of the systemic context. It must be realized that applications of probability sampling to the archaeological context produce estimates of archaeological context parameters and not the systemic context parameters which most seek to estimate. Few questions require only a representative sample of the archaeological context. The discontinuity in sampling domains means that no mechanically simple,

---

*J. Jefferson Reid is indebted to L. G. Ferguson for this distinction.

statistical approach, alone, can be effective in achieving systemic objectives. This does not mean, however, that probability sampling is not applicable to archaeological data retrieval strategies.

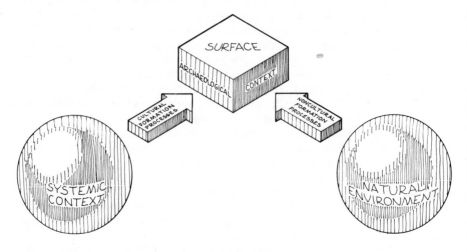

Fig. 12.1. Discontinuity in archaeological sampling domains.

To solve the general sampling problem, we must find ways of partitioning the universe to be sampled into behaviorally meaningful, analytic units of the systemic context. The problem is expressed visually in Figure 12.1. Standing on a site, table of random digits in hand, one is confronted by the realization that only the surface of the archaeological context is visible. Even though the surface may provide some clues to aspects of subsurface remains (Redman and Watson 1970; Redman 1973), it obscures perception of the total, three-dimensional structure of the archaeological context. More serious is how the entire archaeological context distorts the pertinent systemic target populations from which a representative sample is desired. The systemic context cannot be sampled directly since it cannot be directly perceived by the investigator. Thus a *practical* problem is posed: How can we effectively sample the archaeological context to secure a representative sample of systemic context populations within relevant analytic units? The solution to this problem lies first in a consideration of the processes responsible for the discontinuity between the archaeological and systemic contexts.

FORMATION PROCESSES OF
THE ARCHAEOLOGICAL RECORD

The present structure of the archaeological record is a distorted reflection of the past behavioral system. This present structure results from the operation over time of the cultural and noncultural processes which form the archaeological record (see Fig. 12.1). The distortions introduced into the archaeological context can be reduced by explicitly taking into account these formation processes. The reduction of distortion is achieved by means of appropriate "transformation" principles and operations. Transformations identify and model the factors that produced an archaeological context. It is the operation of these formation processes, taken into account by transformations, that are responsible for the discontinuity between the two contexts, and hence the discontinuity between sampling domains.

The use of transformations is not novel. They are embedded in all interpretations of archaeological context phenomena as well as in the more recent attempts to formulate test implications guiding the selection of observational units. However, transformation procedures have not been *systematically* considered by archaeologists in the past. The dual context distinction brings transformations into focus by providing a framework in which general relationships between the two contexts can be established.

The general transformation procedure can be briefly sketched. Research problems are framed within the *systemic context of information*. The systemic context of information includes specific behavioral and cultural variables of the past which are the objects of archaeological descriptions and explanations. These variables are not directly observable in the archaeological record, but are related through *systemic transformations* to specific units of analysis, which in turn, can be operationalized to units of observation in the archaeological context by *identification transformations*. Units of observation are the recovery spaces and material remains recognizable in the archaeological record from their formal, spatial, quantitative, and relational attributes.

At the core of transformation principles and operations are the formation processes of the archaeological record (Schiffer 1972, 1973). All archaeologists have an appreciation for the effects that noncultural processes, such as erosion, decay, and sand deposition, have on the formation and present structure of archaeological remains. The specific principles or relational statements of these processes are termed n-transforms (Schiffer 1973; Schiffer and Rathje 1973). The n-transforms describe the outcome of the interaction between culturally deposited material and environmental variables. For example, textiles, when deposited in a dry cave, will be preserved.

On the other hand, the cultural processes responsible for forming the archaeological record are less well known, except in terms of the temporal sequence of cultural deposition. These processes, such as disposal of the dead, artifact discard and loss, act on the systemic context of materials and transform them into what becomes the archaeological context. The principles which describe the operation of cultural formation processes are called c-transforms (Schiffer 1973; Schiffer and Rathje 1973). These principles relate behavioral and organizational variables of a socio-cultural system to variables describing aspects of the archaeological outputs of that system. For example, as the occupation intensity and population size of a community increase, fewer materials are discarded at their locations of use (adapted from Schiffer 1972: 162).

Taken together, n-transforms and c-transforms allow archaeologists to model the formation of the archaeological record. By this modeling process, we are constructing the means by which we can devise systemic and identification transformations.

Different cultural formation processes produce different kinds of outputs useful for testing different hypotheses and for answering different kinds of questions. Two kinds of cultural formation processes can be defined. The first type consists of activities, such as artifact discard and loss, and disposal of the dead, which result in normal archaeological' outputs from activity areas. Processes of the second type are set in motion by the abandonment of an activity area. When activity areas are abandoned, some usable materials may also be abandoned at the same time, rather than transported to other activity areas.

Two varieties of refuse produced by normal system processes can be delineated. Primary refuse is material discarded at its location of use. Secondary refuse, on the other hand, is removed from its location of use, transported, and discarded elsewhere (Schiffer 1972). These concepts are useful mainly at the intrasite level. When applied at a regional level, all refuse is primary; that is, most items are discarded at the location, or one of the locations, where they were used.

Elements which are output when an activity area or a complete settlement is abandoned are termed de facto refuse (Schiffer 1972). Such materials were still in storage, use, or even manufacture processes just prior to the departure of the human group. As a result, much de facto refuse is not worn-out or broken. When activity areas within a settlement are differentially abandoned, which is most often the case, scavenging activities remove usable de facto refuse from the early abandoned areas (Ascher 1968; Schiffer 1972). Under these conditions, most de facto refuse occurs only in the last occupied behavioral spaces. In the Southwest, de facto refuse is represented archaeologically by material items on late abandoned room floors (Reid 1973a). These formation processes and refuse types do not exhaust all possibilities but they do serve to focus later discussions.

The implications of these different formation processes for acquiring data pertinent to one's required units of analysis in transformation procedures are clear. For example, it would be futile to sample for the spatial distribution of domestic activity areas in secondary refuse since only primary and de facto refuse satisfy the initial requirement — materials discarded at their locations of use — for answering this type of question. Similarly, if one were interested in identifying the total range of past activities through time at a site, de facto refuse, representing only the latest activities, would not be appropriate. A simple example can illustrate how formation processes — in this case, cultural formation processes — can be taken into account by the explicit use of systemic transformations and identification transformations.

In studying the Nunamiut Eskimo throughout their seasonal round, Binford (n.d.a) identifies what he calls "curate behavior." Curate behavior consists of retaining objects in moving from one location to another in anticipation of future use. Curate items are therefore those objects retained and transported. Very few prehistoric communities are abandoned with a complete inventory of cultural remains left as de facto refuse.

Suppose an archaeologist asked the following question of sites in a region: Among prehistoric pueblo groups, how does curate behavior change under different conditions of pueblo abandonment? To answer this question requires the identification of curate behavior at several sites. Our example concentrates on this identification procedure.

By definition, curate items will not be found at the pueblo under study, since they have been removed to another location. But curate items should be identifiable by subtracting the set of artifacts left at abandonment from the complete set of items utilized at the pueblo. For the purpose of this example the simplifying assumption is made that factors of recycling, preservation, and systemic change are constant. The example is further simplified by omitting detailed consideration of procedures for identifying analytic units in the field. Brown (this volume) considers procedures for identifying refuse types.

The problem, then, is to identify the complete range of items utilized at a pueblo and those items left upon abandonment. A set of general systemic transformations specifying relevant units of analysis is that (1) a complete set of material items is represented in primary and secondary refuse, and (2) material culture items left at abandonment are represented by de facto refuse.

After acquiring the basic systemic transformations relating analytic units, our next step is to operationalize these analytic units to units of observation. Identification transformations relate the analytic refuse types to observational units of the archaeological record. Burial goods represent one type of primary refuse while secondary refuse can be identified by deposits of high material density and diversity that contain predominately broken or exhausted items. De facto refuse is found in the last occupied activity areas and requires identification of these areas.

Having established the inventory of items contained within each refuse type, we can employ the systemic transformations to derive the curate items:

1. Complete item set = (primary refuse set + secondary refuse set).
2. Abandonment item set = de facto refuse set.
3. Curate item set = complete item set − abandonment item set.

After investigating curate behavior at several settlements abandoned under different conditions, the archaeologist may derive inferences concerning such questions as probable abandonment rates and distance to the next settlement.

SAMPLING AND FORMATION PROCESSES

At this point the question is: How can we use knowledge of formation processes to sample for the systemic context parameters of interest, and how can we also sample to learn more about the processes that formed the site under investigation (Collins, this volume)? Multistage sampling (Binford 1964; Redman 1973, this volume; Longacre n.d.a; Hanson and Schiffer n.d.; Wilcox n.d.b) provides a vehicle for efficient recovery of data pertinent to the estimation of systemic parameters. In devising a viable multistage sampling program, maximal use of prior knowledge and expert judgment must be made (Longacre n.d.a; Schiffer and Rathje 1973). This expert judgment includes consideration of the formation processes that created the archaeological context to be sampled. These considerations are drawn from the existing knowledge of how similar archaeological contexts were produced, preliminary examination of the context to be sampled, the problem focus of the immediate research, and transformations essential to operationalizing analytic units pertinent to the research. We argue, however, that the transformation principles which comprise this expert judgment be made explicit.

The data collected from a first-stage sample must be evaluated by how well systemic context parameters can be estimated. This, in turn, depends on how closely one has modeled the formation processes of the archaeological record. Continuous evaluation of the data in the field and after a season's excavation is essential in maximizing the potential of multistage sampling strategies (Binford 1964). Every new stage in sampling must be structured in terms of the information gained in the previous stage and the current questions to be investigated.

A point to be emphasized is that probability sampling techniques can be used yet they do not insure at the onset that a representative sample of *systemic context* units can be obtained (Wilcox n.d.b, n.d.c). It is not necessary to know and impossible to insure at the *initiation* of a sampling program that the result will be a representative sample of the systemic context analytic units or the retrieval of relevant systemic context information. On the other hand, it is essential to know at the *conclusion* of a sampling stage whether or not the sample of requisite systemic context units has been obtained. It is anticipated that such an interactive sampling procedure will facilitate the implementation of statistical procedures for the investigation of archaeological questions and thereby provide greater confidence that the sample one ends up with is representative of the systemic units necessary for analysis.

In illustrating some of the above arguments concerning intrasite sampling strategies we draw on data from two research projects carried out in Arizona. These examples should illustrate the important role of expert judgment applied to the archaeological context to be sampled, and how knowledge of formation processes can be used to designate relevant units of observation that relate to systemic context analytic units of interest. In addition, they should demonstrate the importance of multiphase sampling procedures that aim to acquire information about systemic parameters of interest and the formation processes that operated in the past.

THE FIRST EXAMPLE: THE GRASSHOPPER RUIN

Grasshopper (Fig. 12.2) is a 500 room Pueblo IV ruin in east-central Arizona and the site of the University of Arizona Archaeological Field School under the direction of William A. Longacre and Raymond H. Thompson (Thompson and Longacre 1966; Longacre n.d.b; Longacre and Reid 1974). Grasshopper was a large pueblo community occupied from A.D. 1275 to A.D. 1400 by peoples labeled today as Late Mogollon (Rinaldo 1964; Tuggle 1970) or prehistoric Western Pueblo (Reed 1948). As in other southwestern pueblo ruins, it is not unusual to find the floors of habitation rooms covered with whole pots and other de facto refuse as well as to uncover habitation rooms that have little or no de facto refuse on their floors. It is not likely that differences in the activities conducted during the systemic context of these rooms can explain the differences in this de facto refuse. A more plausible explanation accounts for this variability as a product of several formation processes.

At least four cultural formation processes may have operated to produce variable floor assemblages in pueblo rooms. (1) When a habitation room is abandoned while the pueblo is still occupied, usable objects will be retained in moving to another nearby habitation room. (2) Even if all usable objects are not retained, habitation room floors abandoned while the pueblo is still occupied maintain a high probability of being scavenged for usable items. (3) Abandoned habitation rooms may be used for secondary refuse disposal. (4) The last habitation rooms abandoned will not be scavenged nor used as dumps.

The differential effects of these probable cultural formation processes can be expressed as follows:

1. Rooms abandoned while the pueblo was still occupied contain little or no de facto refuse on the last utilized habitation floor but may contain a high density of secondary refuse in the room fill above floor.

2. Rooms abandoned at or near the time of pueblo abandonment have a high density of de facto refuse on the last utilized habitation floor and a low density of secondary refuse in the room fill above floor.*

Assuming that these formation processes operated in the past at Grasshopper, what is indicated about the archaeological context of rooms? Most obvious is the fact that all room floors do not possess equivalent sets of de facto refuse. Late room floors possess many whole or restorable vessels, while early room floors possess no such vessels. All room floors do not possess equally representative sets of material remains and thus do not possess representative or equivalent samples of the past activities performed on room floors. Therefore, comparisons between artifacts from early floors with those of later floors could produce a spurious reconstruction of activities (see Wilcox n.d.c for an insightful discussion of comparability). A simple or stratified random sample of rooms would provide a representative sample of the variability of room floor *refuse;* yet it would not insure that a representative sample of both early and late room floor *activities* would be obtained.

Suppose that an archaeologist were interested in defining the range of variability in early and late ceramics at Grasshopper and would prefer to

---

*This model for estimating relative room abandonment was developed at Grasshopper from distributions of whole pots on room floors and sherds in room fill. The cultural formation processes underlying the model are further supported at Grasshopper by distributions of faunal remains and ground stone artifacts, specifically manos, metates and axes (Reid n.d.). The model has been successfully employed at the Joint Site (Schiffer 1973) and independently derived at Wide Reed Ruin (Teague n.d.), using distributions of chipped stone.

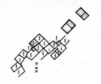

Fig. 12.2. The Grasshopper
Ruin, east-central Arizona.

analyze whole vessels when possible. Whole vessels, when not with burials, are found mainly on the floors of late abandoned rooms. By modeling the operation of probable cultural formation processes, the observational units or proveniences likely to contain early pottery can be identified. One might suggest that until one or more of the earliest or "core" rooms were abandoned, trash would have been deposited on outdoor surfaces. Thus the earliest pottery from the pueblo is to be found below the floors of rooms added to the core, and perhaps in remaining nonarchitectural areas. As rooms within the core unit are abandoned, they may be used as dumps. Thus the fill of early rooms will also contain early ceramics if room abandonment commenced early during the occupation of the pueblo. In short, if one were interested in domestic utility vessels he could obtain a sample of early vessels from preroom surfaces and from the fill of early abandoned rooms. A sample of late utility pottery could be obtained from the floors of late abandoned rooms. Because the probability of finding whole vessels in secondary refuse is small, the sample of early ceramics would be composed largely of sherds.

In the past, probability sampling has been advocated as a procedure for discovering the range of past behavioral and organizational variability that existed in a prehistoric community. Yet this assumes that the range of variability in the archaeological context directly reflects past systemic variability. This may be so sometimes, but, as another Grasshopper example illustrates, many systemic properties can be reconstructed without a representative sample of the archaeological context [Asch, this volume].

The 1971 growth project at the Grasshopper Ruin (Fig. 12.2) sought to explicate pueblo growth and the rate at which it proceeded (Reid and Shimada n.d.). Previous excavation of room corners, under the direction of David R. Wilcox and Michael B. Collins, had provided information on cultural formation processes by demonstrating that the three large room blocks of the main ruin had each expanded from an initial core of rooms. We reasoned that dates obtained from these core rooms could be combined with existing dates for late constructed rooms to delimit the period of room construction at the main ruin. Further, combined with construction sequences outlined through room cornering, these data would lead to general statements on direction and rate of growth.

Since construction of the three large room blocks of the main ruin began with core rooms, these rooms should be the earliest in the room blocks. By definition, all core rooms within a room block were built at one time, therefore excavation of any core room would provide dates for the construction of the set of core rooms and, thereby, date the earliest construction in each of the room blocks. By digging one core room from each room block an estimated date for the initial construction of that block could be determined. The selection of a core room for excavation could have been made through probability sampling techniques. However, since cornering data had provided a basis for estimating that the systemic context units of interest were homogeneous and since there was no further information to estimate which rooms may have contained charred wood suitable for dating, selection procedures based on probability sampling would have contributed little to the estimate of temporal parameters and were, therefore, not employed. Rather, the excavated room from each room block core was chosen on the basis of pragmatic considerations such as depth of fill and disposal of backfill. This example illustrates how, in some instances, the joining of relevant cultural formation processes to specific archaeological questions can reduce systemic variability, thereby making sampling of archaeological context variability unnecessary.

These examples drawn from the Grasshopper Ruin illustrate how one can model the cultural formation processes of the archaeological record to provide explicit criteria by which units relevant to one's systemic context interests can be identified and located. This is not a mechanical or simple process. It forces the archaeologist to muster all the insight gained from experience for designing the sampling strategy to be used at a site. As the archaeologist excavates his initial sample, he must be sampling for information that allows him to test his models about the cultural formation processes. For example, if one believes that rooms constructed late were also abandoned late (thus containing de facto refuse), the first rooms excavated should permit the evaluation of this assumption, and lead to its modification as necessary. Multiphase sampling must involve the acquisition of information about the operation of various formation processes in addition to information about the systemic parameters of interest.

THE SECOND EXAMPLE: THE JOINT SITE

In another example, we illustrate how one can sample for information about the operation of noncultural formation processes in order to facilitate gathering systemic context information. The Joint Site is a 36 room Pueblo III ruin in the Hay Hollow Valley (Hanson and Schiffer n.d.), occupied from about A.D. 1200 to A.D. 1280. The site was excavated in the summers of 1970 and 1971 by the Southwestern Expedition of the Field Museum of Natural History, the late Paul S. Martin, Director. One of the problems investigated there by Schiffer (1973) required the retrieval of data from all or most secondary refuse areas to enable the reconstruction of activities within the systemic context of the chipped stone assemblage (Schiffer 1973). Through familarity with the region it was known that secondary refuse was deposited in the fill of early abandoned rooms, on the surfaces below the floors of late constructed rooms, and in nonarchitectural areas. Two initial strata, consisting of rooms and nonarchitectural areas, were laid out for sampling purposes. Within the two major strata, several substrata were defined. Rooms were randomly sampled within classes defined on the basis of size, and numerous deposits of secondary refuse were located.

This example focuses exclusively on the sampling of nonarchitectural areas. In the first phase of excavation in these areas, a 2% stratified random sample was drawn. The strata corresponded to areas of differential density of surface lithic and ceramic artifacts. In using surface artifact distributions to delineate excavation strata, it has been assumed that noncultural formation processes did not modify the cultural deposits. Accordingly, it has been assumed that what lies on the surface directly reflects the distribution of what lies below. Because this assumption is likely to be inapplicable to many sites (Binford and others 1970), it was tested in the earliest phases of excavation.

By comparing the differential distribution of surface ceramics by weight per unit area (Fig. 12.3) with the distribution of subsurface ceramics plotted as weight per unit area of recovery space from the 2% sample (Fig. 12.4), the assumption of equivalence between the surface and subsurface artifact distributions was evaluated. At the Joint Site the surface is but a distorted reflection of subsurface remains. Many areas of high surface artifact density, especially in the northeast part of the site, overlie sterile soil. Conversely, areas with a low density of materials on the surface — to the south, and just north and east of the large room block — overlie dense subsurface deposits of secondary refuse. There are two ways to use this knowledge gained from the first phase of excavation to structure a second phase of excavation.

The first solution requires one to discover rapidly the nature of the subsurface site. This was accomplished at the Joint Site through a series of 23 backhoe trenches placed in areas not covered well in the first phase of excavation. The major secondary refuse areas not previously sampled were then included within the set of archaeological context deposits containing relevant data. A second stage of excavation resulted in the sampling of these heretofore untouched secondary refuse areas.* The completed sample of nonarchitectural areas at the Joint Site probably includes recovery spaces from every major deposit of secondary refuse. One extensive stage of excavation might have recovered a representative sample of the chipped stone within the archaeological context. It is difficult to see, however, how just a single stage of excavation could have possibly resulted in the retrieval of data from all secondary refuse areas.

Another way to cope with the surface-subsurface differences in distribution is to account by means of n-transforms for the surface distribution and employ that knowledge to define target areas for excavation. Let us examine once more the surface and subsurface pottery densities to see how this solution could have been applied (Figs. 12.3 and 12.4). It is noted that where surface areas of high artifact density occur above sterile soil, they lie downhill from major deposits of secondary refuse. Surface areas of low artifact density are found above deposits laid down near the room blocks, where aeolian sand would have accumulated. By attempting to model the processes of erosion and aeolian sand deposition that operated on the cultural deposits to produce the surface of this site, "target areas" can be defined where subsurface deposits of secondary refuse might be expected to occur. These hypotheses could be tested efficiently and quickly with a few test pits. This solution came to mind only after the Joint Site was excavated (Hanson and Schiffer n.d.; Schiffer and Rathje 1973).

The use of either approach allows the investigator to go beyond his initial discovery that noncultural formation processes produced on the surface

---

*The actual placement of recovery spaces within these newly discovered secondary refuse deposits was based on practical considerations such as finding an area undisturbed by our trenching operation.

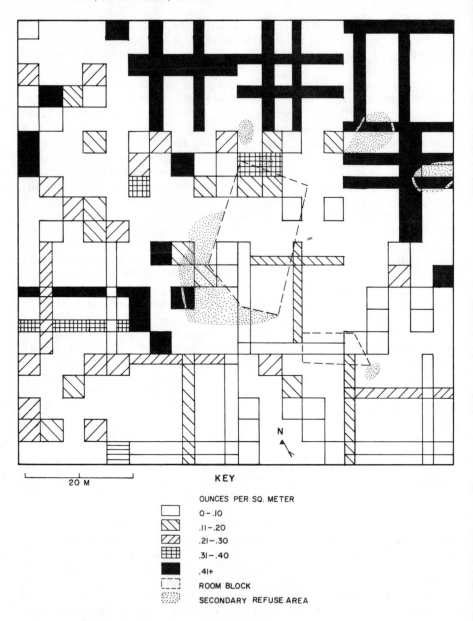

KEY

OUNCES PER SQ. METER

□	0 - .10
▨	.11 - .20
▨	.21 - .30
▦	.31 - .40
■	.41+
⌐⌐	ROOM BLOCK
⋰	SECONDARY REFUSE AREA

20 M

Fig. 12.3. The distribution by weight of surface ceramics at the Joint Site.

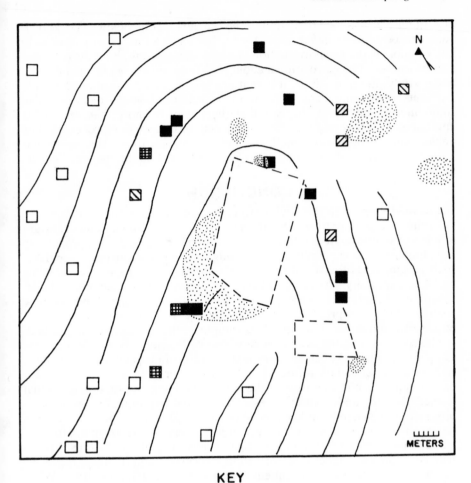

KEY

OUNCES PER SQ. METER

☐	10-20
◪	21-40
▨	41-60
▦	61-80
■	81-100+
⌐⌐	ROOM BLOCK
░	SECONDARY REFUSE AREA

SQUARES NOT TO MAP SCALE

Fig. 12.4. The distribution of subsurface ceramics recovered from the first stage of excavation in nonarchitectural area of the Joint Site. Artifact densities are calculated as weight per unit surface area of recovery space.

of a site are a distorted reflection of the remains that lie below. This knowledge can be used to define areas for further excavation. What is crucial in this example is the rapid evaluation of one's assumptions about these formation processes. The more known about how these processes formed the site under study, the more likely it is that one will be able to locate and sample the units containing data relevant to a systemic context question. The Joint Site example also suggests that there may be more than one viable approach to discovering the effects of noncultural formation processes. The application of alternative methods and techniques for achieving similar systemic context objectives is always contingent upon the site-specific archaeological context.

CONCLUSION

We have attempted to show with examples from the Grasshopper Ruin and the Joint Site how one can specify and locate observational units relevant to one's systemic context interests. The point has been made that probability sampling begins at the limits of expert judgment and in no instance supplants such judgment (Hill n.d.). There are no simple solutions to the sampling problem, especially when it is realized that a representative sample of the archaeological context does not insure a representative sample of the systemic context. Also, a representative sample of the systemic context does not necessarily require a representative sample of the archaeological context.

The formation of the archaeological record provides the key to devising sampling strategies. When an investigator has in mind specific analytic units, such as early secondary refuse, de facto refuse, or even all deposits of secondary refuse, a consideration of the cultural and noncultural processes that formed the site under study is essential. Initial assumptions about these processes are gained from knowledge of similar processes operative in one's region or in comparable archaeological situations. While sampling for systemic context parameters, an investigator must also attempt to test his initial assumptions concerning formation processes and modify these assumptions to structure subsequent stages of the sampling program. When knowledge of formation processes is acquired in the progress of a multiphase sampling design, the probability of successfully locating and retrieving data relevant to systemic context concerns is increased considerably.

ACKNOWLEDGMENTS

We thank Mark P. Harlan, H. A. Luebbermann, Jr., and David R. Wilcox for helpful criticism. Excavations at the Grasshopper Ruin have been conducted by the Department of Anthropology and the Arizona State Museum at the University of Arizona with support from the National Science Foundation (GE-7781; GZ-22; GZ-397; GZ-745; GZ-1113; GZ-1493; GZ-1924; GS-2566; GS-33436). The archaeological research is conducted under an agreement with the White Mountain Apache Tribal Council. We are grateful to the White Mountain Apache for their interest in and encouragement of this program of scientific investigations. The Joint Site investigations were supported by the Field Museum of Natural History and the National Science Foundation (GS-2381 and GY-4601). We thank Sharon Urban and Charles Sternberg for the figures.

PART FOUR

Sampling at the Artifactual Level

The single paper in this section is an example of sampling artifacts and of laboratory, as opposed to field, sampling. Certain deductively based programmatic statements have indirectly argued against the laboratory sampling of artifacts; the argument is that a well-planned research design should consider these contingencies of artifact density prior to excavation. Because such contingencies cannot always be predicted, the recovery of more artifacts than can be realistically analyzed in the laboratory is a common problem. The solution is probabilistic sampling at the artifactual level of analysis and can be achieved because of the ease of constructing a frame of excavated artifacts and of insuring equal probability of selection. If a site has been completely excavated, sampling to solve this contingency avoids the onerous sampling paradox. Another contingency that is difficult to predict is the failure to recover certain artifact classes necessary for the proof of a certain idea or hypothesis. This failure obviously cannot be corrected at the artifactual level of sampling, but requires a modification of the sampling strategy at the site or regional levels as appropriate.

Another contrast between this laboratory level and the previous field levels of sampling is the change in the unit of investigation. In the field, the sampling units are two- or three-dimensional spatial entities that usually contain clusters of cultural elements; in laboratory sampling, the units are cultural elements; e.g. points or flakes. These elements can also be considered as a cluster of attributes. Robert A. Benfer's chapter provides an empirical insight into these methodological and sampling problems.

Additionally, Benfer has opted for one of two possible alternatives in artifactual analysis: the choice of a large number of attribute observations on a small number of artifacts. The opposing option would be the choice of a small number of attribute observations on a large number of artifacts. Of course, there are intermediate options along the continuum. This sampling decision must be, and has been, made consciously or unconsciously by all practitioners of archaeology.

J. W. M.

13. Sampling and Classification

Robert A. Benfer

Robert A. Benfer (Ph.D., University of Texas, 1968) has focused his research on quantitative methods in archaeology and physical anthropology. His very active career includes field research in Peru, Mexico, and Texas; this work has resulted in numerous published articles and reviews, as well as many professional papers. He has held memberships in many scientific societies and has codirected a National Science Foundation grant for the analysis of Tula excavations in Mexico. He also has been Chairman of the Department of Anthropology at the University of Missouri-Columbia.

Excavations directed by Richard A. Diehl of the University of Missouri-Columbia, in the ancient city of Tula, Hidalgo, Mexico, produced over 250,000 provenience-bearing artifacts.* A stratified surface survey of the entire urban area, has added several hundred thousand more artifacts which are presently being processed. Many different analyses are in progress and, of necessity, most involve sampling. For example, the analysis by James Stoutamire of several hundred thousand artifacts, collected by geographically stratifying the urban zone, includes materials from several areas of the zone. The areas are selected both by "common sense" and by formal sampling; samples so derived have been separated for analytical purposes. Work in progress by Robert Cobean has involved the analysis and refinement of ceramic modes by repeated simple random samples taken separately from the excavated and the surface materials. Work by Alice N. Benfer on the over 25,000 obsidian blade fragments from the excavations will include different kinds of samples drawn for different types of studies. Only some of the artifacts can be removed from Mexico, and limitations of time, money, and equipment prohibit study of all specimens of any class of artifact in the Tula laboratory.

Architectural analysis has been partly completed without recourse to sampling (Healan, 1974). Unlike Jelks (1975) and Rohn (n.d.) we find no problems in combining "dissection" or nonprobability sampling with probability sampling. In fact, stratification by nonprobabilistically obtained architectural features is an important part of our research strategy. Appeals to common sense observations leading to a presumably "representative" sample must be carefully considered. Even ethnographers, who spend considerable time in the field and have many more clues for effective nonprobabilistic sampling, find that inferential errors can result from reliance on

*The University of Missouri-Columbia Tula Project has been supported by NSF Grant 2139-2228, as well as grants from the Research Council of the University of Missouri.

judgmental selection (Honigmann 1970: 278–279). Archaeologists may run at least as great a risk by relying on impressions rather than explicit research designs. In practice, both probability and nonprobability samples will always be required if previous experience is to guide – but not completely constrain – new investigations.

One objective of the University of Missouri project is to intensively study obsidian blade fragments in hopes that hypotheses as to their production and use can be generated and tested. Their numbers alone challenge investigators. They are the most numerous category of artifact found at Tula except for ceramics.

Facing the task of ultimately analyzing samples drawn from the 50,000+ obsidian blade segments of the Tula project, the lithic technologist needed answers to important questions (Alice N. Benfer, personal communication). Were the obsidian blade segments a homogeneous set, with variation due to idiosyncratic variations in the stone worker's technique? Or, on the other hand, were the blade segments actually composed of several groups? For example, perhaps obsidian from different source areas possessed properties that caused different kinds of blades to be produced using the same method of production. Or, perhaps alternate techniques for the removal of blades were utilized at the same time, or developed differently through time. And it is also possible that blades were removed in different manners with specific purposes or functions in mind, and these blades would therefore differ in observable characteristics. Since no published work then existed on this problem (A. Benfer n.d.), it was decided to analyze a small available sample of obsidian blade segments. The proximal blade segments alone were chosen as the presence of the bulb of force allowed more technological variables to be evaluated.

If in fact several groups were found, subsequent analysis of samples from the entire collection would be greatly improved by stratifying based on the type of blade. For example, an infrequent type of blade might not be selected at all when samples from individual levels were selected by simple probability sampling. But stratification would ensure its representation, even in small samples. If, on the other hand, no groups exist, a great deal of wasted effort in stratification would be avoided, and the degradation of sample quality by irrelevant stratification would not occur. The present report discusses the logic and techniques used to arrive at a preliminary decision concerning the existence of groups in Toltec proximal obsidian blade segments. While the available sample was small, the information obtained has been helpful in subsequent analyses, and perhaps a review of the entire question of classification and sampling may be helpful to other workers who may be faced with similar problems.

STRATIFICATION BY CONTEXT

With the Tula materials, one sampling problem is immediately posed: how should samples be obtained from the excavated and survey materials in such a manner as to most efficiently allow accurate description of the total collection of blade segments? These tools were obtained (1) by extensive and usually shallow excavations designed to expose large areas of domestic architecture in one small portion of the city, and (2) from an areally stratified surface survey of the rest of the urban zone. While the obsidian tools from the surface survey are not yet analyzed, it is perhaps still of some value to describe the design of this survey, since no other chapter in this book is concerned with surface survey of an urban site.

A .16 percent sampling fraction of 320 surface units was drawn for the entire urban zone. [See Asch, in this volume, for implications of fraction and number of units on reliability.] A 500 × 500 meter grid was imposed on aerial photographs of the urban zone and surrounding areas. Each unit was further divided into 25 100 × 100 meter squares; 4 squares were randomly selected, *without replacement,* from among the 25. A 10 × 10 meter unit in the northwest corner of each larger square was then completely collected. A subsequent trend surface analysis will be used to guide the location of test pits, following Redman's (1973) advice on multistage designs. The interpolations by trend surface analysis may help to locate rarer anomalies missed by the .16 percent sampling fraction. Test pitting in these areas may help reduce the problems of overlooking small but important features. A sample stratified by horizontal location, depth, and context from the excavated material will also be selected to allow placement of the excavated materials in the larger context of the surface materials sampled from the entire city.

Mueller [in this volume] has emphasized the possible artificial inflation of within-group homogeneity when cluster sampling is used. However, I am not convinced that 10 × 10 meter squares in densely occupied urban areas are large enough to qualify as area clusters, or quadrats, in the manner of the 400 × 400 meter squares used by the Cedar Mesa Project [Matson and Lipe, in this volume]. In fact, the 10 × 10 meter square was specifically chosen as the largest area, in the interests of sampling economy to exclude numerous homogeneous elements. While 100 × 100 meter major units with 10 × 10 meter sampling units could be thought of as nested sampling (Mueller), I argue that the sampling units are "points" and will give unbiased estimates of population parameters. [See Judge, Ebert, and Hitchcock, this volume.] For the present, I provisionally accept the stratified areal survey as a point sample.

The choice of square sampling units (quadrats) does not imply commitment to this shape. In another sample, several doughnut shaped bands were collected around conical structures at Tula—to investigate variability near these mounds. However, the results of Judge, Ebert, and Hitchcock [this volume] may be interpreted as favoring square quadrats over rectangular transects for many archaeological purposes. [See also Read, this volume.]

The sampling designs that will be used to investigate the excavated materials will include: (1) a simple probability sample for estimating type frequencies, (2) an architecturally stratified nonprobabilistic sample for detection and verification of areas of specialized activity, and (3) several nonprobability columns for stratigraphic studies. A fourth possibility is discussed below.

STRATIFICATION BY TYPE OF ARTIFACT

Suppose obsidian blade segments were specialized tools to the extent that different types were produced for different purposes, and these types did not occur in similar proportions. If this is so, a sample of the elements, that is, blade segments, should also be selected with stratification by kind of blade. Samples for political opinion polling, to be efficient, must be drawn from various parts of the country, and also must include Democrats, Republicans, and Independents. So also should an obsidian blade segment sample include representatives of each type of blade segment, in addition to being drawn from various parts of the excavations and surface. In the present example, any types of blades, generated from simple measurements and observations could be used as strata from which a small sample could be chosen for such extremely time consuming tasks as microscopic wear pattern and trace element analyses. Redman (1973 and in this volume) discusses the same problem and concludes that a very small obsidian sample would have served him well.

Is there *any* question that subgroups or types exist within the group *obsidian blade segments?* Oxnard (1973: 73) has noted that "the term fundamental group has been taken by some workers to mean that subset of the specimens of whose internal structure one has not yet become aware." Blackith and Reyment, two other biologists, go even further and state, "Indeed, a homogeneous group has been cynically defined as one in whose heterogeneity the experimenter has not yet become interested" (1971: 141). Feynman, a physicist, illustrates the successful technique of "recognizing that the complexity of things at one level is the result of the fact that these things are composed of simpler elements at another level" (1974: 601). However, without experimental control, any hypothesized smaller units would have little utility. Archaeological classification problems are more similar to biological than physical classification problems, where experiments quickly and efficiently weed unsupportable classes from the literature. A more indirect approach is required by biologists and archaeologists where true experimental designs are only occasionally employed. (See Ahler 1971 and Leaf n.d. for two successful examples of archaeological experiments.)

Two broad strategies have been followed by archaeologists to produce or validate homogeneous groups (types). One, identified most prominently with Spaulding (1953), has been to provide some evidence that clusters of attributes (or artifact types) are not totally arbitrary, by rejection of statistically phrased null hypotheses. The other view, perhaps most firmly stated by Dunnell (1971) is to *impose* classes on any given sample by application of contrast sets selected from an examination of materials from the region. Driver (1974: 336) contrasts a similar approach in the strata imposed by Murdock on ethnic units with the biological techniques of numerical taxonomy where units and taxa are *built up* from the data. Obviously sampling is more important in the latter than the former approach. Work reported in this book involves the application of more or less arbitrarily imposed hierarchical classes on the data at coarse levels, and statistical analysis of heterogeneity at finer levels. Hill and Evans (1972) propose an ideal typology of archaeologists where "empiricist" and "positivist" are used in a strange fashion to label models which imply meaning within the data ("empiricist") versus those which confer meaning on the data ("positivist"). The article is confusing, since it seems to favor the latter position, yet structures the argument within the former. "Even though there are archaeologists who subscribe to it in their programmatic statements . . . we know of no archaeologist who really conforms in practice to the tenets of the empiricist model in its *pure* form" (Hill and Evans 1972: 236, emphasis added). Whallon (1974: 28) has additional criticisms of the Hill and Evans position. In any case, I find no such necessary polarity of approaches, and the present chapter is a hybrid of the two, if either exist.

CLASSIFICATORY CONSIDERATIONS

In Theory

Sometimes a distinction is drawn between classes (which are ideational rather than empirical) and groups (which are empirical). Dunnell (1971: 44–45) discusses the contrast at length. For example, a paradigm (as defined in Conklin, 1964: 39–40 rather than the philosophical sense of the word as used by Kuhn 1970) focuses on the intersection of contrast sets. A paradigmatic approach emphasizes all contrasts among the attributes, whether or not particular combinations actually occur on any particular case. On the other hand, a typology—a taxonomic hierarchy where the levels are interchangeable or commutative, and hence, arbitrary—emphasizes actual artifacts as classified by defining contrasts among attributes. There are many, many other structures which can be used to organize data, including dimensional representations which will be discussed below. Degerman (1972) has a very complete discussion of structures useful for analysis. He suggests that paradigms could be rotated and projected into dimensional space for many purposes (Degerman 1972: 202). Formally, paradigms and typologies are not very different (see Dunnell 1971: Fig. 13); paradigms are often portrayed as matrices and include all contrast sets; whereas typologies are more commonly displayed as trees. However, without empirical content, paradigms, typologies, or other kinds of structures do not qualify as appropriate topics for scientific inquiry.

The claim has been made for the priority of the paradigmatic method of organization (Dunnell 1971: 83). A major difficulty with this approach is the problem of sampling among variables, or contrast sets, as they are often called. While the problems involved in sampling *things* are difficult, they do not seem in principle insurmountable. However, to randomly sample variables from even a finite domain is at best difficult. With multivariate procedures, some indication of coverage of a domain with respect to its ability to predict a criterion is usually available. If 85 percent or 95 percent of the variance of a variable or even a linear combination of variables (such as factors, canonical variates, and so forth) covaries with the criterion, then the domain is well sampled with respect to that criterion. A significant body of evidence exists from a number of fields that multivariate techniques such as factor and canonical analysis (Oxnard 1973: 51; Benfer n.d.c; Rummel 1970: Ch. 20) often locate the same *underlying* sources of variance even when different variables or samples are used.

The extreme claim that paradigms can completely serve our analytical purposes loses too much by ignoring folk categories. Feldman (1973: Tables 1 and 2) documents Central Mexican Nahua names for different rocks and minerals. The category *Chalchihuitl* (greenstone) does not include jade while the category *Itzli* (which generally refers to several kinds of obsidian) includes jade as precious *itzli*. Clearly, contemporary geological subdivisions of rocks and menerals may be very misleading in analyses of Aztec stone tools. Perhaps the formal analysis of 'obsidian' used in the present paper has already become too detailed and hence, misleading. Another problem is that major contrasts may be inappropriately selected. For example, a formal account of available subsistence resources may be of little use if most categories are not recognized as available food by members of the society of interest. Ethnographers are protected from such absurd errors by a constant feedback, quasiexperimental situation, where developing ideas (modes) are tested against the data in the observation of daily life.

The experiences of the ethnoscientists with kinship indicate that variability in formal cognitive models within an ethnographically known society is a problem that is ignored at the investigator's risk. (Compare Ackerman 1964 with Geoghan and Kay 1964; or Goodenough 1965 with Schneider 1965.) Intrasociety variation also exists in cognitive models of material items (White and Thomas 1972; Robbins and Pollnac 1974). DeFries and others (1974), using factor analysis, have recently identified nearly identical cognitive dimensions from two different ethnic groups. Multivariate analysis can find and validate major underlying dimensions. Scribner and Cole (1973) present some evidence that extremely abstract categories rarely exist in human minds not exposed to formal schooling. Therefore, elaborate paradigms or typologies may be anthropocentric creations of our educational processes. Randall (n.d.) has suggested that most taxonomic trees are *dwarfs* and that extensive taxonomic trees are not usually stored in a person's memory, but are rather the creation of the ethnographer.

Dunnell's definition of formal archaeological classification is so narrow that near total insulation would be achieved from variability, the use of statistics, and the related troublesome problems of sampling. One is reminded of an earlier, unsuccessful attempt (White 1959) to remove anthropology from the grasping hands of biologists, or worse, psychologists, when cross-fertilization seemed threatening (see Taylor 1972: 32–33 for other criticisms of White's influence on "new" archaeologists). Goodenough (1956) and Lounsbury (1956), ethnographers who refined formal analysis for ethnographic use from the pioneering work of Morgan, Kroeber, and Tax, were also influenced by work in related fields such as mathematical learning theory in psychology and linguistics. While it is possible to argue that White created necessary distance from psychological reductionism, I find the logic strained. Chaney (1974: 1364–1370) advances, in a stimulating essay, a nonreductionist view where problems may be phrased as successively lower levels of conceptualization.

The question of whether the goal of the particular investigation is to find indicators of groups which were cognitively meaningful to the original manufacturers is, in my opinion, a matter of preference rather than dogma. Levi-Strauss (1963: 4), for example, notes the tendency of clan members to try to live up to their clan name in day to day living. Could clan names be discovered from avoidances reflected in material remains? Certainly not, if the question is never asked. The evaluation of cognitive hypotheses with material remains is, of course, going to be difficult, but not impossible (see White and Thomas 1972 and also Robbins and Pollnac 1974 for ethnographic examples). Even "hardliners" such as Hill and Evans (1972: 255) grudgingly allow this possibility.

Lischka (1974: 1716) correctly contrasts the experimental situations often available to laboratory scientists with the nonexperimental situations usually available to archaeologists. The analysis of variance model, so often employed in biological and psychological experimental settings is exactly the case where a paradigm is examined for the significance of the subsets. Since cases are assigned randomly to each cell, any differences greater than chance could account for must be assignable to differential treatments (for example, see Fisher 1954 or Edwards 1960). But random selection of cases, as in probability sampling, is not equivalent to random assignment of cases to groups, and caution is indicated. Uncritical acceptance of models more appropriate to the experimental sciences is still just as dangerous as when I pointed out the problem a few years ago (Benfer 1968). Archaeologists must be careful lest they create the world they wish to examine.

However, even if the loss of information from ignoring folk categories is acceptable in a specific instance, or in general for those who would take archaeology outside of the social sciences, the results still may be dangerous if passed off as though they had some *cultural* validity. Where and how is confirmation of paradigmatic models possible without samples of empirical data? And how are decisions to be made from samples without turning to statistics, the discipline which concerns itself with inferences from samples?

In Practice

While it has been demonstrated that multivariate methods can sometimes recover actual physical groupings of prehistoric artifacts (Benfer and others n.d.) as well as those with common spatial-temporal varying dimensions (R. Benfer 1967 and A. Benfer 1969), what evidence supports *detailed* formal classifications of archaeological data? For example, obsidian blades still possessing part of the proximal end can be divided into those with a prominent bulb of force and those lacking a prominent bulb. But is this dichotomy useful? One criterion of usefulness for the purposes of this study consists of substantial correlation with patterns of wear, for which we do not yet have measurements available. Or, the usefulness of classifications of blade segments might be related to the cultural meaningfulness of the categories to the original manufacturer. But how is cultural saliency judged?

I have suggested and defended (Benfer 1967, 1972) a multivariate approach using factor analysis. White and Thomas (1972: 298) recently demonstrated that principal components analysis could discover significant patterns of covariation not previously suspected—covert types or mental templates. But the complexity of multivariate procedures causes some workers to misunderstand them (Sackett 1969). Still, the search for attribute and measurement patterns must not be abandoned, because success seems very possible. Simon (1974) extends Miller's work in the number of basic categories and finds that 7 ± 2 is still a reasonable estimate. Thus a small, finite "vocabulary" may exist for any specified domain, and it may be discoverable by multivariate procedures even though the number of combinations, or "words" may be very large indeed. In any case, archaeological classes are useful if they tap some part of the culturally meaningful, customary behavior of the original members of the societies whose behavior is in part preserved in the archaeological record [see Collins, in this volume]. Other approaches may find classes that are more useful in understanding the customary behavior of the archaeologist. Dunnell's work resembles biological systematics in the 1940s, when within-species variability was a recognized but poorly resolved problem for static classical taxonomy (Simpson 1945). It is a pity that Dunnell did not follow later developments (Simpson 1961; Sokal and Sneath 1963).

Dunnell would also have us explain artifact variation without making much use of cultural theories, while another kind of processual archaeologist (Flannery 1967) would have us explain cultural changes without making extensive use of the artifactual data. Paleontologists, for example, could attempt to explain changes in, and classification of, fossils without recourse to knowledge of modern adaptive variation. Perhaps a few still do. On the other hand, biologists are not persuasive when they attempt to explain human evolution by appealing to "analogies" with the living apes and producing some slight, often insubstantial evidence for their view. Surely the most productive strategy for archaeologists is to take *cultural, biological, ecological, and other frameworks, modify them so that predictions are centered on material remains, and test the models for goodness of fit with samples drawn from the specified universe.* Recent experiences of paleontologists involved in systematics are of direct interest to archaeologists. After a great deal of not always calm debate (which can be followed in the *Journal of Systematic Biology* over the last ten years), a settling out of strategies has occurred. At the higher, more arbitrary levels of taxonomic hierarchy, where convenience especially determines organization, the classical approach is retained. At the family levels, most numerical techniques concern structures which are present or absent—rather than homologously measurable—and classification techniques tend to center on nominal measurement. At the genus, species, and especially the subspecies level, multivariate techniques based on interval scale measurements predominate (Blackith and Reyment 1971: 275–276). Arguments in archaeology today as to whether formal or statistical approaches are correct will presumably be also recognized as a pseudo problem in time. In this chapter, formal analysis (to the level of proximal obsidian blade segments as one class of obsidian artifacts) is further examined for heterogeneity by statistical means.

The "natural regularities approach" (Flannery 1973) devalues work with only one part of the remains of a cultural system. But, perhaps the systemic view also should be reexamined more critically. In an article titled "The Nature and Sources of Irrationalism" it is noted that the holistic assumption that

All things are internally related in such a way that they are parts of one single organic entity, so constituted that if it changes in one respect it must change in every other respect [while] expressing a hope that many men of great poetic and religious feeling have frequently entertained, is not one on the basis of which anybody can consistently think or act (Frankel 1973: 930).

Relatively simple (Frances 1961; Van de Geer 1971; Blalock 1971) or multivariate (Van de Geer 1971: 196–205; Rummel 1970: 384–385) causal hypotheses can be evaluated even without experimental control. Sabloff and others (1973: 107) see potential in recent preliminary reports of systems application. However, I will leave evaluation of "everything is related to everything" hypotheses to those with more systematic talent. With Sabloff and others (1973: 112), I as yet see no reason to join the building of a "Hempelian superstructure" or the more ambitious task of successfully applying a deductive-nomological strategy to archaeological research. I will return to the classical multiple working hypotheses, a deductive method (Chamberlain 1897), where sampling is required.

CLASSIFICATION OF TOLTEC BLADE SEGMENTS: POSSIBLE PROCEDURES

In order to efficiently sample by stratification, it is necessary to know what kinds of obsidian blade segments do in fact exist. Only by preliminary sampling can we know anything about the total universe of obsidian blade segments at Tula. The sampling "paradox" can be resolved by iteration, as is being done with the ceramic materials. Here I report the results of the first tentative iteration in obsidian blade segment classification.

How should we proceed in the task of discovering Toltec-produced natural groups of proximal obsidian blade segments, if any, from this assemblage? Multivariate techniques are certainly more complicated than univariate and bivariate approaches. I have presented my reasoning for not continuing formal analysis further. But what about simpler statistical techniques?

Univariate Techniques

Univariate techniques usually involve measures of central tendency and variance. Could not the statistical mode be used to indicate that standard which craftsmen were aiming at and explain other results as "errors"? Consider the histogram in Figure 13.1. It is tempting, and possibly correct, to suppose that members of the society whose customary behavior is pre-

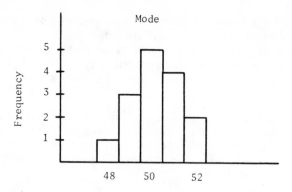

Fig. 13.1.   Hypothetical length of snapped blade segments

served to an unknown extent in these blades were habitually trying to produce blade segments 50 mm. long. But suppose blades for shaving were
longer than blades for cutting food. Figure 13.2b might actually be the
result of two mixed distributions as shown in Figure 13.2a. Notice that
neither tool was intended to be 50 mm. long in this hypothetical example.
The argument could be extended to stylistic changes (51-mm. shaving
blade segments might have gone out of fashion in favor of a more compact
47-mm. model). How can the modal seeking archaeologist know that the
observed mode is not actually the result of mixing? Kruskal (1972) has
suggested the use of a modified measure of the coefficient of variation to
detect mixed distributions. Progress in this work might prove helpful in
resolving the presently unsolved problem.

Rouse's most recent concept of cultural mode (Rouse 1972: 56) is a synonym for types of features. But his earlier definition, that of a community
standard (Rouse 1960: 314), is more appropriate to this discussion. Hill and
Evans (1972: 248) note the difficulty of not always understanding quite
what Rouse has in mind by *mode*, but suggest normative preference as
Rouse's primary meaning. Dunnell (1971: 156) correctly notes that attributes can be the product of human activity while not necessarily being
cultural, that is, behavior directed towards community standards of customary activities. My example (Fig. 13.1 and 13.2) illustrates this possibility
and suggests that it is ambiguously researched with univariate approaches.

Univariate techniques have been extended to a number of variables producing a multivariable but not multivariate approach. Widely available
programs such as BREAKDOWN (Nie and others 1970: 134) and similar
algorithms are only univariate approaches repeated (see Whallon 1972).
Peebles (1972) demonstrates a dramatic failure of this kind of multivariable
univariate approach compared to a more successful multivariate cluster
analysis of the same data. Univariate classificatory approaches might be
safely employed to yield meaningful classifications where very little time,
a small homogeneous settlement, and a general purpose tool (rather than
different varieties for different tasks) are assumed. More powerful methods
are needed in other instances.

Bivariate Techniques

The use of variables (attributes, measurements, scaled observations, etc.) to investigate the distribution of cases (artifacts, dwellings, sites, etc.), or the converse, is a simple bivariate approach. Since I sometimes find it difficult to discuss the two processes separately, I will try to stick with a simpler and more neutral vocabulary than is perhaps customary. In particular, I wish to consider using variables to measure interaction, correlation, or distance among cases.

With a small number of intervals or attribute states, contingency tables are convenient models for examining interactions. Equal interval or ordinal variables are dichotomized or split into a relatively small number of categories (see Sackett 1966: 361–363). Often, contrast sets are actually typological schemes. For example, see Sackett (1966: 364) from which the example in Figure 13.3 is obtained. In my opinion, the pervasiveness of typological thinking at even such very low levels of analysis creates difficulty for many students in learning more powerful measurement scales.

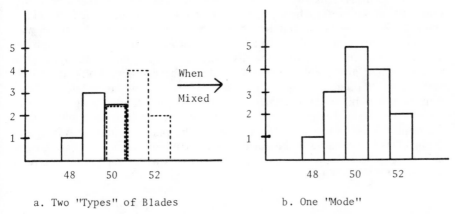

a. Two "Types" of Blades   b. One "Mode"

Fig. 13.2.   Mixed distribution of snapped blade segments

How is the contingency table used to infer "clustering" of cases? Consider the following example where a scattergram and a contingency table are presented. The X and Y axes might represent equal interval measurements, or if the dichotomies are genuine, the continuous probability of the trait being present or absent. Variables X and Y are obviously related, whether one examines the scatter diagram or the contingency table (regression or chi square results might be necessary to convince skeptics). From the contingency table we conclude a significant interaction, and from the scatter diagram a single group is depicted. Consider the next example, Figure 13.5, where a different scatter diagram gives rise to the same contingency table. Three groups appear to be present, judging from the scattergram, whereas the same significant interaction is found in the contingency table. Many different configurations may give rise to similar results.

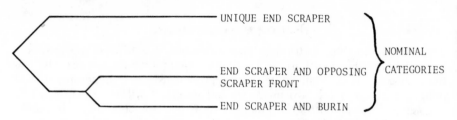

Fig. 13.3.   A typology used as a nominal measurement scale

Spaulding (1953, 1960a), Sackett (1966), Whallon (1972) and perhaps other users of the "statistical clustering" method might assume groups from the contingency table. Williams (1968) does present an actual ethnographic example where heterogeneity is detected by this technique (although his rejection of the homogeneity hypothesis is based on an unusual and seemingly incorrect addition of two chi square values). While it should be obvious from the scattergrams that many possibilities can and do give rise to the same significant interactions, the decision as to whether the data set is heterogeneous, or homogeneous but correlated, is not easily made with bivariate contingency tables. While the bivariate approach is an improvement over the univariate one, the resulting inferences remain ambiguous for two reasons. First, the weakness of nominal measurement scales in locating patterns is implied in Figures 13.4 and 13.5. Second, to infer similarity from nominal bivariate schemes, whether conceptualized as contingency tables, paradigms, typologies, or taxonomic hierarchies, one must make the doubtful assumption that each case can be placed equidistant in space. (Four classes would be at the corners of a tetrahedron, for example, Degerman 1972: 196.) Contrast the contingency tables with their scatter diagrams in Figures 13.4 and 13.5.

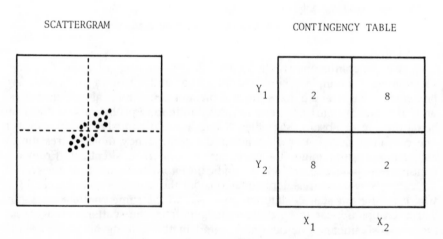

Fig. 13.4.   One group: Significant interaction

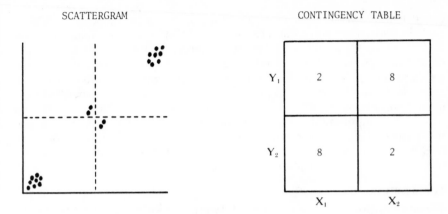

Fig. 13.5.   Three groups: Significant interaction

The weakness of nominal scaling can be compensated somewhat by using many variables. Patterns are more likely to be detectable in n-dimensional equidistant space than in two-dimensional space. A more powerful method of multiway chi square has been used (Sackett 1966). However, Sackett's apparent unawareness of the many methods of assessing similarity among nominally measured things is reflected thusly: "Unfortunately there is no equally satisfactory nonparametric measure of association" (Sackett 1966: 366). This statement is surprising, considering that Sokal and Sneath in 1963 had extensively reviewed matching coefficients, and Driver (1961) described the *early* use of matching coefficients by ethnologists. In any case, contingency table organization of data is probably better reserved for hypothesis testing than for hypothesis generation, and the results of hypotheses tested by the Spaulding method are ambiguous. Simple two-way chi squares should not continue to be used for this purpose. Multiclassificatory chi squares (R. Benfer n.d.a) or the less clumsy log linear models are still useful where a small number of variables are of interest in hypotheses testing. (See Muller and Mayhall 1971, for their introduction to anthropologists.)

Multivariate Techniques

Space does not permit discussion of the various clustering and dimensionalizing techniques available for more powerful detection of groups. Hodson and others (1971) have edited a collection of papers which include many of the presently available tools for producing relatively unambiguous groups with archaeological data. Clarke (1968 and 1972) also presents many possible approaches. Although Davis (1973) addresses his book to geologists, it is an excellent introduction to programming and multivariate statistics for archaeologists. Perrin (1974: 552) illustrates the power of even simple multivariate techniques when he finds 84 percent correct classification of drugs as either sedatives or tranquilizers in an admittedly easy sample. The nearest neighbor approach was used, and similarities were based merely on the number of a's, b's, c's, etc. in the name of each compound. Thus, common structure and activity of drugs are located by extremely unlikely variables. The nearest neighbor approach and, indeed, most clustering techniques depend, as has been recently noted (Machol and Singer 1971) on a hyperspheroid assumption of group composition. I have followed Fillenbaum and Rapoport (1971: 39) in clustering cases in a smaller dimensional space where other patterns of anthropological interest might be observed (Benfer n.d.b). However, all multivariate clustering techniques will usually yield some groups, even if random data are used. How does one avoid producing trivial groups? A provisional solution is suggested below, following a description of the sample.

The Sample

Twenty-six proximal blade segments were collected by Alice N. Benfer from the surface of the general area excavated by the University of Missouri-Columbia at Tula during the 1972 field season. This nonprobability opportunistic collection was selected for attribute analysis as a preliminary sample. On the basis of work described elsewhere (A. Benfer n.d., 1973) and results of the analyses described below, an unprocessed sample has been drawn for the final analysis.

Seventy measurements and observations are available for these proximal segments, and they are described in detail elsewhere (A. Benfer n.d.). Sixty were selected after deleting ten which were either constants or ambiguous.

Sampling Variables

A table of random numbers was consulted to divide the 60 measurements into two sets. One set with 29 variables (from even random numbers) and the other with 31 (from odd random numbers). These two samples of variables are used to investigate the hypothesis that strong groups of blade segments are present. If this hypothesis is correct, then approximately the same groups should be located with each separate set of variables. If the hypothesis is wrong (that is, if the blade segments do not occur in groups), then different clusters of blades may be found with each set. However, before investigating this hypothesis, a more pressing need is to find out whether the distribution of blade segments in 29 dimensional space corresponds to that in 31 dimensional space. The issue here is the reliability of the two different measurement sets in locating the specimens in measurement space, not in the existence of groups.

Reliability Test

Canonical correlation of the two sets* yielded two significant roots ($p < 0.002$ and $p < 0.002$; Program CANON, Veldman 1967). Thus, I conclude the cases have a distribution in 29 variable space that is much more similar to 31 variable space than would be expected by chance. The power of multi-

---

*Actually, loadings from the first seven principal components of each set were used (65% of the variance) as the data matrix could not be inverted.

variate techniques is demonstrated, as two separate sets of variables produced very similar descriptions of the sample. However, nothing is implied about clusters in either sample, as the existence of groups is not directly determined by canonical correlation, but rather whether the coordinates of the blade segments are similar in the two spaces.

Grouping Analysis

Hierarchical cluster analysis of the 26 blade segments first by the 29 variables and secondly by the 31 variables (both sets standardized) produced two separate hierarchical groupings (Program HGROUP, Veldman 1967). Because both sets of variables produced a very large increase in the pooled within variance (greater heterogeneity within groups) when five groups were reduced to four, the two sets of five groups were cross tabulated. Chi square indicates that the marginal predictions do not match the observed values well (p < .005), that is, both sets produced groups similar in composition. These results might appear to force the conclusion that groups do exist in this collection of blade segments, since two different sets of measurements produced similar groups. However, the amount of independence in the two sets of measurements is in doubt. Especially with such a large number of variables, redundant measurements and observations may have occurred in each sample of measurements. Factor analysis is an efficient technique for removing redundancy (R. Benfer 1972; Rummel 1970).

Grouping From Principal Components Scores

Principal components analysis requires *no* assumptions about the data when used to reduce dimensionality and is especially appropriate where heterogeneity is suspected (Gower 1966; R. Benfer n.d.c, n.d.b). On the other hand, common factor analysis is superior where shared variation only is of interest (R. Benfer 1972). Common factor analysis is inappropriate in very heterogeneous samples (Cattell 1965). Component and factor scores are usually similar in any case (Gower 1966: 336). Principal components were extracted from each potentially heterogeneous sample of 29 and 31 variables. Standardized component scores (uncorrelated in the orthogonal Varimax solution used) were input into the grouping program. Several different "shoulders" in the scree test of increasing pooled within variance were present, so the conservative hypothesis of two groups in each sample was tested by chi square.

With six and four component scores, the correspondence between the two groupings (29 and 31 variable sets) approached but did not attain traditional levels of significance (0.05 < p < 0.10). Figure 13.6 illustrates the results. Using larger numbers of components actually decreased the correspondence between the two groupings, presumably as additional components added error to the distances among cases (data not presented).

In summary, sampling of variables does not allow rejection of the alternate hypothesis that strong groups are present when raw, correlated variables are used. The null hypothesis of no groups is rejected. However, the hypothesis that strong groups exist can be rejected by accepting the null

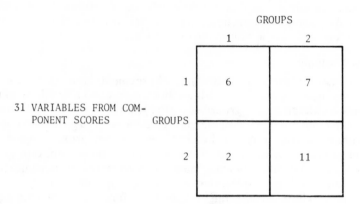

Fig. 13.6. Cross tabulation of groups
from nonredundant component scores

hypothesis when independent linear combinations of the original variables are used. The incredible naivety displayed by Dunnell (1971: 190) in suggesting that "Grouping, since it produces extensionally defined units, is not amenable to testing," is a pity. His lack of even a primitive understanding of multivariate statistics finds him nearly alone, facing backwards to the simpler monothetic days (Dunnell 1971: 53) gone by.

Of course, few researchers have so many variables and so few specimens available; in other cases, tests of the existence of groups, such as multiple discriminant function, are appropriate. However, the small sample pilot technique is recommended where many variables and cases are ultimately available. Preliminary knowledge can be extremely important when an enormous sample is to be analyzed. In a small collection, sampling variables is an alternative to sampling cases.

CONCLUSIONS

Sampling domains of measurement is a practical approach for searching for groups in artifacts. In the present case, no strong groups emerged when independent measures were used. Thus, stratification of proximal obsidian blade segments by groups from measurements does not now seem likely to improve the efficiency of a sample drawn for wear pattern or other types of time consuming lithic studies. Of course, subsequent examination of a larger sample may cause this tentative conclusion to be altered.

Finer Formal Analysis

Further formal analysis of the proximal obsidian blade segments would have produced a tree whose branches could be used to stratify obsidian blade segments for subsequent sampling. Evidence presented above does not suggest this course would prove productive.

Bivariate Analysis

Some of the measurements and observations are significantly intercorrelated (data not presented). These relationships could be found in a single homogeneous group (for example, see Fig. 13.4) or in a sample comprised of several groups (see Fig. 13.5). The bivariate chi square method proposed by Spaulding cannot distinguish the two cases. The more powerful multivariate analysis presented above suggests that these blade segments are a single group. While the significant intercorrelations may suggest cultural preferences, they may also represent mechanical properties of the stone. Further work, in progress, should help in understanding this artifact category, if in fact it is an empirically demonstrable class.

Most univariate and bivariate techniques are not powerful enough to protect users from constructing trivial groups. The greater power of multivariate grouping methods helps somewhat. Sampling strategies for selection of cases and variables can further strengthen analysis, but some problems remain.

Review of the Multivariate Grouping Method

To briefly review the techniques described, I first began with a small sample of obsidian blades, looking for strong groups with an eye towards stratification by groups for a later sampling stage. In order to protect against the creation of groups when in fact none exist—and the Spaulding and Sackett methods have been demonstrated to afford little safety against such mistakes—a multivariate technique was selected. The original 60 variables were first randomly divided into two groups. Canonical correlation found the location of each blade with respect to the other blades very similar for either set of measurements. However, grouping analysis of the two sets of measurements, first transformed to independent linear combinations of the original variables, failed to demonstrate the same clusters at commonly accepted levels of significance.

Strengths of the Multivariate Grouping Method

Division of the available variables allowed rejection of the hypothesis of any groups at all in the sample. *No other method—formal typological analysis, Spaulding or Sackett's contingency table methods, or the application of multivariate clustering methods to the entire data set—would have been able to reject this hypothesis.* On the other hand, were groups to be found by this method, their internally established reliability would demand immediate preference over competing organizations of the data. Further stratification by type of proximal obsidian blade segment is not anticipated on the basis of this evidence. Thus the quality of our ultimate sample will not be degraded by an irrelevant stratification, if the conclusion that no strong groups do exist is correct.

Weakness of the Multivariate Grouping Method

Ambiguous results were obtained when the use of correlated variables was compared to groupings from independent measures. The trouble is that de-correlation of measurements implicitly depends on the equal weighting of each specimen. Yet if the sample is heterogeneous, equal weighting of specimens may be no more correct than the equal weighting of variables. If approximately the same numbers of cases occurred in any existing groups, then the mixing of among and within variances would not be as serious a problem. But in the present case no previous hypotheses were available as to the composition of such groups.

In the extremely heterogeneous case (see Fig. 13.5), both the Spaulding chi square and most multivariate methods will conclude heterogeneity. For multivariate methods this is because the decorrelation of variables will primarily be influenced by the between groups component—a desirable situation where groups are to be subsequently searched for.

In the extremely homogeneous case (see Fig. 13.4), the Spaulding technique will commonly incorrectly infer groups, whereas the multivariate procedures, if protected by reliability estimates, will not make such an error. The intermediate cases are clearly the difficult ones. My co-investigator (Alice N. Benfer) and I are presently examining an iterative method on data from Tula obsidian projectile points which may be of some use under these circumstances.

Independent Versus Correlated Measurements

Only univariate analysis is immune in the consideration of whether to choose independent versus correlated measurements. Jardine and Sibson (1971: 25–28) suggest many problems in such a decision. In classical typology, bivariate chi square, n-way chi square "statistical clustering," and more powerful multivariate methods, the weighting of variables must be decided. If the decision is not made consciously, then, unfortunately, it will have to be made unconsciously.

The argument *for* leaving correlated variables in a grouping analysis is that they have demonstrated their importance by being significantly correlated, and variables uncorrelated with any other variables may merely be noise from the point of view of detecting groups (Sokal and Sneath 1963: 139; Gower 1972: 3). The usual argument *against* leaving correlated variables in a grouping analysis is to remove the (usually unconscious) weighting that is being given to the underlying major sources of variables (for example, see Blackith and Reyment 1971; Rummel 1970; Benfer 1967; and many others). I have noted that Texas dart point typologists weight stem variability more heavily than blade variability, even though both contain important independent patterns of covariation and both sets of patterns vary significantly in time and/or space (Benfer 1967). So naturally I am sensitized to the dangers of unequal weighting; my subsequent work has continued to reinforce this opinion.

Where the group under examination is actually homogeneous, either correlated or uncorrelated measures should usually allow rejection of the heterogeneous possibility. It is this case to which the Spaulding method is often applied with reasonable chances of some success. Despite the title "Statistical Techniques for the Discovery of Artifact Types" (Spaulding 1953), the method actually only allows the ambiguous rejection of group homogeneity. But since either genuine correlation or interaction among the variables or group heterogeneity can influence the decision reached, the results are extremely ambiguous. Much confusion exists in the literature due to this misunderstanding.

On the other hand, consider a group that is actually heterogeneous. Independent measures should efficiently locate subgroups. Correlated measures, since they weight some dimensions too heavily, may or may not produce the desired groups due to skewing from unequal weighting. For example, suppose a collection of heterogeneous boxes, coming in several more or less distinct sizes (such as shoe boxes, cigar boxes, matchboxes, etc.) were measured. If eight or ten different but correlated measurements of length but only one or two of width and height were taken, the use of these measurements would result in a classification greatly exaggerating length. One might find short shoe boxes grouped with cigar boxes of about the same length since width and height would have only a small effect on the results. It is necessary for the analyst to understand the implications of his choice of correlated or uncorrelated indicators. Still, the careful worker will want to hold an open mind on the problem. Perhaps someone will be able to provide an a priori reason for choosing or not choosing independent measures. Until then we will have to settle for a steady accumulation of examples. The obsidian and ceramic types from Tula will be tested for cultural saliency by architectural context and traditional horizontal and vertical provenience. Perhaps these results with both correlated and uncorrelated variables will shed more light on this vexing problem.

SUMMARY

Stratification by types has been suggested as desirable where they exist. Even a nonprobability sample can be examined for groups. If any exist, a subsequent sample should probably be stratified accordingly. Recovery of culturally meaningful classes by univariate and bivariate techniques has been summarized and rejected as weak and usually ambiguous. Multivariate procedures, though not without problems, promise better groups. The rejection of any strong groups in the proximal obsidian blade segments is a surprising result. Since no randomization was employed in the original selection of the blade segments, generalization of these negative results to the total universe of obsidian blade segments at Tula is a risk of unknown proportion. But the results do not support the hypothesis of strong groups in the Tula assemblage. The generalization of classes to a site or region merely because they are logically definable, I will leave to armchair empiricists or the more arrogant theorists – who "examine" the variability of a region, pronounce the major classes, and produce class models which are rarely tested for fit with empirical data. An occasional exception is the ascertainment of whether a matrix is orderable (for example, see Dunnell 1971: 166–167). The rejection of the hypothesis that groups actually do exist in a sample is rarely possible with such methods.

Results of the canonical correlation are also important in contradicting the notion that *basic* attributes do not exist in the data (Hill and Evans 1972: 265). The two similar sets of canonical axes, or underlying *basic* variables, were produced from two sets of different attributes. The second 31 variables added nothing really new to the first 29. Possibly additional variables might be fashioned to add new information, but a point of diminishing returns is reached sooner or later. Multivariate techniques often detect the same major underlying sources of variation, however attributes or variables are scaled or further subdivided. Sometimes, as in the present example, *different* sets of measurements produce the *same* underlying dimensions.

Obviously it is not enough to assert that behavior can be recovered from material remains (Binford 1962: 218–219). It must be demonstrated. Probability sampling and multivariate hypotheses, and where feasible, genuine experimental designs, provide presently available powerful methods for the analysis of archaeological hypotheses. Simulation and cybernetic approaches also hold promise, but both of necessity must also attend to sampling considerations. Regional experts can provide sensitive impressions of important local variations, conveniently arrayed systematically. But these impressions must be evaluated as hypotheses by careful sampling and powerful multivariate classification and prediction techniques.

My original hypothesis that groups did exist in the sample followed the notion that a homogeneous group is one that has not attracted the attention of an investigator. Without independent measures and the canonical correlation reliability test, the literature would end up cluttered with still another nonevaluated hierarchical arrangement of data. Worse, subsequent sampling would probably have been rendered less efficient. Sampling and multivariate tests of classification are at present the strongest defense against appeal to authority as the primary archaeological claim to knowledge.

ACKNOWLEDGMENTS

Richard A. Krause and James W. Mueller made valuable criticisms of an earlier draft of this chapter—criticisms which were helpful in writing this final version. I thank Richard A. Diehl, Director of the Tula Project, for inviting me to join him in what has become a productive endeavor for some students of prehistory.

But I must reserve the bulk of my thanks for my collaborator, colleague, editor, and wife, Alice N. Benfer. While I am responsible for the ideas expressed in this chapter, a great deal of the merit they possess has resulted from our countless discussions which accompanied the development of this report. Without my wife's busy scissors, the organization of this paper would still be in an almost random vector mode. She provided not only raw data but also many excellent suggestions for improving my idiolect into something more nearly approaching standard English.

Finally, I hope the colleagues that I have criticized in this paper will understand that my remarks are not personally directed. Rather I mean to provide an outsider's view of the seemingly narrow provincialism that has, until recently, predominated in classification and sampling in archaeology.

PART FIVE

Commentary

These final two chapters are intended as critical evaluations of the preceding chapters. Hopefully, the theoretical contributions and case studies will be more instructive in light of the discussion by the two commentators. Binford and Cowgill discuss relevant "theoretical issues" from different perspectives as well as specific comments on each of the earlier chapters. The comments by Binford include general discussion concerning the role of sampling vis-à-vis archaeological explanation, decision-making, and methodology. Cowgill's comments are specific and statistically oriented; they may be regarded as a reification of Binford's theoretical discussion. Certainly, these two differing perspectives complement each other nicely.

J. W. M.

14. Sampling, Judgment, and the Archaeological Record

Lewis R. Binford

Lewis R. Binford (Ph.D., University of Michigan, 1964) has been enjoying an intensive and dedicated career as an archaeological practitioner and theoretician. He has practiced archaeology in many parts of the Eastern Woodlands and most recently in Alaska. His extensive bibliography covers a multitude of topics from site reports to radiometric faunal analysis to journal reviews of prehistoric and historic projects. Many of his theoretical contributions have constituted the catalyst in the formation of "processual archaeology." He has been serving as Professor of Anthropology at the University of New Mexico.

INTRODUCTION

In Part One of this book very little discussion has been devoted to sampling. Discontent about the bias in the archaeological record is one nonsampling theme common to several chapters. Such a discussion seems to stem from the naive notion that the archaeological record is directly observable as "meaningful" information about the past; it is not, never has been and never will be.

The archaeological record is a contemporary phenomenon. It is above all a static phenomenon. It is what remains in static form of dynamics which occurred in the past as well as dynamics occurring up until present observations are made. The only meaningful statements we can make about the past are dynamic statements. The only statements we can make directly from the archaeological record are some form of descriptive statics. Getting to the past is then a process in which the archaeologist gives meaning to static phenomena in dynamic terms. This is a cultural process, the assignation of meaning to experience engaged in by the archaeologist. To point out continuously that data do not speak for themselves and that meanings assigned to archaeological observations may be wrong should not be surprising to anyone. Scientists particularly should appreciate that the scientific method was developed to cope with this problem in the first place.

That the archaeologist is surprised or just coming to the realization that data do not speak for themselves tells me something about the lack of scientific development in the field, but nothing about "limitations" on our potential understanding of the past. The limitations on our knowledge of the past derive from our lack of imagination as to how best to operationalize archaeological observations for permitting an evaluation of the meanings which we have given to archaeological facts. Gaining an evaluation of our ideas about the past through the use of archaeological observations of specified relevance is a scientific approach.

Raising objections that the archaeological record may be "biased" seems to stem from some strange expectation that the archaeological record is some kind of fossilized picture remaining to us from the past with built-in and self-evident meanings upon which "times arrow" has played disturbing tricks. No such meaningful picture exists complete with semantic directions as to how properly to read the record. All meanings come from us. All evaluations as to the reliability of those meanings as statements about the past must be made against facts operationalized as relevant and organized so as to permit an evaluation of our ideas about the past. Telling me that the archaeological record cannot be translated mechanically into statements about the past according to some set of rules for assigning meaning does not surprise me or depress me as to our potential for gaining understanding about the past. That only depresses nonscientists.

One general sampling point that has been raised in a contemporaneous publication concerns anatomy and physiology (Jelks 1975). What can you learn about an organized structure from a random spatial sample? My impression is that little can be learned using conventional archaeological grid units (three-meter squares, five-foot squares, etc.). If I am attempting to obtain an unbiased, representative sample of the population of pottery sherds on a site, or flint chips etc., I might come fairly close with a 10–30 percent spatial random sampling in conventional grid units. However, if my target population is the population of houses on a site, I would recover none if my grid units were conventional units, unless of course they were exceptionally small houses! Finally if my concern is with the internal organization of a site, what could I learn from a 10–30 percent random spatial sample? Nothing, or very little. I might be able to define the problem in that I could demonstrate differences and similarities between the sample units. However, the necessary spatial structure of proximity, association with features, and patterns of continuous variation, which provide the linking warrants in the definition of a structure, would still be buried (Jelks 1975). At last we are dealing with a sampling problem. Population biologists have faced similar problems and some knowledge has been gained and some solutions have been suggested. First, a sampling strategy must be evaluated with regard to the character of the target population to be sampled, not in absolute terms. A given strategy may work well for supplying information about the population of small movable items on a site, but not very well for houses. Secondly, to recover data on a number of target populations simultaneously may require a variety of sampling strategies executed in series; this is the reason that long ago I suggested *state excavations*.

Some anti-sampling discussions set up a straw man, a sampling problem, and an inappropriate sampling procedure. Discussions which attempt to argue that sampling has no role or is a cookbook technique to be used by nonexperts have no place in archaeology. Such discussion betrays a naivety about what archaeologists are doing. The demonstration that one procedure does not do what an archaeologist wishes simply indicates that the archaeologist used an inappropriate strategy; it in no way argues that an appropriate sampling strategy could not have been used by an archaeologist who understood sampling and the problem to be solved. The same answer could be made to the person who smilingly objects that the archaeologist using sampling procedures is somehow not using good judgment. For instance, I once heard an objection that if the sampling procedure suggested by me was employed, the crew would have to dig a 10 × 10 out in the middle of Saginaw Bay. Another time it was laughingly said that Binford couldn't dig a particular burial mound because it had been excluded from the area gridded for sampling. Such objections are silly. For instance, one of the assumptions of a sampling strategy is that one can enumerate all those units in the frame from which a sample is to be drawn. If the investigator missed a burial mound, or suggested that some area under water was within the frame, it may well betray a real problem about the archaeologist's competence; it is not, however, a comment on the utility or lack thereof of a sampling strategy. This is one of the largest problems in archaeology—the inadequacy of the archaeologist. Sampling can help the archaeologist overcome these human limitations and uniquenesses which bias his ability to see clearly that the archaeological record is an aid. This is one of the roles of sampling.

SPECIFIC COMMENTS

After this general discussion, I would like to review each of the individual chapters. The major thrust of chapter 2, by Michael B. Collins, is about confusion, confusion between the character of static data, and explanations for the character of that data. All archaeological data are static and importantly *contemporary*. Our observations on the archaeological record are contemporary phenomena, and it is only with these contemporary facts that we learn something either about the character of the archaeological record or in turn what static archaeological facts can do to inform us about the accuracy of our ideas about the dynamics of the past. Any statements about the dynamics of the past or event sequences, which have occurred up until the time the archaeologist makes his observations and which might alter the archaeological record are statements of potential explanatory value for understanding the archaeological facts as seen. Sampling is a procedure which is concerned with providing a representative and unbiased view of the archaeological record as it exists at the time the archaeologists begin making observations. All the problems of erosion, disturbance by rodents, attrition through decay, subsequent destruction by man, etc., which may contribute to the complexity of the archaeological record as it exists at the time the archaeologist begins making observations are potential explanations for the observations which the archaeologist makes. They are in no way relevant to strategy decisions made by the archaeologist as to how best to obtain a representative and unbiased set of observations on the archaeological deposit as it exists. Sampling is concerned with getting as clear a picture as possible, within the limits of stated budget, labor investments, and research goals of the archaeological record as it exists. Discussion of all the factors, which may contribute to distortions in the record between the time of observation and the target time in the past of interest to the archaeologist, do not affect in any way the desirability of obtaining a representative and unbiased view of the archaeological remains as they in fact exist. Viewed from this perspective most of what Collins has to say is of no interest whatsoever to a discussion of sampling. Perhaps his arguments are more relevant to the questions of whether we should even attempt to use archaeological facts in evaluating our ideas about past dynamics or whether it is worthwhile to even do archaeology of any kind!

James W. Mueller's chapter 3 is an argument of "misplaced concreteness." I am suggesting, regardless of the unit specified in the sampling frame, that that unit is known through some idea of a cluster of attributes. Thus, regardless of the units in the sampling frame, one can argue that at least semantically one is cluster sampling. Stated another way, any entity can be analyzed into some set of properties, a cluster of attributes, and if this is done one is cluster sampling, as long as the entity is the unit in the frame. Viewed this way all sampling events are either clusters or not, depending upon the analytical level at which one is working.

Chapter 4, by Dwight W. Read, is fine and requires no comment.

David H. Thomas' chapter 5 appears to be beating a straw man. He seems to be proclaiming that archaeologists have been all wrong, and he has data to prove such a contention. He seems to be saying archaeologists have considered that basic units of meaning in the archaeological record came in site packages. He looked and couldn't find such packages; therefore archaeologists have been wrong all along. Although archaeologists continually speak of sites, this does not mean that they assume sites as basic units of organization. To my knowledge, K. C. Chang and his students, and perhaps Bruce Trigger, are the only archaeologists I know of to whom Thomas' arguments are directed. Chang proposed, as an alleged revolutionary idea, that archaeologists abandon the artifact as the basic unit of observation, and treat the site as such. He never understood, even after I forcefully pointed it out, that the site is a unit of synthesis. One cannot demonstrate the existence of a site until one can demonstrate some spatial clustering of artifacts, which are the units of observation necessary to the definition of a site. As Thomas points out, if one cannot demonstrate a clustering of artifacts, one does not have sites. Only Chang would be distressed to find that archaeology could not be conducted in Thomas' area since the basic units of archaeological observation did not exist! Thomas seems to think his data would somehow distress other archaeologists and demands that they change their ways. That expectation, in my view, could only arise if Thomas felt that K. C. Chang spoke for the field of archaeology. Chang is wrong in his arguments and I think most archaeologists appreciate this, except perhaps Thomas.

Charles L. Redman was kind enough to point out that it is over ten years ago that I read my first paper at a Society for American Archaeology meeting on sampling (Binford 1964). At that time I had a message for archaeologists and they did not like it; I was telling them that their judgments were bad. I suggested that they did not know as much about the archaeological record as they thought they did; it was not as simple as they thought, and that we might try to generate some procedures which would help us learn, rather than assume we knew it all while we were destroying the archaeological record in the meantime. Since that time there have been a number of studies made in which the archaeological record was viewed as a potential set of organized relationships. Applied to its investigation were procedures largely designed to permit the evaluation of one's "judgment" and the traditional "judgment" of archaeologists. The result has been that we have learned some interesting things about the character of the archaeological record, and the inadequacies of our own or traditional judgments for guiding archaeological data collection.

In informal discussions and in the literature, one frequently hears the criticism or suggestion that sampling procedure is a method for idiots, and any archaeologist worth his salt would instead use "good judgment." Such a statement, as I see it is a paradox, since in my view the archaeologist must be continually using good judgment with respect to two sides of an equation. First, he must attempt to use good judgment about the nature of the archaeological record and what he hopes to gain from its investigation. Second, he *must* use good judgment as regards his potential ignorance of the archaeological record. Only when both are considered is "good judgment" evident; if only one or the other is evident, we have naivety or arrogance, but not good judgment. I would say I am in favor of good judgment of all grounds. We must continuously remind ourselves of our ignorance, and if we ever conclude that no ignorance exists, then we are not scientists. Science has the interesting characteristic of being cumulative, and hopefully what we are ignorant about today, we can use good judgment about tomorrow. To argue that having good judgment about the nature of the archaeological record is justification for abandoning good judgment about our potential ignorance of the archaeological record is a fallacy. Sampling is a procedure addressed to the latter; it cannot be abandoned in favor of arrogance. As we learn more of both the archaeological record and our ignorance, we may begin to elaborate and make more complex the techniques based on good judgment.

My findings with respect to feature and artifact distributions at Hatchery West were confirmed by data from the Gilliland Site in Southwestern Colorado (Rohn n.d.). These sites help illustrate my discussion of good judgment in the preceding paragraph. Once we begin to see that there are redundancies between places as widely separated as central Illinois and southwestern Colorado or Upper Paleolithic sites of France and those of contemporary Eskimos, we have the basis for beginning the development of middle range theory dealing with the human use of space, resources, etc.; in short, theory building. As such progress is made and we understand more—have more detailed expectations of the archaeological record—we may use better judgment in the design of excavation strategies. For instance, I am confident that there are certain features and variables common to occupation in rock shelters, regardless of their specific locations and periods of occupancy. Comparative studies of rock shelter occupations from Australia, Southeast Asia, Southern France, the American Southwest etc., would almost certainly uncover much redundancy in the way in which man has made use of such bounded life space. In short, we might expect certain common solutions to common contingencies, such as drip lines, limits of natural light, areas of natural heat radiation, etc. If we know such things, we certainly could excavate rock shelters from a more informed position, with more specific expectations and problems in mind; in short, our excavations could be guided by better judgment. Regardless, we would still be constrained to take precaution so as to insure that the exercise of our good judgment did not bias our results in directions unwarranted by the archaeological realities. No matter how informed we become, no matter how skilled and "expert" as archaeologists we become, we must continue to approach the archaeological record with humility and take steps to insure that our actions do not distort the character of the data we recover. That is one of the primary goals of sampling, particularly when total excavations are out of the question and we must make use of "partial" data.

Chapter 9, by James A. Brown, is a fine example of good judgment. In developing a procedure Brown seeks to use as judiciously as possible our accumulated knowledge and expectations about the archaeological record while also providing for a sampling-based strategy that will permit us to evaluate how good our judgment has been.

Chapter 10, by David L. Asch, provides us with an example of relative use of judgment, and it in no way negates the need for sampling strategies. For instance, Asch makes the point that sampling made little sense in the context of asking questions about a large population of deer represented on his site, and yet he had only 52 mandibles for evaluation as to age. Here is an example of the use of judgment in the context of limited knowledge; expand the knowledge, and the use of good judgment leads to different conclusions. For instance, instead of attempting to obtain information on relative ages of deer from mandibles which are minimally represented, why not examine the abundant remains of long bone articulator ends for an epiphyseal union series and obtain age data on the population in that manner? Good judgment would dictate epiphyseal union studies rather than tooth eruption studies to obtain the desired information. In the latter case if one was convinced that articulator ends were not biased in their presence or preservation, a sampling strategy might well save much time and effort without diminishing the accuracy of one's age estimates of the deer population present. In such a situation we see good judgment used in conjunction with sampling strategies to obtain desired results in the context of both economy of effort and goals of accuracy. Good judgment is always relative to our secure knowledge and understanding; if we have some humility about the latter, then the need for implementing strategies for obtaining some evaluative control over our alleged good judgment is always a necessary part of archaeological strategy — sampling strategies play such a role.

Robert Benfer's chapter 13 is interesting, although it might have been used more profitably elsewhere. His concern is obviously with pattern recognition in data already collected. Stratification is a process of analysis carried out by an investigator in terms of domains of information or areas of concern which the investigator deems important to gather information. The way one stratifies is a function of the assumptions or tentative hypothesis one generates as to the relative independence, dependence, or explanatory potential of dimensions of variation. How one goes about this task is related to how one does theory, and warrants for one method over another are gained from arguing down from theory, or more commonly, poorly formulated biased hunches as to what is important. Once again, no sampling for the latter is the approach used to obtain a representative and unbiased body of empirical material already specified as to its relevance.

The remaining chapters, by Judge, Ebert, and Hitchcock; Matson and Lipe; Morris; and Reid, Schiffer, and Neff (chap. 6, 7, 11, and 12), suggest means to improve and make more flexible sampling strategies. These things we need to know; we don't need to know in graphic terms that some archaeologists are poorly trained in how to do archaeology and the inherent problems associated with that task. Any archaeologist who is going to perform even at minimal acceptable levels in modern archaeology must be concerned with sampling procedures and how best to make use of them. The days of argument about whether sampling is appropriate in archaeology are over, and those engaged in such discussions are in my opinion fossils of a past era—an era in which archaeologists thought of themselves as knowledgeable experts applying their skills and expertise, totally naive about the responsibilities of the scientist. The scientist is continually worrying about his alleged knowledge and understanding. He worries about developing new means of using empirical materials for evaluating his alleged knowledge and understanding, and developing rules for giving meaning to things observed. Sampling plays a role, an important role, in this endeavor to increase the accuracy and breadth of our understanding about the past.

15. A Selection of Samplers: Comments on Archaeo-statistics

George L. Cowgill

George Cowgill (Ph.D., Harvard, 1963) has been serving as Associate Professor of Anthropology at Brandeis University. His fieldwork has been principally in Mesoamerica, in the Maya Lowlands, and especially in the Basin of Mexico. He has been engaged in computerized analyses of data from Teotihuacan, Mexico, supported by the National Science Foundation. His major research interests have been in mathematical and computer methods in archaeology, the comparative study of early civilizations, and the relationships between population and other sociocultural variables.

INTRODUCTION

An autobiographical anecdote by A. V. Kidder illustrates one style in archaeological research design. In 1907 he and two companions were introduced to fieldwork by Edgar Lee Hewitt, who took them to a mesa top in the Colorado Plateau country and casually gave them their instructions. "He waved an arm, taking in it seemed, about half the world, 'I want you boys to make an archaeological survey of this country. I'll be back in three weeks'" (Woodbury 1973: 2). The present book is one piece of evidence, in case anyone still doubts, that archaeology now is not quite the same as it used to be.

Perhaps less obvious is a difference between most (though not all) of the papers in this volume and much of the "avant-garde" archaeological writing of the 1960s. The polemics, while present here, are subdued, and prophets and True Believers are not much in evidence. There are no claims that a particular study has given us, or that a particular technique is bound to provide, quick, deep, and conclusive insights into the details of prehistoric social organization or cultural systems. Parts of some papers are quite technical, but not more technical than is demanded by the issues discussed. There is no mystification for the sake of mystification, and few authors seem out of their depth. Instead, the general level of statistical competence is much higher than was common a few years ago, and there is a "nuts and bolts" tone to most papers. Writers take it for granted that we cannot afford to ignore, or be naive about, matters of research design and the role of probability sampling in research. It is assumed that competence in both theoretical and practical aspects of sampling is a precondition for the effective and convincing testing of important archaeological hypotheses. This is not

[258]

to say that probability sampling per se guarantees highly effective research, or that alternative strategies are not sometimes preferable. Individual writers differ considerably in their enthusiasm for probability sampling; but there is a consensus that *sometimes* at least it can be extremely useful while *sometimes* at least other strategies are better. Insight and sophistication are needed not merely to apply the techniques, but also to judge which techniques are preferable to realize particular objectives in specific situations. There is a relatively high ratio of practice to preaching in these papers, and several of them evaluate substantial amounts of research already accomplished. These include important case studies which compare results of applying different strategies to a given body of known data.

Clearly we need to accumulate much more experience of this kind; and clearly the sampling lessons learned in other disciplines, however instructive for us, cannot entirely substitute for our own experience. Yet these papers indicate that we are well-launched in sampling in archaeology. This is one aspect of applied mathematics in archaeology which, if still very young, is at least beyond infancy; and there are a respectable number of archaeologists now who understand probability sampling fairly well and are doing it, not just talking about it. We will always depend heavily on the advice of professional statisticians. But this must be, and can be, an active collaboration in which archaeological expertise and judgment are brought into creative interaction with mathematical skills.

Nevertheless, the archaeological profession as a whole has only begun to become educated in both the theoretical aspects of probability sampling and its practical role in research design, so that they can evaluate intelligently the results of others, as well as plan their own research. The papers in this book should go a long way toward serving this educational function. However, it would be inadvisable for statistical beginners to try to use the book as either a primer or a source of recipes. It is no substitute for a good general introductory statistics course, preferably followed by a more advanced book on sampling, such as Cochran (1963) or Kish (1965).

In what follows I will not try to repeat or discuss everything of importance in these papers. I will first discuss some important general issues which I think could either be restated more clearly, or have been neglected by other contributors. Finally, I will touch on the relatively few instances where I seriously disagree with writers on points of central importance.

GENERAL ISSUES

First, there is the matter of probability versus nonprobability sampling. I suggest that it is helpful to define two deeper contrasts in strategy. When we know almost nothing about the populations of interest, the most economical strategy may be some form of *probing*, a sort of preliminary exploration to get some notion of the gross characteristics of the population. Probing can include judgmental or systematic or opportunistic pits or borings in a site, but it can also include such things as exploratory surface reconnaissance of a region. Probing may well be a useful strategy in the early stages of research, but the possibilities of deriving trustworthy generalizations from it are very limited, and it needs to be followed by different strategies as research continues. Incidentally, Kidder's work in 1907 was probably quite useful probing, appropriate for what was then known of Southwestern archaeology.

In contrast to probing are all strategies where the population we wish to study can be fairly well defined, and we already have some information, or at least some good hunches, about its structure and variability. These in turn can be divided into *selection* and *sampling* strategies. In all cases, a governing consideration is that we *neglect no observations likely to be important.* "Importance," of course, must be defined with respect to explicit goals, which do not necessarily have to be scientific. For scientific research, "important" data are those needed for decisive choices between two or more competing hypotheses or models, and those of considerable heuristic value for suggesting new hypotheses or new models.

Sometimes our resources, the nature of the data, and the nature of critical test implications derived from competing hypotheses are all such that we can define obvious criteria of relevance, and use these criteria as a basis for picking a manageable number of intrinsically important observations. In these cases, there are other observations we might make but do not make because we are satisfied that they are relatively unimportant for our purposes (always with the ethical proviso that we do not destroy data which may be important for other purposes). This strategy I propose to call *purposive selection.* In the papers here, strategies at least partly or possibly similar are sometimes called purposive sampling, judgment sampling, or nonprobability sampling. I prefer to emphasize the difference between this strategy (at least in its pure form), and any kind of sampling.

There is little question that purposive selection is preferable to sampling whenever selection is feasible, sufficient for one's research objectives, and not wasteful. One of the reasons why improved techniques of data *detection* (aerial photography, magnetometers, etc.) are so important is that they offer new possibilities for feasible and effective data selection. Also, detection and selection offer our best safeguards against what Daniels (1972: 205) calls *gross errors.* These are instances in which our sample statistics fail to reveal or reflect the existence of rare but extremely unusual and intrinsically important elements of the population. Formally, they can be thought of as drastic failures to recognize population heterogeneity. Missing the Pyramid of the Sun in a survey of the Teotihuacan Valley would be a gross error; happily, an error not easily made. Missing the tomb of Tutankhamen was a far more easily made gross error, repeated by grave robbers for many centuries and corrected partly by luck in the 1920s. The nature of archaeological data is such that the risks of missing key data items of major importance are often hard to evaluate. They are greatest for archaeology-as-treasure-hunting, but often not negligible for archaeology-as-science. This is not an argument against sampling, but it is a reminder that purposive selection and new developments in data detection techniques are also important.

In contrast to selection, some form of sampling is preferable in situations (1) where there are more potential observations than our resources permit us to make, or we have reason to think that we do not need to make all possible observations in order to obtain convincing tests of competing hypotheses or acceptable estimates of important parameters, and (2) where there are no indications that tell us which of the possible observations are unimportant or unnecessary. In these cases, we can call the set of all possible relevant observations the *population,* and the set of observations actually picked the *sample.* For better or worse, our criteria for picking observations to include in the sample must be something other than obvious irrelevance of what we omit; in sampling we omit observations because we think they are redundant, rather than because they are intrinsically less relevant than the observations we include. Our interest is less in the intrinsic properties of the sample than in what it permits us to infer about the entire population.

In the case of selection, in a scientific context, the aim is to select observations sufficient for decisive tests of *nomothetic* hypotheses — lawlike generalizations of some sort. In the case of sampling, an additional stage intervenes: we attempt to pick observations in a way which enables us to make *idiographic,* essentially descriptive and phenomenological, inferences about the sampled population which are sufficiently precise, unbiased, and accurate that they can in turn be used for decisive tests of nomothetic hypotheses.

Very often, of course, purposive selection strategies are not feasible or, if we are confident we have not greatly underestimated population heterogeneity, may seem inefficient, and some form of sampling is required or preferable. The catch, then, is to pick the sample so that we have a sound basis for idiographic inferences about the population. Note that, in these terms, purposive *sampling* is practically impossible. In particular, the notion of picking a "representative" sample is ambiguous and apt to be misleading. If one takes it to mean picking items that exhibit extremes in the ranges of variation, or picking at least some examples of all types, or all "diagnostic" types, then this sort of picking is certainly possible and probably useful for limited purposes. The result, however, is most unlikely to be "representative" in any other sense. If, on the other hand, "representativeness" is taken to mean that we are positive that the sample statistics are virtually identical to the corresponding values for the population, there is no way this can be guaranteed without already knowing the population values. Attempts to pick a sample "representative" in this sense by judgment, opportunistic picking, or any other nonprobabilistic strategy founder on the difficulties of estimating bias in the procedures, or prove at best to be some form of covert (and often ill-conceived) selection, rather than sampling at all. In order to know where we stand with respect to idiographic inferences about the population, a reasonable approximation to some form of probability sampling is required.

As numerous chapters in this volume attest, simple random sampling is only one form of probability sampling. Often specific research goals, prior knowledge or strong hunches about the population, or considerations of data-collecting efficiency will argue for some form of cluster sampling, stratified sampling, systematic sampling with random elements, or other variants of probability sampling. Also, research designs that include probability sampling are completely compatible with purposive selection, so long as one keeps good track of when one is selecting and when one is sampling.

For the most part, these papers are reasonably hardheaded about the limitations of sampling, and there are only occasional hints of the notion that in some obscure way sampling per se provides a guarantee that our conclusions will be correct. But among archaeologists in general, there is probably still a tendency either to expect too much or to be disenchanted with sampling because it does not fulfill impossible expectations.

One should always remember that there is *no way,* short of including most or even all the observations in the population, that we can absolutely guarantee the truth of most idiographic inferences of any interest about the population, quite apart from the difficulties of confirming nomothetic generalizations. The advantage of probability sampling is not that it very often enables us to be *sure* about the population, but that it helps us, as I said, to *know where we stand* in relation to various inferences.

One of the most prevalent abuses of statistical reasoning is the tendency to crank out some test of a hypothesis about a population, look up in a table to see if "p" is greater than or less than .05, and then make one of two interpretations. If p is greater than .05, the hypothesis is not rejected, and one feels free to act as if it were certain, for all practical purposes, that all alternative hypotheses about the population characteristic in question were false. If p is less than or equal to .05, the hypothesis is rejected, and one feels entitled to act as if it were certainly false. Aside from the patent absurdity of treating odds of one in twenty as somehow the magic threshold number that separates confident acceptance from confident rejection (a point noted here especially by Redman), there is another less often understood difficulty. Statistical inference is never complete if we only ask whether sample results are consistent with one specific idiographic hypothesis about the population. We always have to think also about with what other hypotheses the results may also be consistent. This concept tends to be underemphasized in elementary statistics texts because there are often an unlimited number of possible alternative hypotheses, and there is no single number that expresses the probability of the observed sample statistic under all possible alternatives. Instead, a power function, a mathematical function of all these alternatives, is required. This is not the place for a lengthy discussion of this problem (cf. Rozeboom 1960 and Morrison and Henkel 1970), but the upshot is that, especially for small samples, a result that does not enable us to reject one hypothesis at a 5% significance level may also be quite consistent, and even more consistent, with very different hypotheses about the population. In general, it seems wiser to focus less on tests of specific hypotheses (especially the traditional "null" hypothesis that what we're looking for isn't there), and more on best estimates and confidence intervals. For very small samples (Asch gives some examples in chap. 10 in this volume) the confidence intervals may prove to be wide enough to warn us that the sample results are consistent with an extremely wide range of hypotheses. On the other hand, very large samples may give results that would be highly improbable if the null hypothesis were *exactly* true, yet provide estimates and confidence intervals which imply that the null hypothesis almost surely differs from the true value by only an inconsequential amount.

If one must think in the significance test framework, one should abandon the simplistic notion that we are committed to, or even entitled to, a two-valued yes/no decision strategy. This commitment is necessary if one is deciding, for example, whether to extend an unproductive exploratory trench another meter. But in terms of idiographic hypothesis testing with a view toward nomethetic theory confirmation, something at least as complicated as pretty-surely-yes/maybe/pretty-surely-no is preferable. This is *not* an evasion or a cop-out. Rather it is appropriate use of statistical reasoning to express what the sample results tell us about hypotheses, rather than to provide a phony aura of certainty for ambiguous data. Ambiguity is where we begin. If we were sure of the answers, there would be no point to research. We try for a research design that we think will settle the questions we started out with, and hope will also lead to new questions. But if some of the answers to our original questions remain ambiguous our response should not be to try to deny this, but to design further research (if it's still possible) that will provide whatever more is needed to shift "maybe" to "pretty-surely-yes" or "pretty-surely-no."

In this vein of belaboring misconceptions, it is probably impossible to attack too often the persistent delusion that there is some special merit in a 10% sample, or in any other preconceived sampling fraction for that matter. A point repeatedly made in these papers is that unless the sampling fraction is more than 20% of the total population, the *proportion* of the population included in the sample is of negligible importance. What is virtually all-important is the absolute size of the sample; that is, the actual number of independent cases (or, in cluster sampling, the effective number) included in the sample. For a population of 40, a 50% sample may be barely adequate, while for a population of 200 million, a 0.01% sample (20,000 cases) may be more than ample. Sometimes I visualize an afterlife in which people who think 10% sampling is a good rule of thumb are set to work drawing such samples from infinite populations. In fact, as several papers here illustrate, selection of a suitable sampling fraction is an important problem in good research design. It depends on prior knowledge or good guesses about the variability in the population, the precision of estimates required for good tests of important hypotheses, and the research resources obtainable.

Five concepts which are used frequently in these papers are *accuracy, precision, bias, representativeness,* and *skewing.* They are generally defined and used correctly (although Read, chap. 4, confuses precision with accuracy), but the definitions may be too brief and possibly confusing. Therefore, I will try to explain them more fully. This seems particularly necessary because many archaeologists appear to confuse bias and unrepresentativeness. Bias is also sometimes confused with the existence of structured relationships within the population, or with skewing.

My explanation of the meanings of accuracy, precision, and bias is intended to be a commentary in less technical terms on the discussion by Cochran (1963: 12–16). I will follow standard practice in calling sample values *statistics* and the corresponding population values *parameters*.

Consider the problem of estimating the true population mean, μ, from a sample mean, $\overline{X}$. If we were to draw a large number of independent samples, following the same sampling procedure in each case, each sample would in general have a different mean $-\overline{X}_1$, $\overline{X}_2$, $\overline{X}_3$, etc. $-$ and these sample means will generally not be exactly equal to μ, the population mean. We can also think of the mean of all the means of the independent samples, and call this mean of means m. It may or may not be true that as the number of independent samples becomes infinite, the probability that m differs by any finite amount from μ will approach zero. If the sampling technique is biased, or if $\overline{X}$ were a "biased estimator" of μ, the expected value of m for a very large number of samples may be substantially different from μ.

Precision is a measure of how widely individual sample means, $\overline{X}_i$, are spread out around m, the mean of these means. In other words, precision is a measure of the probability that the *one* sample mean we actually obtain differs by more than some given amount from m, the mean of all sample means we *would* obtain, if we were to repeat, independently, the same sampling procedure a large number of times (independence here implies that inclusion of an observation in one sample has no effect on its chances of being included in another sample). High precision means that our sample results are highly repeatable, whether or not they are correct. For many forms of probability sampling, the amount of spread to be expected in sample means can be deduced mathematically from known population characteristics, without actually having to draw any samples at all, and it turns out for simple random sampling to be directly proportional to the amount of spread of individual values in the population, and inversely proportional to the square root of the size of the individual samples. Precision can be increased either by increasing the sample size (but 4 times the sample size is needed to double the precision if population variance is known) or by using prior knowledge to define subpopulations which are relatively homogeneous with respect to the variable in question. This is one reason for stratified sampling designs, as is pointed out by many papers here.

Accuracy, in contrast to precision, is a measure of the extent to which the individual sample means are spread out around μ, the true population mean, rather than m. If m is equal to μ, then accuracy and precision are equal, but if m is not equal to μ, then the accuracy will be less than the precision.

Bias, in this example, is the difference between m and μ. More generally, it is the difference between the expected long-run mean value of the sample statistic, if the same sampling procedure were to be repeated a great many times, and the true value of the population parameter which the sample statistic is used to estimate.

There are, so far as I know, two ways in which bias can occur. The first is that, even under probability sampling, the theoretical long-run expected value of the sample statistic is not the same as the corresponding population parameter. For example, for simple random sampling the long-run expected value of the sample variance differs in a known way from the true population variance, and this is why the sample variance has to be multiplied by $n/(n-1)$ in order to obtain an unbiased estimate of the true population variance. However, for simple random sampling, $\overline{X}$ is an unbiased estimator of μ.

The other way in which bias can occur is that our actual procedure for picking observations from the population differs seriously from whatever probability sampling scheme is presupposed by our computations. For example, if we wished to estimate mean size of sites in a region, we might assume simple random sampling, in which the probability of picking any site is independent of its size, and use mean site size in our sample as the estimator of mean site size in the population. But if in fact our procedures are not very carefully designed to give small sites nearly as good a chance of inclusion as larger and more obvious sites, the sample mean is much more likely to be larger than the true population mean, rather than smaller. Even though many repetitions of the same sampling procedure might show quite high *precision,* the mean of all these sample means would be substantially higher than the true population mean—that is, there would be substantial *bias* and the *accuracy* would be low. In fact, if the possibility of bias is not recognized, and the theoretical precision is taken to be a good measure of the actual accuracy, the results will be downright misleading.

Note that it is meaningless to speak of bias with respect to the population. "Bias" should not be confounded with structure or the existence of nonrandom relationships between variables in the population. Note also that (as Asch, chap. 10, and Read, chap. 4, observe), it is not *samples* that are biased, it is procedures that may be biased. If a particular sample happens to be such that $\bar{x}$ is considerably different from μ, it would be best to describe it as *unrepresentative.* I suggest that closeness of specific sample statistics to specific population parameters is the best way of sharpening the ill-defined concept of "representativeness." No sampling procedure guarantees a representative sample. The accuracy of a particular procedure is a measure of the risks of obtaining a sample which is unrepresentative by more than some specified amount.

Finally *skewing,* strictly speaking, has no direct connection at all with bias. It refers to the shape of a frequency distribution, either in the population or in a sample. Its importance is that some statistical procedures presuppose that the population distribution is approximately a symmetrical bell-shaped "normal" curve, while many other procedures do not require this assumption about the population. When the assumption is clearly unjustified (as it often is for archaeological data) or in serious doubt, one should be sure to avoid reasoning which depends heavily on this assumption. In general, the assumption is far more critical for small samples than for large samples.

The most refractory source of bias in archaeology is that the probability or even the possibility of making many observations once potentially available has been drastically altered by events and processes over which archaeologists have no control. This is because some kinds of data are inherently more durable than others, or more durable in some contexts than in others, and because post-occupation events may bury, redeposit, or destroy data in quite nonrandom ways. These are difficulties I have discussed elsewhere (Cowgill 1970), and they are elaborated on here especially by Chenhall (chap. 1) and Collins (chap. 2). These are truly problems, but I should caution readers against overreacting to them. Clearly we are just deceiving ourselves if we try to talk them away or pretend they are not real. However this does not mean that archaeology is hopeless or that uncontrollable bias is so bad that we can comfortably forget all about probability sampling and careful research design, and continue to rely happily on judgmental or opportunistic samples.

What can often be done is to make reasonable estimates of either the maximum likely absolute magnitude of the bias, its direction, or both. If the probable magnitude of the bias is not great relative to the accuracy we require, then its effects will not be too serious (cf. Cochran 1963: 15). If the direction of the bias can be deduced, even though we are uncertain of its magnitude, then we know that tests of significance which ignore bias will be *conservative* tests of hypotheses which assert that the population differs from the sample in the direction opposite to the bias. The troubles in this case are that (a) we cannot tell if we are being far too conservative, and (b) we may be stuck with an interesting hypothesis which predicts differences in the same direction as the bias. At any rate, the things to do are to try to recognize sources of bias and to gain far more experimental evidence about these sources and their effects. We can then design detection and research strategies to overcome the effects where possible. Where this is not possible we still need not despair. Often we can make sensible allowances for bias if the sources of bias are understood.

Another topic alluded to in several papers and which calls for emphasis is the matter of "grain size" of sampling units. It is important that sampling units be substantially larger than significant spatial dimensions of the phenomena we are interested in studying.

If we are primarily concerned with aggregates of items (such as sites or artifacts), the grain size need not be much larger than the individual items. But whenever we are concerned with patterned or systemic relations between diverse items, as we increasingly often are, we require grain sizes (as well as sampling fractions) sufficient to make entire patterns pretty clear. A grain size and sampling fraction quite adequate and efficient for settling the question of whether sites are substantially more abundant in one ecological zone than in another may be very inadequate for revealing settlement systems.

It is relevant here to discuss some instructive results reported by Rohn (n.d.). Density plots of surface sherd counts and weights were compared with the results of total excavation of a Basketmaker III pithouse village which covered about 0.224 hectares (0.55 acres) and was only about 20 cm. in depth. In spite of the shallowness of the deposit, surface sherd concentrations show only a moderate correlation with architectural features. Furthermore, simulations of randomly located 2 × 2 meter squares using 10%, 25%, and 50% sampling fractions indicated that even a 50% sample of test pits would not yield a particularly good picture of site features. One lesson I draw from this is that, as numerous other experiences have demonstrated, test pits are not the way to find out about structures larger than the test pits. In some cases pits may be the best way to *locate* features, but they should then be expanded to reveal more or less the entire feature. A second lesson is that even on relatively undisturbed shallow sites surface artifact concentrations cannot be expected to pinpoint underground structures more closely than within 10 or 20 meters. For a settlement whose maximum dimension is about 50 meters this is a serious limitation. The validity of surface data, relative to the overall scale, seems much greater on sites covering more than a few hectares.

A final important general point, only touched on here by Judge, Ebert, and Hitchcock (chap. 6) is the relevance of sophistication about sampling for salvage, contract, or conservation archaeology. Increasingly archaeologists are being called on to design, to justify budgets for, and to establish guidelines for work in regions where archaeological data are seriously threatened by contemporary human activities. There is a risk that projects which look adequate, judged by conventional archaeological wisdom, will in fact prove inadequate and leave important questions forever moot because the relevant data have been destroyed. Clear definition of objectives and statistical expertise at the planning stage are needed to minimize this risk. At the same time, we have to make the best use of scarce resources, and avoid overemphasis on certain regions, or certain kinds of data, at the expense of other kinds of data or other regions. Our research designs and our budgets should be defensible against the criticism that we are afflicted with a mindless compulsion to find everything, dig everything, and save everything. It is true that whenever we make any judgments that further data would be redundant we have to face the very real possibility that, sometime in the future, they will assume an importance not now recognized. But it should be of very great value to be able to offer a reasoned set of predictions about payoffs for various investments of resources. That is, we should be able to say that, in order to have good prospects of reasonably firm answers to certain basic questions about the prehistory of a given region, approximately X investment of dollars, time, and manpower will be necessary *and also probably sufficient;* while there is little prospect of getting conclusive answers to such-and-such further questions, unless Y further investment is made. Individuals and institutions would then have a much more informed basis for judging or justifying the adequacy of research plans and the merits of budgets.

The outcome of such calculations will probably be that, at least whenever we are concerned with currently important questions about the systemic aspects of the data (let alone when we worry about unimagined future questions), the scale of research required will be considerably larger and the sampling more intensive than has customarily been thought adequate. Certainly the notion that a 10% sample is generally both necessary and sufficient will crumble. A strong argument for more intensive work and a higher level of financial support will be the demonstration that such effort is *needed* in order to solve problems whose importance is already recognized; it is not simply called for because of wasteful research designs or in order to keep archaeologists employed.

SPECIFIC COMMENTS

Chenhall (chap. 1) is pessimistic about sampling, and concludes that in his test case something like a 50% sample was required in order to get representative data. Unfortunately, there are two serious errors in his argument. First, he has converted actual frequencies of sites into percentages, and then computed chi square statistics based on these percentages. This is invalid.

For example, from a known population of 76 sites classified into 14 types, he selected a simple random sample of 30 out of 95 tracts into which the region was divided—a sampling fraction of about 32%. The sample proved to contain 17 sites. Chenhall tabulates the number of sites of each of his 14 types in the population, the number of sites of each type in the sample, converts to percentages, and emerges with a chi square of 98.64. He notes that, with 13 degrees of freedom, such a large chi square has a probability of less than .001, and he concludes that in this case sampling about 32% of the area has yielded a sample of sites which is highly unrepresentative of the population. A second trial, using 48 of the 95 tracts, a sampling fraction of slightly over 50%, was treated in the same way and yielded a chi square of 21.3, which has a probability less than .10 but greater than .05. He concludes that even this 50% sample of tracts is only marginally successful in getting a representative sample of sites.

If chi square for Chenhall's 30/95 sample is recomputed using frequencies rather than percentages, it is only 22.0, rather than 98.64, and the tabulated significance level is between .10 and .05. Actually chi square is a quite inaccurate approximation here, since of 28 expected frequencies, 23 are less than 5, and 14 of these are less than 1. I think the effect is to increase considerably the probability of a large chi square. At any rate, the observed sample seems within the range of probable sampling variation predicted by theory for this situation. An approximate recomputation of chi square for his 50% sample indicates that the value is between 8 and 10. This implies a significance level between .80 and .70 and this sample is very well within the theoretical range of sampling variation.

Parenthetically, if Chenhall's chi square of 98.64 were valid, it would imply that his procedure had not merely failed to pick a representative sample, but that he had succeeded in picking a sample so unusual that, if simple random sampling of sites had indeed been approximated by his simple random sample of tracts, a comparably unrepresentative sample could be expected only once in many thousands of trials. The implication would not be that the sampling fraction was inadequate, but that there was probably some drastic failure of method.

The second serious difficulty with Chenhall's study is that the entire "population" that he sampled consisted of only a 4 square mile region, in which 76 sites were located.

Judge, Ebert, and Hitchcock (chap. 6), who also compared samples with a known population, got considerably better results than Chenhall. In part this is because they avoided his computational errors, but it is also because the absolute sizes of their samples are more adequate. Their population covered 5 times the area of Chenhall's and included 1,130 sites. They used a 20% sampling fraction and located 214 to 227 sites in their various trials. This means that each of their *samples* covered as much territory as Chenhall's *population,* and included about 3 times as many sites. David Thomas' survey area (chap. 5) was nearly 34 times as large as Chenhall's, and the area in his sample (10% of the total) was about 3.4 times the area of Chenhall's population. Matson and Lipe (chap. 7) plan to sample a region about 50 times the size of Chenhall's at an ultimate rate of only about 1.75%, but this still calls for covering about 84% of the area, and several times as many sites, as in Chenhall's total population.

The point is that, irrespective of sampling fractions, Chenhall's samples are extremely small in absolute size, whether measured by total land surface covered or by number of sites discovered. In fact, he is right, although for the wrong reasons, in arguing that, *for the population he has defined,* something much more than a 30% sample is badly needed. This is true, but it is because the numbers of cases in his samples are so small that they are consistent with widely differing hypotheses about the population. The problem with his samples is not that they are biased, but that they permit only extremely *imprecise* estimates of his population parameters. For that matter, his population itself seems much too small to be meaningful except as a pilot study. It is difficult to believe that the inhabitants of any of his sites confined their significant activities and environmental interactions to this 4 square mile tract.

Chenhall also raises difficulties about testing associations between cultural activities and environmental variables. Obviously it is easy to think of enough conceivably important environmental variables to generate, from their logically possible combinations, far more microenvironmental strata than could possibly be used in any feasible research design. But there is no need to prestratify the population by every conceivably important combination of variables. Stratification is, after all, just an intelligent use of prior information or hypotheses to increase sampling efficiency without too greatly increasing design complexity. The effects and possible interactions of many environmental variables can be investigated by a number of multivariate techniques. Chenhall himself does this to some extent.

I do not follow Collins' argument that we always must verify estimates derived from a first sample by taking a second sample. This may be an unnecessary overextension of the quite sound warning that one cannot calculate a large number of association coefficients between many different pairs of variables, selectively weed out the majority which are nonsignificant, and then take seriously the cookbook significance levels of the remaining high coefficients. Spaulding (1973) discusses this well.

Mueller (chap. 3) underlines the point that many of the feasible procedures for archaeological sampling are forms of cluster sampling, which undoubtedly is the case. He also stresses the distinction between spatial and nonspatial calculations. The former are those in which some quantity of excavated volume or surveyed area figures explicitly in the computation of ratios, and the latter are frequencies or ratios in which neither volumes nor areas appear. Mueller argues that nonspatial statistics do not conform to cluster sampling. His point is that if one, for example, excavated 30 rooms in a 100-room pueblo, one should not simply add up all the sherds of type X in all the rooms, find a grand total of sherds of type X, compare this to the grand total of all sherds in all rooms, and treat these numbers as if they were derived from any kind of sampling scheme in which individual sherds were the sampling units. However, this hypothetical case could be treated as cluster sampling with 30 clusters, and cluster sampling concepts and formulas would then be appropriate for this situation.

Read's chapter 4 contains a discussion of bias, errors, precision, accuracy, and considerations entering into choices of sampling schemes and sampling fractions. In general his discussion is very good, although at one point he momentarily confuses precision and accuracy, and he describes small samples as tending to be biased, where I think it would be more correct to say that they tend to be unrepresentative. He goes more deeply than most contributors to this book into the mathematics of cluster sampling, and this should be quite useful for readers who make the effort to follow his discussion here. Especially valuable is his demonstration that cluster sampling may be either more or less efficient than simple random sampling, depending on differences in how data items are distributed in different populations. This leads him to emphasize a point which is also made in many other chapters: the more prior knowledge one has of the population, the better one can design further research. If prior knowledge is not very full, a multistage strategy is advisable, and information gained at each stage can be used in planning subsequent stages.

David Thomas' chapter 5 is another useful case study, coupled with a technically sophisticated discussion. It seems open to at least one spurious criticism. Thomas asks whether his sample data support the existence of certain population differences predicted by his theoretical model, computes certain statistics, and finds that the sample differences are not statistically significant. He then reformulates the question slightly, computes other statistics, and obtains highly significant differences. A skeptic might wonder if this is anything but hocus-pocus, and even be reminded of the unkind aphorism that there are lies, damn lies, and statistics. Put more carefully, the question goes like this: "If we compute 3 different statistics intended to ask substantially the same question of a specific sample, and 2 of them give results that are not highly significant while the 3rd is highly significant, what can we conclude?"

We should remember that computing a multiplicity of statistical tests that ask closely related questions of the same sample is *not* analogous to computing associations between a great many different variables. The statistical tests, even though different, will give highly correlated results. We *cannot* expect that if we ask the same question of random data in 20 slightly different ways, at least one result will be significant at the 5% level just by chance. In fact, Thomas asks only 2 or 3 variants of his basic questions, and gets a number of results which are significant not only at the 5% level, but at the 1% level or better. In the strict sense of testing idiographic hypotheses about phenomenological differences in his subpopulations, I find his results convincing.

Again, it might be well to shift away from one-sided emphasis on tests of significance and think more in terms of estimation of population parameters. I suspect that Thomas' results that were consistent with the hypothesis of no differences between subpopulations might also be consistent with the alternative hypothesis of substantial differences. That is, the computations that do not yield high significances may not be in conflict with those that do give high significance; they may simply be inconclusive. In questions like these reliance on the "cookbook" approach can be very misleading, as Thomas realizes, and the need for full insight into the techniques and the (often partly implicit) reasoning behind them is acute.

On the level of nomothetic theory testing, Thomas' paper is not so satisfying. He presents test implications derived from Steward's theory of Basin ecological adaptations, and presents good evidence from his sample that most of these implications are true of his population. But he does not present test implications derived from any theory other than Steward's, and therefore we are quite unable to judge whether his idiographic inferences about the population might not be just as consistent, perhaps even more consistent, with the implications of some contrary theory. As it stands, he has done only part of the job. Of course, many other reputedly scientific archaeological "tests" of theory have suffered from this same flaw.

Judge, Ebert, and Hitchcock's (chap. 6) comparison of results from 4 different sampling designs for the 20 square-mile (51.8-square km.) Chaco Canyon area is also very instructive. However we should not generalize their results unquestioningly. We need further replications of these same designs on the same population, replications of other designs, and replications on other populations. Read's paper makes this point also. A shift to stratified sampling with unequal fractions, which Judge et al. suggest, would probably produce an improvement in precision far greater than the differences between any of the 4 designs they actually tested. Their Canyon Bottom stratum, which alone included over half the sites in the population, gave estimates of total site density within 20% of the true value for all 4 of their sampling strategies; and in 3 cases within 10%. But the South Mesa, with less than 10% of the area and 1% of the sites, in 3 of 4 cases gave estimates that were off by 60% to 200%. For the other 3 strata nearly half the estimates of site density were off by 20% to 50%. Less intensive sampling of the Canyon Bottom (assuming it is indeed homogeneous enough to justify being treated as a single stratum—note here Thomas' experience with poststratification) and more intensive sampling of the other strata would yield much better overall precision for the same total sampling effort. Nevertheless it is clear that overall deviations of estimates of site density cannot be brought below 10% to 20% for any strategy that does not require a larger total sample. Precision of estimates of site density by phase or other less gross data features will be still lower. As in other papers, the implication is that if we want very high precision, we must draw rather larger samples than we have tended to think.

Judge et al. suggest that interval transects, across the grain of major ecological zones, are a good way to begin a regional survey. This sounds good for most situations. One obvious exception is where tributaries join a main stream at roughly equal intervals. Interval transects might either miss the side valleys and junctions, or else overemphasize them. Common sense should indicate whether this is likely to be a problem in specific instances.

Three technical points in Judge et al.'s chapter need correction. The distribution of sample means does not approach normality when many samples are taken unless either the population distribution itself is normal or the sizes of individual samples are fairly large. The Law of Large Numbers does *not* require a normally distributed population. Simple random sampling also does not require that population parameters have a normal distribution.

Matson and Lipe's work (chap. 7) looks first rate and is certain to provide valuable experience. My only reservation is that I wonder whether their plans to cover about 1.75 square km. in each of several 25 square km. drainages will prove adequate. I am mildly uneasy about this, and await further results.

Redman (chap. 8) offers generally excellent advice, although he leans a little heavily on 10% samples. He gives an example of results from a 10% sample of 1850 obsidian blades, where the sample mean and standard deviation were nearly identical to those from the population. This is so, but note that the standard error is about 3 times as great. It is .49 mm. for the population (thinking of the 1850 blades as themselves a sample), but 1.48 mm. for his sample. In this case the gain in precision is probably not worth the effort needed to measure an additional 1665 blades. Nevertheless, precision requires more explicit attention than it received in this example.

Brown describes efforts to make the best of what remain very refractory problems. For deeply buried strata, both probability sampling and any well-informed purposive selection are practically impossible. I think his strategies alleviate the situation, but the best thing to be hoped for is some drastic breakthrough in sensing devices which will greatly increase the feasibility of "seeing" deeply buried phenomena. Otherwise, there still is no satisfactory alternative to the heavy investments required to clear large overlying volumes without irresponsible destruction of important data in these upper layers.

Asch's (chap. 10) general discussion is lucid and cogent, and I agree with most of what he says. However, he is pessimistic about the feasibility of getting probability samples large enough for acceptably precise estimates. Some readers will be disconcerted by the confidence limits he presents, since in several cases they imply that there is a real possibility that the true frequency of sherds in segments of the Macoupin site is a negative number. This is a consequence of having (apparently) used the t-distribution, which presupposes normality of the population distribution. It is true that confidence limits based on some distribution-free statistic (such as recommended by Matson and Lipe) would be more meaningful here, but I am certain that Asch's point would stand: many of his subsamples would still yield extremely imprecise estimates. Positive skewing in the population means that the lower limit of a confidence interval computed on the assumption of population normality will be too low, but the upper limit will also be too low, and the net effect is generally an underestimate of the total range of the confidence interval (Cochran 1963: 40).

Nevertheless, I think much of Asch's pessimism is unjustified. It seems overoptimistic to have hoped to get useful estimates of internal differences in sherd frequencies in a site covering over 5 acres (about 2.16 hectares) by putting in 155 test pits, each 2.5 × 5 feet (12.5 square feet, or 1.16 square meters). This adds up to a total area of 1937.5 square feet (180 square meters), the equivalent of a single large square 44 feet on a side. The sampling fraction is .83%. Asch does not give the number of sherds recovered. His overall mean of 50.68 for the 155 pits implies a total of 7,855. Means for the 24 individual strata imply totals per stratum ranging from 56 to 1,490, and a grand total of 13,580. It is not asking too much to suggest that we must, and also can, excavate considerably larger areas and deal with several times as many sherds in order to understand 5 acre sites.

It should also be noted that in this case the precision can increase by much more than the square root of the increase in sample size. This is because in the examples of really wide confidence intervals that Asch gives, much of the trouble comes from the fact that the population variance, as well as the population mean, has to be estimated from the sample statistics. Six of his 24 strata consist of 4 or fewer pits, while another 6 strata include only 5 or 6 pits. Much of the imprecision in the estimates of subpopulation means comes from the imprecision in estimates of subpopulation variance, which makes the t-distribution much broader than the corresponding normal distribution. For sample sizes less than about 6 or 7, the precision increases with increased sample size at a rate much faster than the square root. I believe Asch could quadruple the sampling rate in strata where either the small number of original pits or unexpected heterogeneity has led to very wide confidence intervals, and get very substantial improvements in precision within strata by digging less than another 155 pits—although in fact a still larger sample would probably be desirable. Furthermore, I think this could be done without invalidating the assumption of simple random sampling within strata, and without complicating the analysis or interpretation of results.

One further disagreement with Asch concerns his suggestion that we can consider discarding or stripping off material in the plow zone. This layer, however disturbed, may contain unique information about the latest phase of occupation, and we surely risk gross errors by ignoring it altogether. Finally Asch seems to include certain idiographic inferences about population parameters under the heading of "descriptive" statistics, while I have understood this term to refer strictly to the summarization of information explicitly present in the sample observations.

In sum, Asch's is a good paper. I agree with most of his discussion, and his experiences at the Macoupin site are instructive. I agree that we should not blindly expect probability sampling to take the place of judicious selection in all situations. But I think he expected far too much from a probability sample whose absolute size (quite apart from the sampling fraction) was small relative to the interpretive burden it was asked to bear.

Morris (chap. 11) presents a complex strategy for a very large and complex site. It seems to be an excellent pragmatic blend, in several stages, of purposive selection and probability sampling. It is the only paper in this volume which grapples with excavations of the scale and complexity required for the study of truly urban settlements. It seems likely that possible questions about the strict applicability of various computational models will be more than offset by the clarity of the patterns which are emerging. Certainly this is a major advance in the archaeology of complex societies, and will provide experience which cannot be wholly duplicated by regional surveys or excavations in smaller sites.

Benfer's chapter 13 is mainly about multivariate analysis, rather than sampling. He recorded some 60 variables for each of 26 obsidian blade fragments in a "nonprobability opportunistic collection" from a larger collection of over 50,000 blades. Aside from the unresolvable questions about the implications for the population of any results based on an opportunistic sample, the tiny sample size would create serious difficulties even if it had been picked by probability sampling. A feature has to be present on at least 2 or 3 thousand blades in the collection of 50,000 in order not to have a good chance of being absent on all blades in a random sample of size 26. So even moderately unusual features may be totally absent in the sample. And since these features are the direct objects of investigation we cannot use them as a basis for stratifying the population and improving the chances of their inclusion. Also, Benfer concentrates on disproving null hypotheses of the kind which state that there are no patterned relationships or well-defined subgroups in his population. He finds few relationships in his sample which are so strong that they could not easily be due to chance. But, as I took some pains to point out earlier, with a sample this small it is also extremely difficult to disprove alternative hypotheses about the population. Benfer's failure to find strong evidence for clusters or subgroups in the sample does not prove that they are not there and important in the population. It is an inconclusive result, suggesting that there are no immensely strong associations among features common in the population. But there may be moderately strong associations among common features and possibly even very strong associations among moderately uncommon features. One wonders, incidentally, whether any associations strong enough to have attained high statistical significance in a sample of this size would not also have been "obvious" to any archaeologist handling a larger number of the blades and using old-fashioned intuitive and vaguely defined techniques of pattern recognition. Multivariate techniques are very useful when the raw data are too numerous or relationships are of kinds not easily perceived by inspection, but they do not somehow squeeze rich understanding out of tiny samples.

In sum, reflecting on all these papers, they confirm my prior conviction that probability sampling strategies are very useful, but that they should never be applied naively or with a blind faith that they will guarantee "scientific" certainty to our conclusions. Often the best strategies are multi-stage designs with intelligent mixtures of purposive selection and probability sampling. Further, a number of the case studies suggest to me that we have tended to hope for somewhat too much from quite small probability samples. The size and complexity of the sample required depends very strongly on the kinds of questions we ask. For rather simple questions fairly small samples will serve, but for many of the questions we are asking today, especially concerning internal structure and systemic aspects of regions or sites, the samples need to be rather large. The implication is neither that we should forget about probability sampling and rely wholly on intuition, nor that meaningful research is impossible. Rather, it is that statistical expertise can make our research more efficient, but it cannot enable us to work miracles with tiny budgets. These papers help to document the upper limits of what can be achieved by small projects, but they also demonstrate some of the minimal levels of support we need for effective work, however well-designed.

Reference Material

References

Ackerman, Charles, 1964. Structure and Statistics: the Purum Case. *American Anthropologist* 66: 53–65.

Adams, Robert McC., 1966. *The Evolution of Urban Society, Early Mesopotamia and Prehispanic Mexico.* Chicago: Aldine.

———. 1968. Archaeological Research Strategies: Past and Present. *Science* 160: 1187–1192.

Ahler, Stanley A., 1971. *Projectile Point Form and Function at Rodgers Shelter, Missouri.* Missouri Archaeological Society Research Series, Number 8.

Alcock, L. A., 1951. A Technique for Surface Collecting. *Antiquity.* 25: 75–76.

Arkin, A. and R. Colton, 1963. *Tables for Statisticians.* New York: Barnes & Noble.

Arrhenius, O,, 1922. A New Method for the Analysis of Plant Communities. *Journal of Ecology* 10: 185–199.

Ascher, Robert, 1959. A Prehistoric Population Estimate Using Midden Analysis and Two Population Models. *Southwestern Journal of Anthropology* 15: 168–178.

———. 1968. Time's Arrow and The Archaeology of a Contemporary Community. In *Settlement Archaeology.* K. C. Chang, Ed. Palo Alto, California: National Press Books. Pp. 43–52.

Bailey, Vernon, 1913. Life Zones and Crop Zones of New Mexico. *United States Department of Agriculture, Bureau of Biological Surveys, North American Fauna,* No. 35.

Bauer, Harry L., 1936. Moisture Relations in the Chaparral of the Santa Monica Mountains, California. *Ecological Monographs* 6: 409–454.

———. 1943. The Statistical Analysis of Chaparral and Other Plant Communities By Means of Transect Samples. *Ecology* 24: 45–60.

Benfer, Alice N., 1969. Clustering for Maximal Artifact Class Associations. Master's thesis, The University of Texas at Austin.

———. 1973. Preliminary Analysis of the Obsidian Artifacts from Tula, Hidalgo. *In* Interim Report of the University of Missouri Tula Archaeological Project. Richard A. Diehl, Ed. *University of Missouri Museum of Anthropology Reports.*

———. n.d. A Preliminary Lithic Analysis of Obsidian From Prehistoric Tula. Unpublished ms.

Benfer, Robert A., 1967. A Design for the Study of Archaeological Characteristics. *American Anthropologist* 69: 719–730.

———. 1968. The Desirability of Small Samples for Anthropological Inference. *American Anthropologist* 70: 950–951.

———. 1972. Factor Analysis as Numerical Induction: How to Judge a Book by Its Cover. *American Anthropologist* 74: 530–554.

———. n.d.a. Multivariate Chi-square. Unpublished ms.

———. n.d.b. Non-Linnean Taxonomy

(Benfer, *Continued*)
and the Non-Specificity Hypothesis. Unpublished ms.

————. n.d.c. XYZ Coordinates of the Skull. Unpublished ms.

Benfer, Robert A., Melvin Fowler, and Sally Decker, n.d. Programmed Typology as Prehistoric Ethnoscience: The Evidence From Cahokia. Unpublished ms.

Berreman, G. D., 1972. *Hindus of the Himalayas: Ethnography and Change.* Berkeley: University of California Press.

Berry, Brian J. L., 1962. Sampling, Coding, and Storing Flood Plain Data. United States Department of Agriculture, Farm Economics Division, Agriculture Handbook, 237.

————. 1964. Approaches to Regional Analysis: A Synthesis. *Annals of the Association of American Geographers* 54: 2–11.

————. 1968. A Synthesis of Formal and Functional Regions Using a General Field Theory of Spatial Behavior. In *Spatial Analysis: A Reader in Statistical Geography.* Brian J. L. Berry and Duane F. Marble, Eds. Englewood Cliffs, N.J.: Prentice-Hall. Pp. 419–430.

Berry, Brian J. L. and A. M. Baker, 1968. Geographic Sampling. In *Spatial Analysis: A Reader in Statistical Geography.* Brian J. L. Berry and Duane F. Marble, Eds. Englewood Cliffs, N.J.: Prentice-Hall. Pp. 91–100.

Bertalanffy, Ludwig von, 1968. *General System Theory: Foundations, Development, Applications.* New York: George Braziller.

Bettinger, Robert L., n.d. Settlement Change and Stability in Eastern California: A Discussion of Preliminary Results of the Owens Valley Project. Unpublished ms.

Binford, Lewis R., 1962. Archaeology as Anthropology. *American Antiquity* 28: 217–225.

————. 1964. A Consideration of Archaeological Research Design. *American Antiquity* 29: 425–441.

————. 1965. Archaeological Systematics and the Study of Culture Process. *American Antiquity* 31: 203–210.

————. 1968a. Archaeological Perspectives. In *New Perspectives in Archaeology.* Sally R. and L. R. Binford, Eds. Chicago: Aldine. Pp. 5–32.

————. 1968b. Some Comments on Historical Versus Processual Archaeology. *Southwestern Journal of Anthropology* 24: 267–275.

————. 1968c. Post-Pleistocene Adaptations. In *New Perspectives in Archaeology,* Sally R. Binford and Lewis R. Binford, Eds. Chicago: Aldine. Pp. 313–341.

————. 1972. Model Building—Paradigms, and the Current State of Paleolithic Research. In *Models in Archaeology.* David L. Clarke, Ed. London: Methuen. Pp. 109–166.

————. n.d.a. Forty Seven Trips: A Case Study in the Character of Some Formation Processes of the Archaeological Record. Unpublished ms.

————. n.d.b. Interassemblage Variability—the Mousterian and the "Functional" Argument. In *Explanation of Culture Change: Models in Prehistory.* C. Renfrew, Ed. London: Duckworth. (In press).

Binford, Lewis R. and Sally R. Binford, 1966. A Preliminary Analysis of Functional Variability in the Mousterian of Levallois Facies. *In* Recent Studies in Paleoanthropology. J. D. Clark and F. C. Howell, Eds. *American Anthropologist* 68 (No. 2, Pt. 2): 238–295.

Binford, Lewis R., Sally R. Binford, Robert Whallon, and Margaret Ann Hardin, 1970. Archaeology at Hatchery West. *Memoirs of the Society for American Archaeology,* 24.

Blackith, R. W. and R. A. Reyment,

1971. *Multivariate Morphometrics.* New York: Academic Press.

Blalock, Hubert M., 1960. *Social Statistics.* New York: McGraw-Hill.

———. 1972. *Social Statistics.* (2nd ed.) New York: McGraw-Hill.

Blalock, Hubert M., Ed., 1971. *Causal Models in the Social Sciences.* Chicago: Aldine.

Blaut, J. M., 1962. Microgeographic Sampling. *Economic Geography* 35: 79–88.

Bordes, Francois, 1953. Essai de Classification des Industries "Mousteriennes." *Bulletin de La Societé Prehistorique Fran-çaise* 50: 457–466.

———. 1961. Mousterian Cultures in France. *Science* 134: 803–810.

———. 1968. *The Old Stone Age.* New York: McGraw-Hill.

———. 1972. *A Tale of Two Caves.* New York: McGraw-Hill.

Bormann, F. H., 1953. The Statistical Efficiency of Sample Plot Size and Shape in Forest Ecology. *Ecology* 34: 474–487.

Bradley, J. V., 1968. *Distribution-free Statistical Tests.* Englewood Cliffs, N.J.: Prentice-Hall.

Braidwood, Robert J. and Bruce Howe, 1960. Prehistoric Investigations in Iraqi Kurdistan. *Oriental Institute of the University of Chicago, Studies in Ancient Oriental Civilization,* No. 31.

Brainerd, George W., 1951. The Use of Mathematical Formulations in Archaeological Analysis. *Anthropological Papers, Museum of Anthropology, University of Michigan* 8: 117–125.

Brand, Donald D., Florence M. Hawley, and Frank C. Hibben et al., 1937. Tseh So, A Small House Ruin, Chaco Canyon, New Mexico. *University of New Mexico Bulletin, Anthropological Series,* Vol. 2, No. 2.

Brown, James A. and J. L. G. Freeman, 1964. A UNIVAC Analysis of Sherd Frequencies From the Carter Ranch Pueblo, Eastern Arizona (With Comments by Paul S. Martin). *American Antiquity* 30: 162–167.

Brown, James A. and Stuart Struever, 1973. The Organization of Archaeological Research: An Illinois Example. In *Research and Theory in Current Archaeology.* C. L. Redman, Ed. New York: John Wiley & Sons. Pp. 257–280.

Brown, James A. and Bernard Werner, n.d. An Application of a Specialized Data Bank for Analysis and Information Retrieval in an Archaeological Field Lab. Unpublished ms.

Brownlee, K. A., 1965. *Statistical Theory and Methodology in Science and Engineering.* (2nd ed.) New York: John Wiley and Sons.

Campbell, J. M., 1968. Territoriality Among Ancient Hunters: Interpretations From Ethnography and Nature. In *Anthropological Archaeology in the Americas.* B. J. Meggers, Ed. Washington, D.C.: The Anthropological Society of Washington. Pp. 1–21.

Cattell, R. B., 1965. Factor Analysis: An Introduction to Essentials: I. The Purpose and Underlying Models. *Biometrics* 21: 190–215.

Chamberlain, T. C., 1897. The Method of Multiple Working Hypotheses. *Journal of Geology* 39: 155–165. (Reprinted in *In Search of Man.* Ernestene L. Green, Ed. Boston: Little Brown. Pp. 394–402.)

Chaney, Richard P., 1974. Comparative Analysis and Retroductive Reasoning, or Conclusions in Search of a Premise. *American Anthropologist* 75: 1358–1375.

Chang, K. C., 1962. A Typology of Settlement and Community Patterns in Some Circumpolar Societies. *Arctic Anthropology* 1: 28–41.

———. 1967. *Rethinking Archaeology.* New York: Random House.

Chang, K. C., Ed., 1968. *Settlement Archaeology*. Palo Alto, California: National Press Books.

Chenhall, Robert G., 1971. Random Sampling in an Archaeological Survey. Ph.D. dissertation, Arizona State University.

――――. n.d. The Use of Random Sampling in Archaeological Surveys. Unpublished ms.

Clapham, A. R., 1932. The Form of the Observational Unit in Quantitative Ecology. *Journal of Ecology* 20: 192–197.

Clark, J. D., 1966. Acheulian Occupation Sites in the Middle East and Africa: A Study in Cultural Variability. *In* Recent Studies in Paleo-Anthropology. J. D. Clark and F. C. Howell, Eds. *American Anthropologist* 68: 2: 2: 238–295.

Clark, P. J. and F. C. Evans, 1954. Distance to Nearest Neighbor as a Measure of Spatial Relationships in Populations. *Ecology* 35: 445–453.

Clarke, David L., 1968. *Analytical Archaeology*. London: Methuen.

Clarke, David L. Ed., 1972. *Models in Archaeology*. New York: Harper and Row.

Cochran, William G., 1963. *Sampling Techniques*. (2nd ed.) New York: John Wiley and Sons.

Cochran, W. G., F. Mosteller, and J. W. Tukey, 1954. Principles of Sampling. *Journal of the American Statistical Association* 49: 13–35.

Conklin, Harold C., 1964. The Ethnogeneological Method. In *Explorations in Cultural Anthropology*. Ward H. Goodenough, Ed. New York: McGraw-Hill. Pp. 25–55.

Conover, W. J., 1971a. *Practical Nonparametric Statistics*. New York: John Wiley and Sons.

――――. 1971b. Rank Tests for Randomness Without the Assumption of a Continuous Distribution Function. *Kansas State University Statistical Laboratory, Technical Report* 18.

Cook, S. F., 1960. *Comments* on Statistical Description and Comparison of Artifact Assemblages by Albert C. Spaulding. *In* The Application of Quantitative Methods in Archaeology. Robert F. Heizer and Sherburne F. Cook, Eds. *Viking Fund Publications in Anthropology* 28. Pp. 92 ff.

Cowgill, George L., 1964. The Selection of Samples From Large Sherd Collections. *American Antiquity* 29: 467–473.

――――. 1970. Some Sampling and Reliability Problems in Archaeology. *In* Archéologie et Calculateurs: Problèmes Sémiologiques et Mathématiques. Colloque Internationaux du Centre National de la Récherche Scientifique. Paris: *Editions du Centre National de la Récherche Scientifique*. Pp. 161–175.

Daniels, S. G. H., 1972. Research Design Models. In *Models in Archaeology*. David L. Clarke, Ed. London: Methuen. Pp. 201–229.

Daubenmire, Rexford, 1968. *Plant Communities: A Textbook of Plant Synecology*. New York: Harper and Row.

Davies, E., 1969. This is the Way Crete Went – Not With a Bang But a Simper. *Psychology Today* 3: 6: 42–47.

Davis, John C., 1973. *Statistics and Data Analysis in Geology*. New York: John Wiley and Sons.

Deetz, J., 1965. The Dynamics of Stylistic Change in Arikara Ceramics. *Illinois Studies in Anthropology*, No. 4.

――――. 1967. *Invitation to Archaeology*. Garden City, New York: The Natural History Press.

――――. 1968. The Inference of Residence and Descent Rules from Archaeological Data. In *New Perspectives in Archaeology*. Sally R. Binford and Lewis R. Binford, Eds. Chicago: Aldine. Pp. 41–48.

DeFries, J. C., S. G. Vandenberg, G. E. McClearn, A. R. Kuse, J. R. Wilson, G. C. Ashton, and R. C. Johnson, 1974. Near Identity of Cognitive Structure in Two Ethnic Groups. *Science* 183: 338–339.

Degerman, Richard L., 1972. The Geometric Representation of Some Simple Structures. In *Multidimensional Scaling: Vol. 1, Theory.* A. Kimball Romney, Roger N. Shepard, and Sara Beth Nerlove, Eds. New York: Seminar Press.

Deming, William E., 1950. *Some Theory of Sampling.* New York: John Wiley and Sons.

———. 1960. *Sample Design in Business Research.* New York: John Wiley and Sons.

Dittert, Alfred E., Jr., n.d. Archaeological Investigations in the Vosberg Locality, Central Arizona. Unpublished ms.

Dixon, Wilfred J. and Frank J. Massey, Jr., 1969. *Introduction to Statistical Analysis.* New York: McGraw-Hill.

Dorwin, J. T., 1971. The Bowen Site, An Archaeological Study of Culture Process in the Late Prehistory of Central Indiana. *Indiana Historical Society, Prehistory Research Series*, Vol. 4, No. 4.

Driver, Harold E., 1961. Introduction to Statistics for Comparative Research. In *Readings in Cross-Cultural Methodology.* Frank W. Moore, Ed. New Haven: HRAF Press. Pp. 303–331. (Reprinted as Bobbs-Merrill Paper A-53).

———. 1974. Cross-Cultural Studies. In *Handbook of Social and Cultural Anthropology.* John J. Honigmann, Ed. New York: Rand McNally. Pp. 327–367.

Driver, H. E. and W. C. Massey, 1957. Comparative Studies of North American Indians. *Transactions of the American Philosophical Society*, Vol. 47, Pt. 2.

Duncan, O. T., Ray P. Cuzzort, and Beverly Duncan, 1961. *Statistical Geography.* New York: The Free Press.

Dunnell, Robert C., 1971. *Systematics in Prehistory.* New York: The Free Press.

Edwards, Allen L., 1960. *Experimental Design in Psychological Research.* (Rev. ed.) New York: Holt, Rinehart and Winston.

Ember, Melvin, 1973. An Archaeological Indicator of Matrilocal Versus Patrilocal Residence. *American Antiquity* 38: 177–181.

Feldman, Lawrence A., 1973. Stones for the Archaeologist. *Contributions of the University of California Archaeological Research Facility* 18: 87–103.

Feynman, Richard P., 1974. Structure of the Proton. *Science* 183: 601–610.

Fillenbaum, Samuel and Amnon Rapoport, 1971. *Structures in the Subjective Lexicon.* New York: Academic Press.

Fisher, R. A., 1954. *Statistical Methods for Research Workers.* (12th ed.) Edinburgh: Oliver and Boyd.

Fisher, Reginald G., 1930. The Archaeological Survey of the Pueblo Plateau. *University of New Mexico Bulletin, Archaeological Series*, Vol. 1, No. 1.

———. 1934. The Chaco Canyon in 1934. *El Palacio*, Vol. 37, Nos. 15–16.

Flannery, Kent V., 1967. Review of *An Introduction to American Archaeology, Vol. 1: North and Middle America*, by Gordon R. Willey. *Scientific American* 217: 119–22.

———. 1973. Archeology with a Capital S. In *Research and Theory in Current Archeology.* Charles L. Redman, Ed. New York: John Wiley and Sons. Pp. 47–53.

Ford, James A., 1954. Spaulding's review of Ford. *American Anthropologist* 56: 109–112.

Ford, James A. and Gordon R. Willey, 1949. Surface survey of the Viru Valley, Peru. *Anthropological Papers of the American Museum of Natural History* 43, Part 1.

Frances, Roy, 1961. *The Rhetoric of Science*. Minneapolis: University of Minnesota Press.

Frankel, Charles, 1973. The Nature and Sources of Irrationalism. *Science* 180: 927–931.

Freeman, Leslie G., 1973. The Analysis of Some Occupation Floor Distributions From Earlier and Middle Paleolithic Sites in Spain. *Papers: IXth International Congress of Archaeological and Ethnological Sciences*. The Hague: Mouton. (In press).

Fritts, Harold C., 1965. Dendrochronology. In *The Quaternary of the United States*. H. E. Wright, Jr. and David G. Frey, Eds. Princeton, N.J.: Princeton University Press. Pp. 871–880.

Gardin, Jean-Claude, n.d. The Problem of Sorting. Unpublished ms.

Geoghan, W. H. and P. Kay, 1964. More on Structure and Statistics: A Critique of C. Ackerman's Analysis of the Purum. *American Anthropologist* 66: 1351–1358.

Getis, A., 1964. Temporal Land-use Pattern Analysis With the Use of Nearest-Neighbor and Quadrat Methods. *Annals of the Association of American Geographers* 54: 391–399.

Gladwin, Winifred and Harold S. Gladwin, 1928. A Method for the Designation of Ruins in the Southwest. *Medallion Papers*, No. 1. Globe, Ariz: Gila Pueblo.

Gleason, Henry Allan, 1920. Some Applications of the Quadrat Method. *Bulletin of the Torrey Botanical Club* 47: 21–33.

Goodall, David W., 1970. Statistical Plant Ecology. *Annual Review of Ecology and Systematics* 1: 99–124.

Goodenough, Ward H., 1956. Componential Analysis and the Study of Meaning. *Language* 32: 195–216.

———. 1965. Yankee Kinship Terminology: A Problem in Componential Analysis. *In* Formal Semantic Analysis. E. A. Hammel, Ed. *American Anthropologist* 67 (No. 5, Pt. 2): 259–297.

Goodman, L. A., 1961. Snowball Sampling. *Annals of Mathematical Statistics* 32: 148–170.

Goodman, R. and L. Kish, 1950. Controlled Selection – a Technique in Probability Sampling. *Journal of the American Statistical Association* 45: 350–372.

Gower, J. C., 1966. Some Distance Properties of Latent Root and Vector Methods Used in Multivariate Analysis. *Biometrika* 53: 325–338.

———. 1972. Measures of Taxonomic Distance and Their Analysis. In *The Assessment of Population Affinities in Man*. J. S. Weiner and J. Huizinga, Eds. Oxford: Claredon Press. Pp. 1–24.

Gray, P. G., 1957. A Sample Survey with Both a Postal and an Interview Stage. *Applied Statistics* 6: 139–153.

Gregory, H. E., 1938. The San Juan Country. *Geological Survey Professional Paper* 188.

Greig-Smith, P., 1964. *Quantitative Plant Ecology*. London: Buttersworth.

Grigg, David, 1967. Regions, Models, and Classes. In *Models in Geography*. Richard J. Chorley and Peter Haggett, Eds. London: Methuen. Pp. 461–509.

Gumerman, George J., Ed., 1971. The Distribution of Prehistoric Population Aggregates. Proceedings of the Southwestern Anthropological Research Group. *Prescott College Anthropological Reports*, No. 1.

———. 1972. Proceedings of the Second Annual Meeting of the Southwestern Anthropological Research Group. *Prescott College Anthropological Reports*, No. 3.

Hack, J. C., 1942. The Changing Physical Environment of the Hopi Indians of Arizona. *Papers of the Peabody Museum of American Archaeology and Ethnology, Harvard University* 35, No. 1.

Haggett, Peter, 1965. *Locational Analysis in Human Geography*. London: Edward Arnold.

Haggett, Peter and C. Board, 1964. Rotational and Parallel Traverses in the Rapid Integration of Geographic Areas. *Annals of the Association of American Geographers* 54: 406–410.

Haig, I. T., 1929. Accuracy of Quadrat Sampling in Studying Forest Reproduction in Cutover Areas. *Ecology* 10: 374–81.

Hanson, John A. and Michael B. Schiffer, n.d. The Joint Site: a Preliminary Report. *In* Chapters in the Prehistory of Eastern Arizona, IV. *Fieldiana: Anthropology*. (In press).

Hanson, Morris H., William M. Hurwitz, and William G. Madow, 1953. *Sample Survey Methods and Theory, Volume 1*. New York: John Wiley and Sons.

Harvey, D. W., 1966. Geographical Processes and Point Patterns: Testing Models of Diffusion by Quadrat Sampling. *Transactions of the Institute of British Geographers* 40: 81–95.

Hasel, A. A., 1938. Sampling Error in Timber Surveys. *Journal of Agricultural Research* 57: 713–736.

———. 1941. Estimation of Vegetation-type Areas by Linear Measurement. *Journal of Forestry* 39: 34–41.

Hayes, Alden C., 1964. The Archaeological Survey of Wetherill Mesa, Mesa Verde National Park, Colorado. *Archaeological Research Series* 7-A. Washington, D.C.: National Park Service.

Healan, Dan M., 1974. Residential Architecture and Household Patterning in Ancient Tula. Ph.D. dissertation, University of Missouri-Columbia.

Hendricks, Walter A., 1956. *The Mathematical Theory of Sampling*. Brunswick, N.J.: The Scarecrow Press.

Hill, James N., 1966. A Prehistoric Community in Eastern Arizona. *Southwestern Journal of Anthropology* 22: 9–30.

———. 1967. Sampling at Broken K Pueblo. *In* Chapters in the Prehistory of Eastern Arizona, III. Paul S. Martin, William A. Longacre, and James N. Hill, Eds. *Fieldiana Anthropology* 57: 151–157.

———. 1970. Broken K Pueblo: Prehistoric Social Organization in the American Southwest. *Anthropological Papers of the University of Arizona, 18.*

———. n.d. Random Sampling: A Tool for Discovery. Unpublished ms.

Hill, J. N. and R. X. Evans, 1972. A Model for Classification and Typology. In *Models in Archaeology*. David L. Clarke, Ed. New York: Harper and Row. Pp. 231–273.

Hodges, J. L. and E. L. Lehmann, 1964. *Basic Concepts of Probability and Statistics*. San Francisco: Holden-Day, Inc.

Hodson, F. R. and D. G. Kendall FRS, and P. Tautu, Eds., 1971. *Mathematics in the Archaeological and Historical Sciences*. Chicago: Aldine.

Hole, Frank and Robert F. Heizer, 1969. *An Introduction to Prehistoric Archeology*. (2nd ed.) New York: Holt, Rinehart and Winston.

———. 1973. *An Introduction to Prehistoric Archeology*. (3rd ed.) New York: Holt, Rinehart and Winston.

Holmes, J., 1967. Problems in Location Sampling. *Annals of the Association of American Geographers* 57: 757–780.

Honigmann, John J., 1970. Sampling in Ethnographic Field Work. In *A Handbook of Method in Cultural Anthropology*. Raoul Naroll and Ronald Cohen, Eds. New York: The Natural History Press. Pp. 266–281.

Houart, Gail L., 1971. Koster: A Stratified Archaic Site in the Illinois Valley. *Illinois State Museum, Reports of Investigations*, No. 22.

Hudson, J. C., 1969. A Location Theory for Rural Settlement. *Annals of the Association of American Geographers* 59: 365–381.

Isaac, Glynn, 1971. The Diet of Early Man: Aspects of Archaeological Evidence From Lower and Middle Pleistocene Sites in Africa. *World Archaeology* 2: 278–299.

Isard, W., 1956. Regional Science; The Concept of the Region and Regional Structure. *Papers and Proceedings of the Regional Science Association* 2: 13–26.

Jardine, Nicholas and Robin Sibson, 1971. *Mathematical Taxonomy*. New York: John Wiley and Sons.

Jelks, Edward B., 1975. The Use and Misuse of Random Sampling in Archaeology. Gett Publishing Co., Normal, Ill.

Jennings, Jesse D., 1968. *Prehistory of North America*. New York: McGraw-Hill.

Jolly, G. M., 1954. The Theory of Sampling. In *Methods of Surveying and Measuring Vegetation*. Dorothy Brown, Ed. *Commonwealth Bureau of Pastures and Field Crops Bulletin* 42. Bucks, England. Pp. 8–18.

Jones, Kirkland L., 1970. An Ecological Survey of the Reptiles and Amphibians of Chaco Canyon National Monument, San Juan County, New Mexico. Master's thesis, University of New Mexico.

———. n.d. The Ecology of Chaco Canyon. Unpublished ms.

Judge, W. James, n.d. An Archaeological Survey of the Chaco Canyon Area, San Juan County, New Mexico. Unpublished ms.

———. 1973. *The PaleoIndian Occupation of the Central Rio Grande Valley, New Mexico*. Albuquerque: University of New Mexico Press.

Kempthorne, O., 1969. Some Remarks of Statistical Inference in Finite Sampling. In *New Developments in Survey Sampling*. N. L. Johnson and H. Smith, Eds. New York: John Wiley and Sons. Pp. 671–695.

Kenyon, K., 1957. *Digging up Jericho: the Results of the Jericho Excavations 1952–1956*. New York: Praeger.

Kershaw, Kenneth A., 1964. *Quantitative and Dynamic Ecology*. London: Edward Arnold.

Kish, Leslie, 1957. Confidence Intervals in Complex Samples. *American Sociological Review* 22: 154–165.

———. 1965. *Survey Sampling*. New York: John Wiley and Sons.

Kish, Leslie and Martin R. Frankel, 1970. Balanced Repeated Replications for Standard Errors. *Journal of the American Statistical Association* 65: 1071–1094.

Krause, Richard A. and Robert M. Thorne, 1971. Toward a Theory of Archaeological Things. *Plains Anthropologist* 16: 245–257.

Kroeber, A. L., 1916. Zuni potsherds. *Anthropological Papers of the American Museum of Natural History* 18, Part 1.

Kruskal, Joseph B., 1972. Linear Transformation of Multivariate Data to Reveal Clustering. In *Multidimensional Scaling, Volume I: Theory*. Roger N. Shephard, A. Kimball Romney, and Sara Beth Nerlove, Eds. New York: Seminar Press. Pp. 181–191.

Kuhn, Thomas S., 1970. *The Structure of Scientific Revolutions.* (2nd ed.) Chicago: University of Chicago Press.

Lazerwitz, Bernard, 1968. Sampling Theory and Procedures. In *Methodology in Social Research,* (H. M. and A. B. Blalock, Eds.) New York: McGraw-Hill. Pp. 278–328.

Leaf, Gary R., n.d. Debitage in Lithic Analysis: An Initial Perspective. Unpublished ms.

Leone, Mark, 1971. Review of New Perspectives in Archaeology. Sally R. Binford and Lewis R. Binford, Eds. *American Antiquity* 36: 220–222.

Levi-Strauss, Claude, 1963. The Bear and the Barber. *Journal of the Royal Anthropological Institute* 93: 1–11.

Lindsey, Alton A., James D. Barton, and S. R. Miles, 1956. Field Efficiencies of Forest Sampling Methods. *Ecology* 39: 428–444.

Lipe, William D., n.d. Prehistoric Cultural Adaptation in the Cedar Mesa Area, Southeastern Utah. Unpublished ms.

Lipe, W. D. and R. G. Matson, 1971. Human Settlement and Resources in the Cedar Mesa Area, Southeastern Utah. *In* The Distribution of Prehistoric Population Aggregates. George J. Gumerman, Ed. *Prescott College Anthropological Reports,* No. 1. Pp. 126–151.

Lischka, Joseph J., 1974. Problems with Johnson's "Problems in Avant-Garde Archaeology". *American Anthropologist* 76: 1716–1717.

Lloyd, Seton, 1963. *Mounds of the Near East.* Edinburgh, Scotland: Edinburgh University Press.

Longacre, William A., 1968. Some Aspects of Prehistoric Society in East-Central Arizona. In *New Perspectives in Archaeology.* Sally R. Binford and Lewis R. Binford, Eds. Chicago: Aldine. Pp. 89–102.

——. 1970. Archaeology as Anthropology: a Case Study. *The Anthropological Papers of the University of Arizona.* No. 17. Tucson.

——. n.d.a. Statistics in American Archaeology. In *Symposium on Methodology and Theory in Archaeological Interpretation.* Robert Ehrich, Ed. (In press).

Longacre, William A. (Ed.), n.d.b. Multi-disciplinary Research at the Grasshopper Ruin. *Anthropological Papers of the University of Arizona.* Tucson. (In press).

Longacre, William A. and J. Jefferson Reid, 1974. The University of Arizona Archaeological Field School at Grasshopper: Eleven Years of Multidisciplinary Research and Teaching. *The Kiva* 40: 1–36.

Lounsbury, Floyd G., 1956. A Semantic Analysis of Pawnee Kinship Usage. *Language* 32: 158–194.

Ludwig, Emil, 1964. Henri Schliemann. In *Archaeology.* Samuel Rapport and Helen Wright, Eds. New York: Washington Square Press. Pp. 113–131.

Machol, Robert E. and Rolf Singer, 1971. Bayesian Analysis of Generic Relations in Agaricales. *Nova Hedwigia XXI:* 753–787.

MacNeish, Richard S., 1958. Preliminary Archaeological Investigations in the Sierra de Tamaulipas, Mexico. *Transactions of the American Philosophical Society,* Vol. 48, Pt. 6.

Martin, P. S., 1971. The Revolution in Archaeology. *American Antiquity* 36: 162–167.

Matson, R. G., 1971. Adaption and Environment in the Cerbat Mountains, Arizona. Ph.D. dissertation, University of California, Davis.

——. n.d. The results of a stratified surface survey in the Cerbat Mountains, Arizona. Unpublished ms.

Mayer-Oakes, William J. and Ronald J. Nash, n.d. Archeological Research Design—A Critique. Unpublished ms.

McHarg, Ian L., 1969. *Design With Nature*. New York: Natural History Press.

McIntyre, G. A., 1953. Estimation of Plant Density Using Line Transects. *Journal of Ecology* 41: 319–330.

McNitt, Frank, 1957. *Anasazi*. Albuquerque: University of New Mexico Press.

Meighan, Clement W., 1961. *The Archaeologist's Note Book*. San Francisco: Chandler Publishing Company.

Mood, Alexander M. and Franklin A. Graybill, 1963. *Introduction to the Theory of Statistics*. New York: McGraw-Hill.

Morris, Craig, 1967. Storage in Tawantinsuyu. Ph.D. dissertation, University of Chicago.

———. 1971. The Identification of Function in Inca Architecture and Ceramics. *Actas y Memorias del XXXIX Congreso Internacional de Americanistas* 3: 135–144.

———. 1972a. El Almacenaje en Dos Aldeas de Los Chupaychu. In *Visita de la Provincia de Leon de Huánuco (1562), Tomo II.* Iñigo Ortiz de Zúñiga, Ed. Huánuco, Peru: Universidad Hermilio Valdizan. Pp. 385–404.

———. 1972b. State Settlements in Tawantinsuyu: a Strategy of Compulsory Urbanism. In *Contemporary Archaeology: A Guide to Theory and Contributions.* Mark P. Leone, Ed. Carbondale: Southern Illinois University Press. Pp. 393–401.

———. n.d. Reconstructing Patterns of Non-Agricultural Production in the Inca Economy: Archaeology and Documents in Institutional Analysis. In *The Reconstruction of Complex Societies.* Charlotte Moore, Ed. Cambridge, Mass.: American Schools of Oriental Research. (In press).

Morrison, Denton E. and Ramon E. Henkel, 1970. *The Significance Test Controversy: a Reader.* Chicago: Aldine.

Moser, Claus A., and G. Kalton, 1971. *Survey Methods in Social Investigation* (2nd ed.) London: Heinemann Educational Books Limited.

Movius, Hallam L., Jr., 1966. The Hearths of the Upper Perigordian and Aurignacian Horizons at the Abri Pataud, Les Eyzies (Dordogne), and Their Possible Significance. *In* Recent Studies in Paleoanthropology. J. D. Clark and F. C. Howell, Eds. *American Anthropologist* 68 (No. 2, Pt. 2): 296–325.

Mueller, James W., 1972. The Use Of Sampling in Archaeological Survey. Ph.D. dissertation, University of Arizona.

———. 1974. The Use of Sampling in Archaeological Survey. *Memoirs, Society for American Archaeology,* No. 28.

Muller, T. P. and John T. Mayhall, 1971. Analysis of Contingency Table Data on Torus Mandibularis Using a Log Linear Model. *American Journal of Physical Anthropology* 34: 149–154.

Murra, John V., 1962. An Archaeological Restudy of an Andean Ethnohistorical Account. *American Antiquity* 28: 1–4.

Neprash, J. A., 1934. Some Problems in the Correlation of Spatially Distributed Variables. *Journal of the American Statistical Association* (supplement) 29: 167–168.

Nie, Norman H., Dale H. Brent, and C. Hadlai Hull, 1970. *SPSS: Statistical Package for the Social Sciences*. New York: McGraw-Hill.

Noether, Gottfried E., 1972. Distribution-free Confidence Intervals. *American Statistician* 26: 39–41.

Odum, Howard T., 1971. *Environment, Power, and Society.* New York: John Wiley and Sons.

Osborne, J. G., 1941. On the Precision of Estimates From Systematic Versus Random Samples. *Science* 94: 584–585.

———. 1942. Sampling Errors of Systematic and Random Surveys of Cover-type Areas. *Journal of the American Statistical Association* 37: 256–264.

Oxnard, Charles, 1973. *Form and Pattern in Human Evolution.* Chicago: The University of Chicago Press.

Parmalee, Paul W., Andreas A. Paloumpis, and Nancy Wilson, 1972. Animals Utilized by Woodland Peoples Occupying the Apple Creek Site, Illinois. *Illinois State Museum Reports of Investigations* No. 23 and *Illinois Valley Archaeological Program Research Papers* Vol. 5.

Patil, G. P., E. C. Pielou, and W. E. Waters, Eds., 1971. *Statistical Ecology, Volume 1: Spatial Patterns and Statistical Distributions.* University Park: Pennsylvania State University Press.

Peebles, Christopher S., 1972. Monothetic-Divisive Analysis of the Moundville Burials: An Initial Report. *Newsletter of Computer Archaeology* 8: 1–13.

Perrin, Charles L., 1974. Testing of Computer-Assisted Methods for Classification of Pharmacological Activity. *Science* 183: 551–552.

Peters, Charles R., 1970. Introductory Topics in Probability Sampling Theory for Archaeology. *Anthropology UCLA* 2: 33–50.

Phillips, Philip, James A. Ford, and James B. Griffin, 1951. Archaeological Survey in the Lower Mississippi Alluvial Valley, 1940–1947. *Papers of the Peabody Museum, Harvard University* 25.

Pielou, E. C., 1969. *An Introduction to Mathematical Ecology.* New York: John Wiley and Sons.

Pierson, Lloyd M., 1949. The Prehistoric Population of Chaco Canyon, New Mexico: A Study in Methods and Techniques of Prehistoric Population Estimation. Master's thesis, University of New Mexico.

———. n.d. A History of Chaco Canyon National Monument. Unpublished ms.

Plog, Fred, 1968. Archaeological Surveys: A New Perspective. Master's thesis, University of Chicago.

Plog, Fred and James N. Hill, 1971. Explaining Variability in the Distribution of Sites. *In* The Distribution of Prehistoric Population Aggregates. Proceedings of the Southwestern Anthropological Research Group. George J. Gumerman, Ed. *Prescott College Anthropological Reports,* No. 1. Pp. 7–36.

Plog, Steve, n.d. The Relative Efficiency of Sampling Techniques for Archaeological Surveys. Unpublished ms.

Pound, Roscoe and Frederick E. Clements, 1898. A Method of Determining the Abundance of Secondary Species. *Minnesota Botanical Studies* 2: 19–24.

Proudfoot, M. J., 1942. Sampling with Transverse Traverse Lines. *Journal of the American Statistical Association* 37: 265–270.

Quenouille, M. H., 1949. Some Problems of Plane Sampling. *Annals of Mathematical Statistics* 20: 355–375.

Ragir, Sonia, 1967. A Review of Techniques for Archaeological Sampling. In *A Guide to Field Methods in Archaeology,* R. F. Heizer and J. A. Graham, Eds. Palo Alto, California: National Press. Pp. 181–198.

Raj, D., 1958. On the Relative Accuracy of Some Sampling Techniques. *Journal of the American Statistical Association* 53: 98–101.

Randall, Robert A., n.d. How Tall is a Taxonomic Tree? Some Evidence for Dwarfism. Unpublished ms.

Redman, Charles L., 1973. Multistage Fieldwork and Analytical Techniques. *American Antiquity* 38: 61–79.

Redman, Charles L. and S. A. LeBlanc, n.d. Archaeological Research Strategies: Cibola Survey 1972. Unpublished ms.

Redman, Charles L. and Patty Jo Watson, 1970. Systematic, Intensive Surface Collection. *American Antiquity* 35: 279–291.

Reed, Erik K., 1948. The Western Pueblo Archaeological Complex. *El Palacio* 55: 9–15.

Reid, J. Jefferson, n.d. The Archaeologist at Work: Past and Present. Unpublished ms.

———. 1973. *Growth and Response to Stress at Grasshopper Pueblo, Arizona.* Ph.D. dissertation, University of Arizona.

Reid, J. Jefferson and Izumi Shimada, n.d. Pueblo Growth at Grasshopper. Methods and Models. *In* Multidisciplinary Research at the Grasshopper Ruin, W. A. Longacre, Ed. *Anthropological Papers of the University of Arizona.* (In press).

Reid, J. Jefferson, William L. Rathje and Michael B. Schiffer, 1974. Expanding Archaeology. *American Antiquity* 39: 125–126.

Rinaldo, John B., 1964. Notes on the Origins of Historic Zuni Culture. *The Kiva* 29: 86–98.

Robbins, Michael C. and R. Pollanc, 1974. A Multivariate Analysis of the Relationship of Artifactual to Cultural Modernity in Rural Buganda. In *The Human Mirror: The Material and Spatial Configurations of Culture.* M. Richardson, Ed. New Orleans: Louisiana State University Press. (In press).

Robertson, M. G., 1972. Monument Thievery in Mesoamerica. *American Antiquity* 37: 147–155.

Robinson, A. H., James B. Lindberg, and Leonard W. Brinkman, 1968. A Correlation and Regression Analysis Applied to Rural Farm Population Densities in the Great Plains. In *Spatial Analysis: A Reader in Statistical Geography.* Brian J. L. Berry and Duane F. Marble, Eds. Englewood Cliffs, New Jersey: Prentice-Hall. Pp. 290–300.

Robinson, W. S., 1951. A Method For Chronologically Ordering Archaeological Deposits. *American Antiquity* 16: 293–301.

Rohn, Arthur H., n.d. A Test of Density Plots and Random Sampling Procedures at the Gilliland Site. Unpublished ms.

Rootenberg, S., 1964. Archaeological Field Sampling. *American Antiquity* 30: 181–188.

Rouse, Irving, 1960. The Classification of Artifacts in Archaeology. *American Antiquity* 25: 313–323.

———. 1962. The Strategy of Culture History. In *Anthropology Today.* Sol Tax, Ed. Chicago: University of Chicago Press. Pp. 84–103.

———. 1972. *Introduction to Prehistory.* New York: McGraw-Hill.

Rozeboom, William W., 1960. The Fallacy of the Null-Hypothesis Significance Test. *Psychological Bulletin* 57: 416–28. (Reprinted in *Readings in Statistics for the Behavioral Sciences.* E. F. Heerman and L. A. Braskamp, Eds. Pp. 197–212. Englewood Cliffs, New Jersey: Prentice-Hall, 1970.)

Rummel, R. J., 1970. *Applied Factor Analysis.* Evanston, Illinois: Northwestern University Press.

Ruppé, Reynold J., 1966. The Archaeological Survey: A Defense. *American Antiquity* 31: 313–333.

Sabloff, Jeremy, Thomas W. Beale, and Anthony M. Kurland, Jr., 1973. Recent Developments in Archaeology. *The Annals of the American Academy of Political and Social Science* 408: 103–118.

Sackett, James R., 1966. Quantitative Analysis of Upper Paleolithic Stone Tools. *In* Recent Studies in Paleoanthropology. J. Desmond Clark and F. Clark Howell, Eds. *American Anthropologist Special Publication* 68 (No. 2, Pt. 2): 356–394.

———. 1969. Factor Analysis and Artifact Typology. *American Anthropologist* 71: 1125–1130.

Sampford, M. R., 1962. *An Introduction to Sampling Theory.* London: Oliver and Boyd.

Schiffer, Michael B., 1972. Archaeological Context and Systemic Context. *American Antiquity* 37: 156–165.

———. 1973. *Cultural Formation Processes of the Archaeological Record: Applications at the Joint Site, East-central Arizona.* Ph.D. dissertation, University of Arizona.

Schiffer, Michael B. and William L. Rathje, 1973. The Efficient Exploitation of the Archaeological Record: Penetrating Problems. In *Research and Theory in Current Archaeology.* Charles L. Redman, Ed. New York: John Wiley and Sons. Pp. 169–179.

Schneider, David M., 1965. American Kin Terms and Terms for Kinsmen: A Critique of Goodenough's Componential Analysis of Yankee Kinship Terminology. *In* Formal Semantic Analysis. E. A. Hammel, Ed. *American Anthropologist Special Publication* 67 (No. 5 Pt. 2): 288–305.

Schoenwetter, James and Alfred E. Dittert, Jr., 1968. An Ecological Interpretation of Anasazi Settlement Patterns. In *Anthropological Archeology in the Americas.* Betty J. Meggers, Ed. Washington, D.C.: The Anthropological Society of Washington. Pp. 41–66.

Schroeder, A. H., 1965. Salvage Excavations in Natural Bridges National Monument. *University of Utah Anthropological Papers* 75: 85–110.

Scribner, Sylvia and Michael Cole, 1973. Cognitive Consequences of Formal and Informal Education. *Science* 182: 553–559.

Sharrock, Floyd W., 1964. 1962 Excavations, Glen Canyon Area. *University of Utah Anthropological Papers* 73.

Siegel, Sidney, 1956. *Nonparametric Statistics for the Behavioral Sciences.* New York: McGraw-Hill.

Simon, Herbert A., 1974. How Big is a Chunk? *Science* 183: 482–488.

Simpson, G. G., 1945. The Principles of Classification and A Classification of Mammals. *Bulletin of the American Museum of Natural History* 85: 1–350.

———. 1961. *Principles of Animal Taxonomy.* New York: Columbia University Press.

Sjoberg, Gideon, and Roger Nett, 1968. *A Methodology for Social Research.* New York: Harper and Row.

Skinner, G. W., 1964–65. Marketing and Social Structure in Rural China, Parts I and II. *Journal of Asian Studies* 24: 3–43, 195–228.

Smith, Carol Ann, 1972. The Domestic Marketing System in Western Guatemala: An Economic, Locational, and Cultural Analysis. Ph.D. dissertation, Stanford University.

Sokal, Robert R. and F. James Rohlf, 1969. *Biometry.* San Francisco: W. H. Freeman.

Sokal, Robert R. and Peter H. A. Sneath, 1963. *Principles of Numerical Taxonomy.* San Francisco: Freeman.

Spaulding, Albert C., 1953. Statistical Techniques for the Discovery of Artifact Types. *American Antiquity* 18: 305–313.

(Spaulding, *Continued*)

———. 1960a. The Dimensions of Archaeology. In *Essays In the Science of Culture*. Gertrude E. Dole and Robert L. Carniero, Eds. New York: Thomas Y. Crowell. Pp. 437–456.

———. 1960b. Statistical Description and Comparison of Artifact Assemblages. *In* The Application of Quantitative Methods in Archaeology. Robert F. Heizer and Sherburne F. Cook, Eds. *Viking Fund Publications in Anthropology* 28: 60–92.

———. 1971. The Dimensions of Archaeology. In *Man's Imprint From the Past: Readings in the Methods of Archaeology*. James Deetz, Ed. Boston: Little, Brown. Pp. 22–39.

———. 1973. Archeology in the Active Voice: The New Anthropology. In *Research and Theory in Current Archeology*. Charles L. Redman, Ed. New York: John Wiley and Sons. Pp. 337–354.

Spier, Leslie, 1917. An Outline for a Chronology of Zuni Ruins. *Anthropological Papers of the American Museum of Natural History* 18: 209–331.

Stanislawski, Michael, 1973. Review of *Archaeology as Anthropology: A Case Study*. William A. Longacre. *American Antiquity* 88: 117–122.

Stephan, F. F., 1934. Sampling Errors and Interpretations of Social Data Ordered in Time and Space. *Journal of the American Statistical Association* (supplement) 29: 165–166.

Steward, Julian H., 1938. Basin-Plateau Aboriginal Sociopolitical Groups. *Bureau of American Ethnology*, Bulletin 120.

Strong, Charles W., 1966. An Improved Method of Obtaining Density from Line-transect Data. *Ecology* 47: 311–313.

Struever, Stuart, 1968. Problems, Methods, and Organization: A Disparity in the Growth of Archaeology. In *Anthropological Archaeology in the Americas*. Betty J. Meggers, Ed. Washington, D.C.: Anthropological Society of Washington. Pp. 131–151.

———. 1971. Comments on Archaeological Data Requirements and Research Strategy. *American Antiquity* 36: 9–19.

Stuart, Alan, 1962. Basic Ideas of Scientific Sampling. *Griffin's Statistical Monographs and Courses*, No. 4. London: Charles Griffin and Company.

Sukhatme, Pandurang V., 1947. The Problem of Plot Size in Large-scale Yield Surveys. *Journal of the American Statistical Association* 42: 297–310.

———. 1954. *Sampling Theory of Surveys with Applications*. Bangalore, India: Bangalore Press.

Taylor, Walter W., 1972. Old Wine and New Skins. In *Contemporary Archaeology*. Mark P. Leone, Ed. Carbondale and Edwardsville: Southern Illinois University Press. Pp. 28–33.

Teague, George A., n.d. Flaked Stone Items from the Wide Reed Ruin. Unpublished ms.

Thaden, R., et al., 1964. Geology and Ore Deposits of the White Canyon Area, San Juan and Garfield Counties, Utah. *Geological Survey Bulletin* 1125.

Thomas, David H., 1969. Regional Sampling in Archaeology: A Pilot Great Basin Research Design. In *Archaeological Survey Annual Report 1969*. Department of Anthropology, University of California, Los Angeles. Pp. 87–100.

———. 1971. Prehistoric Subsistence-settlement Patterns of the Reese River Valley, Central Nevada.

(Thomas, *Continued*)
Ph.D. dissertation, University of California, Davis.
——. 1972. A Computer Simulation Model of Great Basin Shoshonean Subsistence and Settlement Patterns. In *Models in Archaeology*. David L. Clarke, Ed. London: Methuen. Pp. 671–704.
——. 1973. An Empirical Test for Steward's Model of Great Basin Settlement Patterns. *American Antiquity* 38: 155–176.

Thompson, Donald E., 1968. An Archaeological Evaluation of Ethnohistoric Evidence on Inca Culture. In *Anthropological Archaeology in the Americas*. Betty J. Meggers, Ed. Washington, D.C.: The Anthropological Society of Washington. Pp. 108–120.

Thompson, Raymond H. and William A. Longacre, 1966. The University of Arizona Archaeological Field School at Grasshopper, East-central Arizona. *The Kiva* 31: 255–275.

Treganza, A. E. and S. F. Cook, 1948. The Quantitative Investigation of Aboriginal Sites: Complete Excavation With Physical and Archaeological Analysis of a Single Mound. *American Antiquity* 13: 287–297.

Trigger, Bruce G., 1967. Settlement Archaeology—Its Goals and Promise. *American Antiquity* 32: 149–160.
——. 1968. The Determinants of Settlement Patterns. In *Settlement Archaeology*. K. C. Chang, Ed. Palo Alto, California: National Press Books. Pp. 53–78.

Tringham, Ruth, 1972. Introduction: Settlement Patterns and Urbanization. In *Man, Settlement, and Urbanism*. Peter J. Ucko, Ruth Tringham, and G. W. Dimbleby, Eds. London: Duckworth. Pp. xix-xxviii.

Tuggle, H. David, 1970. *Prehistoric Community Relations in East-central Arizona*. Ph.D. dissertation, University of Arizona.

U.S. Bureau of Land Management, Monticello District, Utah, n.d.a. Homestead Application Evaluations. Unpublished ms.
——. n.d.b. South San Juan Planning Unit Resource Analysis and Land Use Plan. Unpublished ms.

Van de Geer, John P., 1971. *Introduction to Multivariate Analysis for the Social Sciences*. San Francisco: W. H. Freeman.

van der Merwe, N. J. and P. H. Stein, 1972. Soil Chemistry of Postmolds and Rodent Burrows: Identification Without Excavation. *American Antiquity* 37: 245–254.

Veldman, Donald J., 1967. *Fortran Programming for the Behavioral Sciences*. New York: Holt, Rinehart and Winston.

Vescelius, G. S., 1960. Archaeological Sampling: A Problem of Statistical Inference. In *Essays in the Science of Culture, in Honor of Leslie A. White*. Gertrude E. Dole and Robert L. Carneiro, Eds. New York: Thomas Y. Crowell. Pp. 457–470.

Vivian, R. Gwinn, 1970. Aspects of Prehistoric Society in Chaco Canyon, New Mexico. Ph.D. dissertation, University of Arizona.

Wald, A., 1947. *Sequential Analysis*. New York: John Wiley and Sons.

Wallis, W. Allen and Harry V. Roberts, 1956. *Statistics: A New Approach*. New York: The Free Press.

Watson, P. J., S. A. LeBlanc, and C. L. Redman, 1971. *Explanation in Archaeology*. New York: Columbia University Press.

Westman, Walter A., 1971. Mathematical Models of Contagion and Their Relation to Density and Basal Area Sampling Techniques. In *Statistical Ecology, Volume I: Spatial Patterns and Statistical Distributions*. G. P. Patil, E. C.

(Westman, *Continued*)
Pielou, and W. E. Waters, Eds. University Park: Pennsylvania State University Press. Pp. 513–537.

Whallon, R., 1968. Investigations of Late Prehistoric Social Organization in New York State. In *New Perspectives in Archaeology*. Sally R. Binford and Lewis R. Binford, Eds. Chicago: Aldine. Pp. 223–244.

———.1972. A New Approach to Pottery Typology. *American Antiquity* 37: 13–33.

———. 1973. Spatial Analysis of Occupation Floors I: Application of Dimensional Analysis of Variance. *American Antiquity* 38: 266–278.

———. 1974. Working with the "New Paradigm," A Review of *Models in Archaeology*. David L. Clark, Ed. *Reviews in Anthropology* 1: 25–33.

Whallon, Robert and S. Kantman, 1969. Early Bronze-Age Development in the Keban Reservoir, East-central Turkey. *Current Anthropology* 10: 128–133.

Wheeler, Sir Mortimer, 1956. *Archaeology From the Earth*. Baltimore: Penguin Books.

White, J. P. and D. H. Thomas, 1972. What Mean These Tools? Ethno-Taxonomic Models and Archaeological Interpretations in the New Guinea Highlands. In *Models in Archaeology*. David L. Clarke, Ed. New York: Harper and Row. Pp. 275–308.

White, Leslie, 1959. *The Evolution of Culture*. New York: McGraw-Hill.

Wilcox, David R., n.d.a. The cornering project, Grasshopper Pueblo 1969. Unpublished ms.

———. n.d.b. Sampling Pueblos: The Implications of Room-set Additions at Grasshopper Pueblo. *In* Multidisciplinary Research at the Grasshopper Ruin. W. A. Longacre, Ed. *Anthropological Papers of the University of Arizona*. (In press).

———. n.d.c. Sampling Pueblos: The Problem of Comparability. Unpublished ms.

Willey, Gordon R., 1953. Prehistoric Settlement Patterns in the Viru Valley, Peru. *Bureau of American Ethnology Bulletin* 155.

———. 1968. Settlement Archaeology—An Appraisal. In *Settlement Archaeology*. K. C. Chang, Ed. Palo Alto, California: National Press Books. Pp. 208–226.

Willey, Gordon R., Ed., 1956. Prehistoric Settlement Patterns in the New World. *Viking Fund Publications in Anthropology*, No. 23.

Willey, Gordon R. and Charles R. McGimsey, 1954. The Monagrillo Culture of Panama. *Papers of the Peabody Museum, Harvard University*, Vol. 49, No. 2.

Willey, Gordon R. and Philip Phillips, 1958. *Method and Theory in American Archaeology*. Chicago: University of Chicago Press.

Williams, Bobby Jo, 1968. Establishing Cultural Heterogeneities in Settlement Patterns: An Ethnographic Example. In *New Perspectives in Archeology*. Sally R. Binford and Lewis R. Binford, Eds. Chicago: Aldine. Pp. 161–170.

Williams, Frederick, 1968. *Reasoning with Statistics*. New York: Holt, Rinehart, and Winston.

Williams, Leonard, David Hurst Thomas, and Robert Bettinger, 1973. Notions to Numbers: Great Basin Settlements as Polythetic Sets. *Research and Theory in Current Archaeology*. Charles L. Redman, Ed. New York: John P. Wiley and Sons. Pp. 215–237.

Winters, Howard D., 1969. The Riverton Culture. *Illinois Archaeological Survey Monograph I*, and *Illinois State Museum Reports*, 13.

Witter, Dan, n.d. Environmental Data Recording—1971 Chaco Canyon Site Survey. Unpublished ms.

Wood, W. E., 1955. Use of Stratified Random Samples in a Land-use Study. *Annals of the Association of American Geographers* 45: 350–367.

Woodbury, Richard B., 1973. *Alfred V. Kidder*. New York: Columbia University Press.

Woolley, Sir Leonard, 1953. *A Forgotten Kingdom*. Baltimore: Pelican Books.

Zawacki, April Allison and Glenn Hausfater, 1969. Early Vegetation of the Lower Illinois Valley. *Illinois State Museum, Reports of Investigations* 17.

Subject Index

Index
to
People and Places

[299]